THE REICH'S
LAST GAMBLE

THE REICH'S LAST GAMBLE

THE ARDENNES OFFENSIVE, DECEMBER 1944

GEORGE FORTY

CASSELL&CO

Cassell & Co
Wellington House, 125 Strand
London WC2R OBB

Copyright © George Forty 2000

First published 2000

British Library Cataloguing-in-Publication Data
A catalogue record for this book is available from the British Library

ISBN 0-304-35802-9

Distributed in the USA by
Sterling Publishing Co Inc
387 Park Avenue South
New York
NY 10016-8810

Printed and bound in Great Britain

CONTENTS

LIST OF MAPS AND CHARTS

ACKNOWLEDGEMENTS

While researching for this book I was fortunate enough to make contact with a number of American, British and German ex-soldiers who kindly agreed to help me. Their names appear with their reminiscences. One such gentleman was ex-artilleryman Mr. Richard H. Byers of Mentor, Ohio, who sent me a veritable treasure trove of material about the US 99th Infantry Division and the considerable part they played in the 'Battle of the Bulge'. Through him and Mr. Bill Meyer, also of the 99th Infantry Division Association, who led a visit over to England in October 1999 to the nearby village of Piddletrenthide, where they had been stationed in 1944, prior to going to the Ardennes, I was able to contact numerous other 'Ninety-Niners' who have all generously assisted me with the project. Their stories have been included in various chapters of this book and they include: Mr. J. R. McIlroy of Celina, Texas; Mr. B. C. Henderson of The Woodlands, Texas; Mr. Joseph L. Thimm of Salem, Oregon; Mr. Thor Ronningen of Wilmington, North Carolina; Mr. Grant Yager of Bradenton, Florida and Mr. Jett Johnson of Texas. I must also thank my old friend Colonel Owsley Costlow for allowing me to quote from his account of a tank action during the 'Other Bulge' in the Alsace.

On the German side I was indeed fortunate to have a friend living in the Ardennes area – Herr Werner Wagenknetch of Pelm. He had already helped me with a previous book (*Channel Islands at War – a German Perspective*; Ian Alan Publishing Ltd., 1999) and kindly volunteered to do so again. He has been a continual source of help and guidance for which I am truly grateful. It was he who sent me the reminiscences of Frau Agnes Mertes of Gerolstein who served in the German Army Medical Service during the assault. I must also thank Herr Guido Gnilsen, late of 2nd Panzer Division, who allowed me to quote from his. In addition, I must thank the Imperial War Museum,

Sound Archive, for allowing me to quote material from their wonderful Library of Sound Archives. In addition to the IWM sound archive I must thank Thames Television for allowing me to take extracts/quotations from tapes Nos 2713, 2776, 2712 & 3005 all recorded in 1972, reproduced with permission of Pearson Television International Ltd.

Three Englishmen must also be mentioned: Mr. Maxwell Nicholson of Kidderminster and Mr. Peter Parnwell of Dorchester, who have both kindly provided reminiscences, as has my old friend Mr. Lawrence Brooksby of Fellbach, Germany, who, in addition to writing up his reminisences, has been of invaluable assistance translating some of the German ones for me. He knows the Ardennes campaign at first hand because he drove a Sherman in 3 RTR during XXX Corps' defence of the Meuse bridges.

My thanks also to those authors and publishers who have allowed me to quote from their books, in particular the US Army Center of Military History whose definitive histories of the Ardennes and Alsace battles have been invaluable, as have the Garland series of World War II German Military Studies.

Finally, I must thank as always my wife and family for their continued support.

George Forty
Bryantspuddle, Dorset
March 2000

INTRODUCTION

Compared with some of the other major German offensives which were launched during the Second World War, for example, against Poland (1939), France and the Low Countries (1940) and Russia (1941), their surprise counter-offensive, 'Wacht am Rhein', of 16 December 1944, was a relatively small affair, involving as it did only one Army Group of three Armies, containing some 200,000 combat troops, 500 plus tanks and 1,900 heavy guns and rocket-launchers. Indeed, according to one historian,[1] General Dwight D. Eisenhower is reported as saying in late 1945, during a conversation with the American Secretary of War, that the Bulge was: 'a mere incident'. However, I'm sure that he must have been quoted out of context because no one would ever describe an event of such magnitude as being: 'a mere incident' – certainly not the Supreme Commander of SHAEF who must have had a fair number of sleepless nights and worrying days over the assault, especially during the early period, when communication with the front was virtually non-existent and bad weather prevented Allied reconnaissance aircraft from finding out exactly what was happening. The 'Battle of the Bulge' as it is now popularly called, also cost the lives of some 17,000 Germans and more than 8,400 Americans, together with a much smaller number of British soldiers, not to mention the civilians of various nationalities who were unintentionally caught up in the horrors of war, so there were *in toto* well over 25,000 deaths.[2] The counter-offensive could be said to have ended on 23 January 1945, when CCB, of US 7th Armored Division, led by Brigadier General Bruce Clarke, who had defended the key town so bravely less than a month earlier, entered St-Vith, thus removing the 'Bulge' from the Allied front lines. However, one can add a fair number of extra weeks to that date before the Allies had fully re-asserted themselves and resumed their advance to the Rhine.

The total casualties during the offensive by both sides had been 81,834 German and 76,890 Allied, again significant numbers, while countless numbers of armoured vehicles, trucks, artillery pieces, weapons, equipment and other *matériel* had been damaged or destroyed. It would be difficult if not impossible for the Germans to make up these losses, so the outcome really was that the desperate gamble had failed. More importantly, the morale defeat was much greater. Undoubtedly it signalled the beginning of the end of German resistance on the Western Front, and, although there were still more than three months to go before the final surrender, the Fatherland was now very much on its last legs.

With hindsight it is easy to dismiss the basic premises that lay behind 'Wacht am Rhein' as being the last desperate ravings of a madman, still clinging to power despite everything going against him. Nevertheless, what if this last gamble had succeeded and the Germans had reached the Meuse, captured their bridgeheads and gone on to split the Allied armies, even if they had been unable to reach Antwerp? General George S. 'Blood and Guts' Patton was all for letting them do just that so that he and his free-wheeling Third Army could, as he colourfully put it: 'cut their guts out' as the panzers manoeuvred at the end of what would by then have been a very over-stretched supply line. One can imagine what chaos the German armour would have caused in the Allied rear areas, not to mention the alarm and despondency among the recently liberated but still jittery civilians of France and the Low Countries. Hitler had only a very limited number of troops available with which to try to do something spectacular that would have a major impact on a war which he must have already realised that he could not win. Some 200,000 troops would have had only a limited effect upon the situation of the Eastern Front, but in the west it was a different matter. He might even be able to get some of the Allies to consider making a separate peace, especially if he could add to the discord that he knew existed between the senior American, British and French commanders – among whom certain 'prima donnas' with their own agendas were prepared to misinterpret anything that apparently caused them offence. Eisenhower later admitted that the machinations of such 'players' as de Gaulle and Montgomery at that time, had caused him more distress and worry than any similar problems in the entire war; so much then for a 'mere incident'!

It will be seen that as well as covering the major actions which took place in the Ardennes, I have also covered, albeit in outline only, the important flanking actions which took place, namely, the involvement of the British troops of XXX Corps in the north, and of the American and French forces of General Devers' 6th Army Group in the south, against the other surprise German offensive, code-named 'Nordwind'. Both clearly had important effects upon the outcome of 'Wacht am Rhein'.

The 'Battle of the Bulge' is a fascinating subject to study, as is evidenced by the enormous number of books, articles, papers, videos, etc., which continue to be written about every aspect of its relatively short period of action. It was without doubt the most important battle fought by the US Army on the Western Front during WWII. And it showed that, despite getting off to a shaky start, for many understandable reasons, the average young 'green' GI still had all the guts, determination and bravery which his fore-bears had possessed when they established a new country against all the wishes of the old. As one of their severest critics, Field Marshal Montgomery, said of the American soldier: 'He is a very brave fighting man and he has that tenacity in battle which stamps a first-class soldier'. I have therefore devoted a great deal of the space in this book to what was seen in the Ardennes through the eyes of the GIs who took part, rather than describe once again every nuance of each of the many, complex battles which formed the German offensive and the Allied counter-offensive. I hope that I have succeeded in this endeavour in an interesting and readable way.

Notes

1 Miller, Merle. *Ike The Soldier as I Knew Him.*
2 The casualty figures are bound to be vague and different references give different figures, because some sources show 'missing in action' separately, some of whom will have become prisoners of war, while others will have been killed and should there-

fore be shown as 'KIA'. The Allied figure on the other hand is more accurate, the agreed breakdown being:

Formation	KIA	MIA	Wounded
US First Army	4,629	12,176	23,152
US Third Army	3,778	8,729	23,081
British XXX Corps	200	239	896
	8,607	21,144	47,129
Total = 76,880			

TIMETABLE

1944

20 July: Abortive assassination attempt on Adolf Hitler.

25 September: Führer conference at which 'Wacht am Rhein' is first mentioned.

End September–mid December: German build-up in concentration area.

End November–mid December: mock radio traffic and tight radio security in concentration area.

25 November: Original target date for launch of offensive.

1 December: Recce activity along Ardennes Front forbidden from this date onwards.

First week December: Corps commanders informed.

10 December: Divisional commanders informed.

10 December: Hitler leaves Berlin by train to establish HQ at Adlerhorst.

12 December: Attack divisions begin deployment under strict security.

13 December: Americans begin attack on Roer dams.

15/16 December: German troops given detailed orders.

16 December: 'X' Day (also called: *Tag Null*) 'Wacht am Rhein' launched.

17 December: Situation at last light: Sixth SS Pz Army has made small gains, but is now stopped in area Monschau–Elsenborn by determined US resistance; Fifth Pz Army advancing slowly towards St-Vith, but faster to the south; Seventh Army across River Clervé but making slow progress; US troops from Third and Ninth Armies begin deployment to reinforce First Army; SHAEF releases 82nd and 101st Airborne Divs to 12th Army Group and theyare despatched to Ardennes front.

18 December: Target date for Meuse bridgeheads to have been taken. Fifth Pz Army's XLVII Pz Corps has made a sizeable breach in the US front, inflicting heavy casualties on some units (e.g., 110th Inf Regt).

By 19 December: Sixth Pz Army still making slow progress, but attack by leading 'Peiper' battle group halted and isolated; Fifth Pz Army making progress around flanks of St-Vith and has isolated some 8,000 US troops in Schnee-Eifel; Houffalize taken; XLVII Pz Corps reaches outer defences of Bastogne, but main mission of Army to push on to Meuse remains in force; Seventh Army reaches Wiltz; British XXX Corps ordered to get troops down to the Meuse to protect the vulnerable bridges as soon as possible.

19 December: Allied conference at Verdun – Patton proposes to turn US Third Army northwards and attack with three divisions on the 22nd, all agree; in the Ardennes all three German armies continue to advance, although some units, e.g., 12th SS Pz Div, have been without fuel for twelve hours; on their flanks US First and Third Armies regroup.

20 December: Because of Sixth SS Pz Army's lack of progress, von Rundstedt orders shift of main point of effort to Fifth Pz Army which is still progressing towards the Meuse, sweeping past Bastogne which is now all but isolated; Seventh Army advances along Bastogne–Arlon road and finally seizes Diekirch; HQ 21st Army Group (Montgomery) takes command of US First and Ninth Armies from 12th Army Group (Bradley) and First Army launches limited counter-attack towards St-Vith.

21 December: Sixth SS Pz Army still cannot relieve Battle Group Peiper; Fifth Pz Army finally takes St-Vith; Bastogne now completely encircled but McAuliffe of 101st Ab Div, replies 'Nuts' to Germans' call to surrender; Army Group B brings up 9th Pz and 15th Pz Gren Divs as reinforcements; Seventh Army's leading elements reach Libramont. Weather has now turned freezing cold.

23 December: First clear day, so 3,000 plus Allied aircraft fly missions in German combat and rear areas, also supply besieged Bastogne; Fifth Pz Army now only nine kilometres from Dinant and the Meuse, but is halted by US 2nd Armd Div and fuel shortage;

Seventh Army under attack from US Third Army but manages to hold line of the R. Sauer.

24 **December:** Offensive has pushed as far west as it will get; Sixth SS Pz Army now on defensive along line Monschau–Elsenborn–Stavelot–Grandmenil; remnants of Battle Group Peiper manage to break out; Fifth Pz Army now in Conneux–Celles area; spearhead of 2nd Pz Div is attacked by fighter-bombers; Fifth Pz Army unable to mount concentrated attack because of their threatened flank; elements of British XXX Corps now in positions on Meuse between Givet and Liège.

25 **December:** German offensive has ground to a halt from lack of fuel, ammunition and supplies, while everywhere US counter-attacks are making progress; good flying weather persists; spearhead of 2nd Pz Div surrounded and destroyed.

26 **December:** First 'Wacht am Rhein' related message sent using Enigma machine; siege of Bastogne broken by arrival of lead tanks of US Third Army's 4th Armd Div; good flying weather continues and all three German armies suffer major losses from air and ground attack; Hitler refuses to rescind order that Bastogne be taken at all costs.

27 **December:** British XXX Corps halts German advance in the Celles sector; pressure from US First and Third Armies is increasing; Allied High Command propose deep penetration to pinch off the entire German salient; it is clear that the Germans have lost the initiative as more and more of their formations are being forced onto the defensive.

28 **December:** Eisenhower and Montgomery meet at Hasselt, Belgium, to agree counter-measures to be taken in Ardennes; US Third Army prepares for counter-offensive between Rivers Sauer and Wiltz; conference at Hitler's HQ to discuss 'Nordwind'.

30 **December:** US Third Army begins to advance on Houffalize.

1945

1 **January:** Luftwaffe launch Operation 'Bodenplatte'; US Third Army's counter-thrust continues; III Corps counter-attacks around

Bastogne with limited success, while VIII Corps attacks SW face of German salient with considerable success; Germans launch 'Nordwind' – a two-pronged attack by Army Group G in Alsace and towards Strasbourg.

2 January: US Third Army continue advance, taking Gerimont, Mande St-Etienne and Senonchamps; Fifth Pz Army ask for permission to withdraw but Hitler refuses; German pressure in US Seventh Army's sector ('Nordwind') continues and is especially critical in VI Corps' area.

3 January: In Ardennes US First Army mounts offensive towards Houffalize further to reduce enemy salient and link up with US Third Army; 'Nordwind' forces expand their salient towards Bitche; French ordered to garrison Strasbourg, releasing US troops for operations further north against 'Nordwind'.

4 January: Heavy snow prevents Allied attack on German northern flank in Ardennes, but Fifth Pz Army is being slowly pushed back and German attacks on Bastogne come to a halt; Hitler agrees to Sixth SS Pz Army's withdrawal from Eifel area; they are then sent to Eastern Front where a massive Russian assault is anticipated.

5–8 January: Allies launch new assault between Stavelot and Marche.

6 January: Units of US First and Third Armies still pressing forward; withdrawal of Sixth SS Pz Army makes German position even more vulnerable, but Hitler refuses to withdraw east of the Rhine; in south, US Seventh Army still attempting to reduce Bitche salient.

7–12 January: Fifth Pz Army and Sixth SS Pz Army carrying out major withdrawal, while Seventh Army endeavours, unsuccessfully, to hold southern flank; new German offensive in Strasbourg area on 7 January and pressure continues against French First and US Seventh Armies.

13 January: US attacks continue all along Ardennes Front, while British XXX Corps complete their task when 51st Highland Division reaches River Ourthe south of La Roche; in southern sector French troops hold off repeated German attacks around Strasbourg.

16 January: British Second Army launches Operation 'Blackcock' to eliminate German salient between the Meuse and the Rur (the 'Roermond Triangle'); link-up between leading troops of US First Army (VII Corps) and US Third Army (VIII Corps) near Houffalize; German salient has now been reduced to half its former size; in the south, US 12th Armd Div of VI Corps, Seventh Army, opens an offensive against the Gambsheim bridgehead.

20 January: Ardennes salient now reduced to a minimum.

23 January: St-Vith retaken – virtually the end of 'Bulge'.

26 January: End of 'Nordwind' offensive.

By 2 February: German forces are back at the original starting-points along the Siegfried Line from which they launched 'Wacht am Rhein'.

1
THE SEED IS SOWN

The summer of 1944 had proved to be an extremely difficult period for Adolf Hitler and his Third Reich. In the east, the Soviet Forces had been continually exerting more pressure, pushing back the German armies in all areas. The surrender of the Roumanian forces to the Red Army in August 1944, leading to their country's withdrawal from the war early the following month, together with the virtual collapse of Army Group South, had necessitated strong action to prevent a complete disaster, but this had been achieved by the increased use of Hungarian units and a new line had been established in the Carpathians. In the centre, the enemy had reached a line running along the Vistula, to the Narew and thence along the East Prussian frontier. Here they had been held, the only major Russian bridgehead across the Vistula at Baranow having been contained then reduced. In the north, Army Group North was cut off in the Courland, but the front there had also been stabilised. By mid-September, fighting in nearly all sectors had died down and it was clear that the Russian summer offensive was drawing to a close. If all went well there would be no further major sustained Russian effort until February/March 1945 at the earliest.

In the west, the Allies had not only successfully broken through the 'Atlantic Wall' in early June and made highly successful landings in Normandy, but had gone on to establish a firm beachhead, build up their forces so that they could break out from it and then liberate most of France and significant portions of the Low Countries, while being joined by another equally successful landing of more forces in the South of France. All these successes had forced the beleaguered Germans back ever closer to the frontiers of the Fatherland. Nevertheless, the Allied forces were now clearly running out of steam as their supply lines grew longer and longer, while the battered Wehrmacht had withdrawn to the strong, man-made defences of Germany's 'West Wall' which, together with other natural obstacles, would be difficult for the Allies to crack.

In Italy too, after heavy Allied pressure which had included the capture of Rome on 4 June 1944, the Germans had managed to withdraw most of their forces intact and build another stable defensive front along the Gothic Line in the Apennines. The Allied pressure in Italy had of course been weakened by the loss of troops taken away for the landings in the South of France, while the Germans had received reinforcements withdrawn from the Balkans.

Consequently, despite the disasters of the summer, the lull developing on all fronts would give the Germans a breathing-space in which to replenish their losses, re-organise and revitalise their field army which was still, in general, tough, efficient and resilient, despite having suffered grievous casualties in both men and *matériel*. There would also be time to form new units and to re-equip some of them with the new weapons which were surprisingly still being produced in ever greater numbers by the German war machine despite the almost continuous Allied bombing. Perhaps the seemingly preposterous idea that the Germans could regain the initiative was not beyond the bounds of possibility.

To cap the reverses on the battlefield, there had also been the abortive attempt on the Führer's life of 20 July, which had only failed because of the flimsy nature of the room in which the bomb had been detonated. The building, where Hitler had been holding a high-level conference, was in a barracks near Rastenburg in East Prussia, and its weak structure had absorbed much of the force of the explosion, leaving the 'target' with superficial leg, arm and ear injuries only. More importantly, the attempt on his life had exacerbated his deep hatred and distrust for the field marshals and generals of the Army, with whom he had been almost constantly at loggerheads. Lieutenant-Colonel Felix von Stauffenberg, Chief of Staff of the Replacement Army,[1] who had planted the bomb, then went on to commit a major blunder that would cost him his life. Assuming that Hitler had definitely been killed in the explosion, he immediately began to try to put into effect the rest of the plan, namely, to seize control of the state.

Fortunately for Hitler, Major Otto-Ernst Remer, then commanding the Führer's personal guard battalion in Berlin, did not believe the conspirators when they told him that Hitler was dead. After conferring with Goebbels, who managed to get through to Hitler at Rastenburg by telephone (Hitler swiftly confirmed that he was wounded and shaken, but very definitely alive!), Remer received direct orders from his Führer and immediately began rounding-up the conspirators.[2] The witch-hunt against those who were – or appeared to be – involved in any way, including their families, colleagues, friends and acquaintances, would inadvertently incriminate many on the very outer limits of the plot such as Germany's most famous, adored and respected Generalfeldmarschall, Erwin Johannes Eugen Rommel, the 'Desert Fox', hero of North Africa and living legend. Despite the fact that he was himself recovering from the severe wounds which he had received when his car had been attacked in France by a swarm of the dreaded *Jabos*[3] some three days before the bomb attack on Hitler, he would be implicated by a chance remark (made by General von Stülpnagel, a co-conspirator of von Stauffenberg's, while being tortured by the Gestapo) then condemned out of hand and forced to commit suicide to save his wife and son from threatened persecution and possible death.

The failed attempt had also brought to a head the suspicions which Hitler had long held, namely that 'reactionaries', as he described them, had been constantly plotting against him. He was perhaps surprised at the widespread nature of the plot within the Army, but at the same time relieved to find that it did not include a civilian element to any great degree. Having tried and failed, they could now all be rooted out and suitably dealt with. Finally, of course, his miraculous escape from the explosion with only superficial injuries proved the fact that he was protected by 'divine providence' and would survive to lead Germany, whatever the future might hold.

This is not the place to go into further detail about the bomb plot and its aftermath, except to add that Major Remer would have his loyalty rewarded in such a way as to involve him in Operation 'Wacht am Rhein'. It also inadvertently provided the 'target' with a period of recuperation in bed which gave him time to think about the progress of the war and to reflect on past successes and failures. Hitler had been sufficiently superficially injured (e.g., broken eardrum, severe bruising, cuts and lacerations to arms and legs) to keep him bedridden for some weeks during which he sought a solution to the problem of regaining the initiative on the battlefield. Ideally this would involve the staging of a major event, powerful enough to widen the cracks that Hitler was convinced were developing between the Allies (especially between America and Great Britain) and, if of sufficiently earth-shattering proportions, perhaps seriously damage the Alliance. 'Never in history was there a coalition like that of our enemies,' Hitler is quoted as saying, when he was ordering the attack through the Ardennes, 'composed of such heterogeneous elements with such divergent aims … Even now these states are at loggerheads, and, if we can deliver a few more heavy blows, this artificially bolstered common front may suddenly collapse with a gigantic clap of thunder.'

Also, in a strange way, the bomb plot had strengthened Hitler's position as Supreme Commander, so far as his hold over the armed forces was concerned. The fawning Generalfeldmarschall Wilhelm Keitel, Hitler's Minister of War and Chief of Staff of the German Armed Forces since 1938, who had presided over the court which condemned the bomb plotters to death, had even coined a new title for his Führer, namely: 'Grosste Feldherr aller Zeit' or 'Grofoz' for short, meaning: 'Greatest Master of the Field of all Time' – not bad for a one-time infantry corporal! The generals, however, who had seen their earlier victories turn into a string of almost continual defeats, used the new title more as a term of contempt.

'All the world hearkens'

There are a number of scenarios which reportedly seek to explain when and where it was that Hitler first thought of his plan for 'Wacht am Rhein' (Watch on the Rhine), as the assault in the Ardennes was code-named, but it is clear that one of the most likely of these could well have occurred during this period of enforced convalescence. It had become the norm for the Führer to receive regular daily briefings from Generaloberst Alfred Jodl, Chief of the Armed Forces Operations Staff

(*Wehrmacht Führungsstab*), normally accompanied by his aide, Major Herbert Büchs, who would bring a large map of Europe, on which Jodl would explain what was happening in each sector of the fronts. During one of these briefings in mid-September, Jodl made a passing reference to the Ardennes and explained that in this well-forested area of Belgium and Luxembourg, the Allied line was probably at its weakest, with just four American divisions holding the whole area, because the countryside naturally favoured the defence, it being exceptionally difficult going for tracked or wheeled vehicles. Furthermore, these American troops were either 'resting' after heavy fighting elsewhere, or were 'green troops' newly arrived in theatre. At the mention of the Ardennes, Hitler immediately sat up in bed and asked Jodl to repeat what he had said. Clearly this seemingly unimportant fragment of the overall briefing struck a chord with the Führer who it is said, had a formidable memory for facts and figures and often took great delight in castigating any staff officers who misquoted such minutiae as maximum ranges of artillery guns, tank performances and the calibres of their main guns, etc. He must have recalled the way in which he had used the area to advantage in the heady days of 1940. Down the ages, despite unfavourable terrain, the Ardennes and environs had featured in a number of military conflicts involving Germany, the more recent ones being during the Franco–Prussian War of 1870–71 after which Germany had received the regions of Alsace and Lorraine under the Treaty of Frankfurt in 1871; the Great War of 1914–18, when the Schlieffen Plan[4] had formed the basis of German strategy. In 1914, the Plan had involved three Imperial German armies moving on foot through the Eifel then on through the Ardennes, where, after negotiating most of the High Ardennes without fighting, they eventually had to engage the French in the lower, more densely wooded area of the Ardennes Forest in late August.

After the war, the Treaty of Versailles had restored independence to the Grand Duchy of Luxembourg. The German *Blitzkrieg* of May 1940, at the start of their whirlwind capture of France and the Low Countries, had made fullest use of the area for a main armoured advance towards the River Meuse at Sedan.

Selected for this purpose principally because it was the one area through which the French were confident that no major assault could be launched, it had become the centre line for Army Group A, then commanded by General Gerd von Rundstedt. The panzers had moved through the deeply wooded valleys in tightly controlled columns, stretching back a hundred miles, the rear echelons lying well to the east of the Rhine. This enormous mass of armour, comprising more than 2,400 tanks and other armoured vehicles, had swept aside everything in its path and provided the *Schwerpunkt* that would seal the fate of the Allied armies. On that occasion Hitler had followed quite closely behind his armoured columns, reaching Bastogne in the heart of the Ardennes on the morning of May 17 1940, where he had visited von Rundstedt's headquarters. 'All the world hearkens!' he had declared triumphantly, as he walked among his soldiers after an alfresco lunch with them. Since then this moment of triumph had remained at the back of his mind until he was reminded of it by Jodl's passing reference to the same area. If the Germans had used the Ardennes once to secure a great victory, they could do it again. Such an assault was the shortest way to reach the Meuse and once across, they would strike for Brussels, then on to Antwerp, thus cutting the Allied forces in two!

Factors to be considered

If Hitler was to regain the initiative with a devastating attack in an unexpected area, the success of such an operation would depend upon five main factors:

a. strength and speed of the attack
b. response and performance of the opposition
c. terrain
d. weather
e. security

Strength and speed of the attack

It required a force of sufficient size and strength to make an impact on the selected area. This force, he estimated, should be made up of some

25 to 30 divisions, containing a high preponderance of mechanised armour in order to maintain the speed of the assault. The vast majority of the German Army was already committed to battle, so it would be necessary to build up this special force on top of current commitments. To achieve this he needed both additional manpower and *matériel*.

Manpower

As has already been mentioned, the German Army had taken massive casualties on all fronts – three-quarters of a million killed, wounded or taken prisoner on the Western Front alone and even more in the east – so that many of its best and most experienced soldiers were now dead or wounded, leaving great gaps to be filled in many units. Where would the necessary replacement manpower come from? The main sources to be tapped were threefold: first and foremost Industry and the Home Front, then the Navy (Kriegsmarine) and the Air Force (Luftwaffe). Heinrich Himmler, Reichsführer–SS and Minister of the Interior since August 1943, was appointed in mid-August 1944 as CinC of the Replacement Army and directed by Hitler to form and train a people's militia (*Volkssturm*) – the German equivalent of the British Home Guard. More importantly, he had to raise and train a significant number of infantry divisions to be known as *Volks-grenadiers* (lit: people's infantry). To achieve all this the call-up age limits were extended to embrace all males aged from 16 to 60. In addition, reserved civilian occupations were brought under close scrutiny and anyone whose job was not essential or who could be replaced by someone less fit, was immediately called up for military service. This included the 'sick, the lame and the lazy', the sweepings of the prisons, the deaf and those with stomach and other internal disorders. This 'scraping the barrel' must have put impossible strains on the training machine and resulted in some of the newly trained soldiers being more trouble than they were worth. Added to these men from Germany were 'volunteers' from the occupied territories in the east – Poles, Czechs and even Russians. When pressed in battle would they fight well? On the whole, it has to be said, the *Volks* grenadier divisions[5] would perform adequately and fight bravely despite their inadequate training.

At the top of the list of potential new infantrymen, as far as fitness and suitability were concerned, were of course the sailors, for whom no ships were available because the navy's role was rapidly diminishing, and the '*crème de la crème*', those super-fit and well-motivated young men who had already been selected for training as aircrew. Despite having had no previous training as infantrymen, they too would fight with great courage and determination.

The new 'recruits' were given only some six to eight weeks' concentrated training before going to the field army. As well as having less manpower, the new VGDs had a lower scale of such major weaponry as artillery and anti-tank guns (e.g., the anti-tank companies in infantry regiments were equipped with Panzerfaust[6] (hand-held rocket-launchers) in place of the normal anti-tank guns). The new divisions also had smaller reconnaissance and engineer units, but to make up for some of their deficiencies, the infantry units had a higher than normal issue of fast-firing machine-guns and machine-pistols – see Chapter 4 for more information and a detailed organisational chart.

The make-up of these new divisions was thus extremely varied. For example 18th VGD, which was formed in Denmark in September 1944, numbered chiefly redundant naval personnel who had been transferred to the Army, together with members of 571st Grenadier Division which had been first mobilised in September 1944, then dissolved some days later. It also absorbed the remnant of 18th Luftwaffe Field Division which had been badly mauled in the Mons pocket, only about 300 men managing to break out. It would be committed in the Ardennes and fight well. The 212th VGD was formed in Poland, when the shattered 212th Infantry Division was rebuilt to something approaching its previous size, with youngsters mainly from Bavaria, so it had a very high proportion of 17-year-olds. It also fought in the Ardennes and took heavy casualties, losing some 4,000 men from December 1944 to January 1945. In all, some fourteen of these new divisions would be involved in the Ardennes operations (9th, 12th, 18th, 26th, 62nd, 79th, 167th, 212th, 246th, 276th, 277th, 326th, 352nd and 560th VGDs).

Another source of potential power on the battlefield was the Waffen-SS (armed protection echelon) which, despite fighting as normal ground forces, was to all intents and purposes entirely separate from Army. A Party political force, it had been expanded from a pre-war nucleus of regiments (*Standarten*) and had taken part in the Polish campaign as just a handful of regiments, but now comprised some 39 divisions, together with numerous independent formations – more than one million men, a formidable and ruthless fighting force which, unlike the Army, received the best of everything. The Waffen-SS were particularly important to Hitler because they did not answer to the hated, untrustworthy Army generals who had tried to murder him, but rather to the ever-loyal Party members, who were about the only people Hitler was prepared to trust. The Waffen-SS now had made up to strength four élite SS panzer divisions: 1st SS Panzer Leibstandarte, 2nd SS Panzer, 9th SS Panzer and 12th SS Panzer Hitler Jugend, and these crack formations would play a vital role in Operation 'Wacht am Rhein'. All four were completely refitted and retrained deep inside Germany. They would provide a formidable, well-equipped armoured force, capable, it was hoped, of smashing their way through any opposition.

Despite the fact that the newly forming VGDs would absorb much of the new manpower, other selected line divisions would also receive reinforcements of men and *matériel*. In all, some nine other divisions would be earmarked for the coming operation. In the main these were armoured: five panzer divisions (2nd, 9th, 116th, Grossdeutschland Panzer[7] and Panzer Lehr) and two panzer grenadier divisions (3rd and 15th). The Luftwaffe would also make a ground contribution, in that men of both 3rd and 5th Fallschirmjäger (Parachute) Divisions would be called upon to play a special part.

At a higher level, the German staff structure was still fairly well intact and functioning properly. As historian James Lucas comments in his book, *The Last Year of the German Army*, 'The discipline and soldierly qualities of the ordinary German fighting man remained high. The miracle which the newly recalled von Rundstedt was said to have wrought in restoring cohesion and a firm battle line in Belgium had been won for him by ordinary soldiers, NCOs and junior officers directed by superb Staff organisation.'

Matériel

Despite almost continual day and night air raids, the German war industry maintained high levels of production, especially in the areas where it mattered – such as aircraft, armoured fighting vehicles and artillery. One of the main reasons for this was the use of underground facilities and the opening up of many small factories outside the main industrial area of the Ruhr. Another was the wide use of slave labour including prisoners of war – every plant in the Ruhr of any size used forced labour, the various Krupp works alone using more than 100,000 of these unfortunates who were treated appallingly. In his memoirs, Hitler's brilliant armaments and war production minister, Albert Speer, quotes from an output survey issued by the Technical Bureau on 6 February 1945 concerning deliveries of day and night fighter aircraft, during the period January to September 1944. The figures were:

January	1,017
February	990
March	1,240
April	1,475
May	1,755
June	2,034
July	2,305
August	2,273
September	2,878

This steady increase was to some extent achieved by cutting back on other types of aircraft production, the intention being to make more fighters available to deal with the enemy bombing raids, but it does show that despite the concentrated air raids the armament industry was surviving. What is more, the new aircraft included the very first jet fighters with a performance superior to anything the Allies could produce.

German tank production, which had amounted to 6,083 (all types) in 1943, rose by nearly 2.5 thousand to 8,466 in 1944; again, an impressive achievement and another indication that somehow, despite all the Allied bombing, output was more than just being maintained. In addition of course it is worth remembering that tank for tank, the majority of these now being produced were superior on the battlefield to their Allied equivalents. Tanks such as the Pz Kpfw V Panther and Pz Kpfw VI Tiger had already proved themselves and were a byword for power in tank v tank battles. Now in addition there were massive new AFVs such as the Königstiger, Jagdtiger, Jagdpanther, Sturmmörser Tiger, Elefant SP and others in the design stage, though these were produced in relatively small numbers as the war progressed. German tank designers appeared to do little to help themselves and instead of concentrating on their proven battle-winners like Panther and Tiger, they wasted valuable capacity on these behemoths

There was a serious shortage of the most basic firearms; more than 1.5 million personal weapons – rifles mainly – were urgently needed to equip the new infantrymen in the VGDs, so these had to be manu-factured, together with some 100,000 machine-guns. More than 1.25 million tons of ammunition of all natures were also produced. Millions of tons of ammunition, fuel and supplies had to be trans-ported to the front lines without the enemy realising what was happening, and this logistic requirement probably more than anything else, would determine the date by which the assault could be mounted.

Response and performance of the opposition
Detailed organisation and layout of the American forces that would oppose the assault will be covered in later chapters, but it is relevant here to consider the fighting state of the opposition at this point – or more importantly, what the Germans considered to be their fighting state. Holding the Ardennes were troops of Lieutenant General Courtney H. Hodges' US First Army. Like the rest of the leading troops in the Allies' spectacular advance across France and the Low Coun-tries, they had been buoyed up by their success, but they were in fact reaching the end of their tether, as their days in action mounted and

their supply lines grew ever longer. These lines of supply still stretched right back to the Normandy beachheads and would continue to do so until the port of Antwerp (captured on 4 September) could be made operational. This would not be until late November because the entire Scheldt estuary had to be cleared of stubborn enemy resistance. Hodges' leading troops had had the distinction of being the first Allied soldiers to set foot on German soil, when, on 11 September, a small recce party from the 85th Cavalry Recon Squadron, 5th Armored Division, V Corps, had crossed the River Our in the Eifel, the area directly to the east of the Ardennes. It was here that the Germans hoped to make a stand because through it ran their West Wall – known in this area as the Siegfried Line – which comprised deep belts of minefields and anti-tank obstacles, covered by scores of gun emplacements and thousands of concrete pill-boxes.

Almost as soon as they arrived, US V Corps had put in an assault on the West Wall, hoping to break through before the enemy could be reinforced and continue their rapid advance towards the Rhine. The experienced 28th and 4th Infantry Divisions made the assault and it was generally expected that it would be a quick and easy battle, but events proved otherwise. After several days of hard fighting, in which the Americans suffered more than 2,000 casualties, the attack had to be called off and both divisions were withdrawn and rested. Having been reinforced, they were then given the task of attacking Aachen, via the Hürtgen Forest. Once again they failed, this time in what was probably the most costly divisional-level action undertaken by US troops during World War Two – the GIs who fought there now universally refer to it as 'Bloody Aachen!' Once again the decimated divisions were withdrawn and this time sent to a quiet sector to recover from their ordeal. This 'quiet area' was the Ardennes and, while there were rest centres out of range of enemy shelling, which had hot showers, real beds, well-cooked hot food and entertainment such as live USO shows, the front line was still the front line with all the horrors of cold, wet slit trenches, regular shelling and mortaring, etc. Peter Elstob, in his book, *Hitler's Last Offensive*, comments that during the 83rd Infantry Division's one month of 'rest & relaxation' in the Ardennes, they had 26 men killed, 176 wounded and more than 550 non-battle casualties!

In addition to 'resting' divisions, the Ardennes was also used for the 'blooding' of green troops who had recently arrived in the ETO, such as the 106th Infantry Division, who took over the high Schnee-Eifel area from 2nd Infantry Division, and the equally raw 99th Infantry Division, yet to fight its first battle. When Bradley decided to reinforce VIII Corps, he sent them 9th Armored Division which also had never been in action. Much the same situation obtained on the German side of the battle lines, but for very different reasons. Nevertheless, the 'green' or 'resting' German units maintained aggressive patrolling and a far more warlike attitude than did their American counterparts.

Morale

The vicious, abortive battles which had failed to break through the West Wall, plus the high casualties sustained in the Hürtgen Forest and 'Bloody Aachen', clearly had an effect on the morale of both sides. The Germans, despite the rigours of their retreat across France, seemed to have found new strength and determination to resist – heartened no doubt by at last having good static defences in which to fight, coupled with the stark fact that they were now having to defend, for the first time, the beloved soil of the Fatherland. On the Allied side, the 250-mile advance had become very wearing, with ever-increasing shortages of fuel and ammunition to be contended with, plus an enemy who had become even more dangerous and determined as he reached his homeland. Undoubtedly stress and fatigue were affecting the soldiers and their commanders, and this was reflected in an alarming rise in non-battle casualties – what had been called 'shell-shock' in the Great War and was now known as 'combat fatigue'. According to one historian this accounted for a quarter of *all* American casualties at that time, which caused considerable alarm to the higher commanders. Nevertheless, as Elstob succinctly puts it: 'In the three months up to the German attack in December, the Ardennes became a combination of nursery and old folks' home. Here new divisions were sent to be blooded without danger of being destroyed and old, tired divisions sent to lick their wounds and regain their strength.'[8]

Terrain

Although the name 'Ardennes' is the one most closely associated with the 'Battle of the Bulge', strictly speaking both the 'Eifel' which lies to its east and the adjoining 'Hohes Venn' must also be considered in any survey of the general battlefield area, especially when the German forming-up areas are to be included. The whole is, in general terms, difficult country for fighting in, hence the lack of battles there over the centuries. However, on certain significant occasions as has already been explained, the area has been used for the passage of large armies – no surprise really because if one draws a straight line between Berlin and Paris it will bisect both the Ardennes and the Eifel!

Ardennes

The Ardennes (sometimes spelt without the 's') is a wooded plateau which is a part of the ancient Ardennes Forest and now includes most of the Belgian provinces of Luxembourg, Namur and Liège, a portion of the Grand Duchy of Luxembourg and the French *département* of Ardennes. It covers an area of some 3,800 square miles (10,000 square kilometres). Its geological makeup is complex and formed, to quote from *Encyclopaedia Britannica*: 'as a result of intense folding, faulting, uplifts and denudations, older strata of rock had been thrust over younger strata'. The actual name 'Ardennes' strictly only refers to the southern half of the area, where the rugged wooded sandstone, quartzite, slate and limestone hills reach heights of 1,150–1,640 feet. Between the peaks and rocky crags are peat bogs, deep, twisting valleys containing winding rivers and turbulent streams, which emanate from the watershed of the High Ardennes, those flowing north and west going towards the River Meuse, those flowing south and east to the Moselle. Much of the Ardennes countryside was then (and still is) heavily forested, while the rest is covered with thin, waterlogged heathland. The northern part is lower – between 655 and 985 feet – and the land is used as pasture by small-holders, although some cereals, potatoes and clover are grown in the valleys. There are small dairy herds, pigs and other livestock. Two of the region's well-known specialities are Ardennes ham and various types of liver pâté.

Eifel

This is the plateau region of western Germany, lying between the Rhine, the Moselle (Mosel) and the Luxembourg and Belgian borders. It is contiguous with the Ardennes and the Hohes Venn and can be divided into three areas: the Schnee-Eifel, Hocheifel and Voreifel. The first of these, a high, tree-covered ridge, is the most important for this study; it includes the highest point, Hohe Acht (2,451ft), and is drained by the River Ahr which runs through a productive wine-growing area. The Schnee-Eifel is directly to the east of St-Vith and forms a natural barrier in that area. Its thick conifer forests also provide excellent all-year-round cover from air observation.

Hohes Venn

While the Eifel features a complex of fairly high hill ranges, the Hohes Venn is a long area of flat tableland, covered with lakes and marshes. Larger than the Schnee-Eifel, it is bounded by Malmédy and Monschau on the German side and Eupen–Spa on the Belgian, with the Hürtgen Forest adjoining its north-east corner.

Road/rail communications

Running from east to west, the Eifel contains few centres of population larger than small villages. In 1944, the road network was officially described as being 'adequate for a large military concentration', although 'extensive dispersion would be necessary for any large force'. The rail network, however, was very extensive: 'having been engineered and expanded before 1914, for the quick deployment of troops west of the Rhine. The railroads feed into the Eifel from Koblenz, Cologne and the lesser Rhine bridgeheads between the two.'[9] Despite this, the main east–west rail link did not cross the Eifel, but rather followed the Moselle valley to the south. In the Ardennes, the road network had profited from a pre-war boom in tourism, brought about by the arrival of the affordable mass-produced motor-car. The roads were properly surfaced, but still gave rise to some hair-raising motoring as drivers frequently had to negotiate steep gradients, hairpin bends and cross gorges over rushing torrents via narrow, stone-built bridges. In 1944, although there were ten 'all-weather' roads across the German frontier into Belgium and Luxembourg between Monschau and Wasserbillig, there was not a single east–west main road through the Ardennes. As in the Eifel, most of the inhabitants of the Ardennes lived in small villages, with stone-built houses and narrow winding streets, making them ideal strongpoints and obvious bottlenecks. A few of the larger villages had populations of 2,500–4,000, and Luxembourg was the only town of any size.

Three main avenues of approach from the east
In the north, the obvious attack route was from the Aachen area – through the lower part of the Ardennes, via Eupen and Verviers – then south-west keeping well clear of Liège – then on towards Marche and Rochefort – aiming to strike the Meuse in the area of Givet. In the centre, the Losheim Gap offered a route through between Malmédy and St-Vith. Farther south, was the longest of the three routes, between Prüm and Trier – then on through southern Luxembourg, bypassing Luxembourg city well to its south and thus avoiding much of the difficult going, but taking by far the longest route to the Meuse.

Weather
The real 'wild card' to be considered was of course the weather. As one might expect in this generally mountainous/hilly area, one of the main features of the climate was (and still is), considerable precipitation and this was fairly predictable. In the winter this meant heavy rain early on, then large snowfalls later, a foot of snow falling in a 24-hour period is not uncommon. Heavy morning mists and bitter,

raw winds add to the difficulties and on average freezing conditions pertain for about a third of the year. While frozen ground made movement much easier, a sudden thaw, especially if accompanied by heavy rain, soon turned large areas into quagmires which worsened under the passage of wheeled or tracked vehicles. The weather would play a significant part in the coming battle, favouring now attacker, now defender, but it would appear that Hitler did not consider the effect bad weather would have on his troops, but was far more concerned on how it would adversely affect enemy aircraft movement. And no doubt all those who had been at the receiving end of the *Jabos'* attentions, would wholeheartedly agree. The troops were quite prepared to fight in the most atrocious weather if this meant that the dreaded *Jabos* could not fly. Both they and Hitler must have realised that at some point the weather would clear, but all hoped that by then they would at least have taken the vital bridges over the Meuse before that happened.

Security

The Germans had a saying during the war: '*Die Feind hort mit*' (the enemy is listening!) and in general their radio security was much better than that of the Allies. However, they did rely heavily on the Enigma encoding machine,[10] especially at the very highest level, and they had no inkling that the British had broken its code as early as 1940, and could read all of Hitler's and the OKW's most secret communications. Whether Hitler had a sixth sense about this or whether he just decided to be ultra(!) careful is not clear, but none of the operational or administrative details about 'Wacht am Rhein' was ever sent by Enigma until 26th December 1944. This non-reliance upon Enigma was doubly effective, because the Allies, who were so used to getting everything via Ultra (code-name for Bletchley Park's Enigma decryptions), closed their ears to any rumours about possible German attacks right up to the very last minute. As we shall see, there were some in Allied intelligence who did foresee the assault, having read the evidence which was there to be seen by anyone, but they were definitely in the minority and were generally 'pooh-poohed', their evidence not being listened to by anyone save a significant few, like General George Patton.

From the outset, Hitler went to the greatest pains to confine even the smallest details about the coming assault to as few people as possible, swearing the handful in the know to secrecy on pain of death. When it became necessary to increase the circulation, all recipients were required to sign a written oath of secrecy, and defaulters risked being shot. Generalfeldmarschall von Rundstedt, for example, whose name is always linked with the assault – indeed it is known as the 'Rundstedt Offensive', was kept out of the planning until it was *fait accompli*, but this may have been because Hitler knew he would disagree with the plan rather than for security reasons. When von Rundstedt was eventually allowed to see it, Hitler had marked the copy 'Not to be altered!' Von Rundstedt and the other Army generals certainly tried to alter it, but Hitler would brook no argument. Their frustration was clearly demonstrated by von Rundstedt, when he was said to have commented bitterly: 'the only soldiers over whom I have any control are the guards outside my office!'

Low-level security was equally important, hence, for example, the choice of the innocuous code-word 'Wacht am Rhein', which was deliberately chosen to indicate a defensive operation. We will cover details of this level of security a little later, but it is clear that everyone from Adolf Hitler down to the humblest private soldier, took the matter seriously, even though most of the latter had no idea of what they were doing or why!

'Across the Meuse and on to Antwerp!'

To summarise: Hitler had managed to convince himself that he could meet all his criteria by attacking in the Ardennes and was prepared to take a gamble on unforeseen imponderables. He could not or would not see that his plan was fatally flawed from the outset and those who could were either too scared to tell him or unable to persuade him to change his mind. The Führer is said to have informed his subordinates that he was going to make the assault, in very dramatic fashion during a 'Führer Conference' on 25 September. Attending were Keitel, Jodl, Guderian and Kreipe (the latter representing Göring and the Luftwaffe). While they were discussing the current position of the war, the word 'Ardennes' had been mentioned and, rather as he had done some days earlier in his sick-bed, Hitler had come to life: 'Raising his hand, he had exclaimed, "Stop!" There was an abrupt pause. Finally Hitler spoke. "I have made a momentous decision. I am taking the offensive. Here – out of the Ardennes!" He smashed his fist on the unrolled map before him. "Across the Meuse and on to Antwerp!" The others stared in wonder. His shoulders squared, his eyes luminous, the signs of care and sickness gone. This was the dynamic Hitler of 1940.'[11]

Hitler's Plan

No doubt, having considered all the major factors, Hitler would have worked out the basis of a plan which he would have passed to his staff to complete in detail. Certain items, such as location, intention and expected execution, allocation of task forces and timings would have initially been laid down by him. If these were committed to paper, even in note form, they have all been destroyed. However, Major I. G. Büchs, who was one of Generaloberst Alfred Jodl's assistants and who normally took part in the regular 'Führer Conferences', did keep some notes, as did Major Percy Ernst Schramm, who kept the War Diary of the Wehrmacht Operations Staff. Post-war, in the preparation of a series of special reports,[12] these notes were used to assist in writing the study which covered Hitler's initial planning phase. In outline his plan was:

a. Location. Hitler considered that the sector of the Western Front that offered the best chance of success was a 100-kilometre stretch between Monschau and Echternach, because it was so thinly held by US forces. Furthermore, the wooded area of the Eifel which lay to its east would be ideal as an assembly area for the assault forces because they could move up undetected from the air. Once the break-in had been achieved, a rapid thrust by panzer forces would be directed through the Ardennes, to establish bridgeheads across the Meuse between Liège and Namur. The final objective was to be Antwerp, which would be approached bypassing Brussels to the east.

b. Intention. Having crossed the Meuse, the object would be to sever the lines of communication and supply of US First Army, which were thought to lie along the Meuse valley towards Liège. As soon as the assault had reached the Brussels–Antwerp area the British/Canadian 21st Army Group would be similarly cut off, and finally, when Antwerp had been reached, the Allies would have lost their most important available port, which was capable of being used to full capacity almost immediately. This would enable the free-wheeling panzer forces to destroy some 20–30 Allied divisions.

c. Allocation of forces. Hitler's preliminary calculation on the minimum requirement of forces was 30 divisions, at least ten of which had to be panzer. From the outset he had decided that he would denude other sectors of the Western Front of all units that were suitable for reinforcing the attack or defending the extending flanks of the attacking force – units such as anti-tank (especially self-propelled), artillery (as much as possible), including anti-aircraft and smoke-generating equipment. This was taking a considerable risk, but he felt confident that as soon as the offensive began, the Allies would immediately stop all offensive operations and take the defensive everywhere, so as to be able to assemble a suitable force to oppose the breakthrough. As well as the ground troops, Hitler also required the air force to provide maximum fighter–ground attack support over the zone of operations.

d. Breakthrough. To spearhead the attacking force he decided to use two panzer armies advancing abreast. He would have preferred these both to have been Waffen-SS so as to inflict the maximum humiliation on the Army, but this was impossible. The basic make-up of the plan was that after a short but very intensive artillery bombardment, the infantry would break through the enemy front in a surprise attack. Then, led by special forces who would capture the Meuse bridges, the panzers would press on through the disorganised enemy to form bridgeheads across the Meuse by the end of the second day. Although it was appreciated that such a bold advance would leave long, almost unguarded flanks (there being insufficient troops to cover them), it was considered well worth the risk. It had worked in Poland in 1939, then again in France in 1940, so he saw no reason why it shouldn't work again – and besides, hadn't the bold 'gallop across France' by General George Patton's US Third Army shown that it was still a perfectly valid tactic?

e. Timings. Hitler estimated that some six to eight weeks were required to prepare the force, namely: to re-organise the panzer units, activate the *Volks* grenadier divisions (VGDs) plus the *Volks* artillery corps and *Volkswerfer* brigades;[13] obtain the necessary ammunition and POL to sustain the operation; assemble all units in suitable 'jumping-off' areas. It was now nearly the end of September which meant that the earliest date for the operation would be between 20 and 30 November, the Führer is said to have: 'requested maximum acceleration of all preparations in order to meet this deadline as nearly as possible'.

Hitler now gave his senior staff the following tasks:

a. Jodl was to: prepare the first draft of an operations plan, to include accurate estimates of the forces needed; in conjunction with General Walter Buhle, Army COS, to produce a survey of all additional units needed – such as independent tank battalions, artillery corps and rocket-launcher brigades, etc.; prepare a draft order regarding the vital need for security and camouflage during the preparatory period so as to ensure total secrecy.

b. Keitel was to present an overall estimate of ammunition and POL requirements.

c. OB West was given an order to withdraw from the front line I
   and XI SS Panzer Corps with 1st, 2nd, 9th, 12th SS Panzer
   Divisions plus Panzer Lehr Division, and for them to move into
   the region east of the Rhine for re-organisation and training.

'Wacht am Rhein' was under way!

Notes

1 On mobilisation, the German Army had been divided into two branches, the Field
   Army and the Replacement Army. The Replacement Army (*Ersatzheer*) trained
   replacements for the Field Army. This separation extended from regimental level up
   to that of corps.

2 To quote from Robert E. Merriam's book, *The Battle of the Ardennes* : 'Let me speak to
   Remer,' demanded Hitler .... 'only a few officers are involved and we will eliminate them
   from the root. You are placed in a historic position. It is your responsibility to use your
   head. You are under my direct command until Himmler arrives to take over the Replacement Army. Do you understand me?' And so Remer became a German hero.

3 '*Jabos*' was short for '*Jagdbombers*', i.e., 'hunting fighter-bombers'. This was the
   name by which the much feared American and British fighter-bombers were known
   to the Germans. In good flying weather and in sufficient strength, they dominated the
   battlefield and made daylight movement practically impossible.

4 Count Alfred von Schlieffen retired as Chief of the German General Staff in
   December 1905, but left his detailed plan for a future war against France, Russia and
   Great Britain, to be fought on two fronts. The plan was to hold the Russians with a
   small force – he considered that it would take them a long time to mobilise – while
   concentrating most of the German army against the French as they would mobilise
   faster. Schlieffen proposed that the French be encouraged to advance between Belfort
   and Sedan by a feint attack in Alsace–Lorraine, and then to withdraw so as to tempt
   them forward. The major thrust would then be made through Holland and Belgium,
   swinging in a wide arc west of Paris to attack the main body of the French Army in
   the rear, between Verdun and Belfort. Having destroyed the French, troops would
   then be quickly sent to the Russian front.

5 A fair number of existing infantry divisions which had been decimated on both the
   Eastern and Western Fronts, were retitled as *Volks* grenadier divisions, their numbers
   being made up by new recruits. They were then re-equipped to the new scale. In all
   some 60+ such divisions were designated, but some of them were formed in name
   only, then dissolved and their men used to rebuild older divisions that had been
   almost destroyed in 1944.

6 The Panzerfaust was a short-range anti-tank weapon, similar to the American
   Bazooka. It was fired from a disposable tube launcher at a range of, initially, 30
   metres, though later models went up to 100 metres, and could penetrate some
   200mm of armour plate.

7   In the end only a battalion of Pz Kpfw IVs from Grossdeutschland would be used as part of the Führer Begleit Brigade. The rest of the division remained on the Eastern Front, but the presence of some of its panzers and their crews caused no end of headaches to Allied intelligence when identified!

8   Elstob, P. *Hitler's Last Offensive*.

9   Cole, H. M. *The Ardennes: Battle of the Bulge*.

10 Enigma was the German enciphering machine – and the codes it generated. It looked like an electric typewriter and when a key was operated it sent a current through three rotors, the starting positions of which could be varied continuously at each keystroke, so that pressing the same key never produced the same enciphered letter. Ultra (short for 'Ultra Secret') stood for the intelligence information which the British obtained by decoding Enigma.

11 Toland, J. *Adolf Hitler*.

12 Detwiler, D. S. (ed.). *World War II German Military Studies*, 24 vols.

13 The *Volkswerfer* brigades manned rocket-projector batteries. Hitler had ordered five motorised FlaK regiments from the Luftwaffe, twelve *Volks* artillery corps and ten *Volkswerfer* brigades to take part in the offensive.

2
THE GERMANS PREPARE

Doubts about the 'Rundstedt Offensive'

The planning and preparation of the 'Rundstedt Offensive' as it became called – due only to the fact that the 69-year-old field marshal was back in the 'hot seat' as OB West and thus supposedly in charge – did not have the support of any of those senior German officers who would play the leading roles. Von Rundstedt himself is reported to have been both surprised and astonished by his Führer's intentions to attack on a 100-kilometre front with the stated aim of penetrating the Allied lines to a depth of some 200 kilometres. 'I was shocked,' he said later. 'Hitler had not asked me about the prospects of success. I saw clearly that the available forces were much too weak for such an ambitious plan. If we can make it to the Meuse, we should fall on our knees and thank God ...' Post-war, during an interview he gave to the renowned historian Sir Basil Liddell Hart, he showed clearly that he still disliked intensely the fact that it had even been called 'The Rundstedt Offensive'. 'That title acts on Rundstedt like the proverbial red rag, for his feelings about the plan were, and remain, very bitter. In reality he had nothing to do with it except in the most nominal way. Having failed to dissuade Hitler from attempting it, and feeling it was a hopeless venture, he then stood back throughout and left Field Marshal Model to run it.[1]

'Hitler's Fireman', Generalfeldmarschall Walther Model, was in fact equally sceptical. 'To me, the whole thing seems to have a damned fragile basis,' commented the Commander-in-Chief of Army Group B.[2] Indeed, when Model's Chief of Staff, General der Infanterie Hans Krebs, first presented the plan to him, he remarked, 'It hasn't got a damned leg to stand on!' Nevertheless, in his usual way, he would make the best of a bad job and buckle down to the task. Model's newly arrived Operations Officer, Gunther Reichlem, recalled in John Eisenhower's book, *The Bitter Woods*, how, having reported to HQ Army Group B, 'disillusioned and despairing', he found his spirits lifted and his morale restored by Model who had: '... committed himself completely to the offensive and to the training and instruction of his new officers and new units'. Reichlem accompanied his commander when he visited the various formation headquarters in the three armies under his command, carrying out map exercises with each one in turn, and he makes the interesting point that Sepp Dietrich failed to attend many of Model's discussions, being normally represented by General der Waffen-SS Willi Bittrich who would command II SS Panzer Corps in the offensive. He was even absent for the map exercise for his own SS Panzer Army HQ – but then, his lack of soldierly expertise was well known – hence the appointment of the very capable Fritz Kraemer as his deputy.

The three commanders-in-chief of the chosen attack armies were all equally as pessimistic about 'Wacht am Rhein'; they considered that Hitler's objectives were too far-reaching to be achieved with the forces that would be available. General der Panzertruppen Hasso von Manteuffel, undoubtedly the most brilliant soldier of the three, wrote later: 'We were absolutely sure that – although the plan for the offensive was ingenious and well conceived – such a plan at this point in time with the available forces in their current state could not be conducted success-fully.' Even the Führer's favourite, SS Oberstgruppenführer 'Sepp' Dietrich disliked the plan intensely: 'All Hitler wants me to do', he remarked bitterly, 'is to cross a river, capture Brussels and then go on and take Antwerp! And all this in the worst time of the year through the Ardennes where the snow is waist deep and there isn't room to deploy four tanks abreast let alone several panzer divisions! Where it doesn't get light until eight and it's dark again at four and with re-formed divisions made up chiefly of kids and sick old men – and at Christmas!'[3]

Von Rundstedt, Model and von Manteuffel quickly realised that they were all equally opposed to the plan as it stood, their main objections being:

a. The strategic dispositions were faulty and there would be grave risk to the flanks unless extra troops reinforced the shoulders of the assaulting armies.

b. Ammunition and fuel supplies were insufficient for such extensive aims.
c. Allied air superiority presented far too great a threat to achieving the long-range objectives.
d. The Allies apparently had strong reinforcements available, including airborne divisions, and the good network of roads behind the Allied front line would make their counter-moves easier to achieve.

Having formulated their disagreements they drafted a proposal to OKW explaining the main arguments against Hitler's plan and suggesting a modified one which did not have such grandiose aims. Briefly it would hope to:

a. Deliver an attack north of Aachen towards Maastricht. (This attack would need strong right flank protection.)
b. Push the American forces back from Aachen as far as the River Roer.
c. Attack south of Aachen with a view to establishing a bridgehead over the Meuse in the Liège area.

If all these aims were achieved, an advance toward Antwerp would still be possible, but the risks could be limited if something went seriously wrong.

Hitler rejected their proposals out of hand and as they were clearly all too scared of his rages to continue to voice their objections too loudly or for too long, they all appear to have decided that discretion was the better part of valour and that they would accept the plan with all its inherent problems and try to 'massage it' in order to make it work. Von Manteuffel, for example, was able to introduce has own tactics into the opening moves with considerable success. In actual fact, Hitler of course had hardly taken any notice of their fears and criticisms; he was already making plans to move himself and his headquarters from the *Wolfsschanze* (wolf's lair)[4] in the Görlitz Forest, some eight kilometres east of Rastenburg in East Prussia, to the *Adler-*

horst (eagle's nest) in the wooded hills quite close to Schloss Ziegenberg, exactly the same location as he had used to direct his first offensive against the west in May 1940.[5] He would not actually leave Berlin until 10 December, when he departed on the Führersonderzug 'Brandenburg' at 0500 hrs for the 22-hour train journey, followed by a 4½-hour car ride to 'Amt 500' (Exchange 500) which was the part of FHQu Adlerhorst that contained his special bunker.

His state of mind at this time was undoubtedly bordering on the unbalanced. At times he was perfectly lucid, at others almost crazy. Guderian commented in his autobiography that Hitler's mind at the time: '... remained active but there was something unhinged about this activity because it was dominated by constant wanderings'. Undoubtedly he was convinced that the offensive was the only way left to achieve victory.

Secrecy and Deception

From the outset, Hitler had stressed that the success of the offensive would depend upon complete surprise and this could only be achieved by strict security. It would be useful here, therefore, to summarise the main aspects of the web of secrecy and deception being spun by the Germans to disguise the preparations for the coming offensive. These were:

a. The use of misleading code-names. In addition to the obvious use of 'Wacht am Rhein' to suggest that the operations were defensive not offensive – it later became known as Operation *'Herbstnebel'* (Autumn Mist). Other code-names employed were equally baffling such as: *Feldjägerkommando z.b.V* (Military Police Command for special assignments) – this was the name given to Fifth Panzer Army, while Sixth Panzer Army was called 'Refresher Staff 16'.

b. Simulated deployment and mock radio traffic. The simulation of a significant deployment to the east of the Rhine to give the impression that counter-attack forces were concentrating there against the anticipated major attack which the Allies were planning. For example, Sixth SS Panzer Army moved quite openly

by day into an assembly area on the plains near Cologne –
apparently to forestall Allied operations aimed at that area.
They did not move into their correct assembly area in the Eifel
region until 72 hours before the offensive was due to begin –
and then their 35-mile journey was made exclusively by night.
Coupled with this type of movement, was a mass of spoof radio
communications between a non-existent HQ Twenty-fifth Army
and nine non-existent divisions all located to the west of
Cologne. (This was not dissimilar to the mock radio traffic
which the Allies had established in the UK prior to D-Day,
known as Operation 'Fortitude', which had General George
Patton at the head of a mythical army group in Kent that would
land on the northern French coast, the intention being to keep
the Germans thinking that the main assault would come in the
Pas-de-Calais, and not in Normandy.) At the same time, all
genuine telephone and radio traffic concerning the operation
was strictly forbidden, even if using Enigma. All 'Wacht am
Rhein' information was carried by messenger or liaison officer
(*but they were forbidden to travel by aircraft!*), and because the
Allies were so confident that Ultra would provide them with
everything they needed, the lack of such messages reinforced the
belief that nothing major was being planned.

c. Reconnaissance limitations. Reconnaissance activities were
initially carefully monitored, then severely restricted all along the
front in September and November, and were *entirely* forbidden
from 1 December on. These restrictions did not prevent commanders like the diminutive von Manteuffel (known as '*Kleiner*' to his
friends!) from personally carrying out his own recces, but he did
so in disguise, wearing the uniform of a colonel of infantry and
then, for example, spending a night in a pill-box overlooking the
River Our. From this vantage-point he confirmed that the
infantry regiments of the US 28th Infantry Division had withdrawn their outposts and that his leading troops would be able to
assault across the river without a preliminary bombardment and
thus gain surprise. During an interview in 1972, he said of this

reconnaissance: 'I went to the front-line troops disguised as a colonel of infantry and was there for 33 hours I think. I hoped to get some hints and I was right – the Americans ... well I think one hour after darkness they went to the villages, to their rooms or their girls, I don't know, then one hour before the sun came up they came back to their trenches. ... so there was no one covering their positions during the night. It was for this reason that I proposed to Hitler that we begin early, so we formed strong troops from each division and began to attack at five o'clock in the morning ... we slipped through the American positions and at about 8 or 9 o'clock when the sun came up we strengthened our attack.'[6] Such individual reconnaissance was rare, so the ban resulted in the major drawback that there was little if any up-to-date information about the Allied dispositions all along the Start Line and this would inevitably hinder the assault.

On the other hand, US reconnaissance activity provided some heart-stopping incidents. For example, in early December a strong night recce patrol penetrated the forward observation officers' post of an artillery battery of I SS Panzer Corps and, in the morning, it was found that two men were missing. Everyone was on tenterhooks, expecting the worst, but when there was no further reaction it was assumed that the two men must either have been killed or had refused to give any more than the required name, number and rank during interrogation.

d. Troop movements. A considerable amount of troop movement took place, both genuine and bogus, the latter obviously by day. Operational movement took place only by night when no lights or rest halts were permitted; straw was put down on roads close to the front lines and aircraft flew low over enemy positions to mask the noise of ground traffic.

e. Markings on supply transport. Road and rail transport received incorrect markings to disguise the destinations of ammunition, fuel and supplies, misleading signs were posted at some railway stations, and there was much deceptive loading and unloading activity.

f. 'Need to know' severely restricted. The number of personnel involved in the planning was extremely restricted and each one 'in the know' was registered by name and threatened with the death penalty for security violations, irrespective of rank. Charles B. MacDonald in *The Battle of the Bulge*, gives a graphic account of the scene when the divisional and corps commanders were gathered for briefing at von Rundstedt's head-quarters in Schloss Ziegenberg at the end of the first week in December 1944. They were first ordered to remove their personal weapons, then their briefcases, then put aboard a bus which took them on a circuitous half-hour journey through the darkness, wind and rain, to reach the *Adlerhorst*, which was actually only a three minutes' drive away! The final indignity came when they left the bus and had walked through a double row of armed SS guards down into the deep underground conference room where: '... as they sat down around a large square table, an SS guard assumed a position behind each chair, glowering with a ferocity that made at least one of the generals, Fritz Bayerlein, fear even to reach for his handkerchief.'

g. Low-level operational briefings left to the last minute. *Tag Null* (Zero Day) was set for Saturday, 16 December and it was only on the night of the 15th/16th that the troops of the attacking forces were briefed on the operational plan. This meant that no artillery targets could be pre-registered and the opening barrage was severely restricted, but as has already been pointed out, this did add enormously to the assault coming as a complete surprise to most of the Allied troops facing them.

How much did the Allies know?

It would be wrong to imagine that the German security was so good that absolutely no one on the Allied side suspected that something big was about to take place. In fact two of the major 'players' in the Intelligence field, had worked out for themselves that all was not well. One of these was the redoubtable Colonel Oscar W. Koch, G-2 section head of Patton's US Third Army. Patton had brought him to

2nd Armored Division soon after the 'Hell on Wheels' Division had been established, then taken him to North Africa as Chief of Staff of one of the task forces. Later he became his G-2 in Third Army: 'Koch is the greatest G-2 in the US Army,' wrote one of his contemporaries. 'His record is without equal in every phase of intelligence ... Koch was the spark plug of HQ Third Army. Because of his exceptional abilities, unfailing effectiveness and the wide range of G-2 activities, he was constantly being tossed the ball. Patton and the COS were constantly assigning him tasks outside his sectional duties.'[7] As we shall see, it was thanks to Koch's insistence that the Germans were about to launch an all-out offensive in the Ardennes and Patton's eminently sensible orders to plan for every emergency, that his Army was 'ready to roll' almost immediately, much to the surprise and disbelief of Eisenhower and Bradley!

Oscar Koch was not the only senior intelligence officer to come to the correct conclusion about what was going on, The other was Colonel Benjamin Abbot Dickson, known as 'Monk' by his associates at HQ First Army. A reserve officer who had been recalled to active duty in 1940, he had been selected for intelligence initially because of his ability to speak French and German. On 10 December he had issued his G-2 Intelligence Estimate No. 37 in which he had directly referred to the distinct possibility of the enemy's mounting an all-out counter-offensive: 'Von Rundstedt, who obviously is conducting military operations ... has skilfully defended and husbanded his forces and is preparing for his part in the all-out application of every weapon at the focal point and the correct time to achieve defense of the Rhine west of the Rhine by inflicting as great a defeat on the Allies as possible.' Clearly Dickson felt that what he had put in his intelligence estimate should have been sufficient to alert the senior Allied commanders (Eisenhower and Bradley), so that they would at least take some emergency action. However, apart from Third Army nothing happened and this was undoubtedly at least partly due to the fact that 'Monk' had his problems with those 'above', which included a clash of personalities between himself and First Army's COS, Major General William B. Kean, whose imperious manner had earned him the nickname of 'Captain Bligh'! Instead of taking any notice of Colonel Dickson's suspicions, he branded him an alarmist and a pessimist – as did Brigadier General Edwin L. Sibert, G-2 at HQ 12th Army Group – with whom Dickson was also continually at daggers drawn. This was nothing new, the animosity between them being deep-seated. It could probably be traced back to the fact that Dickson had been part of Bradley's staff in North Africa and had then been taken back by him to UK to prepare for D-Day as G-2 of HQ First Army. Dickson had always assumed that he would continue to be Bradley's G-2 when the latter moved up to command 12th Army Group, so he felt that General Sibert was now occupying the appointment that was rightfully his – and naturally Sibert did not agree! This caused Sibert to pour scorn on all that Dickson did, including the all-important contents of HQ First Army's G-2 Estimate No 37 and to aver that in his opinion there would be no enemy counter-attack until after the Allies had achieved a major breakthrough towards the Rhine. This view was of course supported by the evidence coming from Ultra, which was being interpreted to suit what the Allies wanted to happen, so anything that could have been construed as obvious warning signs of the enemy build-up was unfortunately interpreted wrongly. For example, there were a number of intercepted requests for air reconnaissance in the Ardennes around Malmédy, but these were ignored and instead the Allies fixed on a number of requests for similar recces around Aachen. On 11 December von Rundstedt's HQ sent a message to OKW which Ultra deciphered as follows: 'Large-scale attack against western Germany might begin in the very near future. Allies will probably try to seize Rhine crossings by air landings on a large scale. It is most important that defences at the Rhine bridges be maintained in a constant state of readiness.' This was taken to support the theory that the Germans were really only interested in defending their Fatherland and not in launching a major counter-thrust.

Writing about this period after the war, Group Captain Winterbotham, CBE, who was one of the remarkable band of people responsible for the inception of Ultra, explained how when he had returned to London after an important trip to Australia and America, he had: '... got the first news of the apparent failure of Ultra to warn either

Eisenhower, Bradley or Montgomery of Hitler's offensive in the Ardennes.' He goes on to say that, while initially he had no definite explanation as to why Ultra had apparently failed, it was very clear to him that the Germans had imposed tremendous secrecy prior to the 'Wacht am Rhein' operation and that this was evidenced by the fact that once the operation had started it was 'business as usual' as far as Ultra was concerned. In fact he makes the very relevant comment that perhaps because Ultra had been so helpful during the previous year, some Intelligence staffs had 'begun to rely on it almost entirely' and had ignored information coming from other sources such as battlefield prisoners. (For example, on 13th December, a fairly high-ranking prisoner had reported that he had been told sometime back in August that it was impossible to supply the infantry divisions fighting on the Western Front with fresh troops, because all potential reinforcements were be required to join the newly forming *Volks* grenadier divisions that were then being established to become part of a massive assault army under 'Sepp' Dietrich. The target then was for seventy such divisions to be formed, some ten or so of which would be used for holding 'blocking' positions, while the rest were going to be used for a massive counter-attack on the Western Front, scheduled towards the end of December. The prisoner went on to say that the OKW had high hopes of achieving a major breakthrough, because of the lack of depth of the Allied positions in France and the fact that they had few reserves).

Group Captain Winterbotham also comments that from all the intelligence appreciations put out by the various G-2s in the month before the offensive, it was apparent that there were plenty of clues which could have been gleaned from the statements of POWs, from captured documents, from photo-recces and from logistical Ultra, but that only one man, namely 'Monk' Dickson, did so and reached the right conclusion in his now famous 'Intelligence Estimate No 37'. To be fair to Colonel Oscar Koch, Patton's G-2, he also merited similar praise. 'I think that these two old-timers', writes Winterbotham, 'even without the high-level signals from Hitler and the OKW that they were used to, had put their bits and pieces together correctly despite the extraordinary precautions that Rundstedt had taken to cover up his troops' movements. Once the battle had started Ultra had confirmed the presence of our old enemies the Fifth and Seventh Panzer Armies as well as the SS divisions and there had been enough Ultra to follow the lines the attack was taking.'

Specialised troops

While the organisation, weapons and equipment of the attacking force will be dealt with in detail in a future chapter, it is perhaps relevant here to mention a special force which Hitler had dreamed up for a special role in his offensive. It would be led by his protégé, Sturmbannführer (now to be promoted to Obersturmbannführer) Otto Skorzeny, who was also known as: 'The most dangerous man in Europe'. He had earned his promotion and been awarded the German Cross in Gold from the hands of his grateful Führer for his latest escapade, which had even topped his miraculous rescue of Benito Mussolini the year before. He and his men had seized the citadel in Budapest, thereby preventing the Hungarian government from signing a separate peace treaty! 'Don't go, Skorzeny,' Hitler had said as the blond giant was ready to leave. 'I have perhaps the most important job in your life for you. So far very few people know of the preparations for a secret plan in which you have a great part to play. In December, Germany will start a great offensive, which may well decide her fate.'[8] Hitler went on to give Skorzeny a very detailed explanation of the top secret operation. 'I am telling you all this so that you can consider your part in it and realise that nothing has been forgotten,' Hitler continued. 'One of the most important tasks in this offensive will be entrusted to you and to units under your command, which will have to go ahead and seize one or more bridges over the Meuse between Liège and Namur.' Hitler explained that Skorzeny and his men would have to wear British and American uniforms, speak English, drive Allied vehicles and generally behave like them, so as to fool the enemy. They should also give false orders, upset communications, misroute convoys and generally cause as much chaos as possible. Having digested everything Skorzeny felt it necessary to raise some of his misgivings, in particular the lack of time in which to prepare. Hitler, while agreeing with him, said that he must do the best he could in the time available. He also explained once again that the most important thing was secrecy, so Skorzeny should keep his own men in complete ignorance until the very last minute – 'You can mislead them by allowing it to be known that the German High Command is expecting a big enemy attack in the Cologne–Bonn area this year, and all these preparations are for the purpose of defeating it.'[9]

One detail with which Skorzeny was most unhappy was the wearing of foreign uniforms, because they would risk being shot as spies if captured. Eventually it was agreed that they should wear German uniforms beneath the Allied ones, so they could take off the latter before actually opening fire. This was a great relief to him, but the next shock came when he heard that OKH proposed to issue an order throughout the entire army, that all English-speaking officers and men should report for a 'special operation'. He protested, was told that the order had been cancelled, then was shattered to receive a few days later a copy of the very order headed: 'SECRET COMMANDO OPERA-TIONS' which contained a paragraph to the effect that units should send in the names of all those who wished to transfer voluntarily to a formation to be commanded by 'Obersturmbannführer Skorzeny in Friedenhall, near Berlin!' The order was in fact issued to all units of the Wehrmacht both at home and at the front. Skorzeny knew that Allied intelligence was bound to pick this up – it is said that they did so in about eight days – but then did nothing whatsoever about it! Skorzeny protested that his cover was completely 'blown', but the only answer he got from above was: 'It's idiotic, but it has been done. We cannot hold up your operation now.'

The Skorzeny operation now had its own code-name, 'Greif' (Griffon) and Skorzeny's 150 Panzer Brigade was approved to have a strength of some 3,500 all ranks and to consist of:

a small brigade headquarters
two tank companies each of ten tanks
three reconnaissance companies each with ten scout cars
three motorised infantry battalions, each with two rifle and one heavy machine-gun company

one light anti-aircraft gun company
two anti-tank gun companies
one mortar section
one intelligence company
one Commando company

Skorzeny asked General Burgdorf, chief of the army personnel office at OKH, for the loan of three battalion commanders with front-line experience which was agreed. In addition he was promised two Luft-waffe parachute battalions, one army tank company and one communications company.

If hundreds and hundreds of 'fast-talking phoney GIs' was what Skorzeny optimistically expected the appeal would produce, what he actually received must have been a great disappointment. After his force had assembled and undergone two weeks of language instruction, he estimated that his volunteer force had some 500 'English speakers', but only a mere ten of these were able to speak the language fluently and had a good working knowledge of American slang. A further 30 to 40 could speak English well enough, but knew no American slang; 120–150 spoke English fairly well; the rest had learned a little English at school so had a smattering of English words. Everyone else in 150 Panzer Brigade could only, as Skorzeny himself puts it, 'just about say "Yes"!'

With regard to vehicles, weapons and equipment the situation was not much better. For example they started training on the Grafenwohr Training Ground, with just two US Sherman tanks (and one of these would break down with transmission troubles in the Eifel before the operation started!). These were supplemented by thirteen Panthers which had been 'doctored' cosmetically to look like Shermans (anyone who knows what the two tanks look like will realise this was impossible to achieve – Skorzeny commented that they would only deceive: '... very young American troops, seeing them at night from very far away!') – but the shape of the false armour which had been added to the turrets far more resembled the US M10 tank destroyer which, although it was based on the Sherman, had an open-topped, low sloped turret, which was far easier to mock-up than the high rounded turret of the Sherman. They also received just ten Allied scout cars, only four of which were American; the six British cars all broke down during the training period, which solved the problem of disguising them as US cars! So far as 'B' vehicles were concerned, some 30 Jeeps arrived in dribs and drabs, but they had only fifteen genuine American 2½-ton trucks, so had to make up the rest of their requirements with German Fords painted green. Weapons were equally impossible. They started off with just 50 per cent of the US rifles they needed, and they had no ammunition for their US anti-tank guns and mortars. When a few ammunition-filled railway wagons arrived, they blew up as a result of faulty stowage! In the end they had to make do with German weapons for everyone except the Commando company.

The state of vehicles, weapons and ammunition was bad enough, but that did not compare with the clothing situation, which of course was vital if they were going to masquerade as GIs. Most of the first consignment to arrive was British, then the Head of the POW Section sent them a supply of US field jackets, but all were adorned with the tell-tale triangle peculiar to POWs, so had to be returned! Skorzeny comments: 'It was an eloquent comment on the way the business was handled that the commander of the brigade – myself – got nothing but an American army pullover in my size.'

Despite all these problems, 150 Panzer Brigade carried on with its training and because they were not permitted to know the true details of 'Greif', all manner of weird and wonderful notions were dreamed up among the men. Some said that the brigade was going to be sent at top speed to rush across France and liberate the beleaguered garrisons of Brest and/or Lorient. Others were firmly convinced that they were heading for Paris to capture Eisenhower and his SHAEF Headquarters – the RV for this one being the Café de la Paix! This extraordinary flight of fancy percolated through to the Allies, who it is said, concentrated defence measures on that point for some months! (See later for the effects which such rumours had on Eisenhower's personal freedom of movement). More about 'The Most Dangerous Man in Europe' and his assault force in due course.

Deployment

Despite the need for maintaining tight security, a very large mass of men, weapons, ammunition, fuel and rations simply had to be moved, so rail and road transport had to work as efficiently as possible at all times and in all areas. In spite of Allied air interference, the *Reichsbahn* for example, managed to move some 500 trainloads of equipment, fuel and ammunition across the Rhine quickly and efficiently, despite continual attacks on the railway bridges and marshalling yards. Delays due to Allied attacks were kept to a minimum. In his official US Army history, Hugh M. Cole quotes as examples of the *Reichsbahn*'s expertise the situation at Koblenz where, on 10 December, an air raid had left a hundred bomb craters, yet twenty-four hours later they had all been filled in and the trains were running on time. Next day the main double-track line between Cologne and Eusenkirchen, which supported Sixth SS Panzer Army's deployment, was badly hit and all traffic was stopped. By the very next day everything was running again without a hitch. Two of the railway bridges over the Rhine were hit during November and four others were under repair as a result of bombing raids the previous month, yet at least one line per bridge was kept open. In the concentration area, only fifteen carloads of the entire 500 trainloads were actually destroyed by direct enemy air attacks. By far the greatest aerial threat to the *Reichsbahn* operations came from the *Jabos*, the dreaded fighter-bombers which attacked the tracks, rolling-stock, stations and marshalling yards. Such air attacks achieved 125 breaks in the railway lines feeding the Western Front in the first two weeks of December, 60 of which were in the concentration area. Despite all these problems, the *Reichsbahn* somehow managed to maintain an equilibrium between Allied damage and their railway repair capability. Hugh Cole comments that the story of this German success merits close study, especially because it was achieved in spite of complete Allied dominance in the air.

Fuel problems

There were some serious problems which seemed to have escaped notice, as is evidenced when considering the all-important fuel requirements. It had been estimated that some 4.49 million gallons would be needed to support the offensive. Despite a deterioration in POL production, it was considered perfectly feasible for OKW to raise the reserves to the required level by the time the attack was planned to start. On 28 October an order was issued concerning the establishment of POL reserves in the west. The aim was to accumulate 660,000 gallons of oil and 3.96 million gallons of petrol – a total of some 4.62 million gallons of fuel. On top of this of course, the Germans anticipated that they would be able to capture further supplies from the enemy. The major problem was to get this fuel up to where it was needed. By mid-December, only 1.98 million gallons had been delivered to the Eifel assembly area, the main cause of the delay being the transportation system. The road transport was probably the worst part, the convoys consisting of worn-out trucks, being driven over bomb-damaged roads, at night and under severe blackout restrictions. The camouflaging of storage positions was a continual headache, while nearer the front line, horses had to be used to tow guns and ammunition limbers, so as to eliminate engine noise. By the time the offensive began, some 3.17 million gallons of POL had been delivered to the Armies and their subordinate units. A further 2.11 million gallons was on its way, and 792,000 gallons had been promised as a reserve.

This all sounds as though Keitel and his staff, who were in charge of providing the fuel (and ammunition) for the offensive, had worked a major miracle. And so they had, but what they hadn't allowed for was the greater fuel consumption, especially of the tracked vehicles, which would result from hilly terrain, ice-covered roads and all the other hazards to be faced in the Ardennes. In most of the planned attack areas the AFVs would have to move mainly in low gear, thereby using at least twice as much fuel as planned. The fuel consumption estimates were hopelessly wrong so supplies were totally inadequate from the outset. As the German/US study of the campaign comments: 'Thus, the scope of the Offensive had – in reality – been limited in advance by the POL situation, which also hampered the preparations at every stage because of the enforced fuel conservation.' It also goes on to explain that although the fuel supplies had been procured: 'It had, however, not been possible to deliver them sufficiently close to the front to make them immediately available, and it proved to be even less possible to assure their timely delivery during the course of the Offensive.'[10]

And ammunition too

Hitler had allocated 100 ammunition trains from his own special reserve to 'nourish' the offensive. On top of this the *Oberquarter-meister*, Generalmajor Alfred Toppe, reckoned on scraping together three units of what was considered in German practice to be a basic load. Of these units, one was allocated to the artillery for the opening preparatory barrage; a ½-unit was for the break-in battle; then the further 1½ would be allocated to the fire needed to keep the offensive rolling forward. Toppe planned to have two basic loads in the hands of the troops before they began the attack and these deliveries were made on time, but he had not allowed for the fact that Allied counter activity had also to be catered for, so that by the second week of December the two allocated loads were down to 1½ and this was never made up. The figures used for ammunition consumption were based upon a fast-moving exploitation scenario, once the initial break-through had been achieved, and as this did not happen, they would prove to be far too optimistic.

Nevertheless, miracles were performed. During the period 9 September to 15 December the main concentration area received 1,502 troop trains and some 500 supply trains, the vast majority of which was allocated to 'Wacht am Rhein'. The Eifel rail system had unloaded 144,735 tons of supplies during the same period, but saturation-point was reached on the 17th when OB West was forced to detrain incoming reserve divisions on the west bank of the Rhine – and this would have serious consequences as the battle progressed. Much of this great achievement was: 'the product of an almost psychotic drive by Hitler to put every last man, gun and tank that could be stripped from some part of the declining German war establishment into the attack. Thirteen infantry and seven armored divisions were ready for the initial assault. Five divisions from the OKW reserve were on alert or actually *en route* to form the second wave, plus one armored and one mechanised brigade at reinforced strength. Approximately five additional divisions were listed in the OKW reserve, but their availability was highly dubious.'[11]

Training

For some years now the German commanders in the west had been training their troops to fight static, defensive battles against an invading force; since 6 June 1944 they had actually been fighting defensively, in a series of withdrawals against a much better and more lavishly equipped enemy, who, most of the time, had managed to force them steadily back. It was now necessary to retrain these same commanders into the *Blitzkrieg* frame of mind of the early war years. However, this had to be done using subterfuge, again for security reasons. Night operations were practised and map exercises held, to remind staff officers of how to control and regulate traffic columns in winter, especially by night. A certain amount of individual training was necessary, especially for tank drivers, who were generally unused to driving in winter weather – indeed, tank losses had meant that a fair proportion of AFV drivers were being misemployed as infantry and some had become casualties, so new drivers had to be quickly trained. Units such as Skorzeny's 150 Panzer Brigade required specialised training, which inevitably would have to be somewhat sketchy given the short time available and the paucity of Allied uniforms, arms and equipment.

Preparations for deployment

Certain improvements to the existing infrastructure had been in hand almost from the time when the plan had been first mooted, being justified on the grounds that these measures would have been equally necessary had there been an impending major enemy attack, so nothing would be given away by their being reported to the Allies. These included:

a. Reinforcing the various road and rail bridges over the Rhine so that they could carry heavier loads over longer periods.
b. Concealing bridging equipment in strategic places on the banks of the Rhine for immediate availability if bridges were destroyed by enemy action.

c. Improving existing forward storage installations for POL, ammunition, rations, medical supplies and non-expendable items.

d. Restructuring the railway system .

On 12 December the attack divisions began their deployment under a strict blanket of security. Over the last 5 to 8 kilometres many of the guns were towed by horses to cut down engine noise. Such noise that was noted by GIs opposite was put down to normal unit movement. 'Camouflage officers' ensured that units' camouflage was maintained at the highest level, by day or night. Undoubtedly, the long, dark nights and the prevailing dull autumn weather with thick, low clouds, which was the norm in the Eifel at this time of year, helped enormously with the cover and concealment of the attack force.

The Luftwaffe

To support the Ardennes offensive Reichsmarschall Hermann Göring had promised one thousand aircraft. This was small beer compared to what had been achieved in the past; for example, 2,500 front-line aircraft had been available to support Operation 'Barbarossa'. Even Hitler was extremely sceptical about this figure, so he reduced it to 800–900 when he briefed the OKW. In fact this lower figure would *just* be reached by the Luftwaffe, but only for one day, and by then the ground battle had already been decided! Is it any wonder that the Führer gambled on bad weather, so that the massive Allied air superiority could not play a proper part in events. However, even this token gesture by the German Air Force was really more than they could or should have made. To produce his 800 aircraft, Göring had taken the fighter reserves away from the defence of Germany, and casualties among the fighter squadrons were to be out of all proportion to the damage they would inflict on the Allies. 'The Luftwaffe received its death blow in the Ardennes,' Adolf Galland would later write. This fighter ace with more than 100 air-to-air victories to his credit, one of the select 27 members of the Wehrmacht who had received the coveted Diamonds to his Knight's Cross, was to be one of the main losers in the murky politics which now surrounded the once proud Luftwaffe.

For some time he had been planning for the 'Big Punch' against Allied bombing raids and had some 2,700 fighters assembled to strike at the leading waves of American bombers over their targets deep inside Germany and continue the attacks during the raids and while they were returning to their bases in England. These attacks would continue even when the enemy aircraft were trying to break off and escape. His plan would come to naught, swept aside by Göring who heaped a tirade of abuse on Galland's fighter pilots: '... questioning their courage, insulting their honour, assaulting their pride. Men who had more than 1,000 combat sorties in their logbooks, men with more than 200 air-to-air victories, men with tortured limbs and ugly burn scars on their faces, hollow-eyed, chain-smoking men wearing the highest decorations for valour their country could bestow; men who were now the only survivors of their training school classes – these men were forced to listen while the porcine Reichsmarschall hurled reproaches and irrational accusations in their faces.'[12]

Perhaps Galland would have been all in favour of an offensive like the one that was being planned by Hitler and his generals, but he was not given a chance to get involved. Instead he was sidelined – relegated to looking after the Me 163 and Me 262 technical evaluation projects. The fighter aircraft which he had so carefully husbanded would be frittered away in the murky skies of the Ardennes, in a low-level battle for which they had not been trained. 'Galland understood at once that it would be a massacre, and that it would bring about the final defeat of the Luftwaffe.'[13]

Notes

1 Liddell Hart, B. H. *The Other Side of the Hill*

2 Model had initially taken over both as CinC Army Group B (from Rommel) and as CinC Army Group West (vice von Rundstedt), but found the two jobs extremely difficult to manage and so was relieved when von Rundstedt was reinstated as OB West.

3 As quoted in MacDonald, C. B. *The Battle of the Bulge*.

4 Called the 'wolf's lair' because Hitler's undercover code-name before he came to power was 'Wolf'.

5 The *Adlerhorst* had been the very first *Führerhauptquartier* to be constructed, in the autumn of 1939, and would now be the last of Hitler's field headquarters to be occupied.

6   IWM Sound Archive Tape No 2713 (recorded in 1972).
7   Colonel Robert S. Allen in his book, *Lucky Forward*.
8   Skorzeny O. *Skorzeny's Special Missions*.
9   Ibid.
10 *World War II German Military Studies*, vol. 10.
11 Cole, H. M. *Ardennes: the Battle of the Bulge*.
12 Baker, D. *Adolf Galland, The Authorised Biography*.
13 Ibid.

3
ON THE OTHER SIDE OF THE HILL

The Western Front

By early December 1944 the Allies had made some progress all along the Western Front, inflicting heavy casualties of the order of two/three to one which would be increasingly difficult for the enemy to replace. However, they had not yet inflicted a decisive defeat upon the Germans, nor cleared them from their positions west of the Rhine, except in the far south. Hitler's forces had re-organised their defences and recovered from the trauma of being defeated in Normandy, then swept out of the rest of northern France. The 'Gallop across France', was now over and everywhere the Allies were faced with stiffening German resistance. Reading from north to south, the situation was roughly as follows.

a. In the north, despite the failure of the Arnhem operation, 21st Army Group had still made considerable gains. The advance by British XXX Corps had led to the liberation of a large part of Holland; the primary aim now was the freeing of the area between Arnhem and the Zuider Zee, which had been partly flooded by the enemy. Operations near the coast had included the clearance of the Scheldt Estuary which was achieved by early November, so that the port of Antwerp could be properly used the first convoy berthing there on 28 November. The freeing of the port would certainly help to ease the continuing supply problems which had so adversely affected all Allied plans for too long. By early December British Second Army had cleared the remaining enemy footholds over the Meuse, but the Germans had blown a dike on the Lower Rhine near Arnhem, causing severe flooding and forcing Canadian First Army to withdraw across the River Waal – a tributary of the Lower Rhine.

b. In the centre 12th Army Group had gained ground in the direction of both Bonn and Cologne, with troops of Patton's Third Army now up to the River Saar. During the second week of November they had begun the 'Battle for Germany' including a massive assault on Metz on the 8th, but this was hampered by severe flooding in the area of the Moselle. Once the weather had improved, the mighty US Eighth Air Force sent in nearly 1,500 heavy bombers to help break the Metz deadlock, but 'The Bastion of the East', as it was called, was not finally subdued until the very end of the month. Progress continued on the 10th and 11th, with the Germans fighting a series of delaying actions in the forests and villages. On the 11th, despite Third Army's progress, the Army Group commander (Bradley) took 83rd Infantry Division away from Patton and it reverted to US First Army command. This prevented Saarbrücken being taken, which, in Patton's opinion, was one of the direct causes of the Germans' early success in the Ardennes.[1]

c. In the south, 6th Army Group had made good progress, US Seventh Army capturing Strasbourg, while French First Army had liberated Belfort and trapped a sizeable force of the enemy in the Colmar pocket.

A number of senior commanders, including Bradley and Montgomery, met with Eisenhower at Maastricht on 7 December, to plan future operations. All were generally in agreement that a major offensive should be launched early in the New Year, but, as in the past, the arguments for a narrow thrust strategy rather than the broad front assault, remained as bitter as ever. Montgomery still favoured the single strong thrust approach (as he had done for the past three months), aiming to cross the Rhine north of the Ruhr, for which he would expect (and require) massive support, but this would mean holding up all other operations, especially those scheduled farther south. While Eisenhower was prepared to go as far as putting US Ninth Army under HQ 21st Army Group's control for such an operation, he was not willing to abandon the other part of his 'one-two punch' strategy, which would

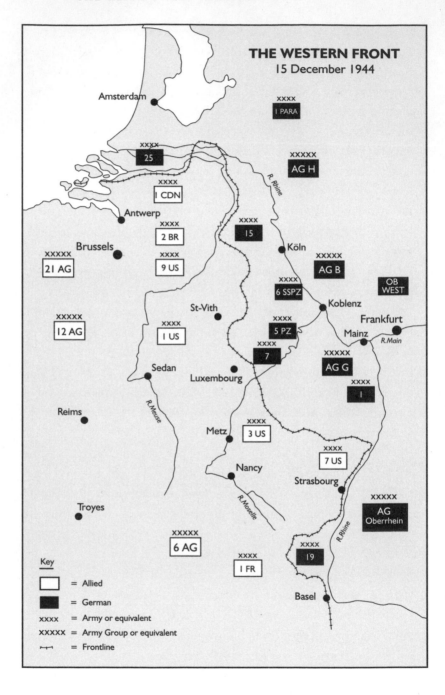

THE WESTERN FRONT
15 December 1944

Amsterdam

xxxx
1 PARA

xxxx
25

xxxxx
AG H

xxxx
1 CDN

R. Rhine

Antwerp

xxxx
2 BR

xxxx
15

Köln

Brussels

xxxxx
21 AG

xxxx
9 US

xxxxx
AG B

OB WEST

xxxx
6 SSPZ

Koblenz

Frankfurt

St-Vith

xxxxx
12 AG

xxxx
1 US

xxxx
5 PZ

Mainz

R. Main

xxxx
7

xxxxx
AG G

Sedan

Luxembourg

xxxx
1

Reims

R. Meuse

Metz

xxxx
3 US

Nancy

xxxx
7 US

Strasbourg

R. Moselle

Troyes

xxxxx
AG Oberrhein

xxxxx
6 AG

xxxx
19

R. Rhine

xxxx
1 FR

Basel

Key

▢ = Allied

■ = German

xxxx = Army or equivalent

xxxxx = Army Group or equivalent

⊢⊣ = Frontline

require Patton's US Third Army of Bradley's 12th Army Group to make a major assault towards Frankfurt. The meeting did not resolve the argument and Eisenhower continued to plan to inflict as much damage on the enemy along a broad front, before considering launching the main assault in the north.

In the Ardennes

Here an uneasy calm reigned. Defended by troops of General Hodges' US First Army, it was considered to be a quiet, unimportant area where badly mauled units could recuperate, or 'green' ones receive a 'blooding' without have to take part in heavy fighting. The forests were considered to be virtually impassable for major troop movement. It is strange that no one ever appeared to consider that it was via this route that the Germans had unleashed their assault on the west in May 1940. Little did virtually anyone guess of course, that this 120 kilometres of difficult, seemingly impenetrable forest, which was presently held by just five infantry divisions and one armoured division – about 83,000 men in total – would shortly be facing an assault by nearly three times that number! In the meantime it was considered more important to maintain the status quo, with neither side doing anything to 'rock the boat'.

The outline layout from north to south along the Ardennes Front was as follows:

2nd Inf Div (around Monschau)
99th Inf Div (Monschau Forest)
106th Inf Div (Schnee-Eifel)
28th Inf Div (east of Bastogne)
4th Inf Div (Echternach)
9th Armd Div (in reserve around Vianden)

The 2nd and 99th Infantry Divisions were part of V Corps, the remainder were all VIII Corps formations. See Appendix 3 for background details of all these formations. The other major formations in

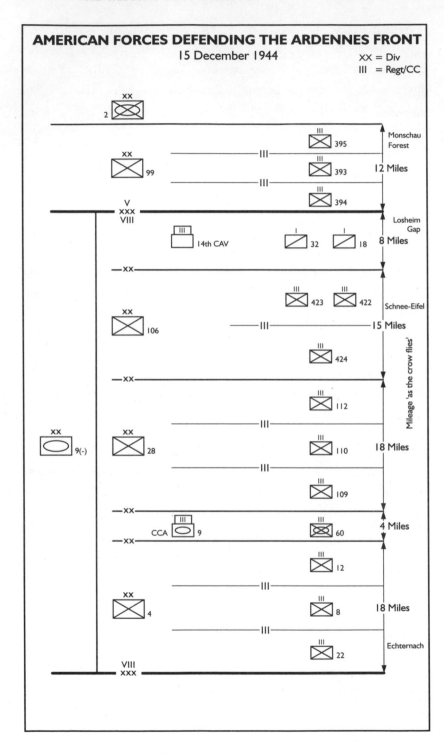

AMERICAN FORCES DEFENDING THE ARDENNES FRONT
15 December 1944

XX = Div
III = Regt/CC

V Corps were 1st, 9th, 30th and 78th Infantry Divisions. Of these 1st and 30th were enjoying some well-deserved 'rest and relaxation' behind the front lines, after more than two weeks of continuous action in the Hürtgen Forest – some of the bloodiest and toughest fighting they would ever experience. The remainder, together with 2nd Infantry and 3rd Armored Divisions, would soon be embroiled in an equally bruising battle for the Roer and Urft dams.

2nd Infantry Division

The Indianhead Division was the most northerly of these US formations. Together with 9th and 78th Infantry Divisions, plus 3rd Armored Division, they had been sent by General Gerow, CG V Corps, to assault the Roer and Urft dams in an offensive which began on 13 December. The 2nd had been ordered to outflank Monschau from the south-west while 9th Infantry and 3rd Armored advanced in the centre and 78th Infantry converged with them from the north-west. The intention was to capture the dams before the Germans decided to open the floodgates and turn the region into an impassable sea of mud (as they had done earlier around Antwerp). Since late September, 2nd Infantry had been located in the Schnee-Eifel to the east of St-Vith as part of VIII Corps, but they reverted to V Corps for the dams operation. The Schnee-Eifel had been a quiet area with little enemy activity apart from exchanges of artillery fire from time to time and a few patrol clashes. On 11 December, the GIs of 2nd Infantry were pulled out of their foxholes in the middle of a heavy snowstorm, to be replaced by the men of 106th Infantry Division (see later). The 2nd Inf Div then moved to assembly areas close behind 99th Inf Div's lines to their south, near a Belgian Army barracks, Camp Elsenborn, where they would prepare for the coming attack against the dams. The attack began at first light on the 13th. The infantry pushed forwards slowly through thick forest and heavy snow, initially encountering no enemy. As they left the tree line they came within range of the first enemy pill-boxes and, being now out in the open, drew heavy fire. This, and the swathes of barbed wire and anti-personnel minefields which were invisible under the deep snow, made progress painfully slow, the engineers having to sweep every inch of the way, but 2nd Div made gains, as did the other attacking divisions. One of their main objectives was the village of Wahlerscheid which 9th Infantry Regiment captured on the night 15/16 December. A gap in the enemy wire having been cut the previous evening by a patrol, one company after another passed through in single file without alerting the enemy. When two complete battalions were through they began a full-blooded assault: 'The men moved swiftly, blowing the doors of pill-boxes with explosive charges, killing or capturing the occupants, prodding sleepy Germans from their foxholes and capturing seventy-seven in one sweep.'[2] Having captured Wahlerscheid, however, the GIs of 2nd Infantry were now unwittingly 'out on a limb' and would find themselves in great danger when the German assault on the Schnee-Eifel began in the early hours of the 16th.

99th Infantry Division

Below 2nd Infantry's original positions, holding a 19–20-mile stretch in the Monschau Forest area, was 99th Infantry Division, with their three infantry regiments all up in the line (north to south: 395th, 393rd, 394th). The men of the 'Checkerboard' Division, who were almost totally without combat experience, were occupying the area between Höfen in the north and Lanzerath in the south, in positions which they had taken over from 9th Infantry and 5th Armored Divisions. J. R. McIlroy of Celina, Texas, was then an enlisted man in the 34th Platoon, F Company of 393rd Infantry Regiment. He recalled that they had sailed from England to Le Havre on about 5 November, moved on to Aubel in Belgium where they spent about four days, then were brought into the line on 10 November:

> We replaced a company of the 39th Infantry of 9th Division man for man, foxhole for foxhole. These log covered foxholes were not near each other – in fact they were more like outposts. Although they had logs over the top they did not protect us from melting snow or rain. It was snowing the day we moved into the line – little did we know that was to be the case for the next 90 days! Our positions faced east overlooking the international highway – Germany and its pill-boxes

and dragons' teeth lay on the other side. For the next 30 days there was very little close-up combat. We went across into Germany on patrols and exchanged mortar fire, but no attacks from either side. We had moved and located north to another holding position, when on 11 December we pulled back to about one mile north of Krinkelt. On the 13th we of the 2nd Battalion stacked our duffel bags (these were never seen again) and moved out to the north-west. As I found out later we were going with the 1st and 2nd Battalions of the 395th Regiment and most of the 2nd Infantry Division and other attached units on a push to take the Roer River dams. This movement was all uphill and many dropped out. There was a light snow that morning, but other than the steep climb what bothered us was the wet snow dropping off the trees. At that time I was first scout, BAR [Browning Automatic Rifle] man and acting squad leader. Our BAR man (Shuman) was sent back with concussion after a direct hit on his foxhole; the first scout (Mussey) made sick call with trench foot, while our squad leader (Rhineheart) was older and not in good shape. He could not keep up – in fact he told me to take over the squad – he could not do the job.

Late on the 13th, after reaching the top we began to hear mortar fire up ahead about where E Company was. We stopped and began digging foxholes. About the time we got a foot dug in the hard frozen ground we were ordered to move up and dig in again after dark. We slept by just lying on the cold ground. The next day (14th) they told us BAR men – Hillenbrand, Jordan and myself – to go to the front and fire at an enemy pill-box on our right. At the same time a flame-thrower team slipped into the ravine to our right and were to take out the pill-box. The flame failed to ignite. The next day they tried the same thing but with a Bangalore torpedo, but with the same result. We had still not moved past the pill-boxes on the 16th.

We will catch up with McIlroy in a later chapter.

One battalion of 395th Infantry Regiment was occupying Höfen and was rather 'out on a limb' because of the gap which had been created to allow the passage of 2nd Infantry Division through their lines. Their artillery was deployed ready to support the 2nd's coming attack, and from 8 to 13 December, their engineer combat battalion had been hard at work improving a narrow north-south track through their positions. This track would prove most useful in the coming battle. This is how Richard H. Byers, a forward observer with C Battery of 371st Field Artillery Battalion, recalled those early days:

The map of the road from Losheim to Losheimergraben clearly shows the location of our first observation post. The railroad tracks run roughly parallel to this road on the south side then cross underneath the road at the foot of a rise just short of Losheim. We were in a patch of trees and brush bounded on the south and east sides by the railroad cut and on the north by the Losheim–Losheimergraben road. Out to our left was a blown bridge over the tracks. Across the road to the north of the OP, also on the brow of the hill, were the shattered remnants of a forester's house.[3] In this little patch of woods with us were a few infantrymen, members of the 394th Infantry Regiment Cannon Company's observation team.

Things were quiet, snowy and soggy throughout November and the first week of December. Around 10 December we had several days of inactivity due to the heavy fog. It was a drab world except for the underlying excitement and tension of occasional danger. I wrote to my wife: '– the countryside is similar to England: rolling hills, hedgerows and all that, but it lacks the coloring, the bright greenness of England. And all the woods are of tall pines, dark and gloomy inside. After a snow it is all in black and white, black hedgerows and roads, drab houses scaled with grey asphalt shingles and pine forests with white fields of snow.' This was the 'Forest of Arden' from Shakespeare's *As You Like It*.

We spent a lot of time out of our holes trying to keep dry and talking to each other. We would get the occasional mortar fire in on our position when we became too careless and too many of us gathered too closely out of our holes. Our observation post consisted of one large dugout, about four feet square, with a log roof and floor. It was large enough for two men to slide into from the rear and look out [of] a front slit. Each of us also dug slit trenches scattered through the trees.

After one particularly soggy night all the holes were filled almost to the brim with icy water so everyone was out in the open when mortar rounds suddenly started crashing in on them. They all ran and scattered back into the woods until the shelling stopped. Shortly, Corporal Cleon Janos came out of the woods, but his buddy, Corporal Bill Johnson, was nowhere to be seen. Janos became very concerned and began going from slit trench to slit trench feeling down inside each one, for all the world like he was hunting for soap in a bathtub, saying: 'Johnson, are you there? – Johnson are you there?' This struck us as hilarious, particularly when Johnson eventually came ambling out of the woods, having stopped to answer a call of nature.

While our party was manning the observation post over-looking Losheim only three men actually went forward and one usually stayed in Losheimergraben to take care of our night-time quarters. These quarters were in one-half of a duplex house, part of a little development of fairly modern duplexes in the south-east quadrant of this crossroad village. We assumed these were second homes belonging to more affluent Germans, judging by the quality of the furnishings and the two fur coats left behind (we used the sleeves of the coats as mittens!). The house still had most of the amenities including beds with mattresses, silverware, china, glasses and cooking utensils. There was a large pile of coal briquettes in the basement. We used them constantly for cooking and maintaining a fire for warmth. After a time we noticed that the pile was diminishing at an unusually fast rate; far faster than we were using them, but there was no way into the basement except through the front door which we watched. Finally the pile dropped to the point that the mystery was explained – the Cannon Company men next door had tunnelled through the basement wall and had been raking out coal from the bottom of the pile for their own use. We discussed painting a hand-grenade black and adding it to the pile but we never got that nasty.

The man who stayed behind was responsible for preparing the evening meal. We supplemented our 10-in-1 rations[4] with cabbages and onions salvaged from the garden. With the stove and its bake oven we were able to come up with some unusual dishes from a few raw materials. My speciality was grinding hardtack biscuits and tropical chocolate together. This mixture made either a chocolate pudding or a chocolate cake, depending on how much clean water you were able to melt from the snow. It was topped with a lemon sauce or lemon icing made from the crystallized lemon powder that was also part of our rations. After our evening meal we read, wrote letters or played cards by the light of our Jeep's headlight. We removed it nightly and hung it from the ceiling, wired to the battery of the Jeep parked outside.

The increase in German activities during the final week before they launched their 'Ardennes Offensive' greatly increased the number and length of the daily intelligence reports we observers turned in on this section of the front. These reports were bucked up to Division or higher where they were digested into a G2 Report, a few copies of which filtered back down to our level. We were told that we faced the 277th *Volks* Grenadier Division, made up of old men, young boys, ex-Luftwaffe, ex-Navy and convalescents from the Russian front. There was really no reason to be concerned that we were stretched out for 20+ miles because our opponents were there only to keep us out of Germany. We wanted to believe this and up until then, in spite of a few dangerous incidents, there was a feeling of being on an adventurous camping trip which would be over just as soon as the German Army faced up to the inevitable and collapsed. Nobody realised that Hitler had ordered the massing of most of the best of what was left of the German Army. This massed force was gathering just over the horizon from us. The 'air-raids' were just a diversion to cover the sound of all of their armor being moved up at night. In a letter home, two days before reality struck, I joked, 'if anyone said I'd be sitting in a warm house in Belgium eating fried chicken with french fries, I'd say they were crazy. I'll be getting fat if this deal lasts.' Famous last words!

More from Dick Byers later. Little did he suspect that it would be the dogged defence of his 'green' division that would prevent the push towards Eupen by the German LXVII Corps or that of I SS Panzer Corps towards Malmédy.

Another member of the 99th 'Checkerboard' Division was B. C. Henderson, from Texas, a reinforcement to B Company of the 394th, who had arrived from Camp Elsenborn and who recalled life on Elsenborn Ridge as follows:

As I remember I wore longjohns and two pairs of OD pants, two shirts, a knitted sweater and a field jacket. I also had gloves and a knitted cap to wear under my helmet, plus two extra pairs of socks. Each GI had a blanket and poncho. I kept the extra socks inside my shirt for a dry change as the combat boots were no match for the deep snow and cold (my foxhole buddy and I would often sit facing one another and rub each other's feet, trying to keep the circulation going so as to prevent trench foot). The first few nights we were busy trying to dig additional foxholes for new replacements to come in later. The ground was so frozen that we couldn't dig with the tools we had, so we would try to get a hole large enough to place a charge of TNT in it and then blast out a hole from which we could shovel the loose dirt and thus finish digging the foxhole. The foxhole had become our home, such as it was, we dug small holes in the walls for personal items, such as cigarettes, writing material, the next tinned meal, even extra grenades and ammo. When the Kitchen brought up food, they would leave a jerrican of gasoline for our use, we filled a C-Ration can half-full of dirt and poured gasoline in and lit it with a match for heat and light in the foxhole. As a result of using the gasoline in such a confined space our exposed skin soon became black with the soot, while our clothing kinda glazed over also with soot. We left a small opening at the top of the foxhole just large enough to get in and out, but we kept it covered most of the time. Sometimes the snow was so heavy on the top that we had to use our feet to push off the lid! From time to time the Kitchen would come up to a point near our foxholes in a depression out of sight to the enemy, bringing Coffee and French Toast. There was no way they could keep the toast hot, however, the coffee did a little better, so we had warm coffee and cold toast – still they did the best they could.

During the six weeks we were on the Elsenborn Ridge the temperature was continually zero degrees and below, while the snow was always about knee deep. It has been said that the winter of 1944–45 was the worst that the Belgian Ardennes had experienced in fifty years and it is not difficult for me to believe that! We got back to Elsenborn village once during that time, where a tent had been set up for showers and a place to shave. We also got a clean change of clothing, so when we got back to our foxholes our buddies didn't recognise us minus all the black soot and whiskers! The soot I breathed during those weeks on Elsenborn Ridge stayed in my lungs for many years and each time I would get a chest cold I would cough up black soot.

Joseph L. Thimm, yet another 'Checkerboard' infantryman, was in the 2nd Platoon of K Company, 3rd Battalion, 395th Infantry Regiment, protecting the eastern edge of Höfen. He was first a rifleman, then later BAR man. His recollections of the days before the German assault were very similar to those of B. C. Henderson, being mainly concerned with improving his foxhole.

I'm vague about the details of what happened over the next few days, but I do remember we began the job of shoring up the roof of the hole, using personal gear or anything laying about that would plug the holes. If I recall accurately, the hole was not very large or deep and so we began to dig the hole deeper and improve a firing position in the side of the hole, at the hole entrance, and another a few yards down the hedgerow. Over the next two or three weeks, as we began to adjust to this caveman existence, we made trips back to Höfen to 'requisition' household improvements. On one occasion, Bob Warner and I unhinged a large shed door and carried it back to the hole and installed it as a new roof – just as we did as kids! We piled old and new dirt on top and shovelled fresh snow over it for camouflage. I believe we also picked up a couple of blankets and rugs to cover the dirt floor and the entrances to the firing positions. The final touch, which took place a good time later, was the installation of a small iron stove and a rigged-up chimney. At the same time we were able to pick up coal briquettes in Höfen and usually managed to keep a couple of coals burning most of the time with little or no visible smoke.

At the same time as improving their personal living space, they also improved all their defensive positions:

... anything that would improve our chances of survival ... mortar and machine-gun positions were dug in, in support of the line platoons. I remember early on, for instance, accompanying a forward artillery observer team out beyond our line to view the area in front so they could fix their co-ordinates on likely targets. As far as I can remember, most of this activity occurred over the five-week period between November 10 and the German attack on December 16.

Trench foot

One of the nastiest aspects of living like cavemen in the winter conditions was that men began to suffer badly from trench foot, as Joseph Thimm explains:

... after a few days on the line we began to experience our first trench foot casualties. With our leather shoes and boots, we were ill-prepared to deal with the wet and cold of those first few days and weeks on the line. We all had swollen feet, but some guys experienced almost intolerable pain, were unable to put on shoes or walk, and had to be evacuated. Bill Sheppard has related to me his own experience which began when he was carried from our hole in the middle of the night. He eventually ended up in treatment at Camp Carson, Colorado, one of two military hospitals in the States set up to handle the most serious trench foot cases. Eventually, rubber boots replaced the leather shoes and heavier socks were issued with instructions on how better to care for our feet … all of this only after hundreds of men had become trench foot victims.

106th Infantry Division and the 14th Cavalry Group

Below 99th Infantry Division was V Corps' boundary with VIII Corps, and the next 21 miles were defended by, first, 14th Cavalry Group (spread over some 9,000 yards), then 106th Infantry Division on the line Lanzerath–Krewinkel–Roth– Kobscheid. This meant that a lightly equipped Cavalry Group was responsible for the all-important north-eastern entrance to the Losheim Gap. They had taken up their positions with 18th Cavalry Reconnaissance Squadron and a company of 3in tank destroyers, covering the mouth of the gap. Their positions – which they had inherited from the infantry division previously occupying the area – were in some of the little groups of homesteads which had been built in depressions, where they could gain as much shelter as possible from the raw winds sweeping through the Ardennes. There were about eight separate little positions spread out across the front, some almost as much as a mile apart, so a homogeneous line of defence was impossible. Furthermore, to the north of 14th Cavalry Group there was a 2-mile gap between their northernmost position and the southernmost position of 99th Infantry Division. This gap was patrolled every two hours, by a small party from the attached TD company, in conjunction with an I & R Platoon from the 99th. Hugh Cole describes this type of defence as being: 'small islands of resistance, manned usually in platoon strength'. He goes on to point out that the mechanised cavalry were thus committed to positional defence – a cardinal sin because they did not have the staying power to maintain defence in depth and should not have been given such a task. There were plans in the pipeline to reinforce 14th Cavalry Group, but these did not come to fruition before the enemy attacked.

Below 14th Cavalry Group were 106th Infantry Division (422nd, 423rd and 424th Infantry Regiments), their positions following an irregular north-east–south-west line through the central and southern section of the heavily forested Schnee-Eifel. One of their infantry regiments (the 422nd) occupied a salient, which jutted out into the enemy lines and was part of the West Wall positions that had been captured some weeks earlier. This made their location somewhat exposed, but it did mean that they occupied a wedge of the West Wall which might be a good jumping-off area for future operations. There were three main routes through the divisional area, the most northerly one running from the village of Hallschlag into the Our valley thence to St-Vith. In the centre, the road ran from Roth south-westwards through the Losheim Gap, while the southernmost road followed the valley of the River Alf from Prüm, but then turned north-west through Winterspelt to St-Vith. Both the northern and southern routes were good tarmac roads, more than 20 feet wide and leading through the divisional positions directly to the key town of St-Vith. When the 106th had taken over on 11/12 December, they had moved into well-prepared positions, built to withstand the worst of the Ardennes winter, so there were log dugouts for the rifle and weapon squads. The two divisions had exchanged their heavy weapons, so that the 106th took over the emplaced mortars and heavy (.50 cal) machine-guns. A comprehensive communications network was in place with wire running to nearly every squad and outpost (although the 106th lacked the abundance of power microphones held by the veteran division). These were all pluses, but on the minus side, the 'green' 106th had already lost more than 60 per cent of their original enlisted men who had been taken away to meet the heavy demands for trained personnel both before and after D-Day, so their men were in many cases newly arrived replacements. At least they were taking over well-prepared positions, with elaborate bunkers, foxholes and trenches in what had been until now a quiet part of the front. But even this was not all it seemed; for example, the battle-experienced men of 2nd Division had taken many of their 'creature comforts' (e.g., stoves they had 'liberated' from local houses) with them and, even more worrying, as these were in many cases the old German positions of the Siegfried Line, they could be easily pinpointed by the enemy, which would have disastrous consequences in the coming early morning barrage.

A tragic story

The official US history of the 'Battle of the Bulge', prefaces the chapter on this part of the battle with the following words, which I believe it is both relevant and important to quote here verbatim:

> The story of the 106th Infantry Division and the attached 14th Cavalry Group is tragic. It is also highly controversial. Since the major part of the division was eliminated from combined operations with other American forces on the second day of the German counter-offensive, information from contemporary records is scanty and, as to particulars, often completely lacking. The historian, as a result, must tread warily through the maze of recrimination and highly personalized recollection which surrounds this story. It should not be concluded that reminiscence by those caught up in this disaster is consciously tendentious. But the officers and men of the 106th Division who so narrowly escaped the German trap or who spent months in German prisons would be less than human if they did not seek to discover the cause of this débâcle in either human error or frailty. Since the author has been forced to depend in so great degree on the human memory, unaided or unchallenged by the written record, the scholar's old rule 'one witness, no witness' has been generally applied. Even so, some relaxation of the rule is necessary if a sustained and sequential narrative is to be presented. Fortunately, the picture as seen

from the German side of the Schnee-Eifel is fairly complete and can be applied as a corrective in most of the major areas of controversy and contradiction.[5]

28th Infantry Division

On the right of the ill-fated 106th Infantry Division was 28th Infantry Division, occupying the southern portion centre ground of V Corps' positions – a distance which stretched over some 18 miles 'as the crow flies' – but was more like 25 miles plus on the ground. In order to cover this sector the division was three regiments 'up' with 112th Infantry Regiment on the left, 110th in the centre and 109th on the right. This was perhaps the quietest sector of the Ardennes front and, as the veteran 28th had just lost more than 6,000 men in the bloody fighting in the Hürtgen Forest, they fully deserved a 'quiet' location for a change. They had taken over in mid-November and were now stretched 'paper thin' along the River Our, all the way south to where it joined the Sure in little more than what could be described as a line of small outposts.

4th Infantry Division

Below the 28th was 4th Infantry Division, again fully stretched like the 28th in little more than an outpost line. They too had suffered badly in the Hürtgen Forest, having incurred more than 7,500 casualties, 2,500 of whom were suffering from trench foot and exposure. They were still some 2,000 under strength when they moved to Luxembourg that: 'quiet paradise for weary troops' as it had been called. They had taken over 83rd Infantry Division's positions on the far right flank of VIII Corps. Their 35-mile front lay along the west bank of the rivers Sauer and Moselle. On the opposite of this river line were, supposedly, a heterogeneous collection of German units which did not appear to offer much opposition, so the 4th were confident of getting the rest they needed and deserved. They had completed their concentration in Luxembourg on 13 December. The division's three regiments had now taken up their positions with 12th Infantry Regiment on the left along the Sauer; 8th Inf Regt were in the centre, deployed both on the Sauer and the Moselle; to the south was 22nd

Inf Regt, spread along the Moselle all the way down to the inter-Army boundary with Patton's Third Army which was just beyond the Luxembourg border.

As soon as they had reached 'paradise', the battle-weary 4th had immediately begun to send leave-parties to Paris and other fleshpots, some of the more fortunate even getting back to the USA. A system of rotation was arranged so that men could spend a few hours in Luxembourg City, enjoying: 'ice cream in several flavors, well-watered beer, and the dubious pleasure of hearing accordionists squeeze out German waltzes and Yankee marching songs of WWI vintage.'[6]

The 4th had been fighting hard ever since Normandy, so many of its weapons and much of its equipment had become decidedly battle worn. The attached tank battalion (the 70th) for example, had only eleven of its total complement of 54 medium tanks in running order when it arrived. Some of the division's B vehicles had broken down *en route* for Luxembourg, and some of their artillery was in divisional ordnance repair shops. Manpower shortages were especially acute among infantry units, many companies being under half strength. The divisional commander, Major General Raymond O. Barton, had ordered his regimental commanders to maintain just a small number of troops manning the river outpost line, while holding their main strength – generally in complete companies – close at hand, but not committed, in nearby villages. Each regiment also had a battalion as a mobile reserve at four hours' notice to move; other mobile support was provided by the tanks, the SP tank-destroyers of 803rd TD Bn and the towed anti-tank guns of 802nd TD Bn. Barton considered that the enemy might well try to send a raiding force to seize Luxembourg City, and when the battle began on the 16th he still considered the capital to be the main German objective.

9th Armored Division

This arrived in VIII Corps in October 1944 and on the 15th became General Middleton's mobile reserve. As the tankers of the armoured division had no previous battle experience, the corps commander decided to use one of its three armoured infantry battalions (the

60th) to hold part of 28th Inf Div's frontage, intending to rotate it with the other two – the 27th and 52nd in turn. The tanks of CCA were kept concentrated in a leaguer area a few miles to the rear. CCB and CCR were kept in reserve even further to the rear, but on 13 December CCB was ordered to move up to provide tank support for the assault on the Roer dams.

XVIII (Airborne) Corps

Although not committed until 'Wacht am Rhein' began, it is perhaps relevant here to mention what the other corps which would fight within First Army's area, was doing prior to 16 December. Major General Matthew Bunker Ridgway's XVIII (Airborne) Corps was SHAEF's only immediate emergency reserve. There were other divisions in the UK, completing their training, but XVIII Corps was the only formation with troops immediately available on the continent. Its main components, 82nd and 101st Airborne Divisions, were then in reserve near Reims, recovering from their recent long operational stint in The Netherlands, which had of course included the Arnhem operation. In fact Ridgway was not with his corps, but in England, where he was involved with the final part of the training of what was to become his third airborne division, namely 17th Airborne Division. His deputy, Major General 'Slim Jim' Gavin was in command, and 101st Airborne Division was also without its regular CG, Major General Maxwell B. Taylor, who was in the USA. In his place was his deputy Brigadier General Anthony C. McAuliffe, shortly to have fame thrust upon him. The two veteran airborne divisions would soon be on their way, by road, as would 7th Armored Division which initially was under command of VIII Corps 16–19 December, then would join XVIII Corps on the 20th, as would 30th Infantry Division from V Corps on the 21st. Finally, 75th Infantry Division, which had only landed in France on 13 December, earmarked for XVI Corps in US Ninth Army, would be re-assigned, first to VII Corps (22 December) and then to XVIII Airborne (29 December). A British officer who happened to see some of the last of these moving up to the front in a long convoy of

6x4 cargo trucks commented that they all : '... seemed so young – full of anticipation and certain that now "We Brits" could take it easy and let them take care of Hitler and his Generals.'

Notes

1 Patton was to record that he considered this to be one of the major errors of the campaign. 'If Bradley had not welshed on his agreement,' he wrote in his diary, 'we would have taken Saarbrücken within 48 hrs after we got Koenigsmacker. Once we had [Koenigsmacker] they couldn't have stopped us from taking Trier, and if we'd had Trier it would have been impossible for the Germans to launch their Ardennes offensive.'

2 MacDonald, C. B. *The Battle of the Bulge.*

3 Some months later Dick Byers heard that when the area had been retaken at the end of the offensive, a patrol had explored the forester's tumbled-down house at their leisure: 'They found a tunnel from the house down the embankment to the railroad tracks. Apparently the German observers came up the tunnel into the basement, watched and shelled us whenever warranted, then simply disappeared back down into the town before we retaliated.'

4 This was the Field Ration C which had been developed just before the war. It consisted of small cans of meat and vegetables (10 in all, such as meat and beans, meat and vegetables, meat and spaghetti, meat and noodles, etc.). Jam, crackers, powdered drinks, sugar and cereals were also included.

5 Cole, H. M. *The Ardennes: Battle of the Bulge.* He goes on to explain that while the records and reports of the HQ 106 Inf Div and of 424th Inf Regt were intact though rather scanty, those of the 422nd and 423rd had been destroyed before the regiments were captured. This loss has been partly rectified by interviewing a large number of personnel from these two regiments as soon as they were released from POW camps.

6 Ibid.

4
A COMPARISON OF STRENGTHS AND WEAKNESSES

From D-Day until the launch of the German counter-offensive, the Allies on the Western Front had known mainly success in their offensive operations, especially once the constraints of the Normandy bocage had been broken and the 'gallop' across the more open French countryside had begun. Perhaps this relatively easy progress had given them the false idea that the enemy had nothing more to offer apart from a dogged defence based upon continual withdrawal back to the Fatherland, albeit as slow as possible, but withdrawal nevertheless. Couple this with the obvious lack of activity in the Ardennes area and one can well see why the mood of the GIs there was over-optimistic, considering that the war was as good as won and that nothing could possibly happen to spoil their undoubted feeling of general well-being as Christmas approached. Those 'green' units who were the new arrivals, lacked the knowledge of how quickly events can change on the battlefield, while the seasoned warriors who did know, had been lulled into a false feeling of security to a greater degree than at any time since they had landed in NW Europe. This undoubtedly had an effect upon their morale when the battle began. The Germans on the other hand were buoyed up by the knowledge that it was now or never for them and that they were 'gambling everything' as von Rundstedt told them in his pre-battle message. Would their seemingly high morale wither on the vine when the battle did not go the way they had been told?

There were additional factors which affected the troops' morale on both sides, one being their state of training, another the state of their arms and equipment, and perhaps most importantly, the nature of the men themselves and their loyalty to the cause they were fighting for. Although the defenders were, as has been mentioned, a mixture of 'green' and seasoned troops, they had all been through the same induction and basic training, which was, now some four years into the war, more thorough and more efficiently organised than that which could now be given in Germany where shortages of everything had begun to bite with a vengeance. Interviewed in 1972, Generalleutnant Siegfried Westphal, von Rundstedt's brilliant Chief of Staff, had this to say about life in Germany in December 1944: 'Life in Germany at that time was already terrible. The food was strictly rationed – the rations were very few, very little. The railways were handicapped by bomb attacks. We had no trucks, no petrol, no coal and the population – women and children – had to suffer very, very much. When Hitler reproached me, saying that the situation on the Western Front had not got any better since my arrival I said to him: "You must know of the terrible life the people have, especially in the Ruhr area," and, I added, "you must have seen it." Then there was silence.'[1] In addition to these problems of *matériel* shortages, many of the latest Wehrmacht recruits had received very little training simply from lack of time. On balance, therefore, the German troops were under-trained as compared with the GIs, apart, that is, from the 'old hands' who were now becoming few and far between. After the war, Generalmajor Walter Warlimont, Jodl's deputy at OKW, had this to say about the state of training before the Ardennes offensive: '... the main sources for offensive action of the kind Hitler had in mind were not at hand anymore, no troops had been trained sufficiently and there was insufficient means of moving troops and armaments. The bad winter weather was just as it had been in 1940, when Hitler tried to start the campaign in France too early.'[2]

However, the senior German staff were amazed that the American defences were so weak in the Ardennes. After the war, Generalleutnant Siegfried Westphal, asked whether he was surprised that the Americans hadn't learned the lesson of the French in the Ardennes in 1940 replied, 'Yes, we did not understand. We were astonished and could not understand why they were so weak in this area.'[3] Nevertheless, the initial panic which gripped some of the American troops when the assault began, soon gave way to displays of courage and sheer obstinacy, which proved the true mettle of the majority of the GIs, who fought bravely and with great determination against seemingly impossible odds. As Brigadier General Hal C. Patterson says in the foreword to the official history: 'The mettle of the American soldier was tested in the fires of adversity and the quality of his response earned him the right to stand shoulder to shoulder with his forebears of Valley Forge, Fredericksburg and the Marne.'

Opposing strengths
On the morning of 16 December 1944, the opposing strengths were:

a. American defending forces holding a frontage of some 104 meandering miles, in the direct path of the assault – four and two-thirds divisions, with an effective strength of approximately 83,000 men. Their heavy weapons comprised some 242 M4 Sherman medium tanks and 182 tank-destroyers of various types supported by 394 artillery pieces in the divisional and corps artillery regiments.
b. German assaulting forces on a 60-mile frontage – five armoured and twelve and two-thirds infantry divisions, with an effective strength of more than 200,000 combat troops. Their heavy weapons comprised 500 medium, or heavier, tanks, and the fire support of 1,900 guns and rocket-launchers.

Although it is difficult to work out an exact average of attacker to defender, because this varied so much over the battlefield, the probable figures as given in the official history are:

Infantry. Overall ratio of German to American infantry, 3 to 1, rising to 6 to 1 at certain points of concentration.
Armour. Overall ratio of German tanks (and SP guns being used in the tank role) to American, 4 to 1.

By early January 1945, when the Allies were in a position to begin to destroy the 'Bulge', the Germans had deployed a total of eight armoured and twenty infantry divisions, plus two independent mechanised brigades, against which the Americans had eventually deployed eight armoured, sixteen infantry and two airborne divisions.

Weapons Comparison

In the following comparison of the weapons of both sides, it will be evident that some German weapons, such as their tanks, were individually superior to the Allied equivalent. In general terms, however, Allied *matériel* (the vast proportion of which was produced in the USA) was superior to that of their opponents – this includes uniforms, equipment and rations. etc.

Armour

Because of its importance to the attacking force, we will start by comparing the organisation and equipment of the tank divisions of the two sides. The Germans had initially amassed more armoured divisions than had the Americans and British in the Ardennes and its immediate vicinity, but of course as there were more tanks in an American or British armoured division than in its German equivalent, a simple divisional count does not tell the whole story. Nevertheless, there was clearly far more armour concentrated in the attacking force than was immediately available to the defenders. Apart from the armoured divisions, they had other independent formations of tanks, assault guns and SP anti-tank guns (for example in the Führer Begleit Brigade and 150 Panzer Brigade); on the Allied side there were independent tank and tank-destroyer battalions and tank brigades, all of which are detailed in Appendices 1 and 2. Although practically no German units were anywhere near up to full strength (Hitler had attempted to make up for this disparity by ordering the attachment of separate Army tank battalions to panzer divisions), they did manage to field a large number of medium, medium heavy and heavy tanks (mainly Pz Kpfw IV, V and VI), probably more than had ever before been assembled in one place on the Western Front. Furthermore, the vast majority of these tanks were – tank for tank – technically superior to anything the Allies could field

US 'LIGHT' ARMORED DIVISION 1944

HQ-(HQ Coy)

TANKS	ARTILLERY	ARMORED INFANTRY

HQ + HQ Bty

Bn Bn Bn	Div Air Sect	Armd Field Arty Bn	Armd Field Arty Bn	Armd Field Arty Bn	Bn Bn Bn

CCA CCB CCR Div Band

Armd Eng Bn   Cav Recce Sqn (Mech)   Sig Coy   Div Trains

HQ + HQ Coy

Ord Bn   MP Plat   Med Bn

		Principal Armament and Vehicles	
Entire Division	10,937	Rifles .30cal.	2,063
Div HQ	164	Carbines .30cal.	5,286
Tank Bns (3)	729	MGs .30cal.	465
Inf Bns (3)	1,001	MGs .50cal.	404
CC HQ & HQ Coy (2)	184	Mortars 60mm	63
Div Trains HQ & HQ Coy	103	Mortars 81mm	30
CCR HQ	8	A-Tk Rocket-Launchers	607
Field Arty	1,623	Hows 57mm	30
		Hows 75mm	17
Auxiliary Units:		Hows 105mm	54
Cav Recce Sqn (Mech)	935	Med Tanks	186
Engr Bn	693	Lt Tanks	77
Med Bn	417	Armd Cars	54
Ord Bn	762	Halftracks Carriers	455
Sig Coy	302	Halftracks 81mm	
MP Plat	91	Mortar Carriers	18
Div HQ Coy	138	Vehicles All Types	
Band	58	(except boats & a/c)	2,650
Attached Medical	261	Less Combat Types	1,761
Attached Chaplain	8		

at that time, in two of the three most important characteristics of tanks, namely firepower and protection. But where mobility was concerned, the lighter, more manoeuvrable, mechanically more reliable, American medium tanks had the edge in the difficult winter conditions.

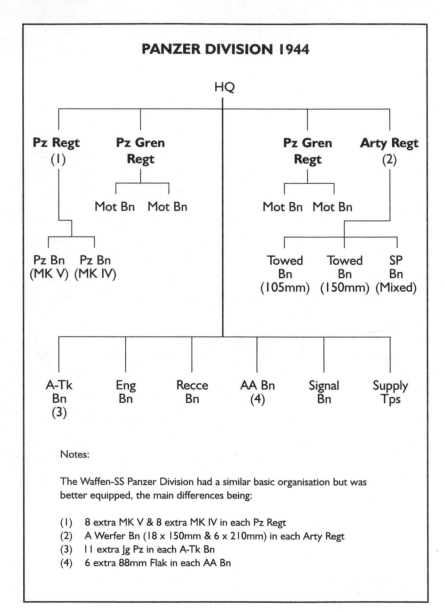

PANZER DIVISION 1944

HQ

Pz Regt (1) — Pz Gren Regt — Pz Gren Regt — Arty Regt (2)

Mot Bn   Mot Bn

Mot Bn   Mot Bn

Pz Bn (MK V)   Pz Bn (MK IV)

Towed Bn (105mm)   Towed Bn (150mm)   SP Bn (Mixed)

A-Tk Bn (3)   Eng Bn   Recce Bn   AA Bn (4)   Signal Bn   Supply Tps

Notes:

The Waffen-SS Panzer Division had a similar basic organisation but was better equipped, the main differences being:

(1) 8 extra MK V & 8 extra MK IV in each Pz Regt
(2) A Werfer Bn (18 x 150mm & 6 x 210mm) in each Arty Regt
(3) 11 extra Jg Pz in each A-Tk Bn
(4) 6 extra 88mm Flak in each AA Bn

In the lightning 'Gallop across France' the Americans had achieved much of their success not only because they had more AFVs than the Germans, but also because they had complete air superiority, the dreaded *Jabos* being able to deal with anything the enemy could field – witness the carnage in the Falaise Gap. As far as numbers were concerned, however, an experienced American tanker in 3rd Armored Division, told me that many of the panzer crewmen they captured had a stock joke which went like this: 'Von off our tanks iss better than ten of yours'. Then, just about when you had decided to punch the guy in the whiskers, he would shrug, grin and say, 'But you always haff eleven!' This time, it would be the Germans who initially had superior numbers of superior AFVs and for much of the early part of their counter-offensive the weather prevented the *Jabos* from flying. However the snow and ice of the brutal winter weather in the Ardennes did work against the heavier, less manoeuvrable German AFVs, which somewhat evened up the balance, as did their POL supply problems which got worse and worse as the attack proceeded and their supply lines became over-extended and the roads and tracks hopelessly jammed.

The main American armoured division of the period was based upon the organisation: 'TO 17 of 14 September 1943', known as the 'Light' armored division, with 186 medium tanks and 77 light tanks – the former being the M4 medium Sherman, the latter the M5A1 light Honey.[4] As the latter were armed with a 37mm gun only, they cannot be counted as being of much use in the tank v tank battles in the Ardennes. They were used for other purposes; for example the British armoured regiments used them in their reconnaissance troops, and the 37mm gun did prove capable of knocking out heavy AFVs as will be recounted later. The Shermans were organised in three battalions and were a mix of various Marks and Types, but all too many still mounted the M3 75mm gun or the 105mm close-support howitzer. The new 76mm gun had started to come in and re-gunning had begun to take place, but even the new gun as mounted on the Sherman M4A3 would still not penetrate the frontal armour of either the Tiger or Panther.[5] There was only one type of

PRINCIPAL ALLIED AND GERMAN TANKS

Type	Weight (tons)	Crew	Armament	Remarks
ALLIED				
M 5 series Light Tank Stuart (Honey)	} 14.73 to 15.13	4	1 x 37mm 3 x MG	} Used for recce, etc., rather than as main battle tank
M 24 Chaffee	18 tons	5	1 x 75mm 3 x MG	replaced M5 in some cases
M 4 series Sherman	29.68 to 32.5	5	1 x 7.5mm or 76mm 3 x MG	Main Allied medium tank. There were also: a. Firefly – with Br 17pdr gun; b. Jumbo – added armour put up weight to 42 tons
GERMAN				
Pz Kpfw IV Ausf H/J	25	5	1 x 7.5cm KwK L/48 2 x MG	End of PzKpfw IV series which had been in constant production since 1937
Pz Kpfw V Panther	45.5	5	1 x 7.5cm KwK 42 L/70 2 x MG	Approx 450 Panthers were in Army Group B for 'Wacht' am 'Rhein'
Pz Kpfw VI	57	5	1 x 8.8cm KwK 36 L/56 2 x MG	Not many Tiger Is were used
Pz Kpfw VI Ausf B	68	5	1 x 8.8cm KwK 43/L71 2 x MG	Also known as Tiger II or the *Königstiger* (King Tiger)

Sherman that could deal effectively with the heavier German tanks and that was the British version which mounted a high-velocity 17pdr gun. Known as the Sherman Firefly, the upgunned tanks were issued on the basis of one per troop in British armoured regiments and none was in service in American armoured regiments. There were a few heavily armoured Shermans (M4A3E2 Assault Tank), known as 'Jumbos', which had additional armour of up to 100mm thickness, but these were few in number and only seen on the US Third Army front. It is all the more remarkable therefore that American armour did so well in the Ardennes, although the short ranges of engagement probably helped, as did the manoeuvrability and reliability of the Sherman. Colonel Bruce C. Clarke's masterly defence of St-Vith with CCB of 9th Armored Division was a classic example of what could be done by an armour expert even when outnumbered and outgunned.

Two of the American armoured divisions (2nd and 3rd) were in fact still based on the old 'square' organisation which had a strength of 14,620, with a total of 232 medium and 158 light tanks. The British armoured divisions which were involved towards the end of the offensive, were on the point of being re-equipped with the new Comet tank, which mounted a 77mm gun and had armour up to 101mm thick. It was an excellent tank and came near to matching the Panther in performance and gun power, but in the emergency situation that 'Wacht am Rhein' had sparked off, the British armoured regiments had to hurriedly re-draw their battle-worn Shermans and motor swiftly to the Meuse in their dilapidated old 'Ronson Lighters'.[6]

On the German side, as I have shown in the charts, there were also two types of panzer division: the Waffen-SS panzer division and that of the Heer. The former was considerably stronger in every respect than its army equivalent and much better equipped, Adolf Hitler having made quite sure that they got the best of everything – as far as that was possible.

Armoured Infantry

Also within the 'light' armoured division, were three armoured infantry battalions who rode into battle in halftracks, but fought on their feet like normal infantry. The Germans likewise had panzer grenadiers, in fact in larger numbers, but only some of these were lucky enough to travel in halftracks; the others had to cling on to tank turrets and back decks, making them much more vulnerable to enemy fire. The armoured infantry of both sides were skilled at working with tanks. The American armoured division also had three self-propelled artillery battalions, an armoured engineer battalion, cavalry recon squadron, signal company and the normal 'divisional trains' (i.e., the administrative 'tail') making up the rest of the divisional manpower total of 10,937 all ranks. Normal attachments included tank-destroyers and mobile AAA guns. As will be seen, the majority of these 'Other Arms and Services' were similarly represented in panzer, SS panzer and panzer grenadier divisions in roughly similar numbers, although the size of individual units naturally varied.

Tanks

The German tanks were mainly Pz Kpfw IV and V. The former was undoubtedly still the backbone of the *Panzerwaffe*, having been in continuous production throughout the war. This shows how excellent the original design must have been as it had come off the drawing-board in 1935, with the Model A entering production the following year. It went on being improved, uparmoured and upgunned year by year, and remained in production throughout the war. It was the Ausf H (Sd Kfz 161/2) of which more than 3,700 were built between April 1943 and July 1944, together with the Ausf J, the last model to be built (1,750 plus produced between June 1944 and March 1945) that was mainly used in the Ardennes. In June 1944, most of the 750 Panzer IVs in France were Ausf H, and to those remnants left after the battles in June to September, were added some 260 newer Ausf J, plus a number of other, older models that had been scraped together from training establishments and reserve units especially for the Ardennes offensive. It was undoubtedly the Panzer IV on which the German commanders, like Dietrich and von Manteuffel, relied to spearhead their operations, because its reliability, suitability to the terrain and, most importantly, lower fuel consumption, than the heavier Pz V and VI. In addition to ordinary gun tanks, there were anti-aircraft Flakpanzers, command versions, bridgelayers, recovery vehicles and a range of assault guns (e.g., Sturmpanzer IV, Sturmgeschütz IV and Panzer IV mounting 7.5cm guns up to the Nashorn with its 8.8cm gun), all based upon the Pz Kpfw III/IV chassis.

Next in importance was the Pz Kpfw V, Panther, which had made its début in the battle of Kursk in July 1943. Probably the best all-round medium-heavy tank of the war, Panther had a lethal combination of gun and armour and was to be found in considerable numbers in both the Heer and Waffen-SS formations. For example, 2nd Panzer Division in von Manteuffel's Fifth Panzer Army, which was reckoned to be the best panzer division in the Heer, had more than 100 tanks and assault guns, of which one complete battalion was all Panthers; while 2nd SS Panzer Division Das Reich fielded a total of 58 Panthers. Mention has already been made of the thirteen Panthers inadequately disguised as Shermans in Skorzeny's 150 Panzer Brigade, but all these were destroyed before the end of the operation.

Few of the dreaded Pz Kpfw VI Tigers were deployed in the offensive and they did not perform well, being really too big and cumbersome, and they guzzled precious fuel at an alarming rate. It was the even larger and heavier Tiger II, Pz Kpfw VI Ausf B Königstiger (King Tiger) which was more often seen – indeed it has gone down in popular history as being the 'tank of the offensive' (although many sightings were figments of the GI imagination in which every enemy tank seen became a Tiger!). It could deal with any Allied armour with ease and Hitler had great hopes for its success. For example, he had ordered the Waffen-SS 501st Heavy Battalion back to Germany so that it could be re-equipped with these 68-ton monsters which mounted the very latest 8.8cm KwK 43/3 L71 gun. Their thick armour (150mm on the front glacis) made them almost impervious to enemy fire, so it was their problematic automotive performance and the ever-worsening shortage of fuel which accounted for most of their battlefield failures. A typical example of their uselessness is given by an examination of Battle Group Peiper, which was spearheading the Waffen-SS advance. His task was to exploit any breakthrough as quickly as possible before the Allies could react. So he chose to lead his battle group with a mix of

Pz Kpfw IV and V; the King Tigers brought up the rear, keeping up as best they could. Inevitably they soon fell far behind and only ten of the thirty that had started managed to reach the spearhead when it was held up on the 20th. Four King Tigers were lost in the next two days and when, by the night of 23/24 December, the force had completely run out of POL and ammunition, the remaining six were destroyed together with 29 other tanks. One post-battle estimate is that only some 50 plus Tiger IIs were ever fully employed in the Ardennes – about one-third of the total then in service, so obviously their impact on the battlefield was limited.

Assault guns

Because of the general shortage of tanks within panzer divisions, assault guns (e.g., the StuG III and IV) were used to supplement tank battalions both in the Heer and the Waffen-SS. For example, both panzer regiments in 2nd and 9th SS Pz Divs each had two tank companies entirely equipped with StuG III, while 2nd Pz Div had a complete StuG battalion of three companies, each having fourteen StuG IIIs.

Tank destroyers

The US Army had reacted strongly to the lightning successes of the *Blitzkrieg* in 1940, and embraced the doctrine 'Seek, Strike and Destroy' as enshrined in the Tank Destroyer (TD), whose sole task was to kill enemy tanks. The TD Force grew rapidly and when it reached its peak in 1943, there were no less than 106 TD battalions active – only thirteen fewer than the total number of tank battalions! TDs therefore played an important role in the Ardennes, the main American ones being the M10 (3in gun) and the M36 (90mm gun). Both had open-topped turrets as did the third type, the M18 Hellcat, which mounted a 76mm gun and was the only one of the three designed from scratch as a tank destroyer. The Germans also used numerous types of tank destroyers in order to get a larger anti-tank gun onto a mobile chassis – one of the best being the Jagdpanther with its deadly 8.8cm which could deal with most tanks on the battlefield at ranges up to 3,000 yards. Others included the Jagdpanzer IV (7.5cm gun) and various Marders including Marder II (based upon the Pz Kpfw II chassis), and Hetzer (based on the Czech 38(t) chassis), which were in service both in the Heer and the Waffen-SS. Such TDs being generally lighter, faster and more manoeuvrable than tanks, were able to jockey for position along the winding roads in the Ardennes and yet were just as difficult to destroy as tanks.

Infantry

The standard US infantry division of the Ardennes period was based upon T/O and E7 and allied tables of 15 July 1943, and had a total

PRINCIPAL ALLIED AND GERMAN TANK DESTROYERS

Type	Weight (tons)	Crew	Armament	Remarks
ALLIED				
GMC M18 Hellcat	17.86	5	1 x 76mm 1 x MG	Built from scratch as a TD
GMC M10 Wolverine	29.47	5	1 x 3in 1 x MG	British version with 17pdr and was called Achilles
GMC M36	27.7	5	1 x 90mm 1 x MG	
GERMAN				
Panzer IV	25.8	4	1 x 7.5cm PaK42 L/70 1 x MG	Improved version of Jagpz IV
Jagdpanther	46	5	1 x 8.8cm PaK43/3 L/71 1 x MG	Based on Panther
Jagdtiger	70	6	1 x 12.8cm PaK44 L/55 2 x MG	Based on Tiger but with fixed turret

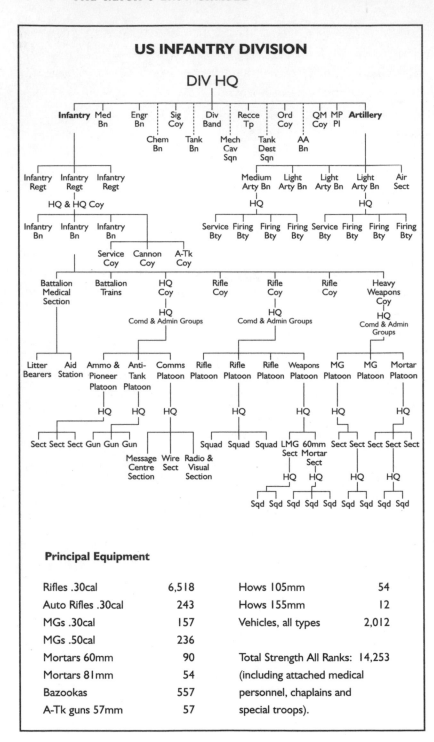

US INFANTRY DIVISION

DIV HQ

Principal Equipment

Rifles .30cal	6,518	Hows 105mm	54
Auto Rifles .30cal	243	Hows 155mm	12
MGs .30cal	157	Vehicles, all types	2,012
MGs .50cal	236		
Mortars 60mm	90	Total Strength All Ranks: 14,253	
Mortars 81mm	54	(including attached medical	
Bazookas	557	personnel, chaplains and	
A-Tk guns 57mm	57	special troops).	

complement of 14,253, so it was some 4,000 men stronger than a *Volks* grenadier division. The 'bayonet' strength of the American division was 9,354, being based upon the triangular organisation of three infantry regiments (each of 3,118) which were themselves divided into three battalions. Support for the rifle companies was at two levels, some within each battalion in their heavy weapons company, and some within the regiment in the additional, more powerful cannon and anti-tank companies. In support were the normal elements of artillery, engineers, signals, medical and all the rest. The normal German infantry division of the period also had three infantry regiments (each of two battalions), but the *Volks*

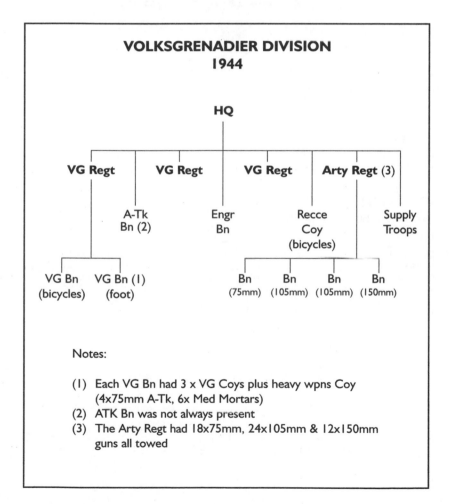

VOLKSGRENADIER DIVISION 1944

HQ

VG Regt — VG Regt — VG Regt — Arty Regt (3)

A-Tk Bn (2) — Engr Bn — Recce Coy (bicycles) — Supply Troops

VG Bn (bicycles) — VG Bn (1) (foot)

Bn (75mm) — Bn (105mm) — Bn (105mm) — Bn (150mm)

Notes:

(1) Each VG Bn had 3 x VG Coys plus heavy wpns Coy (4x75mm A-Tk, 6x Med Mortars)
(2) ATK Bn was not always present
(3) The Arty Regt had 18x75mm, 24x105mm & 12x150mm guns all towed

grenadier division had just one people's rifle regiment of about 2,000 men, which was divided into two battalions of about 700 men each. One of these battalions was motorised, the other marched. Although their internal supporting weapons were nowhere near as lavish as those of the Americans, the *Volks* artillery regiment had four battalions like their American equivalent and all the other supporting elements were there. To make up for the lack of infantrymen, the *Volksgrenadiers* were quite lavishly equipped with machine-pistols; this augmented firepower was used to considerable

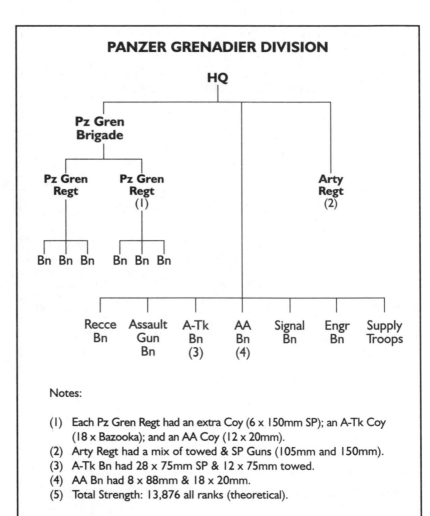

PANZER GRENADIER DIVISION

HQ

Pz Gren Brigade

Pz Gren Regt

Pz Gren Regt (1)

Arty Regt (2)

Bn Bn Bn   Bn Bn Bn

Recce Bn — Assault Gun Bn — A-Tk Bn (3) — AA Bn (4) — Signal Bn — Engr Bn — Supply Troops

Notes:

(1) Each Pz Gren Regt had an extra Coy (6 x 150mm SP); an A-Tk Coy (18 x Bazooka); and an AA Coy (12 x 20mm).
(2) Arty Regt had a mix of towed & SP Guns (105mm and 150mm).
(3) A-Tk Bn had 28 x 75mm SP & 12 x 75mm towed.
(4) AA Bn had 8 x 88mm & 18 x 20mm.
(5) Total Strength: 13,876 all ranks (theoretical).

advantage in special assault companies within infantry regiments. However, as far as mortars, machine-guns and other personal weapons (rifles, pistols, carbines) were concerned, there was little to choose between the two and it was more a question of who was able to maintain a plentiful supply of ammunition. Of course, at the lowest level, the guts, determination and fighting ability of the individual soldier made all the difference.

Hand-held anti-tank weapons

Fighting a winter campaign at close quarters in difficult conditions gave both sides maximum opportunity to attack enemy armour at close range. The US Bazooka (the rocket-launcher M1 and M9) and its German equivalent, the *Raketepanzerbüsche* (RPzB 54), also known as the *Panzerschreck* (tank terror), and the earlier *Panzerfaust* 30, 40 and 60, were all effective weapons if the firing team (usually two men) could get close enough – and there were always brave men on both sides willing to risk their lives to knock out an enemy tank. Take for

---

HAND-HELD ANTI-TANK WEAPONS

Type	Weight	Range	Penetration	Remarks
AMERICAN				
M1 and M9 Rocket Launcher Bazooka	5.96kg	max – 640m fighting – 150m approx	4.7in	M9 could be broken into two halves for carrying
GERMAN				
Panzerfaust 30, 60 and 100	up to 6.4kg	30 to over 100m depending on type	4in	Greatly feared by the Allies
Panzerschreck 8.8cm Rakettenpanzerbüsche 43	9.2kg	150m	8.25in	Revised version increased range to 201m

example, Staff Sergeant Isadore S. Jachman of Company B, 513th Parachute Infantry Regiment, who won a posthumous Medal of Honor at Flamierge, Belgium, on 4 January 1945. His company was pinned down by enemy artillery, mortar and small-arms fire, when two hostile tanks attacked the unit inflicting heavy casualties. S/Sgt Jachman, seized a Bazooka from a fallen comrade and, leaving his foxhole, dashed across open ground through a hail of fire from the two tanks which concentrated their fire on him. Firing his Bazooka at them, he managed to damage one and forced them both to withdraw. His heroic action, during which he was fatally wounded, disrupted the entire enemy attack.

Artillery

Calibre and performance of medium and field artillery guns on both sides were much on a par, except that the Germans had introduced the multi-tube rocket-launcher (*Nebelwerfer*) after suffering from these weapons at the hands of the Red Army. They had the advantages of being easy to manufacture and were more mobile than conventional

EXAMPLES OF AMERICAN AND GERMAN ARTILLERY (TOWED)

Type	Wt in action	Shell wt	Max Range	Remarks
AMERICAN				
75mm howitzer M1A1	980.6kg	6.63kg	8,930m	light/pack
105mm howitzer M2A1	1,934kg	14.98kg	11,438m	field
155mm howitzer M1 and M1A1	5,432kg	43.1kg	14,640m	medium
240mm howitzer M1	29,354kg	163.3kg	23,000m	heavy
GERMAN				
7.5cm FK38	1,365kg	5.8kg	11,500m	light
10.5cm LeFH 18	1,985kg	14.8kg	10,675m	field
15cm sFH 36	3,280kg	43.5kg	12,300m	heavy

towed normal artillery pieces. Their performance was excellent; for example, the 15cm version (*Nebelwerfer* 41), which weighed only half a ton), could fire the equivalent of half its own weight in HE in less than ten seconds. The larger, 21cm model (*Nebelwerfer* 42) weighed 1½ tons and had double the performance of the 150mm version. The weapons were not very accurate and the 4-man crew had to take cover some ten yards away because of the back-blast. Both were easily towable on their integrated two-wheel carriage.

In past offensives such as the first *Blitzkrieg* on Poland, then on France and finally on Russia, the dive-bomber had been used as 'air artillery' to punch holes through which the armour could then burst. Despite all Göring's promises, this would be lacking in the Ardennes, so conventional artillery had to be used instead – within the bounds of secrecy and of ammunition supply, so a prolonged pre-attack barrage was impossible. The offensive therefore was preceded by a short, sharp artillery bombardment, before dawn, from only some twenty artillery pieces per kilometre of front. Nevertheless this barrage was successful in helping the initial assault to penetrate the American positions, but the German artillery then lacked the ability to maintain the same level of support. This was not only because of ammunition shortages, but also the difficulty of getting artillery pieces and ammunition forward along the congested roads; for example, it took the artillery corps that was supporting II SS Panzer Corps five days to reach their selected firing positions just to the rear of the original American line. Fire support for the assaulting infantry thus came mainly from the direct fire of tank guns and infantry assault guns rather than from massed artillery pieces.

Once the initial trauma of the first few hours was over, the Americans had massive superiority as far as artillery was concerned and used it to great effect. However, at first they too had to depend on the direct fire of weapons such as tank destroyers, in some cases attached to artillery units, to defend the gun lines.

Self-propelled artillery
Without a doubt the mobile, tactically agile SP artillery proved its worth over and over again, because it was able to influence the battle

quickly and effectively, far more swiftly than its towed counterpart. SP artillery – and towed also for that matter – was often used in the anti-tank role at close range, the HE shells fired by US field artillery accounting for a large number of 'kills', even though the actual damage to the individual enemy tank might have been quite minor, e.g., to the suspension (broken track, damaged sprocket/idler).

Anti-tank

I have mentioned the Tank Destroyers under 'Armour', but of course there was also a range of towed anti-tank guns on both sides, the smaller ones (57mm) were of little use, the most effective being in the 75mm calibre range. However, towed guns suffered from the extremely difficult conditions which made handling in the mud and snow very hazardous, with the result that many guns were lost. In addition, in the close battle conditions, the towing vehicle (or horses in some cases on the German side) could well be shot up and badly damaged or destroyed, leaving the gun intact but immovable.

Anti-Aircraft

With the bad weather restricting flying, many LAA guns were used in the ground role, thus making up for a lack of other weapons. As the details in Appendix 3 show, most US divisions had AAA AW battalions attached.

EXAMPLES OF SELF-PROPELLED ARTILLERY

Type	Chassis	Weight	Calibre of gun
	AMERICAN		
HMC M8 howitzer	M5 light tank	15,700kg	75mm
GMC M12	M3 medium tank	26,750kg	155mm
	GERMAN		
Hetzer	Pz Kpfw 38(t)	17,400kg	7.5cm
Hummel	Pz Kpfw IV	23,500kg	15cm

Proximity fuzes

One new 'secret' weapon which the Americans had recently developed was the VT or POZIT fuze, which detonated projectiles close to targets yet without the need for actual contact, thus producing highly effective airbursts. Originally designed for AA work, it was used in the ground role for the first time during the Ardennes offensive. It was not on wide distribution and was only used on a few occasions prior to the Allied counter-attack – and then mainly in bad weather or at night – so it was difficult to gauge the results. According to the official history, post-war claims that it had played a major part in halting German attacks are grossly exaggerated.

Battlefield illumination

The Canal Defence Light (CDL) searchlight mounted on tanks which were to have been used on D-Day had not been employed since and, although the British CDLs would still have their moment to 'shine' during the Rhine crossing, they were not used in the 'Bulge', while the six US battalions of CDLs had already been converted back to gun tanks on the grounds that there was no operational use for them. Therefore it is interesting to note that it was the Germans who, having produced a large number of searchlights for use in support of flak batteries around major potential targets in Germany, decided to try them out in a ground role. Tests proved satisfactory and large numbers of searchlights both small and large were used to illuminate the initial attacks. These would prove to be very successful in providing 'artificial moonlight' (by cloud reflection), direction-finding (by following the beams) and the actual illumination of US front-line positions. However, none of the large searchlights (150cm and 200cm) were mobile, so they had to be left behind at the Start Line when the assault began to move into the Ardennes.

Engineers

The defensive positions built for the American troops in the Ardennes were on the whole adequate and the engineers had done their usual excellent job so far as building linking roads and tracks was concerned. Perhaps the most important aspect of the combat engineers which came to the fore during the Ardennes offensive was the requirement for them to put down their shovels, pick up their rifles and fight as combat infantrymen. In addition to constructing and manning roadblocks, they would be required to hold them against savage enemy attacks, many earning unit citations for their bravery. As the CG of 30th Infantry Division, Major General Leland Hobbs, would, for example, write of the 291st Engineer Combat Battalion: 'Not only did the Engineers hold out against continuous enemy assault, but they strengthened their position locally in depth every day during their occupancy.'[7]

While the American engineers were showing that they were equally adept at fighting, those engineers in the assaulting forces were often found wanting, the paucity of their training and their lack of equipment causing them continual problems. For example, it took the engineers of 212th VGD forty-eight hours to erect a relatively simple 16-ton bridge over the River Sure, which resulted in the infantry elements along the German Seventh Army front being forced to assault without the support of their heavy weapons for the first three days. Ineffectual bridge building and the inability to repair quickly bomb-cratered roads or clear roads blocked by abatis (felled trees, barbed wire entanglements, etc.), exacerbated the problems of the attack force.

Communications

It may seem surprising to us now, but communications on the Allied side of the line in the Ardennes and beyond, was still almost entirely dependent upon line communications ('wire' as the Americans call it) rather than upon radio. This was because the standard tactical radios of the period lacked the required range and were constantly being screened by the trees and the contours of the ground – deep, winding valleys for example. In addition, both sides used jamming, but this often affected friendly transmissions as well as those of the enemy. To this can be added the unfortunate lapses in radio security that were endemic among the American radio operators.[8] Thus the control of weapons and the effectiveness of their fire depended upon line communications. These, of course, had been laid before the battle started, so, for example, artillery Forward Observation Officers were in touch with Regimental and Battery Command Posts. But the initial bombardment wrecked many of the carefully strung telephone lines in many areas, so that forward troops were out of touch with their battalion command posts at the critical moment.

At a higher level the dependency on line was just as critical. For example, HQ 12th Army Group had some 50 important line circuits between Luxembourg and First and Ninth Armies. These lines extended laterally to link the three headquarters in sequence and comprised a mixture of buried cables and open line stretching from Aubange, near Luxembourg, to Namur and Liège, via a repeater station at Jemelle, near Marche. This station was therefore the key to the whole northern network and it was lost when its protection force was ordered out when the enemy were in sight of the station. The Germans subsequently cut both the line and cables. This left communication solely by VHF radio, which had limited range. These too had to be moved farther west to avoid capture. Despite these difficulties, the US Signal Corps were able to maintain a minimum service – except for short lapses – but, as the official history puts it: 'Whether this would have sufficed for the 12th Army Group to exercise administrative as well as tactical control of the First and Ninth Armies from Luxembourg is problematical.'

On the German side, general radio silence was imposed on the newly arriving divisions so they had no chance to check their nets, test in advance the radio network which had been prepared for the offensive, or give operators the regular practice they needed. This, of course had been done so that there would be no obvious increase in the volume of radio traffic, but it would clearly affect the smooth running of unit radio nets once battle commenced and trouble was therefore expected. This is exactly what happened in the first few days of the attack, until the difficulties were gradually overcome. As far as line was concerned, no new line was allowed to be laid until the corresponding positions had been occupied. Civilian telephone traffic behind the front line was either stopped or carefully monitored to ensure that nothing was given away.

The Air

I have already mentioned the broken promises made by Reichs-marschall Hermann Göring concerning the number of aircraft that would be available to support the offensive, but if one considers the Luftwaffe's other problems, the assistance they provided was not inconsiderable. OB West estimated that about 850 ground-attack sorties were flown on 18 December and this was the largest recorded number, though there is no indication of how many actually reached the battle area. For example, six days later, when the Luftwaffe supposedly put in their heaviest assault since D-Day, US Third Army, which by then was counter-attacking and must have presented many likely targets, reported seeing only one enemy squadron active in their airspace. Once the skies cleared and the Allied aircraft were able to fly, the 'boot was very firmly on the other foot', the USAAF, for example, flying 1,138 tactical sorties on 24 December, of which 734 were ground-support missions, plus 2,442 bomber sorties. On the same day the British 2nd Tactical Air Force flew 1,243 sorties. Allied tactical air operations would be mainly directed against armoured fighting vehicles, motor transport and large troop concentrations and it is very clear that they played a major role in defeating the offensive – for example, on 26 December Model had to issue an order forbidding any major daylight movement.

Notes

1 Extract from IWM Sound Archive Tape NO 2776 (recorded in 1972).
2 Extract from IWM Sound Archive Tape No 2712 (recorded in 1972).
3 Extract from IWM Sound Archive Tape No 2776 (recorded in 1972).
4 The tank was in fact the M5A1 light tank, the latest derivative of the M3 light series. The British called it the Stuart, the Americans the M5, but tank drivers universally still called them 'Honeys' the name they had been given in the Western Desert because of their excellent handling capabilities.
5 'You mean our 76 won't knock these Panthers out?' General Eisenhower exclaimed angrily. 'Why, I thought it was going to be the wonder gun of the war.' 'Oh it's better than the 75,' replied Bradley, 'but the new charge is much too small. She just hasn't

the kick to carry her through the German armor.' Ike shook his head and swore. 'Why is it that I am always the last to hear about this stuff? Ordnance told me this 76 would take care of anything the Germans had. Now I find you can't knock out a damn thing with it!' This quotation comes from Bradley's autobiography, *A Soldier's Story*, and must epitomise the anger and frustration which the discovery had already engendered. Much later in the war a high-velocity AP round was perfected, but this could still only penetrate the Panther at under 300 yards.

6 This was an unfortunate nickname given to the Sherman, because of the fact that it was prone to bursting into flames when struck by enemy anti-tank rounds – even more sinister was its German nickname, 'The Tommy Cooker'!

7 His letter of commendation would earn the Battalion a Presidential Citation.

8 Prior to the offensive the Germans had three communications intelligence companies working under Army Group B which reported that: 'American carelessness in the use of radio and commercial telephone nets was up to par, and that no reinforcements were en route for the Ardennes.' (quotation from the official US Army history).

5
THE FINAL PLAN

'Wacht am Rhein'

In broad outline the offensive envisaged an early morning assault by three armies, preceded only by a short, sharp artillery barrage so as to gain maximum surprise, aimed at breaking through the American defences in the Ardennes between Monschau in the north and Echternach in the south. Once through, the German forces would press on as fast as possible to capture crossings over the River Meuse (Maas) between Liège and Namur, then, bypassing Brussels, they would aim to capture Antwerp. All this was to be achieved within seven days.

General

In 1947, the Office of the Chief Historian at HQ European Command received various documents which had been written by a Major a.D. Percy Ernst Schramm. He had been responsible, for taking notes at meetings of the *Wehrmacht Führungsstab* WFSt) – the Armed Forces Operations Staff. From these documents, part of the OKW War Diary (covering the period 1 April–18 December 1944) was translated into English by the Historical Division HQ US Army, Europe. Initially classified, this document was de-restricted in 1968 and now forms one of a series of *World War II German Military Studies* (see Bibliography), Appendix No. 2 of which contains the attack orders for the three assaulting armies which took part in the Ardennes Offensive – reconstructed in outline according to data furnished by the Army Chiefs of Staff. This chapter gives a résumé of that document, enlarged where possible, with the orders received from Model's Army Group B and those of the individual Army commanders.

Sixth SS Panzer Army

'After strong artillery preparations, Sixth SS Panzer Army will – on "X" Day (16 December 44) – break through the enemy front on both sides of Hollerath, and will relentlessly thrust across the Meuse towards Antwerp. For this purpose, Army will make full use of its motorised forces.' The following explanatory instructions then detailed the tasks of the various corps in Obergruppenführer 'Sepp' Dietrich's Sixth SS Panzer Army:

a. I SS Panzer Corps. SS Gruppenführer Herman Priess' panzer corps would start its attack at 0600 hrs on 'X' Day (16 December 1944) and break through enemy positions along the front in the Monschau–Losheim sector, taking the Elsenborn Ridge and breaking through the Losheim Gap. To achieve this frontal assault Dietrich deployed three divisions: 3rd Panzer Grenadier Division, 12th and 277th VGD, on the right against the main American positions (99th and 2nd US Inf Divs), with 3rd Fallschirmjäger (Parachute) Division on the left to open up the Losheim Gap. Subsequently, with 12th SS Panzer Division on the right and 1st SS Panzer Division on the left, they would thrust forwards, cross the Meuse and continue the attack towards Liège–Huy. Thereafter the corps' mission would be: 'Relentlessly to pierce towards Antwerp, by making full use of its motorised elements, or to be available for the protection of the right flank along the Albert Canal.' It goes on to order that a number of carefully selected advance units, led by 'particularly daring commanders' were to advance as rapidly as possible to capture the bridges over the Meuse before they could be blown by the enemy. This would be the main task of the leading battle groups which were:

(i) Leibstandarte Adolf Hitler – Battle Group Peiper. In addition to his own SS Panzer Battalion (72 mixed Pz Kpfw IV and Panthers) of his 1st SS Panzer Regiment, Jochen Peiper was given 501st SS Heavy Panzer Battalion (45 Tiger II), 3rd SS Panzer Grenadier Battalion (mounted in halftracks), an artillery battalion of 18 x 105mm towed guns, an

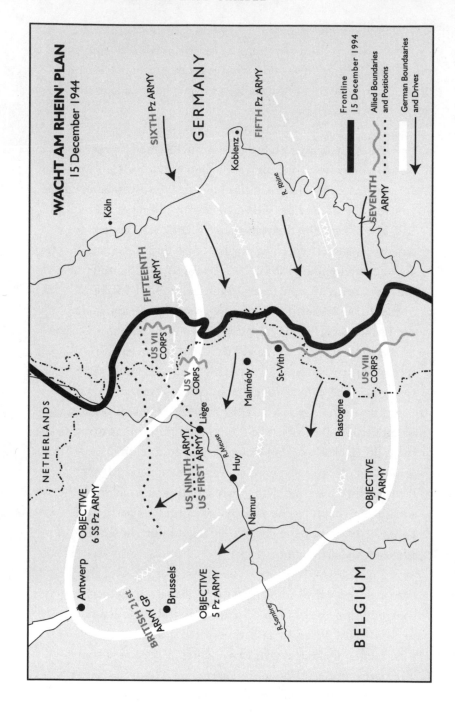

'WACHT AM RHEIN' PLAN
15 December 1944

infantry gun company (150mm), part of 84th Light Flak Battalion equipped with some twenty 20mm and 37mm guns, plus his normal engineer, AA, etc., units. In total the battle group comprised some 4,800 men and 800 vehicles (nearly 25 per cent of which were tanks). All it lacked was engineer bridging support, but this was intentional because it would clearly slow down movement and in any case the group had the task of capturing bridges before they could be demolished!

(ii) Hitlerjugend – Battle Group Kuhlmann. This group had a similar organisation, its 1st SS Panzer Battalion containing some 80 (37 Pz Kpfw IV, 37 Panther, 4 command and 2 recovery) tanks, and 560th SS Heavy Panzer Battalion (14 Jagdpanther, 26 Jagdpanzer) plus additional artillery, infantry gun company, AA, etc., with a total strength roughly equivalent to Peiper's force.

Attached to Priess' corps would be: 277th VGD, 12th VGD and 3rd Parachute Division, the last two of these returning to army control once the breakthrough had been achieved.

b. II SS Panzer Corps. SS Obergruppenführer Wilhelm Bittrich's panzer corps was to be held in readiness close behind I SS Panzer Corps and would immediately follow on during the advance, the corps' mission being : 'To thrust together with I SS Panzer Corps towards the Meuse, cross the river and continue its advance on Antwerp, disregarding any enemy contact on its flanks.' It was stressed that it was vital for them to remain in constant liaison with the leading panzer corps, with advance armoured detachments close up behind the leading troops' rear elements. They were also given the task of keeping the 'roads of advance' (i.e., the Centre Line) open behind I SS Panzer Corps.

c. LXVII Infantry Corps. Generalleutnant Otto Hitzfeld's infantry corps was given the task of breaking through the enemy positions on both sides of Monschau, with 326th and 246th *Volks* Grenadier Divisions, then crossing the Mützenich–Elsenborn road, turning north and west, to build up secure defensive positions along a line: Simmerath–Eupen–Limbourg–Liège, so as to protect the northern shoulder of the offensive. Their orders went on to explain that 12th VGD and 3rd Parachute Division would be committed to this defence to the west of Limbourg and that HQ Sixth SS Panzer Army would be responsible for moving them up once they had completed their tasks with I SS Pz Corps. 'Road-blocks, supported by armoured detachments, will be established far to the north across the main roads and across the lines of communication leading from north to south. The hilly terrain around Elsenborn will be seized and firmly held.'

d. Artillery. Special orders were issued for the artillery which specifically regulated the pre-'X'-hour barrage, also the support which could be given during the attack and to additional artillery tasks, plus the allocation of artillery while the attack was in progress. As will be seen from Appendix 1, Sixth SS Panzer Army, like the other two, was allocated additional artillery to boost its organic batteries.

The 'main effort'

'Sepp' Dietrich's panzer army was thus tasked with the 'main effort', and for this reason it was equipped with more tanks and other AFVs than either of the other two armies. Army Group B's orders stated that Sixth Panzer Army would break through to the north of the Schnee-Eifel and would then: 'resolutely thrust forward on its right flank with fast-moving units for the Meuse crossing-points between Liège and Huy. Following this they will drive forward to the Albert Canal between Maastricht and Antwerp'. To assist them in achieving their missions, two individual co-ordinated operations had been planned: Operation 'Greif' and Operation 'Stösser'.

a. Operation 'Greif'. This was designed to capture selected bridges over the River Meuse and was to be carried out by Otto Skorzeny's 150 Panzer Brigade, as already mentioned in Chapter 2.

b. Operation 'Stösser'. This was to be a Parachute landing in the mountain area north of Malmédy, with the aim of securing the important road junction at Baraque Michel through which the armoured spearheads of 12th SS Panzer Division would need to advance on their way to Liège.

In their final orders OKW stressed three objectives which had to be taken initially:

a. in the north, the vital Elsenborn Ridge.

b. in the centre, the Schnee-Eifel.

c. in the south, the confluence of the Rivers Sauer and Our.

Fifth Panzer Army

On 10 December, General der Panzertruppen Hasso von Manteuffel issued detailed: 'instructions on the assembly and fighting', which were divided under three headings: (1). The enemy; (2). Intentions of the Army Group and the adjacent units; (3). Mission of Fifth Panzer Army which was as follows:

'The mission of Fifth Panzer Army is, to break through the enemy positions in the Ölzheim–Gemünd sector under cover of darkness, and to thrust across the Meuse on both sides of Namur up to Brussels.'

The first objectives of the attack were the bridgeheads across the Meuse. It was stressed that it was vital to break through any enemy resistance, to keep going by day and night: 'to advance relentlessly disregarding prescribed routes of advance; if necessary, the advance will be continued on foot.' (These orders are reminiscent of General Patton's to his US Third Army when faced with POL shortages during the 'Gallop across France'!)

In order to achieve their mission against US 28th and 106th Infantry Divisions, the various formations were given the following tasks:

a. LXVI Infantry Corps. On the right flank, using 18th and 62nd VGD, General der Artillerie Walther Lucht's corps was to execute a double envelopment of the enemy forces in the Schnee-Eifel to 'nip out' that salient, after which they were to capture St-Vith. This achieved, they would press on, echeloned in depth, reach the Meuse and cross in the Huy–Andenne sector, or else be moved to cover the left wing of the Army.

b. LVIII Panzer Corps. In the centre, using 116th Panzer Division and 560th VGD, General der Panzertruppen Walter Krüger's panzer corps was to force a crossing of the River Our on a broad front on both sides of Ouren, then push forward to the Meuse via Houffalize, thrust across the Meuse in the Andenne–Namur sector and establish bridgeheads.

c. XLVII Panzer Corps. On the left flank, south of Dasburg, using 2nd Panzer Division and 26th VGD, General der Panzertruppen Heinrich von Lüttwitz's panzer corps was to force a crossing of the River Our on a broad front in the Dasburg–Gemünd area, bypass the Clerf/Clervaux sector, capture Bastogne and finally, echeloned in depth, thrust towards and across the Meuse in the vicinity and to the south of Namur.

d. Panzer Lehr Division and Führer Begleit Brigade. Initially they were to be held in readiness as Panzer Army reserve, then, as soon as one of the corps had succeeded in breaking through, they would be launched in a rapid thrust toward the Meuse.

There followed more instructions which dealt with points of detail in the execution of these tasks, such as details of boundaries, instructions for the conduct of the battle, the mission of the artillery and engineers, the commitment of the Luftwaffe and the Flak, signal communications, special administrative instructions for the supply services, the maintenance of secrecy and camouflage measures, the plan for the assembly, a time schedule for the orientation of the troops taking part, and, finally, a description of the terrain, instructions on the locations of command posts and a complete series of the requisite maps.

Seventh Army

The mission of General der Panzertruppen Erich Brandenberger's Seventh Army on 'X' Day was: 'to cross the Rivers Our and Sauer, break through the enemy front in the Vianden–Echternach sector, then, with its reinforced right wing, to thrust towards the line Gedinne–Libramont–Martelange–Mersch–Wasserbillig in order to protect the southern flank of Fifth Panzer Army. The Army will then gain ground beyond this line, will advance up to the Semois sector and the Luxembourg area and will – by fluid conduct of battle – prevent any enemy thrust into the southern flank of the Army Group.' In essence, therefore, Seventh Army had two principal tasks, the first being to protect von Manteuffel's left flank, the second to threaten Luxembourg so as to tie down enemy reserves.

The following instructions were issued to the corps:

a. LXXXV Infantry Corps. General der Infanterie Baptist Kniess' Infantry Corps will start its attack at 0600 hours on 'X' Day, crossing the River Our and breaking through the enemy front in the area Vianden–Ammeldingen. The 5th Fallschirmjäger Division on the right and the 352nd VGD on the left, will: 'relentlessly thrust to the west' and then turn off towards the line Gedinne–Libramont–Martelange–Mersch, where they will first adopt a defensive posture. Advance mobile detachments will keep contact with the southern elements of Fifth Panzer Army which will be advancing to the north of the corps via Bastogne. These detachments are to advance beyond the objective of the operation up to the Semois and block its main crossing-points.

b. LXXX Infantry Corps. General der Infanterie Franz Beyer's Infantry Corps would also start its attack at 0600 hours on 'X' Day, crossing both the Rivers Our and Sauer, breaking through the enemy front in the Wallendorf–Echternach area. Then with 276th VGD on the right and 212th VGD on the left, they would: 'relentlessly thrust towards the line Mersch–Wasserbillig where their main forces will adopt a defensive posture. Advance mobile detachments will cross the Sauer, advance into the Luxembourg area and prevent enemy forces from advancing via Luxembourg.' It was vitally important that enemy artillery positions in the Christnach–Alttrier area be quickly neutralised. Special mention was also made of the role of the penal battalion (*Bewährungsbataillon*) which was committed to the River Sauer front west of Trier, and was to be held in readiness for the thrust across the Sauer.

c. LIII Infantry Corps. Commanded by General der Kavallerie Graf von Rothkirch und Trach, it was to remain 'available' to HQ Seventh Army.

Air Support
Göring's Luftwaffe had been ordered to support the operation in three main ways:

a. Close air support for the attacking troops, so as to provide local air superiority in the battle area of Fifth and Sixth Panzer Armies – in view of the bad weather which was normal at this time of year in the chosen attack area, this would be impossible to achieve, indeed Hitler had deliberately chosen to time his offensive so that it coincided with the worst weather possible!

b. A special operation, code-named 'Bodenplatte', designed to seek out and destroy Allied aircraft on the ground. As we shall see, this operation would not take place until 1 January 1945.

c. Operation 'Stösser' – as already mentioned, the use of Paratroops to facilitate the advance of the leading elements of SS Sixth

Panzer Army by securing key road junctions ahead of the ground advance and then holding them until link-up.

As always Göring had promised far more than he was able to provide, boasting that he had some 3,000 fighters available to support the ground forces, when the actual *entire* strength of the Luftwaffe at that time was only about 2,000 aircraft.

6
THE ASSAULT BEGINS

Orders of the Day 16 December 1944
The following daily order was issued by OB West from CinC West:

> Soldiers of the Western Front!! Your great hour has struck. At this moment the veil which has been hiding so many preparations has been lifted at last. Large attacking armies have started against the Anglo-Americans. I do not have to tell you anything more than that. You feel it yourself: *We are gambling everything!* You carry with you a holy obligation to give everything to achieve things beyond human possibilities for our Fatherland and our Führer!
>
> Signed
> Von Rundstedt.
> Generalfeldmarschall.

This ringing call to arms was endorsed by the CinC Army Group B.

> We will not disappoint the Führer and the Fatherland who created the sword of retribution. Advance in the spirit of Leuthen.[1] Our battle-cry must now more than ever be 'No soldier in the world can be better than we soldiers of the Eifel and of Aachen!'
>
> Signed
> Model
> Generalfeldmarschall

And again at Army level there were yet more Orders of the Day, such as this one from CinC Fifth Panzer Army:

Forward at the double! In remembrance of our dead comrades and therefore on their orders and in remembrance of the proud tradition of our Wehrmacht!

Signed

Von Manteuffel

General der Panzertruppen

The assault begins

On the night of 15/16 December 1944, *Gefreite* (L/Cpl) Guido Gnilsen was a radio operator in a command halftrack belonging to one of the battalions of 2nd Panzer Grenadier Regiment in 2nd Panzer Division of XLVII Panzer Corps of von Manteuffel's Fifth Panzer Army, so he was right at the centre of the German assault. Their headquarters was initially in the town of Dahnen and at about midnight they had their last meeting with all the other radio and telephone operators while being briefed on what was to come. He recalled later:

> We were all sitting quietly by the light of candles, looking around the walls of our shelter you could see the white and serious faces of my comrades. We had all been issued with winter camouflage suits and rations for three days in a bread bag. Then we left carrying our heavy kitbags in long lines, one after the other down a small wet lane to the river that was also the border. I helped the telephone troop to lay their cable, then went back to check it so as to ensure there were no breakages and that we had good communications. Our halftrack was 'telephone central' so it had to stay on the east bank until we had crossed in rubber boats and had established a bridgehead over the other side.

The initial crossing of the River Our (which was in full flood) by XLVII Panzer Corps took place at Dasburg and began at 0530 hrs on the wet, cold and foggy morning of the 16th, with the infantry of 26th VGD in the lead. They had many ex-Navy personnel in their lower ranks, so their level of infantry training and combat experience was low. However, their senior NCOs and officers were experienced and well trained. Although surprise was total and initial success was achieved, the Americans unexpectedly offered strong resistance along the Hein-erscheid–Hoscheid road, which was known to the GIs as 'Skyline Drive'. The positions there were manned by men of US 28th Infantry Division, together with Combat Command 'A' of 9th Armored Division. Guido Gnilsen continues:

The thoughts that were going through our heads at that moment were how we were going to get over the high hills and what would be waiting for us on the other side. The night passed and we slept fitfully in the halftrack. Then, at about 5 o'clock we were woken by tremendously loud explosions. I thought that the world was coming to an end! It was our mortars shooting rockets out of their many barrels with deafening explosions and screaming, the earth trembling as if there was an earthquake.[2] You could see the glowing rockets flying in the direction of the enemy while searchlights turned night into day on our side. As far as you could see everywhere were the flashes from artillery fire. It was like being in Hell, something you can never forget – and it must have been a lot worse for the enemy.

The tension was rising as the minutes ticked by, we would have to get moving, win or lose. The first reports were favourable, many places had been taken, you could see blue smoke in the distance where villages were on fire, our push was going well.

We were waiting for our air force to appear – we had been told that they had a new weapon and plenty of them – maybe a jet that could fire rockets – we were told you could recognise it by its yellow trail.[3] We could see specks in the sky coming towards us, then flying over our heads, but they were the hated 'Light-nings' with the double fuselage,[4] but they didn't have anything to laugh about this time, as the anti-aircraft guns were waiting for them and did not stop firing until they decided to get moving.

We had taken the bridge at Dasburg before the enemy had time to destroy it, so we had no trouble getting our tanks, ammunition carriers, artillery and reinforcements, etc., over to the other side. Now we could widen our bridgehead. We got the order to move the halftrack over as quickly as possible. There were lots of things for me to see – burning houses, knocked out tanks, vehicles burning and all around exploding ammunition – it was a real picture of war.

In fact, although they had taken the bridge site at Dasburg, the bridges had been destroyed by German forces during their withdrawal in the autumn, so there was a delay while two Class 60 combat bridges were laid – and these took longer than expected because of adverse water and river bank conditions, so it was not until 1600 hours that the first tanks could cross at Dasburg, and even later at Gemünd.

Problems with Operation 'Stösser'

The great offensive did not get off to a particularly good start every-where, certainly not so far as the parachute operation 'Stösser' was concerned. It had been designed to drop Paratroops in the Hohes Venn, their tasks being: to block the roads Eupen–Malmédy and Verviers–Malmédy, capture the vital Baraque Michel crossroads and hold them until the arrival of the leading elements of the panzers – Battle Group Peiper. When the Paratroop commander, the highly decorated and exceptionally able Oberst Freiherr Friedrich August von der Heydte, arrived at Bad Lippspringe airfield in the early hours of 16th December, having briefed his officers at their training base and then driven ahead to one of the two departure airfields (the other was Paderborn), he thought that he would not have long to await the arrival of his Battle Group von der Heydte, because their drop was scheduled to take place between 0430 and 0500 hrs that morning. However, when they still hadn't arrived by 0400 hrs, it was clear that there would be no drop that day and his operation would have to be postponed by at least 24 hours.[5] Poor von der Heydte, his rag-tag Paratroop force was a pale shadow of the 'Storming Eagles' which he had led so bravely in Crete in 1941. It had been formed as a result of Hitler (via OKW) ordering every Parachute Regiment in II Para Corps, to send a hundred of their best soldiers to form the new unit for a mission which could not be disclosed. As anyone who knows 'the Army Game' might expect, without any knowledge of what the unit was being set up to achieve (on account of the secrecy surrounding 'Wacht am Rhein') the commanding officers took it as an ideal opportunity for getting rid of their 'sick, lame and lazy'! It was not until von der Heydte's old unit, 6th Parachute Regiment, learned about the intended mission of the force, that they were able to persuade the powers that be to let some 250 of them join in. Von der Heydte was also permitted to select his company and platoon commanders. His force, which numbered some 1,200 men in total, was to be organised along the lines of a normal battalion, with four rifle companies, a heavy weapons company of twelve machine-guns and four mortars, plus signals and engineer platoons. Von der Heydte had precious little time to prepare his *ad hoc* battle group, some of whom had never even made more than one practice jump, so he was filled with foreboding from the outset, especially after he was told about the difficult, heavily wooded, broken country on which his inexperienced force was expected to land – and by night! To top it all, he discovered that many of the aircrew of the air transport squadron detailed to fly the mission had neither night flying experience nor experience in dropping Paratroops!

The operation got under way on the night of the 16th, with all 80 aircraft taking off safely – but that was to be the end of their good luck. Many of the inexperienced aircrew were totally at a loss what to do or what corrections to make when they experienced strong headwinds over the target area. Consequently, the Paratroopers were dropped at random all over the place; some, for example, landed near Bonn on the Rhine, others in Holland, others crashed into the tops of neighbouring mountains, and some were shot down by American AA fire. Only ten aircraft found the correct drop zone, so there were eventually only some 300 men at von der Heydte's rallying-point. As it would turn out all these problems didn't really matter, because Sixth SS Panzer Army's 'point' failed to reach its first-day objectives, so there was no link-up. However, there was an unexpected bonus which the general chaos and haphazard spread of the German Paratroopers would have upon their opponents, namely the spreading of alarm and despondency on a very wide scale, far outweighing the strength of the actual force and its true purpose, which added considerably to the morale-sapping effect that Skorzeny's Operation 'Greif' would have initially, again out of all proportion to the size and nature of 150 Panzer Brigade's operation.

'Everything has changed in the west!'

The blistering early morning barrage on *Tag Null* (Day Zero) took the vast majority of the defenders by surprise all along the 104 'meandering miles' of front line – it was the kind of 'wake-up' call that the thousands of sleeping GIs had never expected to receive in their Ardennes 'rest area'. Some of course were already awake in their forward OPs and had been reporting the hundreds of 'flickering lights' – which a few seconds later were explained as enemy artillery gun flashes as the 'incoming mail' began to arrive! Then, where the phone lines/radios were still working and it was possible to get through to higher headquarters, came reports of enemy infantry moving slowly forward, clearing lanes in the minefields in front of the American positions. They would be followed by the panzers which, once the infantry had breached the American positions, would burst through and sweep westwards along their selected *Rollbahnen* (Centre Lines). This is what the 'big picture' must have looked like on the OKW, OB West and Army Group B battle maps, but at the sharp end it was initially just a confused jumble of individual, apparently unconnected actions, which few of the defenders recognised as being individual segments of a massive front-long assault. 'I told the Führer on the first day of the attack that the surprise had been completely achieved,' said Jodl in a post-war interview, while 'Just a local diversion', is how more than one American intelligence officer reported the attack on his part of the front, and no doubt that was the opinion of numerous more senior intelligence officers all the way back to SHAEF. With the overall breakdown in communications which the opening barrage had caused and the highly successful German pre-attack security, the delay in appreciating the true size and nature of the assault can be explained, but not excused. The first long situation report from Army Group B (sent at about 1245 hrs) contained numerous extracts from radio intercepts which had picked up frantic messages from hard-pressed American forward units that had been bypassed or were in danger of being overrun. All appeared to suggest that the attack was going completely according to plan and certainly Hitler was clearly caught in the mood of the moment as a conversation he had with General Hermann Balck (CinC Army Group G, which was located to the south of Army Group B) that afternoon shows: 'Balck! Balck,' Hitler rasped. 'Everything has changed in the west! Success – complete success – is now within our grasp!'[6]

However, the Führer had spoken far too soon.

Holdups in the north

In the far north, the right wing of Dietrich's SS panzer army, 'Korps Monschau', as LXVII Corps was sometimes called, did not get off to a good start. It did not help matters that, acting on orders direct from Feldmarschall Model, the opening barrage was not permitted to include the ancient timber-framed buildings of Monschau itself. Also, many of the assault guns, so vital in providing close infantry support, had been taken away from 326th VGD (supposedly because of 'expected terrain difficulties'), and despite the consider-able barrage there was still strong American opposition everywhere. The assault failed and the troops had to be withdrawn back to their Start Lines that evening. They would begin again before dawn next day, but only limited gains were made before American fighter-bombers arrived on the scene. By the evening of the 18th it was realised that the original mission was impossible to achieve and that they would have to make do with blocking off the exits from the Hohes Venn astride the Eupen road, thereby protecting the northern flank of the attack. After the war Dietrich's Chief of Staff, Fritz Kraemer, put their failure down to the non-arrival of a heavy panzer battalion (the trains carrying the tanks had been attacked from the air on a number of occasions) and to the inexperience and lack of training of the *Volksgrenadiers*. Monschau and Höfen would thereafter be left relatively in peace and the divisions involved in the failed assault mainly redeployed elsewhere.

J. R. McIlroy, First Scout, BAR man and acting squad leader of the 2nd Squad in 34th Platoon, F Company, 2nd Battalion of the 393rd Infantry Regiment, which had accompanied 2nd Inf Div's push to take the Roer dams, whom we met earlier, was still bogged down trying to take a German pill-box line. He recalled:

We could hear all kinds of noises – the sounds of war – artillery, rifle and machine-gun fire, et cetera, but we never saw a single German. As luck would have it we were in a position where the Germans did not attack. This was a location where the terrain was so bad that tanks could not have moved – in fact it was so bad that they hadn't built any dragons' teeth here. Early on the seventeenth we were told to hold in place, that something was going on. About noon Colonel Ernest Peters, our battalion commander, made the announcement that the Germans were breaking through and we were to leave anything we could not carry easily and get back to Litchenbret (known as the Hasselpat Trail). I think we got all our wounded out – I'm not sure if we got Sergeant Rhodes' body (our first killed) out. About the middle of the afternoon we reached the trail. After a little way we took a break on the side of the track by a big bulldozer that had lost its tread. About that time I was told to lead us east into the forest until we encountered the Germans – we knew they were near because spent bullets sailed over our heads and the rifle fire was near. We moved out and advanced probably about five hundred yards – I was leading followed by the Second Scout (Alvin Swisher). When we moved over a hill we would wave the company on. After going over two hills safely, we started down the third when I noticed several Germans coming around the bend. They had seen me first and they fired before I could move. Their shots hit my BAR and I promptly hit the ground! Alvin, not finding a place to get behind, lay across me and fired at the Germans. In just a second he was shot between the eyes. I lay there a little while with bullets hitting my pack. At that time some of my group began firing at the Germans and they took cover. During this time I shed my pack and ran back up the hill with the Germans firing at me all the way. Alvin's body was recovered after the 'Bulge' and he is now buried in the Henry Chappel Cemetery.

We were told to hold at all costs, that the Germans were advancing and that the Second Division on our left would be trapped if the road behind us was not held open. We held in place that night and on the eighteenth we moved a little south. After digging in we soon encountered opposition. German troops were trying to advance but we repulsed all their attacks that day. About dark that day we were told that we had held long enough and we started pulling back. At this time we had several wounded and five killed. All the rest of us were very tired – the lack of sleep and food was beginning to get to us.

One of the GIs defending Höfen against the VGD assault was Joseph L Thimm, a rifleman in 2nd Platoon, K Company of the 3rd Battalion, 395th Infantry Regiment of 99th Infantry Division, who had taken over some weeks before from sub-units of 5th Armored Division. The battalion had all three companies (I, K, L) in a semi-circle on the eastern edge of the village, facing the enemy-held village of Rohren. He recalled:

The Second Platoon had the good fortune to locate its platoon CP in an honest-to-goodness German pill-box about fifteen or twenty yards from the Höfen/Rohren road. The rest of the platoon moved into previously dug positions to the front and right of the pill-box. I'll never forget the look of relief on the face of the Fifth Armored guy as he welcomed us to his hole. And I'll never forget my reaction (sinking depression) that this can't be real! After all the elaborate training and preparation for war, here we stood staring into a muddy hole with a make-shift roof of shelter staves, branches and whatever else was handy to keep the rain and snow out. To the front of us was a bleak snow-covered field, and to the rear was another field leading back to Höfen, with dead, bloated cattle lying about. Before he left us, I remember the Fifth Armored GI saying something about where the Germans were located and to follow the path to the pill-box since mines and booby-traps had probably been planted all around the area by the Germans. And off he went, leaving three disbelieving GIs to consider what a heck of an introduction this was to front-line combat!

The soon to be launched German assault on Höfen was detected along the front late on the night of December fifteenth – engine noises could be heard by those of us in the foxholes and we passed this information back to platoon and company. Our own artillery and mortar fire began before midnight and continued for a couple of hours, but before dawn on December sixteenth, we were on the receiving end of heavy German artillery, mortar and rocket fire which lasted about half an hour. Then again we could hear the sounds of engines which meant tanks were on the move in front of us. The main German thrust struck I and K Companies. These attacks were met by small arms and concentrated mortar and artillery fire. The Germans backed off until about midday then began to attack again directly on the K Company front. Small arms fire and artillery blunted the attack. Fortunately, the tanks never appeared on the Höfen road, either taken out by artillery fire or bogged down in the snow and mud.

With the exception of air activity and flares, December seventeenth did not see a repeat of the German infantry attack. On the early morning of December eighteenth, the Germans launched an attack on I Company, and later in the morning K Company was again on the receiving end of an infantry/tank assault preceded by another heavy artillery, rocket and mortar concentration. The German infantry and tanks were met with heavy artillery and mortar fire that drove the foot soldiers back and prevented the armor from moving up. The German attack continued on the I Company front until late morning when their penetration into Höfen was stopped and the German infantry forced to retreat. German combat patrols struck I and L Companies later in the evening, and succeeded in infiltrating L Company lines and inflicted casualties, but eventually were forced to pull back. After three days of fighting, the battle of Höfen was largely over, and although German patrols continued to pressure the Battalion front from December nineteenth to twenty-fourth, another full scale attack never developed.

Thor Ronningen of Wilmington, North Carolina was a member of I Company of the 3rd Battalion and ascribed much of their success to their outstanding battalion commander, Lieutenant Colonel McClernand Butler. He told me:

> Having come on line ninth November 1944, we had the advantage of time to prepare our positions. Colonel Butler saw at once that we would not be able to form a solid line so he had us prepare a series of strong points. He insisted that we install a solid roof on each position which would protect us from anything except a direct hit. Six times during the battle he ordered five minute concentrations on our positions from our own artillery as he knew we were well protected. No American troops were killed by this fire. Our artillery was a fantastic advantage and we could not have held without them.

The 3rd Battalion was awarded a Presidential Unit Citation for its gallant defence of Höfen. Despite being outnumbered at least five to one, they had held their positions, inflicting heavy casualties on the enemy and denying them the road to Eupen. If they had not made their gallant stand undoubtedly the Germans would have been able to get behind the troops on the Elsenborn Ridge, where another brave defensive battle was fought.

Action at Lanzerath

Another desperate, yet determined action, took place on the extreme southern flank of the 'Checkerboard' Division's thinly-held positions, right on the inter-corps boundary with VIII Corps. Here, near Lanzerath, the eighteen men of Intelligence and Reconnaissance Platoon of the 394th Infantry Regiment, plus four artillerymen, occupied a commanding position on a knoll to the west of the village, which completely overlooked the road farther south, through the Losheim Gap (see photograph). They occupied positions which had been dug originally by 2nd Inf Div, well-protected foxholes with overhead cover. Fortunately they had plenty of ammunition for their weapons, which included a .50cal machine-gun mounted on a Jeep. The .50 is a formidable weapon with a muzzle velocity of some 2,900fps and a rate of fire of 450 575rpm, fed by a 110-round metal link belt. It is said to have been produced in larger quantity than any other American machine-gun. (I had one mounted on top of the turret of my Centurion Mark III in Korea and can vouch for its devastating firepower.) The I&R Section position was in fact located just over the inter-corps boundary, the nearest other unit being a section of tank destroyers belonging to A Company of 820 TD Battalion attached to the 14th Cavalry Group, VIII Corps, which was in the village of Lanzerath.

On 12 December, Richard Byers, forward observer with C Battery of the 371st Field Artillery Battalion, whom we met in Chapter 4, had moved with his battery about a mile to the north of their previous location, to the village of Murringen, which was not far from Lanzerath within the 394th area. The howitzers had their gun lines on the east side of the village and the men of the Survey & Observation Section were snugly billeted in a house near the centre of the village. In the normal style of country building in the area, the barn adjoined the house, so that the farmer could step directly from his kitchen into the cow byres and he and his family could share the warmth emanating from their animals in the bitter winter weather. The upstairs room occupied by the section shared the back wall and roof in common with the barn, and was of a solid stone structure. He recalled the morning of 16 December in his memoirs, entitled 'Out of the frying pan, into the frying pan':

Just before dawn, on the morning of the 16th, we were awakened by a muffled explosion and a slight tremor of the house. None of us thought enough of the occurrence to get out of a warm sleeping-bag to investigate, but, as far as our group was concerned, this incident was the start of the Battle of the Bulge. One of our section finally got up to go downstairs and out to the latrine. By the early light he saw a delayed fuse artillery shell had gone through the roof of the barn, just two feet from the wall of our bedroom. The round had buried itself in the haymow before exploding. Later a series of German shells came marching across the fields directly at one of our gun positions. The gunnery sergeant panicked and started to scramble out of the dugout. His men restrained him. The next round exploded just behind the entrance to this gun section's dugout. The Sergeant was sent to the 5th Evacuation Hospital as a 'slightly ill non-battle casualty – not yet diagnosed', per Section III Circular 69, never to return.

Throughout the morning shells hit at random around the village. One exploded among a group of infantrymen lined up for breakfast outside their headquarters house and killed several men. By mid-morning we realized there was a pattern to the explosions. They fell close to houses occupied by American troops. Later, we heard that a captured German artillery observer had a marked map showing all the occupied houses. If true, this information must have been given to him by someone planted in the area by the Germans when they retreated in October or infiltrated through the forest at night.

I don't recall many events of that hectic day except in the afternoon I drove with Lieutenant Mayer to the 3rd Bn, 394th Inf Regt command post near Losheimergraben for a briefing. While the Lieutenant was in the crowded dugout we were hit by the first and worst barrage I've ever been in, before or since! Sergeant

Fletcher and I were caught flat-footed in the open in a pine forest without a hole or any adequate cover. The shells were hitting the treetops and spraying the ground all around us with sharp steel fragments. I do believe I pressed a slit trench into the snow and frozen ground with my body, trying in my terror to become as small and as flat as possible. The noise was so incredibly loud it could not be heard, it rang in our ears and vibrated our bodies. Just imagine putting your head up inside an enormous bell while giants pounded it with sledgehammers. The only thing that keeps you going at moments like that is the youthful sense that you are invulnerable; that while others could be getting slaughtered all around you it wasn't going to happen to you. With my back so exposed I lost the sense of invulnerability and sheer terror took over until the shelling stopped. I barely kept control.

Back on their knoll near Lanzerath the I&R Platoon had a spectacular view of the barrage, as they witnessed the scores of muzzle flashes light up the early morning sky. Sensibly they were at the bottom of their foxholes and thus well protected before the 'incoming mail' arrived! The barrage lasted for about an hour, then everyone stood to, expecting the enemy to attack immediately. Instead, all they saw – much to their annoyance – was the hasty departure to the rear of the tank destroyers. Lieutenant Bouck reported this on his radio and was ordered to send a patrol into Lanzerath to find out what was going on in the village. So, taking three men, he set off down to the village by a circuitous route and having got there safely, made for the house where he had seen the TDs' OP based and from its windows saw a great mass of German troops moving towards them from Losheim. Ordering two of his men to remain in the house to observe for as long as they could (i.e., until the enemy were about a mile or so away), Bouck got back to his platoon position as quickly as he could and tried to reach 1st Battalion HQ on the telephone, but found the line broken. So instead he got on to Regt HQ on the radio. The officer at the other end was incredulous. 'Damn it,' Bouck hollered. 'Don't tell me what I don't see! I have twenty-twenty vision. Bring down some artillery, all the artillery you can, on the road south of Lanzerath. There's a Kraut column coming up from that direction!'

Much to his disappointment no artillery came down as the guns were themselves under heavy counter-battery fire. Then the two men whom he had left in the village telephoned (using the line which had been left behind by the TDs); they were sure that the enemy were already in the village and had just entered the house they were in, so they were trapped! Fortunately, just as Bouck readied a party to go down to try and extricate them, the two men appeared and jumped into their foxholes – the 'Krauts downstairs' had turned out to be Belgian civilians looking for shelter in the cellars. However, they were able to confirm that the enemy was now very close indeed, so Bouck readied his men for battle. They had plenty of firepower, adequate ammunition stocks and good positions, but this was their first proper test in action – how would they perform?

Richard Byers recalled:

We began to hear confused stories just ahead of us in the forward area. We were worried about our Forward Observation party which was now in Lanzerath, outside the Division's boundary line. Their only protection was a tank destroyer group and the 394th Infantry Intelligence and Reconnaissance Platoon which screened the two-mile gap between the south end of our lines and the north end of the 106th Division's. This party included Lieutenant Warren Springer, Sergeant Peter Gacki, T/5 Billy Queen and T/4 Willard Wibben. They had been watching Losheim from the south through a gap in the forest. Their OP was on the second floor of a house on the edge of Lanzerath. On the night of the fifteenth Gacki observed and reported that Losheim was lit up like a Christmas tree. Later Sergeant Gacki wrote: 'We were awakened by an artillery barrage early in the morning of the 16th. We were in contact with the Battery and I don't remember what our orders were but when we began to get ready to leave we found that the Tank Destroyer Company had already left town ... I guess it was strange considering the circumstances but we didn't feel any sense of urgency at that time. We left some food and a package I had received from home. As far as I know, we were the last to leave town. We started back to the Battery and then stopped to help the I & R Platoon. I guess we stayed too long.'

By staying too long they became involved in the crucial day-long battle with the German 9th Para Regiment of 3rd Parachute Division whose mission was to clear them out of the way for the armoured columns of Battle Group Peiper and I SS Panzer Corps.

They stopped to help just as the point of the column of Paratroopers marching out of Losheim reached Lanzerath. While in the dugouts with the eighteen men of the I & R Platoon, they tried to call artillery fire from C Battery directly on their own heads to help fight off the hundreds of Paratroopers attacking them. Corporal Billy S. Queen died during the fighting. By dusk, the German Paratroopers finally decided to hit them from the sides instead of attacking straight up the hill. All radios were dead, all ammunition was gone, so the Germans finally succeeded in overwhelming them.

The I & R Platoon battle at Lanzerath was typical of the intense, low-level battles that were taking place all along the Ardennes front, so it is worthwhile looking at it in some detail. To do this I have used a report on a hearing held some 30 plus years after the event in which one of those who took part, William James Tsakanikas, was recommended for the award of a posthumous Medal of Honor for his bravery that day.[8] 'Sak', as he was called by the other members of the platoon, was a born soldier, always volunteering for the dangerous jobs, despite his age (he was just nineteen). He was the runner for the platoon commander, First Lieutenant Lyle J. Bouck, who obviously placed a great deal of trust in him. In a letter to Lieutenant Colonel Robert L. Kriz, 394th Infantry and former S2, written at the end of March 1945, and quoted from the Medal of Honor submission, 'Sak' recalled the battle as follows:

On the morning of 16th December at 0520 they started shelling our position on the hill, it lasted exactly one hour. No casualties from that first shelling, but it messed up our telephones. During the morning 1st Lt Bouck, Pfc Robinson and myself scouted out the draw on the left of town leading towards Losheim. There were no Jerries, but we heard small arms fire in the distance. We went back to the hill and everybody was on the alert in their holes. The TDs had pulled out of the town sometime during the morning and the artillery observer pulled back to our hill.

At that point Lt Bouck sent two men (or rather they volunteered) to establish an OP where the TDs had theirs. The small arms fire kept getting closer. Then Sgt Slape and John Creger who were manning the OP phoned back and said there were some Jerries in the same house downstairs. We listened over the phone and nothing came over. Lt Bouck took off with some men to rescue the two men. They all got back up the hill.

Then I posted myself at the point of the woods to observe, and there they came, a battalion of infantry, marching up the road in closed formation. I observed a girl talking to one of their officers and pointing up the road.[9] I reported to Lt Bouck and we held our fire since the houses were between us and them. A mortar section would have had a field day. Our radios went dead and there we were with no communications. The FO couldn't bring in any artillery. Before we knew it we were surrounded.

Lt Bouck made a last minute check on all the holes, ducking and dodging. He and I took over the newly built BAR [Browning Automatic Rifle] hole. We could have retreated easily, but Lt Bouck said that our orders were to hold the hill and we were determined. We held them at bay during the afternoon.

Then just as it was getting dark, they started their main attack. We received three bursts and all hell broke loose. Sgt Slape jumped up on the .50 caliber and opened up and we were all firing. I don't know if they got Slape, but the .50 was silenced. After a while the battle started to die down. They must have knocked out some of our holes on the forward slope. Some crazy

Jerry yelled at us to surrender and he stood up. All of a sudden he must have had a heart attack. The grenades started exploding near our hole – we could tell ours was the only hole still resisting. We were going to make a break for it when all of a sudden a burp gun tears into my face. I could just remember being taken down the hill by this Jerry aid man and Lt Bouck. The hill was strewn with German dead. They put me in this house with German wounded all over the floor and I remember seeing Louis Kalil wounded. The last I remembered was Lt Bouck giving me my Bible and two pictures of my girl. He told me they were separating us: I don't remember anything after that until I woke up in a German hospital.

'Sak' was naturally reticent about his part in the battle, but in fact he had played a major part as this account from the Medal of Honor submission explains:

A major attack seemed in the making. The members of the platoon were not sure from which direction the attack would come, but it made little difference. The platoon was disposed in a beautiful tactical position, a perimeter defense at the edge of the wood line. At the point nearest Lanzerath was the foxhole occupied by Bouck and James [Tsakanikas had dropped his last name after the war and was simply called Bill James]. A couple of .30 caliber light machine guns were covering the Honsfeld road junction to the north and many of the men had Browning Automatic Rifles. James had a special weapon of his own. He had taken the liberty of appropriating a 'grease gun' [submachine-gun] from supply after the last patrol six days earlier. The .50 caliber machine-gun on the jeep, protected from direct fire, could put down devastating fire, but whenever artillery came in, whoever was manning it would have to hop down into a foxhole.

They waited for the German troops to arrive. They were not disappointed. When the Germans approached the Americans gasped in amazement; two columns marching on both shoulders of the road in close order, weapons slung, looking to neither side; no security had been put out on either flank. James, waiting with the rifle he had kept (along with his grease gun) let the group go past. The Germans were in mottled uniforms. James was surprised at this regalia, but Bouck, having been an instructor for two years at the Infantry School, Fort Benning, recognised them as Paratroopers' uniforms and later reported this to the Regimental-S2 section, now much concerned.

When to open fire? Sergeant Slape, sharing a foxhole on the left flank, picked up his rifle and took aim on the lead German as he entered Lanzerath. 'Your mother's going to get a telegram for Christmas,' he mumbled. Bouck knocked the rifle aside. 'Maybe they don't send telegrams. Besides,' Bouck went on, 'I don't want to get the point, I want to get the main body.' Slape chuckled.

They let some 300 Paratroopers go by, then came three figures, walking separately, clearly the commander and two of his staff. James chose to fire at them, but before he could do so, the little blonde girl appeared and, worried that he might hit her, James held his fire and the opportunity for an ambush passed, because the German officer gave a shout and the Paratroopers dived for cover.

The fire fight began; the Germans were pinned down. Fortunately for Bouck's men, the road to the south was exposed and the parachutists could never reinforce their isolated battalion without coming under heavy .50 caliber fire from the Americans some distance off. The fire fight never ceased all day. James dashed back to man the .50 calber machine-guns and staying down on his knees for protection, fired by observing the strike of the bullets in the snow. He began raking the ditches and woods to the north and south. He also took an inventory of his grease gun; five magazines of nineteen rounds each. By noon some of the I & R men were wounded, but none seriously. Repeatedly James screamed at Bouck to bring in artillery with the new proximity fuse.[10] Bouck in turn, kept screaming to Regiment on his radio. but for the moment no artillery came in.

'What shall we do then?' Bouck demanded of Regiment.

'Hold on at all costs.' That was the last conversation Bouck would have with Regiment, because just then a bullet struck the radio, destroying it and knocking him to the ground. Fortunately he was unharmed and was dragged into a nearby foxhole by a couple of his men. There was no letup in the German assault, wave after wave of Paratroopers came up the hill, only to be mown down by the defenders, James's .50 caliber and the other machine-guns and BARs wreaking havoc, but the enemy did not break or retreat. About mid morning, the Germans raised a white flag and under its protection, their medics dealt with the dead and wounded, while James lifted his fire on to enemy activity farther away.

The next assault came as soon as the stretcher-bearers had taken away the last of the casualties (the I & R Platoon had also taken casualties, but they were surprisingly light). This time the attack was supported by mortar fire, but when it lifted Lieutenant Bouck and Sergeant Slape toured the position checking on their men. When the next attack came in, three Paratroopers managed to crawl up close enough to threaten the light machine-gun which was guarding the left flank. James cut them down with his 'grease gun', emptying an entire magazine into the corpses, the heavy .45 calibre slugs rolling at least one body clean over.

During the next lull, Bouck shouted to James: 'Sak, I want you to take the men who want to go and get out.' 'Are you coming?' 'No, I have orders to hold out at all costs. I'm staying.' 'Then we'll all stay.'

According to the record books there were precisely eight hours and five minutes of daylight on 16 December 1944, sunset coming at 1635 hrs, with just another 38 minutes of twilight bringing the short winter's day to a close. However, it must have seemed an eternity to the men of the I & R Platoon before the light began to fade. They were almost out of ammunition, so Bouck felt justified in planning a withdrawal. Some of his men were wounded, but only one had been killed. But the fading light brought new dangers as it enabled the Germans to infiltrate the position. Then their most valuable weapon, the .50 calibre heavy machine-gun, was knocked out, just as the enemy made yet another frontal assault. It was during this last assault that James was wounded – the right side of his face being shot away, his right eyeball hanging in the hole where his cheek had been. The enemy were now on top of them and Bouck and he were saved from certain death by a German officer who shouted 'Nein!' and jumped between his men and the two GIs. Could this have been the officer he had so nearly shot wondered James, as he passed out.

That was the end of the platoon's heroic defence, which had held up the German assault for the entire day. Perhaps it is fitting to end this small-scale battle with the words which were whispered to James Tsakanikas, as he was being interrogated in a cafe in Lanzerath, drifting in and out of consciousness. 'The German, giving up the interrogation, leaned over and whispered in English, 'Ami, you and your comrades are brave men.' In spite of everything, James felt good for a moment.'

A Medal of Honor for the 99th

In the centre of the assault against 99th Infantry Division's positions on the Elsenborn Ridge, the action was just as hot and heavy. Here 277th VGD had the task of taking the villages of Krinkelt and Rocherath, while 12th VGD were to assault Büllingen and Nidrum on the main centre line. As already mentioned, they were short of infantry assault guns, and although initially they made good progress, by afternoon the attack had ground to a halt, with heavy casualties from mortar and machine-gun fire. Typical of the heavy fighting was an action near Krinkelt which resulted in the 'Ninety Niners' winning their first Medal of Honor. T/Sgt Vernon McGarity of 393rd Inf Regt had been wounded during the opening artillery barrage, received treatment at the aid station, but refused to be evacuated, choosing to return to his hard-pressed men instead. They were soon without any communications and were being heavily attacked by tanks and infantry. Armed only with a Bazooka, McGarity braved heavy fire in order to get to a suitable place from which to engage the leading tank. He knocked it out while the combined firepower of his hard-pressed squad drove the accompanying infantry back. Eventually the remaining enemy tanks withdrew. McGarity then rescued, under heavy fire, a wounded GI and directed devastating fire on a light cannon which the enemy had brought up. When the squad's ammunition began to run low, McGarity, remembering an old ammunition bunker some 100 yards away, braved a concentration of hostile fire to replenish supplies. When the enemy managed to bring up a machine-gun to the rear and flank of the squad's position cutting off their withdrawal route, he unhesitatingly took it upon himself to knock it out. He left cover and, while under steady enemy fire, killed or wounded all the machine-gunners with accurate rifle fire, then prevented all attempts to re-man the gun. Only when the squad's last round had been fired were the enemy able to advance and capture McGarity and his men. The citation closes with the words: 'The extraordinary bravery and extreme devotion to duty of T/Sgt McGarity supported a remarkable delaying action which provided the time necessary for assembling reserves and forming a line against which the German striking power was shattered.'

All in all, the 'Battle Babes' of the 99th did extremely well in their first day of action. They had held the full weight of the initial attacks of Dietrich's Sixth SS Panzer Army, involved as they had been with 326th VGD in the north, 277th VGD in the centre and 12th VGD in the south, and of course also with 3rd Parachute Division coming up from the south as well. While all these attacks were taking place, 2nd Infantry Division had continued with the first phases of its assault on the Roer dams, via 99th Div's northern positions, making good progress towards Wahlerscheid and apparently intending to press on with the attack on the 17th. At that time they still assumed that the enemy assault was merely a spoiling attack to hamper their offensive.

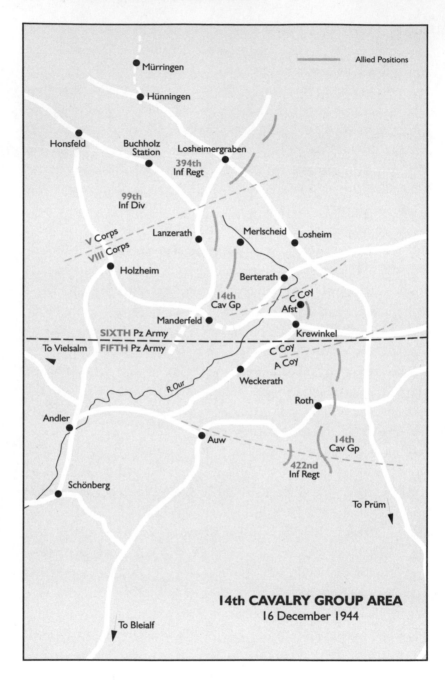

Allied Positions

Mürringen

Hünningen

Honsfeld

Buchholz
Station

Losheimergraben

394th
Inf Regt

99th
Inf Div

V Corps

VIII Corps

Lanzerath

Merlscheid

Losheim

Holzheim

Berterath

C Coy

14th
Cav Gp

Afst

Manderfeld

SIXTH Pz Army

Krewinkel

To Vielsalm

FIFTH Pz Army

C Coy

A Coy

R. Our

Weckerath

Roth

Andler

Auw

14th
Cav Gp

422nd
Inf Regt

Schönberg

To Prüm

14th CAVALRY GROUP AREA
16 December 1944

To Bleialf

Trouble in the Losheim Gap

Below the 99th's positions, however, it was a different story. The task of holding the Losheim Gap area was in the hands of Colonel Mark Devine's 14th Cavalry Group, which consisted basically of the 18th and 32nd Armored Cavalry Squadrons. While designed to take on armoured reconnaissance and to screen areas with small mobile patrols, an armored reconnaissance squadron was not equipped to hold ground against a determined and well-equipped enemy – and certainly not when the area which it had to protect was more than 9,000 yards wide – the type of frontage that would normally be allocated to a full infantry division.[11]

Colonel Devine endeavoured to make the most of his Group's main attributes of speed and mobility by keeping one of the two squadrons (32nd) complete and in reserve, although it was placed rather far back, some 20 miles behind the front at Vielsalm. The 18th Squadron therefore was spread thinly across the nine-mile front, although it was reinforced by A Company of 820th TD Battalion, but was minus its B Troop which had been taken away to carry out a similar screening task between two of the Infantry Regiments of 106th Infantry Division, who were located farther south (see later). As the sketch map shows, unbeknown to Colonel Devine and his men, his thinly spread Cavalry Group were not only at one of the main *Schwerpunkte* of the coming German attack, but also in the unfortunate position of covering the boundary between Fifth and Sixth Panzer Armies, so would receive the full force of two major assaults. Indeed, Hugh Cole in the official US History, after explaining what was about to hit that part of the front line makes the comment that: 'On no other part of the American front would the enemy so outnumber the defenders at the start of the Ardennes counter-offensive.'

For example, one of the platoons of C Troop, 18th Squadron, was located in the important village of Krewinkel (see map overleaf). When the GIs had recovered from the pounding their positions had received during the opening early morning barrage on the 16th, which put out all their line communications, they 'stood to' in their foxholes and waited for the enemy to attack. They must have been somewhat surprised, however, to see a large column of German troops – five abreast– marching along the road towards them, singing and talking together, just as though they were on a peacetime route march! The GIs held their fire until the enemy were almost on top of their defensive positions, then opened up with devastating light automatic fire, which cut the German column to pieces. For the rest of the morning they were under continuous attack, but held off the Paratroopers, inflicting severe casualties without taking many themselves.

However, it soon became very clear to Colonel Devine that his greatly outnumbered group could not continue to hold their exposed positions much longer, indeed some had already been outflanked – they were so thin on the ground that in some cases the enemy had infiltrated behind them without either side seeing the other! And not only were these just infantry attacks, enemy tanks were soon engaging them at close range. He requested the commander of 106th Infantry Division, Major General Alan Jones, whose HQ was at St-Vith, to put in a counter-attack to help restore the position, but there were no reserves available, nor did Jones consider the situation serious enough at that time for such an attack to be mounted. Somehow Colonel Devine managed to extricate his hard-pressed force and to bring most of it back to the high ground on the Manderfeld Ridge, but it was soon clear that they could not stay there for long because the enemy had already begun to bypass Manderfeld and was moving on towards the River Our. At about 1600 hrs he was given permission to withdraw to the line Andler (on the Our)–Olzheim. The Losheim Gap was now open wide.

Trouble for the 106th

Somewhat belatedly General Jones realised that his inexperienced 'Golden Lion' Division was now in danger of being outflanked to the north of their positions on the Schnee-Eifel, where the 422nd and 423rd Infantry Regiments were holding positions in what had been the old Siegfried Line. There was then a 3-mile gap between the southern end of the 423rd's and the beginning of 424th's positions at Winterspelt (see sketch map). To defend this gap an *ad hoc* force had been

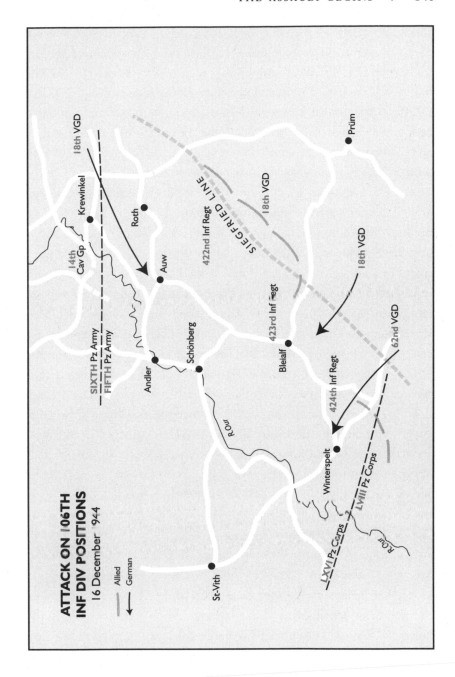

ATTACK ON 106TH
INF DIV POSITIONS
16 December 1944

Allied
German

formed from the 423rd which comprised an anti-tank company, part of a cannon company, one rifle platoon and a TD company. Below them was 18th Cavalry Squadron's B Troop, which, as already explained, had been detached from the hard-pressed 32nd Cavalry Group in the Losheim Gap. If the Cavalry Group had an impossible task to cover their 9,000-yard front, the 'green' 106th Division had an even more massive frontage to cover. However, all had been lulled into a false sense of security when they had taken over this supposed back-water where nothing was expected to happen, so the gaps had been accepted along with everything else. Towards the end of the afternoon, General Jones had a change of heart after talking to the corps commander, General Middleton, and decided to send his only reserve (2nd Battalion, 423rd Infantry, then located at Born, some 5,000 yards north of St-Vith) to cover the northern flank around Schönberg. Middleton also told him that he was sending elements of 7th Armored Division to St-Vith and that they should, on arrival, be immediately sent up to Schönberg. What was not made clear was that this force would not arrive for some time. By the end of the first day the 106th were still occupying most of their original positions, but the enemy (LXVI Corps) had made significant progress in the Winterspelt area, penetrating between the 423rd and 424th, and had worked their way around the left flank and rear of the 422nd. By last light they were undoubtedly in a position to take out the Schnee-Eifel area, but this would not take place until the following day.

And worse for the 28th

Below Schnee-Eifel lay the even more extended positions of 28th Infantry Division, once again holding an impossibly massive frontage along the Our, in a supposedly quiet area, where they were being given the chance to recover from the heavy casualties they had received in the Hürtgen Forest in November. The battle-hardened 'Keystone' Division was in the process of assimilating its new replacements under the watchful eye of tough Major General 'Dutch' Cota, whose outstanding performance on the Normandy beaches had earned him his command appointment. They would face the main *Schwerpunkt* of von

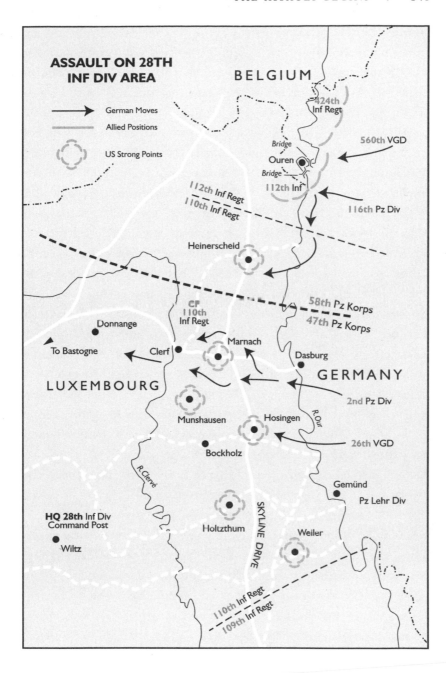

ASSAULT ON 28TH
INF DIV AREA

→ German Moves
━━ Allied Positions
⟲ US Strong Points

BELGIUM

424th
Inf Regt

560th VGD

Bridge
Ouren
Bridge

112th Inf

116th Pz Div

112th Inf Regt
110th Inf Regt

Heinerscheid

58th Pz Korps
47th Pz Korps

CP
110th
Inf Regt

Donnange

To Bastogne   Clerf

Marnach

Dasburg

GERMANY

LUXEMBOURG

2nd Pz Div

Munshausen

Hosingen

R.Our

Bockholz

26th VGD

Gemünd

Pz Lehr Div

HQ 28th Inf Div
Command Post

Wiltz

Holtzthum

Weiler

R.Clervé

SKYLINE DRIVE

110th Inf Regt
109th Inf Regt

Manteuffel's Fifth Panzer Army, where he intended to use not just one but two panzer corps! In the north, LVIII Panzer Corps would try to capture the bridges over the Our at Ouren with 116th Panzer Division, while 560th VGD crossed in the same general area. To the south, XLVII Panzer Corps was to assault in the area known to the Americans as 'Skyline Drive' – the north–south road which connected St-Vith and Diekirch (see map) – with 2nd Panzer Division and 26th VGD in the lead, and Panzer Lehr Division following up. US 28th Division was deployed with 112th Infantry Regiment in the north, joining with 106th Division's most southerly regiment, the 424th. Both were responsible for a bridgehead over the Our which included the two bridges at Ouren. Next came the 110th along 'Skyline Drive', then the 109th who were in what was perhaps the best defensive position of the three regiments. The main weight of the German assault would fall upon the centre regiment, the 110th, commanded by a WWI veteran, Colonel Hurley Fuller. One of his battalions (the 2nd) formed the divisional reserve at Donnange, some four miles west of the Regimental CP which was at Clerf, one of the main crossings over the River Clervé. John Eisenhower in *The Bitter Woods*, says that Colonel Fuller was known for two things: 'his fighting qualities and his cantankerous disposition'. Unfortunately his irascibility had begun to 'overshadow his virtues' and he had been relieved of his command after Normandy, but had then been given a second chance by his corps commander (and old friend) Major General Troy Middleton.

As in the other front line areas, the forward troops would first be puzzled by the 'pinpoints of light' appearing all along the enemy front, then blasted by the totally unexpected heavy enemy barrage which fell upon their positions, cutting off their line communications. While the GIs held their positions and fought back stubbornly, the Germans were infiltrating around the widely spread American strongpoints. Nevertheless, by last light 2nd Panzer Division had still not taken Marnach or Clerf, so their road through to Bastogne was still blocked. Given that 2nd Panzer had two full-strength panzer battalions, with a total of some twenty-seven Mark IV, 58 Panthers and 48 Sturmgeschütz, together with adequate wheeled vehicles for road movement (they only lacked tracked cross-country vehicles), one might be surprised that their progress was so slow, but this was a consequence of the appalling state of the roads and tracks plus the generally stubborn defence of the GIs in their well-sited positions. General Cota had ordered two companies of the 707th Tank Battalion, which was attached to the division, to reinforce Fuller's hard-pressed 110th, but would not release the Regiment's 2nd Bn which was his only divisional reserve. On the face of it his division was still doing well, and was holding its own in many places – the official history quotes as an example, the sterling work of one M16 anti-aircraft halftrack belonging to 447th AA (AW) Battery, in defending a hard-pressed field artillery battery near Bockholz. The M16 had been standing at a cross-roads early on the 16th, when a German company had marched up apparently intending to deploy and attack the battery position: 'Seeing the vehicle, the enemy column paused. One of the crew thought fast and waved the Germans forward in a friendly fashion. When the .50 caliber machine-guns on the halftracks ceased fire nearly one hundred German dead were counted.'[12] The advancing German infantry had so far been forced to fight without the support of their heavy weapons because the engineers had not yet completed the heavy bridging needed to cross such waterways as the Our and the Clervé, but clearly this situation would not last much longer.

The Southern Shoulder holds on

Below Fifth Panzer Army was Brandenberger's Seventh Army, which had a much more limited mission than either of the two panzer armies to its north, namely to cross the Our and press forward in the direction of Luxembourg so as to protect the southern flank of the offensive. The area in which he would make his assault with LXXX and LXXXV Corps abreast, was held by three different units/formations: in the north, where LXXXV Corps attacked with 5th Para Div on the right and 352nd VGD on the left, both were faced by the hard-pressed 109th Inf Regt of 28th Infantry Division. In LXXX Corps' sector, 276th VGD on the right, faced the 60th Armd Inf Regt

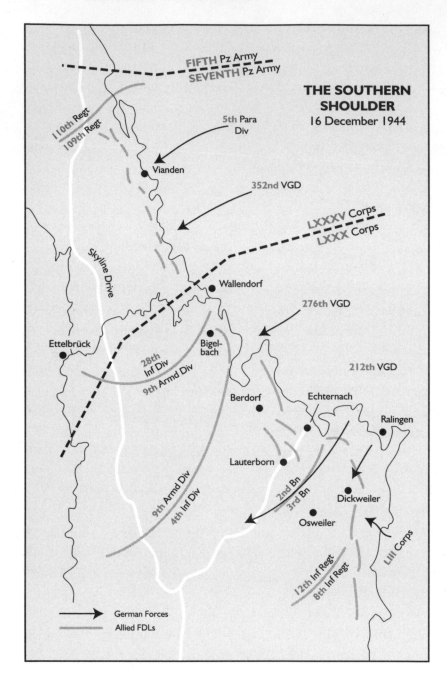

FIFTH Pz Army
SEVENTH Pz Army

**THE SOUTHERN
SHOULDER**
16 December 1944

110th Regt
109th Regt

5th Para
Div

Vianden

352nd VGD

LXXXV Corps
LXXX Corps

Skyline Drive

Wallendorf

276th VGD

Ettelbrück

Bigel-
bach

212th VGD

28th
Inf Div
9th Armd Div

Berdorf

Echternach

Ralingen

9th Armd Div
4th Inf Div

Lauterborn

2nd Bn
3rd Bn

Dickweiler

Osweiler

LIII Corps

12th Inf Regt
8th Inf Regt

→ German Forces
━━ Allied FDLs

of 9th Armored Division, while 212th VGD faced 4th Infantry Division's 12th Inf Regt. Finally, to the south, LIII Corps faced 8th Infantry Regiment's positions. The odds by any standard were firmly in the German favour, but the Americans somehow held on and inflicted heavy casualties on the attackers. Nowhere was this done more effectively than in 60th Armd Inf Bn's area, where the battalion had call upon the fire of the entire divisional field artillery battalion as well as tank support.

Summary of Day One

The opening barrage at 0530 hours had come as a complete shock to the Americans – a triumph of German planning and security! The attack had been launched on time, but in the north Sixth SS Panzer Army had only managed to advance some two to three kilometres in the direction of Elsenborn, against unexpectedly strong American resistance. The roads in the front line area were now so muddy after the assault guns had passed through, that no other large vehicle movement was possible. In the centre, Fifth Panzer Army had made better progress, advancing to the Schnee-Eifel and crossing the River Our between Dasburg and Gemünd, but progress had been slower than anticipated because of bridging problems. By midnight Marnach had been captured, clearing the route towards Clervaux, but Hosingen remained in American hands and the first day's objective (the River Clervé) had not been reached. In the south, Seventh Army, which had a more limited mission than the other two armies, had not made the progress that had been anticipated. Although the attackers had made penetrations between the American units all along the front, and 5th Parachute Division had seized the Diekirch–Hosingen road, most of the American defenders in other areas had managed to hold their positions. What was clearly not yet apparent, was the true size of the German offensive and the fact that what seemed to be just localised attacks were in fact all part of a major assault. Perhaps the most telling factor, which had not come to light because the weather had grounded aircraft in the battle area, was the fact that the Germans were completing heavy bridging across the main waterways which stood in their path. Once these were finished and the full might of the *Panzerwaffe* released, the situation would be radically altered.

Meanwhile at the top

It is surprising that so much enemy activity on this hitherto quiet sector did not prompt an immediate reaction from the higher levels of the Allied command. It is possible that the 'top brass' convinced themselves that it was merely a feint to put the Allies off their stride. It certainly did not produce much immediate action. At SHAEF, the Supreme Commander had been entertaining General Omar Bradley, Commander of 12th Army Group, to celebrate Eisenhower's fifth star which raised him to the highest rank possible in the US Army. They had been discussing ways to overcome the acute shortage of infantry which constantly bedevilled SHAEF. In his memoirs Eisenhower says that he was: '... immediately convinced that this was no local attack; it was not logical for the enemy to attempt merely a minor offensive in the Ardennes, unless of course it should be a feint to attract our attention while he launched a major effort elsewhere. This possibility we ruled out.'[13] He goes on to say that he and Bradley were sufficiently convinced that a major attack was developing in the centre of 12th Army Group to begin moving formations from the flanks towards the embattled sector. These words were written some few years later and with the best will in the world I think that at the time neither Eisenhower nor Bradley had immediately recognised the scale of the problem which was about to face them. General Bradley had dismissed it as being just a 'spoiling attack', but at least General Eisenhower had the good sense to tell him to take some precautions, namely to move his two reserve armoured divisions into more suitable positions (7th Armored down from the north and 10th Armored up from the south). At one level lower, General Courtney Hodges, the taciturn commander of US First Army and General 'Simp' Simpson of US Ninth Army, having discussed the situation, agreed that a further 'north–south' reinforcement should take place, namely that elements of the uncommitted US

1st Infantry Division (26th Infantry Regiment) should be moved down into First Army territory, to Camp Elsenborn, where it arrived at 0700 hours on the 17th. Simpson had also generously offered both 5th Armored and 30th Infantry Divisions on his own initiative. On the following day the only available theatre reserves (82nd and 101st Airborne) would also be deployed.

Notes

1   The Battle of Leuthen, which took place on 5 December 1757, during the Seven Years' War, was one of the great battles of German history in which Frederick the Great with a force of some 33,000 Prussians, heavily defeated 90,000 Austrians, killing and wounding more than 7,000 and taking 20,000 prisoners and 134 guns.

2   Presumably he means the multi-barrelled Nebelwerfer 41 and 42 – known as 'Moaning Minnies' by the Allies because of their distinctive sound in flight.

3   The rockets with 'yellow trails' were most likely the V1 which was used against mainly civilian targets in England and elsewhere, rather than a new jet aircraft.

1   The Lockheed P-38 Lightning was an American single-seat long-range fighter, normally used for bomber escort.

5   The Paratroops had been delayed because of chronic fuel shortages, which had meant that only about a third of the battalion could be transported at a time.

6   As quoted in *The Battle of the Bulge Then and Now*.

7   As quoted in Eisenhower, John. *The Bitter Woods*.

8   Hearing on HR 3407, held before the Military Personnel Subcommittee of the Committee on Armed Services, House of Representatives, Ninety-Sixth Congress, First Session, 11 July 1979.

9   There were conflicting reports about this 'young, blonde German girl', Anna Christen, who still lives in Lanzerath. After considerable research, Dick Byers has come to the conclusion that she did not give away the American positions. The German officer asked her: 'Are there any Americans here?' She replied, 'No' and pointed up the road in the direction she had seen the American TDs and the artillery forward observers leave. Lieutenant Bouck agrees with this interpretation saying: '... I still think she was showing them which way the TDs went. I don't believe she knew we were even there.'

10 As we now know and as explained in Dick Byers' memoirs, the new fuse was not yet on general release.

11 A US armoured cavalry squadron numbered just under 1,000 men. The three recce platoons in each of its three recce troops were equipped with M8 armoured cars, halftracks and Jeeps; it had a light tank company with some seventeen light tanks (M5A1 which mounted the tiny 37mm gun as its main armament); an assault gun troop with four platoons each of two M8 75mm carriage howitzers.

12 Cole, Hugh M. *The Ardennes: Battle of the Bulge*.

13 Eisenhower, General Dwight D. *Crusade in Europe*.

7
THE ASSAULT CONTINUES

SIXTH SS PANZER ARMY'S FRONT

150 Panzer Brigade and Battle Group Peiper go to work

The first elements of Skorzeny's 150 Panzer Brigade to go into action were the small number of English-speaking members of the Commando unit *Einheit Stielau*, who were (as far as possible) wearing American uniforms and equipped with American vehicles, arms and equipment, in order to facilitate their role of sabotage, reconnaissance and the spreading of alarm and confusion. This was a highly dangerous mission and all those who undertook it must have realised that if they were discovered they would very likely be shot as spies. Post-war Skorzeny said that some 44 men in total had been sent out on these missions and that all except eight of them had returned safely. They undoubtedly had some success, but it is very difficult now to separate 'fact from fiction'. The news that there were enemy soldiers dressed as GIs, roving behind the lines did spread like wildfire and even affected the freedom of movement of senior Allied Generals such as Eisenhower and Bradley, so this aspect of the operation was undoubtedly successful. This was all helped rather than hindered by the Americans' capturing a set of plans for Operation 'Greif'.[1]

Also integral to the success of Dietrich's assault in the north was the task of the main body of Otto Skorzeny's special force, which had to bypass the leading elements of I SS Panzer Corps, in order to get ahead of the main attacking forces and then to go hell for leather for the vital Meuse bridges. Close on their heels would be the powerful Battle Group Peiper, based upon 1st SS Panzer Regiment, which, together with Herbert Kuhlmann's similar hard-hitting battle

group, was to lead the main bodies of Leibstandarte and Hitlerjugend Divisions respectively, and link up with Oberst von der
Heydte's Paratroopers in the concluding part of Operation 'Stösser'.
However, as we already know, the Paratroop operation had gone
awry Peiper and Kuhlmann would have just as frustrating a time as
von der Heydte.

The 150 Panzer Brigade had been moved into its final assembly
area near Münstereifel two days before the attack, and during the
afternoon of the 16th its three battle groups closed up behind the
leading elements of the three attack divisions (1st SS Pz Div, 12th SS
Pz Div and 12th VGD). One can imagine the traffic problems which
this great mass of armour, infantry, engineers, artillery and other
weaponry, not to mention the administrative 'tail', produced, clog-
ging up the narrow country roads, which were by now almost
impassable in mud and slush. In one place Skorzeny says that he
found a huge Luftwaffe transporter more than 10m long, which had
become wedged into other traffic on a narrow road – some thirty
men were desperately trying to manhandle it out of the way. It was
carrying parts for long-range V1 rockets – just what was needed for
the initial attack! Skorzeny made everyone get out of their vehicles
and tip the contents of the transporter over the side of the road and
into a nearby lake, followed by the transporter itself – in fifteen
minutes the road was clear again – but not for long! It rapidly
became clear to Skorzeny that, apart from the leading 'Commandos'
who had already infiltrated the American lines, his operation was
not going to get off the ground so, in the evening of 17 December,
while attending a conference at HQ Sixth SS Panzer Army, he
suggested that his force be reconstituted as a normal brigade and
thereafter employed coventionally. This was agreed and the panzer
brigade was told to concentrate south of Malmédy and Skorzeny
was ordered to report to HQ 1st SS Pz Div at Ligneuville. The
capture of Malmédy and its key road junction – vital for opening
Rollbahn C – would be the task given to his brigade, but only two
of his battle groups ('X' and 'Y') had as yet arrived, so Skorzeny
planned a pincer-attack with 'X' on the left from Ligneuville, while

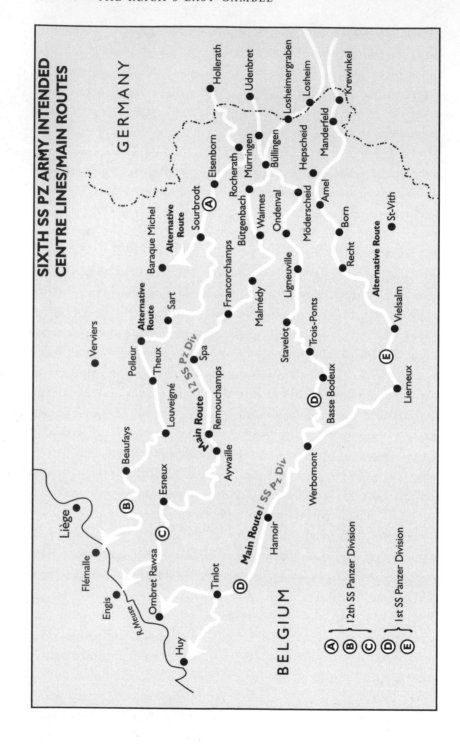

'Y' moved along the road from Baugnez. The attack was timed to begin in the early hours of 21 December.

Peiper's advance is stalled

When the early morning barrage began on 16 December, Peiper's battle group was preparing to advance out of its assembly area in the Blankenheim forest and close up behind 12th VGD. Their commander was up at 12th VGD's command post and must have been getting more and more frustrated at the *Volksgrenadiers'* slow progress. As has already been mentioned, Peiper had chosen to lead with his lighter, more manoeuvrable Pz Kpfw IVs and to relegate the heavy Tiger IIs of 501st SS Heavy SS Panzer Battalion to bring up the rear behind the rest of the battle group. Peiper rejoined his force at about 1430 hrs and immediately ordered his column to get forward as quickly as possible, physically pushing everything else out of its way as it pressed on towards Losheim. Despite all his efforts, however, it was late evening before his leading troops reached the village where they were ordered to divert through Lanzerath. Here Peiper found his way blocked by an old German minefield which had not been cleared. As his mine-detection equipment was some way back in the column he decided to accept the risk of losing some tanks and to press on through the minefield – losing three tanks in the process. He then pushed on along Rollbahn D and by first light was at Honsfeld, taking the American troops there – a mix of 14th Cavalry Group and 99th Infantry Division – by surprise, having calmly joined the tail of a stream of American trucks as they moved slowly through the village. Peiper captured a considerable amount of equipment, weapons and vehicles in Honsfeld, including seventeen SP anti-tank guns and more than 100 trucks, reconnaissance vehicles and halftracks. Some 300 GIs were taken prisoner and, it was later alleged, fifteen of them were shot after they had surrendered. Having moved on westwards, the battle group was then attacked by *Jabos*, which damaged a number of vehicles and knocked out two anti-aircraft tanks.[2]

The column then pressed on to Büllingen where there was a US Army fuel dump from which Peiper knew he could replenish his vehicles – it had been a major administrative centre for the Americans in the area, having both fuel and ammunition dumps, plus two airstrips from which light observation aircraft had operated. There was a battle in Büllingen in which both sides sustained casualties, but eventually the battle group was able to gain the upper hand and to seize sufficient fuel to replenish all its vehicles. One of the GIs in Büllingen at that time was Grant Yager, now of Bradenton, Florida, then an ammunition section chief (buck sergeant) in the Service Battery of 924th Artillery Battalion of 99th Infantry Division. He told me:

'Early in the morning of the 17th we were awakened and told to get dressed at once. When I walked out the front of the house I was met by our ammunition sergeant, S/Sgt George Zoller, who handed me a Bazooka and told me to take two privates, Art Romaker and Santos Maldonado, and proceed out of town on the Honsfeld road and set up a road block as – and I repeat what Zoller said – a German tank had broken through our lines. Actually this was Peiper's SS column which contained perhaps 75 tanks and 100 halftrack vehicles! It was about 0730 when I walked out of the house and was handed the Bazooka. We were captured about 0800.

'Romaker, Maldonado and myself proceeded south on the road towards Honsfeld and stopped alongside of the road just as we arrived outside of town. In just a few minutes as we were determining what to do we heard tracked vehicles approaching from the direction of Honsfeld and as the first tank came into view we saw a black cross on its front. At this time we thought it was the single tank Zoller had told us had broken through our lines. We were standing near a small amount of brush and dropped behind it out of sight. I had Romaker arm the Bazooka and attempted to take aim at the tank but discovered the sights had broken off the weapon and the tank passed on into Büllingen. A second tank appeared and I determined I could aim without sights by looking along the barrel as I had done for so many years bird hunting with a shotgun back in Michigan. By doing this I was able, with one shot, to disable the second tank in the column. As the tankers exited the tank through the hatch I fired at the first two but my carbine jammed as I attempted a third shot. I was unaware the entire column had stopped behind the disabled tank and reached for Romaker's carbine to continue firing, but he stopped me and pointed to the column, the first vehicle behind the tank was a halftrack full of infantry. We were sitting ducks, no place to go and only a few yards from the half-track. Had I continued firing we would have been killed at once. At this point we only had two choices, die or surrender. As we could do no more good for our cause we surrendered.

'At this time we were under guard standing on the road near the lead halftrack when one of the young Germans pointed to a wounded American soldier … we were allowed to administer first aid, but when the column was ready to pull out one of the Germans shot him in the head so that they wouldn't have to care for him. While standing on the road a young German officer walked up to me, stuck a pistol in my stomach and began to question me in German, which I didn't understand nor did he understand American so he turned and walked away. Years later while standing on the same spot with Will Cavanagh, another British author, I described the event and mentioned the officer had on a light-colored leather jacket. At once Cavanagh said that it was Major Diefenthal [Jupp Diefenthal was commanding the 150mm gun company in Rudolf Sandig's 2nd SS Panzer Grenadier Regiment], the only officer in the column out of uniform as the SS all wore black. Why he failed to shoot me I can't understand as they had already killed prisoners in Honsfeld and a few hours later and only a few miles distant the same officer was one of the SS responsible for the Malmédy Massacre.'

Grant Yager and his two comrades were put onto the hood of the leading halftrack and they proceeded into Büllingen where he was loaded with other prisoners into an American GMC truck with a German driver and began the long journey to Germany and POW camp.

Now also began Peiper's fateful advance, which would end for him, not in victory or even in a hero's death on the battlefield, but rather would see his name being reviled as responsible for an infamous massacre of prisoners, for which he would first be sentenced to hang, then serve more than ten years in prison and finally, be murdered in France some 31 years later.

The Malmédy Massacre

The German column had moved on at about 0900 hrs and was soon attacked again by P-47 fighter-bombers which knocked out at least one of the slow, heavy Tiger IIs that by now had caught up with the column. Peiper was keen to press on because he had discovered from interrogating a captured American officer that there was a large US Army headquarters at Ligneuville (it was actually the HQ of 49 AAA Brigade). Progress was not easy – due to the state of the going rather than strong enemy opposition, but the leading tanks eventually reached the Baugnez cross roads, where they met a column of American vehicles belonging to 285th Field Artillery Observation Battalion. The German tanks immediately opened fire with their main armament, then with machine-guns, moving along the column firing at the vehicles, as the Americans tried desperately to find cover in the roadside ditches. As one can imagine there was total confusion, some of the GIs sought cover and began to return fire, others tried to escape into nearby trees, while others threw away their weapons and surrendered. Eventually the Germans herded the majority of them – about 150 in all – back towards the cross-roads and into a nearby field, where they were lined up in rows under guard, ready to be loaded into some of their own vehicles, while the German column got ready to move off under the urging of their commander who was following closely behind and anxious to press on at best speed. What then occurred has been told and retold in numerous books and articles. In his book, *Men of Steel*, Michael Reynolds tells how after the war Peiper described what happened, saying that he saw three groups of Americans – the first were standing with their hands up, the second lying on the ground or in nearby ditches pretending to be dead, and the third who, after pretending to be dead, suddenly got up and tried to run to the nearby woods. He said that his men then fired warning shots at the latter two groups. Whether or not that was true, the awful result was that of the 113 unarmed American prisoners in the field, 77 died in or within 200 metres of the field and 46 managed to escape although four of them died later. In the entire short engagement a total of 84 Americans were killed and a further 25 were wounded, while 56 men survived the whole brutal affair, of whom only seven became prisoners of war. There were no German casualties.[3]

Ligneuville did indeed contain numerous American units including the administrative 'tail' (known in US Army parlance as 'divisional trains') of 9th Armored Division which had moved south the previous night. Fortunately they did receive some warning of the German approach and most were able to escape before the head of the enemy column arrived. In the short fire fight which followed the Germans lost one Panther, the Americans three AFVs (two Shermans and an M10), numerous trucks and more than twenty men were taken prisoner – some of whom were also later shot. Peiper's battle group now paused to re-organise before resuming the advance to Stavelot at about 1700 hrs. Peiper did not accompany them, but stayed in the village waiting to talk to his divisional commander, Wilhelm Mohnke, who was coming forward with a small tactical HQ. It would have been far better had Peiper gone on with his column because they allowed themselves to be held up by a road block manned by a small party of GIs with a Bazooka, a machine-gun and some anti-tank mines – though to be fair the road block was excellently sited on a severe bend, with a sheer cliff towering upwards on one side and a precipitous drop to a raging torrent below on the other. In pitch darkness the German column halted after a short exchange of fire and waited for Peiper to rejoin them. This he did at about 2300 hrs, but decided that he would delay attacking Stavelot until daylight. He and his men had been on the go for more than forty hours and were exhausted, so there was ample reason why he decided not to blast his way through the road block and take the town. However, he undoubtedly missed a golden opportunity because the only bridge on the road leading into Stavelot had not been prepared for demolition, nor was it properly defended. By waiting he not only allowed the Americans to prepare a proper defence, but lost vital hours in which he might have continued to advance and thus might have reached the vital Meuse bridges on the 18th. After the war he wrote: 'We approached the outskirts of the town, but bogged down because of stubborn American resistance at the edge of Stavelot. We suffered fairly heavy losses, 25–35 casualties, from tank, mortar and rifle fire. Since I did not have sufficient infantry, I decided to wait for the arrival of more.'[4] At least one historian who has studied the battle carefully (Major General Michael Reynolds) questions this statement because it belies the true facts. Nevertheless, whatever the reasons why, it was fortunate for the Allies that this, the strongest of the battle groups, which might have had a dramatic influence on the early days of the 'Battle of the Bulge', allowed this opportunity to slip through its fingers. Elsewhere the story was much the same. On the Hitlerjugend front, the gains had been only a few kilometres, and requests to shift the main emphasis of First SS Panzer Corps' attack some 10 kilometres farther south on to better going and easier routes, was refused. It was almost as though the Germans wanted to do it the hard way!

The American resistance in Stavelot comprised a company of 526th Armored Infantry Battalion, 7th Armored Division, plus a platoon of M10 tank destroyers. The Germans attacked before the defence was entirely ready, but they were able to hold the town for more than two hours. More importantly, they were also able to prevent Peiper from reaching the nearby fuel dump at Francorchamps, by the simple expedient of pouring some of the vast quantity of fuel[5] into a deep road cutting and putting a match to it! More than 120,000 gallons were burned, but the enemy was prevented from getting around the flames and thus never reached the precious fuel stocks which would have taken them all the way to Antwerp! Peiper's battle group, which in fact did not go anywhere near the burning fuel, wasted no more time, moving instead towards Trois-Ponts. While he was moving part of his armoured column at best speed, the US troops in Trois-Ponts (so named because of its three

Above: General Dwight D. Eisenhower, with some of his most senior American generals. These include, front row left to right: William H. Simpson (CG US Ninth Army); George S. Patton, Jr. (CG US Third Army); Carl A Spaatz (CG USATAF); Eisenhower (Supreme Commander); Omar N. Bradley (CG 12th Army Group); Courtney M. Hodges (CG US First Army); Leonard T. Gerow (CG US Fifteenth Army). (US Army)

Below: The Supreme Commander studies his map with two of his Army Group Commanders, Field Marshal Montgomery and General Omar Bradley. It was the switching of US First and Ninth Armies from Bradley's 12th to Monty's 21st Army Group, to end the confusion of command on the northern shoulder of the 'Bulge', that caused the most friction between American and British commanders. (US Army)

Above: Amid the ruins of Bastogne after its relief, Eisenhower confers with Generals Bradley (left) and Patton. (US Army)

Left: Brigadier General (later General) Bruce C. Clarke, the hero of St-Vith, which he defended at the head of CCB, 7th Armored Division. This photograph was taken in the USA in 1942, when he was the CO of CCA, 4th Armored Division. (Patton Museum)

Above: Lieutenant Colonel (later General) Creighton W. Abrams, CO of 37th Tank Battalion, 4th Armored Division, whose tanks relieved Bastogne. According to General Patton he was the best tank commander in the US Army. (Patton Museum)

Right: On 29 December 1944, General Patton pins a Distinguished Service Cross to the tunic of Brigadier General Anthony C. McAuliffe, deputy commander of 101st Airborne Division and hero of the garrison of Bastogne, which withstood the German siege. His one-word reply of: 'Nuts!' sent to the Germans when they called on him to surrender has gone down in history. (US Army)

Above: Generalfeldmarschall Gerd von Rundstedt. As CinC Army Group West, he was ostensibly the instigator and then the unwilling commander of all the German forces involved in 'Wacht am Rhein'. Taken prisoner on 2 May 1945, he is seen here with Major General John E. Dahlquist, CG 36th Infantry Division. (US Army)

Left: Generalfeldmarschall Walther Model, GC Army Group B, which commanded the 'Bulge' operation. Known as 'Hitler's Fireman', he was an able and competent soldier and one of the few top ranking German generals prepared to argue with the Führer. After the failure of the Bulge counter-offensive he committed suicide rather than surrender. He is seen here wearing his Knight's Cross with Oakleaves and Swords. (Tank Museum)

Left: SS Obergruppen-führer und General der Waffen-SS 'Sepp' Dietrich, Commander of Sixth SS Panzer Army. He is seen here wearing the Waffen-SS winter dress and his Knight's Cross with Oakleaves only. He would go on to become one of only two members of the Waffen-SS to be awarded the Diamonds, to add to the Oakleaves and Swords. A rough, tough 'bully-boy', who lacked military knowledge, he was a brave and fearless individual, much respected by his troops. (Tank Museum)

Right: General der Panzertruppen Hasso von Manteuffel, Commander of Fifth Panzer Army, was a bundle of energy despite his small stature, and one of the most brilliant of all the German tank commanders. He would receive the Diamonds to his Knight's Cross for his bravery and leadership during the Ardennes offensive. This photograph was taken on the Eastern Front early in 1944. (Tank Museum)

Above: General der Panzertruppen Erich Brandenberger, Commander of Seventh Army, which assaulted on the left flank of 'Wacht am Rhein', but whose role was minor compared with that of the other two armies. Bespectacled and looking more like a school teacher, he was nevertheless a competent panzer general. (IWM–OWIL 67969)

Left: SS Oberststurmbannführer Otto Skorzeny. A burly giant of a man, he became Hitler's favourite commando after rescuing Mussolini. During the offensive he commanded a special task force – 150 Panzer Brigade – with mixed results. (IWM–HU 46178)

Above: A well-known, probably staged, photograph of one of the Schwimmwagen in Obersturmbannführer Jochen Peiper's special task force reaching the Kaiserbaracke cross-roads. The passenger looks not unlike Peiper, but is more probably SS-Unterscharführer Ochsner, which has led to the photograph being incorrectly captioned on numerous occasions. (US Army)

Below: A Panther tank carefully endeavours to get past a column of halftracked vehicles in the snowclad Ardennes, showing vividly the chaos resulting from traffic congestion. (Tank Museum)

Right: Lanzerath, Belgium. The I&R platoon/394 vs the 9th Parachute Regt 16 December 44 (see page 129)

(1) I&R Platoon dug-in positions: 18 Infantymen plus 4 Artillerymen vs two battalions of paratroopers (trees logged off after battle)

(2) Separate bunker with 3 I&R men

(3) Route of 9th Parachute Regt, 3rd Para Div

(4) German Govt refugee house from which little girl ran out to warn Paratroop officers

(5) Direction of repeated attacks, during the day

(6) Route and dlrection of final attack at dusk

(7) Café Palm

(8) Christophe and Adolph Schur house

(9) Anna Christen House: C Btry/371 F.A. Bn observation post

(10) School and A Co/820th Tank Destroyer Bn command post

(11) 2nd Plt and Recon Plt/A/Co/820th T.D. Bn sleeping quarters

(12) Scholzen house: I&R/394 observation post

(13) Café Scholzen

(14) Nicholas and Sany Schugens house

(15) View of Losheim across valley

(16) Road used by Kampfgruppe Peiper to Buchholz, Honsfeld, Bullingen

(17) Road to Losheimergraben. Blown bridge over deep R.R. cut

(18) Silvola. Robinson and McGehee cut off. Try to escape north. Captured by 27th Fusiliers at R.R. cut

(from the Hatlem Collection file of the U.S Army Military History Institute. Carlisle Barracks, PA. Coding and Key by L. H. Byers. C/371)

Left: Luftwaffe personnel looting American corpses at a crossroads in Honsfeld. Note that the GI on the left has had his boots taken. (US Army)

Right: The aftermath of the fiery barrier above Stavelot on the Francorchamps road, where thousands of gallons of fuel from a major US fuel dump were set on fire to form an ad hoc road-block. It brought the Germans' advance to a halt there and thus prevented them from getting to the fuel they so desperately needed. (US Army)

Left: Taken prisoner at Honsfeld on 17 December 1944, these GIs of US 99th Infantry Division look suitably dejected and shell-shocked. They are led and flanked by troops of 3rd Fallschirmjäger Division as they are marched back to POW staging camps well behind the lines. (US Army)

The series of photographs starting on the left and continuing on the following two pages, were staged after a real battle had taken place between troops of Battle Group Hansen, which included SS panzer grenadiers and Luftwafffe personnel, and the 14th Cavalry Group, 7th US Armored Division, north of Poteaux, on 18 December 1944.

Left: An SS-Rotten-führer (file-leader) of the battle group, urges his men forward. (US Army)

Right: An excellent shot of an SS panzer grenadier, with his entrenching tool, leather map case and his shelter quarter rolled up and tied on his back. Burning American vehicles are on the road to his front. (US Army)

Below: Three panzer grenadiers launch an attack across the road – note all the knocked-out American vehicles in the background. (US Army)

Left: More panzer grenadiers and Luftwaffe personnel, smoking looted American cigarettes. Note the American M8 'Greyhound' armoured car in the background. (US Army)

Below: Three members of the battle group – the one in front carrying an American carbine – advance past the camera. The strut is part of a static radio mast. (US Army)

Above: Men of Company M, 18th Infantry Regiment, 1st US Infantry Division, lying in wait for German paratroopers being flushed out of woods near Sourbrodt, Belgium, 19 December 1944. (US Army)

Below: GIs inspect a Focke-Wulfe 190 which was shot down by American multiple .50cal anti-aircraft fire, near Rotgen, Germany, on 23 December 1944. (US Army)

Above: GIs of 393rd Infantry Regiment, 99th Infantry Division, digging in on Elsenborn Ridge on 19 December – before the snows came – and came – and came! (US Army, via Richard Byers)

Below: Life on the gun positions at Camp Elsenborn; Richard Kaplan beside his dugout. (Richard Byers)

Above: One of several German assault guns (Sturmgeschütz III Model G) knocked out while assaulting the Elsenborn Ridge. (Richard Byers)

Below: Two of the ten-barrelled version of the 15cm Nebelwerfer 41 (rocket-launcher) moving forward to support the assault. (Author's collection)

Above: Carol Service in besieged Bastogne. Enemy shells scream overhead while carols are sung by men of 101st Airborne Division on Christmas Eve 1944. (US Army)

Below: Troops of 75th Infantry Division move past a Sherman tank in the village of Bussanville, Belgium, on their way to deal with pockets of enemy resistance, 26 December 1944. (US Army)

road bridges: two over the Salm and one over the Amblève) were hastily preparing their defences. These comprised Company 'C' of 51st Engineer Combat Battalion which had only arrived there at about midnight on the 17th,[6] plus a lone 57mm anti-tank gun belonging to 526th Armored Infantry Battalion and which had got lost on its way to Trois-Ponts. The engineer company's commander, Major Robert B. Yates, took over the weapon and its crew and positioned it on the Stavelot road where a small belt of mines had been laid. At about midday, Peiper's leading tank appeared and was disabled by the anti-tank gun. There was a brief skirmish while the Germans dealt with the road block which gave the engineers time to blow the vital bridges and fall back on the village.

This left Battle Group Peiper with only one way out of the Amblève valley, namely the northern route towards La Gleize where they found an intact bridge which would enable them to continue westwards. However, it was a very narrow, twisting road and when the weather cleared *Jabos* knocked out a number of tanks and halftracks which completely blocked the road for a considerable time. By last light, however, the head of the armoured column was only some three miles from Werbomont on the Liège–Bastogne road. But all was not yet plain sailing. American engineers blew up the only bridge across the Lienne (there were other bridges across this large stream which was in full spate, but none would take the weight of the Tiger tanks). Those troops that did manage to cross were ambushed and destroyed near the village of Chevron by a battalion of 30th Infantry Division which had been sent to intercept Peiper's column. Peiper now retraced his steps, having decided to re-organise during the night and move his column towards Stoumont at first light, leaving the Panthers of 1st SS Panzer Company, which had so far led for much the way, to form a firm base at La Gleize.

On the Hitlerjugend front the situation was just as difficult, because of the terrible state of the roads and the much stronger American resistance, particularly in and around Rocherath and Krinkelt, which led to the loss of a considerable number of tanks and assault guns.

American reinforcements on the way

Early in the morning of 17th December, V Corps' commander, Major General Leonard T. Gerow, was given permission by his Army Commander (Hodges) to halt the next phase of his Roer dams offensive and go on the defensive. Gerow immediately cancelled the intended morning attack and ordered Major General Walter M. Robertson, CG 2nd Infantry Division, to take command of the hard-pressed troops of 99th and 2nd Infantry Divisions who now, inextricably mixed up and 'way out on a limb', faced the full might of Dietrich's Sixth SS Panzer Army. Gerow had decided to make his defensive line some five to six miles behind the current FDLs (forward defensive localities) on the Elsenborn Ridge, which ran north–south through Elsenborn. In addition, as has already been mentioned at the end of the last chapter, the Army Commander released to V Corps the 'Big Red One', the US Army's premier infantry division, which had fought longer than any other American division, having taken part in the 'Torch' landings in North Africa, the amphibious assault on Sicily 'Bloody Omaha Beach' and all the way to the equally bloody Hürtgen Forest. One regiment was to report to CG 99th Division without delay with the task of blocking Rollbahn 'C', the remainder to follow as soon as possible. The 26th Infantry Regiment was the chosen one and by last light on the 17th they had taken position on the high ground south-west of Bütgenbach, to be followed by 16th Inf Regt on the high ground north of Waimes, while the third, 18th Inf Regt, went to the Eupen area to deal with the Paratroops landed during Operation 'Stösser'. Their routes had been over icy roads on which, according to one observer, '33-ton tanks spun crazily on the gentlest slopes, sometimes turning completely around two or three times before they came to rest.'[7] The 'Big Red One' did not go into action until 20 December when the enemy launched an attack on 2nd Batt of the 26th, only to be beaten off with the loss of some eight tanks. This would be followed on the 21st by another assault, after a heavy artillery bombardment. This time, despite knocking out another five panzers, the American lines were breached and the enemy got to within 75 yards of the Regimental Command Post before they were stopped by HQ personnel manning anti-tank weapons. The Germans would try again unsuccessfully next day, then, after a total loss of at least 44 panzers, they would resort to a holding battle which went on for the rest of the month.

US airborne forces on their way

At this time SHAEF also released to Bradley their only theatre reserve, the 82nd and 101st Airborne Divisions. Both divisions were at Reims resting and refitting after the abortive Arnhem operation, and were given a warning order to prepare to move. No location was given although, even then, Bastogne, one of the most important road network centres in the area, was an obvious choice.

FIFTH PANZER ARMY'S FRONT

Von Manteuffel achieves a partial breakthrough

We left CG US 106th Infantry Division, Major General Alan Jones, sitting in his command post at St-Vith, watching his world collapsing about him. Two of his regiments, 422nd and 423rd, in their positions on the Schnee-Eifel, were in imminent danger of being surrounded and destroyed and – to make it even harder for him to bear – his son was at that time serving in the headquarters of one of the two regiments. Jones' third regiment (424th) was a little farther south at Winterspelt where it would shortly be joined by 9th Armored Division's Combat Command 'B'[8] under Brigadier General William Hoge. Neither Jones nor Hoge knew that a third 'player' was about to enter the scene, namely Brigadier General Bruce C. Clarke, CG of 7th Armored Division's CC 'B', whose name would shortly become inextricably linked with St-Vith from then on. 'Clarke of St-Vith' as he came to be called, had been all set to go on a few days' Rest and Recuperation leave in Paris, having just been promoted to Brigadier General. He was also suffering considerable pain from gallstones so a few days' rest would have been perfect. However, this was not to be because at the last minute his divisional commander, Brigadier General Robert Hasbrouck, had rung him, explained that 7th

Armored had been ordered to move to Bastogne, told him to get his CC 'B' on the move as quickly as possible and go there ahead of them, so that he could find out exactly what VIII Corps Commander, Major General Troy Middleton, whose HQ was then at Bastogne, had in store for them. Clarke was quickly on his way and arrived at Middleton's CP at about 0400 hrs next morning. There he was briefed on the situation as far as the corps staff knew it, namely that the Germans had attacked in some force, that there had been a break-through in the Losheim Gap area and that the American positions around the St-Vith–Schnee-Eifel area, were in a bad way. General Middleton told him to get some sleep and then go to St-Vith with his Combat Command to see how he could help General Jones' belea-guered 106th Division. Clarke slept for a few hours, had a decent breakfast and then got on the radio to 7th Armored. After outlining the situation he explained why his combat command must go directly to St-Vith, where he would meet them. In fact there was a hold-up in obtaining road clearance for the move, so the division did not leave its assembly area in Holland until 0500 hrs. This meant that they would not arrive at St-Vith until much later in the day, which would give him plenty of time to get there and assess the situation.

Clarke arrived at St-Vith at about 1030 hrs and must have been very worried by what he saw and heard. General Jones was completely out of touch either by wire or radio with the two regi-ments surrounded on the Schnee-Eifel. The 14th Cavalry Group, which had been defending the Losheim Gap, was no longer in a state that could be described as being in any way fit for combat; indeed, when its commander, Colonel Devine, reached St-Vith at about 1330 hrs, he was in a very highly stressed, panicky state.[9] Clarke tried to calm him down and suggested that he go straight on back to Bastogne, to give the corps commander a first-hand briefing on the situation. Devine left the HQ, but did not go to Middleton's HQ and was eventually evacuated on medical grounds. Clarke knew that his own combat command would not arrive for some hours, so it would not be able to break the German stranglehold on Jones' regiments that day, nor provide a defence for the vitally important road communications centre of St-Vith. However, it was clear that Clarke's Combat Command represented the most viable force to defend St-Vith – when it arrived – and this appears to have persuaded Jones to hand over command of the town to Bruce Clarke then and there. Actual 'troops on the ground' to carry out this defence comprised elements of two engineer battalions (the HQ and Service Companies of 81st and 168th Engineer Battalions) plus HQ 106th Division's protection platoon. They were soon in action a mile or so to the east of St-Vith on the Schönberg road, where a mixed force of engineers, anti-tank weapons from the protection platoon (including two 57mm anti-tank guns and some Bazookas) were fortunately joined by a platoon of six tank destroyers, in a small village. They were attacked by an enemy force of tanks and infantry at about 1500 hrs. Both sides sustained casualties, until an air-to-ground liaison officer with the defenders managed to bring in fighter ground-attack aircraft which, despite the poor weather, succeeded in knocking out at least one enemy tank. The enemy then broke off their attack – first blood to the Americans.

Movement problems for 7th Armored Division

If the Germans were having their problems trying to get forward on the clogged, muddy roads, the situation on the American side of the front lines was even worse. Clarke's CCB with the rest of 7th Armored still strung out behind them, was having to cope with an endless stream of traffic all 'bugging out' westwards as fast as they could, along the narrow twisting roads. Progress was slow – even the sight of 30-ton Sherman tanks occupying most of the carriageway, thundering along in an easterly direction, did not put off the panic-stricken drivers who were trying to get westwards. As one observer (the S-3 of 38th Armd Inf Bn) put it: '… It wasn't orderly; it wasn't military; it wasn't a pretty sight – we were seeing American soldiers running away.'[10] Brigadier General Clarke was to witness the traffic chaos at first hand when he went out to see what was holding up his Combat Command's arrival. He had sent his operations officer (Captain Owen Woodruff) out ahead of him to guide them in from a cross-roads just to the west of St-Vith. When Clarke got there he found the road completely blocked by the vehicles of a medium field artillery battalion, which had abandoned its guns and was monopolising the entire road in their determination to escape. Woodruff explained that the artillery CO had threatened to shoot him if he got in his way, so he had been powerless to stop them. One can imagine the effect which these words had upon Bruce Clarke! Swiftly he cornered the artillery commander, ordered him to get his trucks off the road so that the tanks could get through and intimated that if there was to be any shooting that afternoon then he would start it! The cowed artillery commander gave in, the artillery trucks were quickly run off the road and Clarke's tanks moved eastwards! Fortunately not all the American artillery was as anxious to leave the battlefield and the St-Vith defenders were lucky enough to be able to enlist the support of 275th Armored Field Artillery Battalion (late 14th Cavalry Group) under its CO, Lieutenant Colonel Maximillian Clay, who came up to Clarke and volunteered his services. They provided Clarke's only artillery support for the first few days of his epic defence of St-Vith.

The leading elements of Clarke's CCB arrived at about 1600 hrs in the shape of the M8 'Greyhound' armoured cars of B Troop, 87th Cavalry Reconnaissance Battalion. One of these little 7.5-ton armoured cars would later during the defence, pull off the remarkable feat of knocking out a 68-ton King Tiger! The M8 was in a concealed position when the Tiger approached along a track which ran directly in front of the armoured car's hide. As it passed, the Greyhound slipped out unobserved and began to tail the massive tank. However, in order to keep up, the car had to accelerate and the increased engine noise caused the tank commander to look round. He immediately saw the little armoured car, so began to traverse his turret to bring his enormous 8.8cm gun to bear. It was now a race between the driver of the Greyhound, who was attempting to get the M8 close enough so that its tiny 37mm main armament would be effective against the relatively thin armour on the rear of the Tiger, and the German turret crew who were trying to traverse their massive turret to the rear. Fortunately for the Americans, the M8 was able to close to within 25 yards and fired three quick rounds from its 'peashooter' before the Germans could fire. An eye-witness reported: 'The massive Tiger stopped, shuddered and exploded. Flames burst out of the turret and engine ports, The armoured car returned to its hide.'[11]

Later that afternoon Brigadier General Hasbrouck, CG 7th Armored, arrived at St-Vith. He had come via Bastogne, so was in the picture as far as Clarke's task was concerned and was also well ahead of the rest of his division. It was clearly too late in the day to contemplate any endeavour to rescue 422nd and 423rd Infantry Regiments from their desperate plight in the Schnee-Eifel. Instead, as the elements of Clarke's Combat Command began to arrive, Clarke spent a busy night getting them into defensive positions around the town. It was fortunate that during the 17th and the night of 17th/18th that the Germans did not mount a major assault upon St-Vith. This appears to have been because the German Corps Commander, General der Artillerie Walther Lucht, had chosen 18th VGD to carry out the encirclement of St-Vith, rather than one of his panzer divisions, so they lacked the mobility necessary for a swift attack. By first light on the 18th Clarke's CCB had been disposed by its commander, with part of 38th Armored Infantry Battalion, plus A Company, 31st Tank Battalion, now supporting the engineer group to the east of St-Vith, while the remainder of 31st Tank Battalion, together with 23rd Armored Infantry Battalion, plus B Company, 33rd Engineers was providing a mobile reserve to the west of the town. Major General Jones pulled his Div HQ out of St-Vith and back to Vielsalm, quite near, but not co-located with HQ 7th Armored. It cannot have been easy for all the various commanders to work in harmony, because there were now – all commanding troops in the same area – Major General Jones (106th Inf), Brigadier General Hasbrouck (7th Armd), Brigadier General Hoge (CCB 9th Armd) and Brigadier General Clarke (CCB 7th Armd), but that was the way in which the corps commander chose to work and they appear to have managed it successfully. Nevertheless, it was very clear that Clarke was now solely in charge of the defence of St-Vith.

Over the next few days, Bruce Clarke conducted a masterly defensive operation. He later explained: 'As commander of CCB, I analysed the situation and decided that the probable objective of the German attack was not St-Vith or a bridgehead over the Salm River, but rather a decisive objective far to my rear, probably toward the English Channel. I could well afford to be forced back slowly, surrendering a few kilometres of terrain at a time to the German forces while preventing the destruction of my command and giving other units to my rear the time to prepare a defence or a counter-attack. Therefore by retiring a kilometre or so a day, I was winning and the Germans, by being prevented from advancing many kilometres a day, were losing; thus proving my concept that an armored force can be just as effectively employed in a defense and delay situation as in the offensive.'[12]

Surrounded on the Schnee-Eifel

While Brigadier General Bruce Clarke was working his personal magic on the problems at St-Vith, the situation in the Schnee-Eifel deteriorated from bad to worse. As I have already mentioned in Chapter 3, in describing the fate of Major General Jones' 106th Infantry Division and the attached 14th Cavalry Group, the US Army official history goes to some lengths to explain that the story is even now highly controversial, principally because of lack of hard evidence from the American side. One of those who was 'right in the thick of it' was Henry Broth, a combat infantryman in 106th Infantry Division, who was captured by the Germans. In an interview recorded by the Imperial War Museum in 1972,[13] he explained how, when they had first taken over the Schnee-Eifel positions from men of the veteran 2nd Infantry Division they had been told that things were '... pretty quiet and that it was like a "country club", with nothing much to do – just real nice living.' None of them expected the German offensive of the 16th, although they did appreciate that they were somewhat 'out on a limb'. 'They [the officers] told us that we were going to hold the lines until they could be strengthened, more divisions brought up and the line straightened out, ... because we were, as we say in America, sticking our noses too far into Germany ... without support on either side. True we had some support, but they were so far away from us.' His recollections of the 16th were not untypical of those from anywhere on the American front line. 'They started to shell us during the night with all kinds of gunfire from tanks, artillery and real heavy stuff. Having all that fall on us we became kinda confused, not knowing what was happening, we didn't know that a major offensive was in the making.' More from Broth later, though it seems clear that the young GIs of 106th Division had their 'tails up' when they entered the line. They had had no battle experience, but they had all been well trained and were adequately armed – although they did not have the considerable excess of numbers of light machine-guns and Browning Automatic Rifles which the veteran ETO divisions now carried as a matter of course.

The assault begins

The assault troops of 18th and 62nd VGDs had been moving from their Start Line towards 106th Division's positions since 0500 hours on the 16th and now began to push against the regimental sectors (424th in the Heckhuscheid and Winterspelt areas; 423rd in Bleialf area; and 422nd on the Auw–Schönberg road). They also would endeavour to turn the 106th's exposed northern flank. The 62nd VGD had not arrived in the line until after last light on the 15th so had had no time to carry out any pre-assault recces. Typical of the German assault is this account of the actions in 424th's sector:

> The 3d Battalion of the 424th Infantry received the first German blow in its positions north of Heckhuscheid. After a 20-minute concentration of artillery and mortar fire, a shock company of the 183rd Regt, 62nd VGD drove in on Companies K and L about 0645. Although the defenders got word back to their own artillery, when daylight came the enemy had penetrated well into the position. The 3d Battalion, however, was on ground which favoured the defender and not unduly extended. The most serious threat developed to the north on the weak flank screening the switch position. Here the regimental cannon company (Captain Joseph Freesland) armed only with rifles and machine guns was deployed at the Weissenhof cross roads blocking the main road to

Winterspelt. Guided by flashlights and flares the Germans made their attack in column, advancing erect, shouting and screaming. The cannoneers, nothing daunted, did well in their infantry role, holding for several hours against assault from front and flank. Col Reid, the regimental commander, ordered his 1st Battalion, in reserve at Steinebrück, to the support of the threatened north flank. Company C arrived to reinforce the cannon company and the rest of the reserve battalion hurriedly established a defensive position to the rear at Winterspelt.[14]

There were many acts of bravery and some remarkable displays of good shooting – one being by Pfc Paul C. Rosen, a gunner in an M10 tank destroyer, who saw five enemy tanks and a truck moving north of Lützkampen. He engaged them at a range of some 2,000 yards and destroyed all six vehicles, using just eighteen rounds of HE and AP capped ammunition! However, the pressure soon began to tell and the gallant cannoneers, for example, were forced to make a fighting withdrawal to Winterspelt, with fire support from Company C and the platoon commander of 2nd Platoon (Lieutenant Crawford Wheeler) who stayed behind with a Bazooka to engage the leading Sturmgeschütz and was killed by point-blank fire. By the night of the 16th, General Jones had committed all his reserves, apart from the engineers now helping in the defence of St-Vith. When 2nd Inf Div had handed over the area to the 106th, they had taken their armoured support – CCB of 9th Armd Div – with them, north into the V Corps area. The 9th Armd's CCR was thus the only mobile counter-attack force left available to VII Corps and they were located about twenty miles south of St-Vith. However, it was clear that they could not cope alone and at 1025 hrs, First Army released 9th Armd's CCB to VIII Corps, so Middleton was able to move CCR to 'backstop' his 28th Inf Div and attach CCB to the 106th, the tanks thus going back to their old, familiar location.

Throughout the early hours of darkness on 17 December, mortars and artillery hammered the front-line foxholes of the 424th, while patrols crept forward, cut through the barbed wire and began lobbing grenades into the American positions. Then, an hour or so before first light, the German searchlights were switched on and the rain of shells and 'Moaning Minnies' began again. The main thrust was at Winterspelt and by daybreak 1st Battalion had been driven out of the village by troops of 62nd VGD, but the 424th still blocked the main road to the Our. To speed up the attack the German Corps Commander, Walther Lucht, personally drove to Winterspelt to get the 62nd moving on towards the river. They had suffered considerable casualties and were somewhat disorganised. Under his urging they advanced, but were finally stopped by a scratch force from the 424th, led by First Lieutenant Jarrett M. Huddleston, Jr., who held the Steinebrück bridge over the Our against all comers.

Meanwhile, Brigadier General Hoge's CCB of 9th Armd, which had been ordered back to the Winterspelt area, arrived at St-Vith just before dawn on the 17th. Their orders were to seize the high ground near Winterspelt with 27th Armored Infantry Battalion, while 14th Tank Battalion assembled west of the Our, to be committed as the situation dictated. News of the loss of Winterspelt did not reach CCB until the two leading rifle companies had begun to move towards the Our. By 0930 hrs they had crossed and had made contact with the enemy dug in along the high ground overlooking the village of Echterach, about a mile from the Steinebrück bridge. It would be another two hours plus before CCB had all their supporting artillery and tanks coordinated, which of course meant that the enemy had had time to bring up reinforcements of his own. The battle for the hills flanking Echternach was a bloody one on both sides, but by 1500 hrs the Americans had achieved their objective and taken some ninety prisoners. Notwithstanding this success, it was decided to withdraw both CCB and the 424th across the river that night (17/18 December), but the infantry regiment had to leave much of its equipment behind. Although the intervention by CCB had not entirely achieved its aim, it had allowed the 424th to withdraw successfully and had undoubtedly delayed the enemy drive toward St-Vith.

Nevertheless, the 17th had been the 'fateful day for the 106th Division' with the Germans striving to close the trap around them and the Americans trying desperately to prevent this. Undoubtedly there was also some misunderstanding of the situation and how it should be resolved, between the corps commander and the divisional commander. Middleton had told Jones by telephone as early as the night of the 16th, that he was worried about the security of the 422nd and 423rd Infantry Regiments, but at the same time he had stressed the importance of maintaining the Schnee-Eifel position and Jones had perhaps given the wrong impression that he could and would hold firm. Later Jones made a tentative suggestion that, given the increased enemy pressure, perhaps it would be wise to pull them back to a less exposed position. Middleton's answer seemed to suggest that such a decision had to be left to the 'man on the ground', but in a post-war interview he stated categorically that when he had ended their telephone conversation he had been fully convinced that Jones was going to withdraw the beleaguered regiments. Jones, on the other hand, had apparently read their conversation entirely differently and felt he was being told that he must hold on at all costs and therefore decided not to withdraw them. With hindsight, this type of misunderstanding and indecisiveness is almost impossible to imagine, but given the stress under which both commanders were working it is perfectly understandable. Clearly the 'fog of war' had also descended over the battlefield and Jones' troops were in a similar predicament as Henry Broth remembers:

After about a day, a day and a half, when we realised they were trying to break through, trying to break us up into smaller pockets so that they could get us out of the way ... we started gathering whatever kind of gear we could gather together and started to move out from the positions we were holding. We did not think that there would be any problems getting back to St-Vith, where our headquarters were. However, in trying to work our way back we found that we were surrounded on all sides by German tanks and other panzer outfits. No matter which way we turned we were stopped. In our particular sector the communications were not too good, because we were spread too far apart. We didn't know where the other elements of our division were ... we ourselves didn't even know where we were, we were just wandering about trying to get out of the trap. One particular instance I remember very distinctly, where I had to take a message to another officer with a group of men in the woods a little way across from where we were and there was a clearing and in order to get there I had to crawl along on my stomach. Up at the top of the clearing there happened to be a German machine-gunner and he took aim at me and fired. Of course he didn't get me, I'm still here. But that was typical, no matter which way we tried to go we were stuck. The countryside was mountainous, hilly and so forth and it was always snowing or raining so our planes couldn't drop any ammunition or food to us or any other supplies.

Finally it was the superior German firepower that stopped all movement away from the area. Tanks were heard approaching from the north, which turned out to be Otto Remer's Führer Begleit Brigade, which was to support LXVI Corps' assault on St-Vith. Remer's panzers arrived just as the German infantry disgorged from the woods and it was soon all over for the bewildered GIs: 'The lieutenant went down and made arrangements with the German officer in charge,' recalled Henry Broth, 'then came back and told us that we had one hour to dismantle and destroy our weapons, or dig holes and bury whatever we wanted to bury and be ready to come off that hill within one hour. So we dismantled our weapons, took the firing mechanisms apart and so forth and just threw parts of the rifles helter-skelter so that they couldn't put them back together again.'

It is difficult to be exact about the actual number of American troops who capitulated from the two regiments, probably somewhere between seven and nine thousand, while the loss of weapons and equipment was also considerable. As the official history states: 'The Schnee-Eifel battle, therefore, represents the most serious reverse suffered by American arms during the operations of 1944–45 in the European theater. The Americans would regard this defeat as a blow to Allied prestige. The Germans would see in this victory, won without great superiority in numbers, a dramatic re-affirmation of the Schlieffen–Cannae concept.'[15]

28th Infantry Division is also attacked by Fifth Panzer Army
Below the doomed 106th Infantry Division, the line was held by the
veteran 28th Infantry 'Keystone' Division. As has been explained, they
were facing the might of two panzer corps which contained some of
the best tank units in the German Army. Despite their competence, the
Germans were still finding progress difficult, as this excerpt from the
reminiscences of Gefreite Guido Gnilsen, an operator in the command
halftrack of a battalion in 2nd Pz Gren Regt, 2nd Panzer Division, who
were leading on the right flank, recalls:

> We were beginning to hear of our own losses, our battalion had
> many casualties when the Amis made a counter-attack from
> Fischbach. They did not give us much of a chance, we were
> defenceless against such a powerful force and they came in the
> night. We had to withdraw and wait for help. We lost many good
> men – San.-Fw (medical sergeant) Bacher killed, our communica-
> tions sergeant also dead; the Adjutant, Leutnant Feitner and his
> clerk Corporal Winterer, our 'Sparks' Wegner and Schwedler
> wounded. Richard Schmitt missing. The company also had heavy
> losses, with two platoon commanders killed, and today is only
> the first of the advance. We were beginning to ask ourselves when
> our number would be up.

Gnilsen does not appear to have allowed the horrors of war to get him
down. He could see that the American ration stores were burning and
was told that they were crammed with 'goodies':

> ... the infantry chaps showed us the way and we landed in one of
> the offices of the Amis who had just received parcels from home
> – with chocolate, sweets and a nice cake box. On it it said "For
> my Darling". There was [sic] also lots of paper and letters for
> Christmas, but we did not have time to read them, oh and not
> forgetting the cigarettes. I tried to carry too much and in my
> greed let half of it fall on the floor, but I also got a new pair of
> boots from a pile that was lying about. Then we went back to

share our loot with the others. I was very happy with what I had got and packed them under my seat, then I started eating the chocs and sweets until I couldn't eat anymore – and I couldn't eat my rations either! At this moment I was enjoying the war, but we didn't know how long it would stay like this.

We reached Clervaux (Clerf), the first big town and a very important rail junction, just at the right time … we had received a wireless message from Major Monschau that the bridge was still in one piece and we were able to take our tanks over, including the Panthers. For this success he was later awarded the Knight's Cross. Then there was a lull in the fighting until midnight. Prisoners were brought in and the wounded cared for. Then the fighting started again and by the next morning Clervaux was free of all enemy, a few hundred prisoners were brought in together with lots of booty.

In one of his many books about the Battle of the Bulge, British historian Charles Whiting tells how two German signallers were despatched before the offensive began, to go secretly to Clervaux, establish a radio station there, so that they could call down German artillery with pinpoint accuracy once the assault to capture the vital bridges started – and this is exactly what they did. Clervaux was also the location of the headquarters of Colonel Hurley Fuller's 110th Infantry Regiment, whose troops were holding the 'Skyline Drive' positions. Fuller made a determined attack with whatever reserves he could muster, to retake the village of Marnach, just to the east of Clervaux, but his attack coincided with 2nd Panzer Division's assault on Clervaux: 'It was an amazing spectacle: a couple of infantry companies and one company of light tanks versus substantial elements of an entire panzer corps.'[16] The outcome was inevitable and despite their brave attempt, the Americans had to withdraw with heavy casualties. It was the same at Hosingen and in the other positions along 'Skyline Drive', the Americans fighting until their ammunition was exhausted and being forced to surrender. However, this gallant stand by the men of 28th Infantry Division ensured that the German thrusts towards the key town of

Bastogne would be significantly delayed, allowing time for the defenders, elements of 101st Airborne Division and 10th Armored Division, to arrive and establish a perimeter.

> The cost had been high, much higher than American units expected to pay at this stage of the war: the 110th Infantry virtu- ally destroyed, the men and fighting vehicles of five tank compa- nies lost, the equivalent of three combat engineer companies dead or missing, and tank destroyer, artillery and miscellaneous units engulfed in this battle. In the last analysis the losses inflicted on the enemy may have equalled those sustained by the Americans – certainly the Germans paid dearly for their hurried frontal attacks against stonewalled villages and towns – but the final measure of success and failure would be in terms of hours and minutes won by the Americans and lost to the enemy.[17]

SEVENTH ARMY FRONT

Slow progress farther south

The assault by Brandenberger's Seventh Army still lacked the impetus of von Manteuffel's panzer forces to their north. Granted his army was much weaker than the other two (it was lacking both in armour and artillery), but it still did not make the progress which might have been expected. For example, three of its four divisions were involved in the initial surprise attack across the Sauer, and they were faced by just two infantry regiments: the 109th of 28th Inf Div and the 12th of 4th Inf Div, with 60th Armd Inf Batt and CCA of 9th Armd sandwiched between them. In total the Americans were at a numerical disadvan- tage of at least one to three, but their stubborn, highly successful forward defence, effectively held off the enemy onslaught. Limited penetration between American positions was achieved, but the centres of resistance in villages and other key locations, were bypassed and remained generally intact. This was only achieved at considerable loss; the US casualty estimate in killed, wounded and missing for the southern shoulder defenders was estimated at more than 2,000 for the six days 16–21 December. However, German casualties were even greater and in addition they suffered severely from frostbite and trench foot, because the defenders generally were sheltered from the elements.

Tutti Fratelli (All men are brothers)

In battle, the badge of the Red Cross reaches across frontiers and shows no distinction between enemies – medical staff of both sides treating the sick and wounded of the enemy should the situation require them to do so. And it was thus in the Ardennes. One such 'guardian angel' was Frau Agnes Mertes of Gerolstein, whose husband had been killed on the Yugoslav Front earlier in the war. Despite her advancing years she still does voluntary work for the Red Cross and was recently decorated in recognition of more than sixty years of service in the German Red Cross. In early December 1944 she was serving in the German Army medical services (*Sanitätsdienst*) in Yugoslavia, when her unit was transferred to Western Germany as she recalls:

> Our unit prepared for action at Gerolstein in the Rhineland, on Christmas Eve 1944. On this very day we suffered one of the heaviest air-raids by the Allied Air Forces in the region Gerolstein–Pelm–Büdesheim. Because of my experience as a seasoned campaigner, the head physician of the Civil Central Hospital at Gerolstein gave me the order that I should transfer the wounded German soldiers from the partly destroyed hospital to an emergency sick bay that had been set up in a local inn for wounded American soldiers who had been captured. We had to care for many Americans and bedded the German wounded down in the same rooms. We also had some motor ambulances and I received another order, this time to transfer the wounded from another hospital in Büdesheim to our 'inn' in Gerolstein. The road between the two places was under heavy bombardment from Allied aircraft and when the alarm was given we had to stop, unload the wounded and hide them (and us) in the roadside ditches. One day while unloading the stretchers at our emergency hospital, a bomb exploded near the inn 'Zur Linde'. A wall caved

in and fell upon the wounded soldiers and the nursing staff. I was working nearby and was slightly wounded, but after a short treatment I as able to carry on with my duty.

The MO then handed over to me the remnants of the ambulance medical kits and field dressings and we got another order, this time to transport all the German and American wounded to the Main Military Dressing Station at Neuwied. We didn't ask the wounded soldiers: 'Are you American or are you German?' instead we just loaded them all up together, because they all needed urgent help and all were worried about the bombing.

ALLIED COMMAND PROBLEMS

Higher Command Problems

It is not easy to decide when exactly the senior Allied commanders realised that the German onslaught was a major threat. Certainly they did not do so on the first day, despite what has been written since: 'I was immediately convinced that this was no local attack ...' wrote General Eisenhower in his book, *Crusade in Europe*, in the chapter in which he deals with the Ardennes offensive. Later he says that Bradley and he were convinced: '... that a major attack was developing against the centre of the Twelfth Army Group...' However, Robert E. Merriman, who served first as a field member, then as chief, of the US Army Historical Division in the Ardennes, says: 'Although claims have been made that Eisenhower instantly gauged the seriousness of the situation, the truth is that none of the Allied commanders, from Eisenhower down, realised the true extent of the German attack on that first day. Eisenhower *did* suggest to Bradley that he send an armored division to each side of the apparent attack area. So the 7th and 10th Armored Divisions from Ninth and Third Armies respectively were ordered to move during the night of December 16/17 to the Ardennes.'[18] To be fair, however, Eisenhower certainly reacted faster and more decisively than did Bradley or Hodges once the true impact of what was happening became clear.

Operation 'Confusion'.

The rumours and hysteria spread by the haphazard arrival of von der Heydte's Paratroopers, coupled with the grossly exaggerated doings of Skorzeny's Commandos and a lack of information about enemy movements, led to a wave of near panic behind the lines. Typical was the hurried evacuation of the headquarters of US First Army from Spa on the 17th, when it was thought that they were in the path of the onrushing SS panzer divisions. To quote Robert Merriman again: 'On the seventeenth the headquarters had been hastily evacuated; those of us who were there later found many secret documents left by various hastily departing staff divisions. Others found new pistols and other types of equipment left behind in the departure.' He goes on to explain also the reaction of local civilians to the hasty departure still further westwards of the same headquarters from its next location at Chaudfontaine, near Liège: 'Stark fear gripped the faces of those dazed peasants as the last trucks vanished around the final gentle curve in the road. "Is there no one who can help us?" one of them asked me. I could only stammer helplessly and vanish into the distance myself.' It is indeed fortunate that so many of the front-line GIs were made of sterner stuff. Merriman goes on to liken the German attack to a shot of insulin injected under the American skin: 'Stung by the surprise punch of the Germans, we staggered and then rebounded. Our minds suddenly cleared.'

'Let the sons of bitches go all the way to Paris!'

There was one American commander who was 'ahead of the game', thanks to his intuitive staff and his own innate feel for warfare, and that was the charismatic US Third Army Commander, General George S. Patton, Jr. His brilliant Intelligence Officer, Colonel Oscar Koch, who had been faithfully following the piecemeal reports of the German build-up, ignored by most other intelligence officers, had become convinced that there would be a major enemy counter-attack – probably well to their north in First Army's sector – very soon, probably in mid-December 1944. Patton had taken notice of what his 'spark-plug' had told him and as early as 12 December had ordered his staff to make contingency plans for pulling Third Army out of its present east-wards attacking mode (i.e., into the Saar) and changing its direction northwards by 90 degrees, so that they could attack the exposed flank of any enemy offensive through the Ardennes. Thus, when he was ordered to attend Eisenhower's top level conference at Verdun on the morning of the 19th, GSP had a pleasant surprise up his sleeve for the worried Supreme Commander! Patton's last words to his staff before he left were to tell them to 'polish up the plan' and be ready for his phone call. Patton was supremely confident of his own abilities, but it is doubtful that even he could have foretold the dramatic effect his words would have at that conference.

Everyone there except for GSP (those attending included Bradley, Devers and Tedder) was in a sombre mood, which was not helped by the surroundings – described as being 'cheerless, smelly and freezing cold'! Eisenhower began the conference by getting the SHAEF G-2 to give an up-to-date briefing on the situation and to explain how serious the enemy threat was. Patton's early contribution was both positive and upbeat: 'Hell, let's have the guts to let the sons of bitches go all the way to Paris. Then we'll really cut 'em up and chew 'em up!' As one can imagine, such bravado was not appreciated by any of those present, in particular Eisen-hower, who was determined not to allow the enemy to cross the Meuse. Ike went on to say that he wanted Patton to '... get to Luxembourg and take command of the battle and make a strong counter-attack ...' Then came what his biographer, Martin Blumenson, describes as being: 'the sublime moment of his career. Ike said, "When can you attack?" I said, "On December 22, with three divisions; the 4th Armored, the 26th and the 80th."'[19] Later GSP added that his positive statement had created '... quite a commotion'. Most of those attending probably thought he was just being boastful and doubted that such a complicated operation could be undertaken so quickly – but of course they didn't know that Patton's staff had already done most of the planning.

Monty takes charge of the northern flank
Another revelation came to GSP next day, when he visited Bradley's HQ in Luxembourg. While he was there, Eisenhower phoned to say

that he was going to put Field Marshal Montgomery in operational command of all the American troops on the northern shoulder of the Bulge, namely US First and Ninth Armies. As might have been expected, this was not a decision that had been decided upon lightly, but came as the result of a period of lobbying by the British field marshal as it became clearer and clearer to him that Bradley had lost control. Of course Monty's desire to take over control of land operations had been nascent for some time; one of his biographers (Nigel Hamilton) quotes him as having told Field Marshal Alan Brooke, the British CIGS, in confidence in late November, that as a commander in charge of land operations: '... Eisenhower is quite useless. There must be no misconception on this matter; he is completely and utterly useless.' Later he commented, 'First Army is struggling forward slowly, but here again there are no reserves.'[20]

Monty was probably the best informed senior commander on the entire front; he had his own personal team of specially trained, able and intelligent young liaison officers who would constantly be going out from Monty's Tac HQ, wherever and whenever their master required them to go, bringing back first-hand, up to the minute reports. When the German assault began, the 'fog of war' descended, and there was very little information coming in on what was happening, so Monty sent out his LOs to investigate everywhere – in the American sectors as well as on their own front. One of these was Captain (later Lieutenant-Colonel) Carol Mather, MC, of the Welsh Guards, who set out with two companions on the morning of 19 December, bound for General Hodges' First Army HQ at Spa to find out what was happening. One can imagine his surprise when he found the HQ completely deserted: 'A hurried evacuation has evidently taken place. We walk in. The tables in the dining-room are laid for Christmas festivities. The offices are deserted, papers are lying about. Telephones are still in place.' Mather goes on to liken it to a *Marie Celeste*-type situation, then the truth begins to dawn: 'The German attack is more serious than we thought, for the evacuation of the headquarters shows every sign of a panic move.'[21] Mather eventually found Hodges at his Rear HQ, considerably shaken and unable to give a coherent account of what had happened. He was also out of touch with Bradley's 12th Army Group HQ. One of the party, Lieutenant-Colonel Tom Bigland, who was Monty's LO at HQ 12th Army Group, went off immediately to Luxembourg to establish contact with Bradley, while the rest returned post-haste to report to Montgomery.

Mather was given the task of returning immediately to see Hodges once again (at Chaudfontaine), telling him that he *must* block the Meuse bridges: 'I was to demand of General Hodges that he take every precaution immediately to hold the river crossings and I was to tell him of the movements of 21st Army Group to meet this threat.' Mather asked Monty how he was expected to give General Hodges these orders when he was not under command: 'Just tell him!' replied Monty and went on to explain how vital it was that the enemy were not allowed to capture any crossing over the river and how important it was that Hodges realise what had to be done. Finally, he told Mather to tell Hodges that by first light on the 20th there would be 90 SAS Jeeps and officer patrols from Phantom[22] covering the crossings as recce; that XXX Corps would 'sidestep' into the area to the north of the Meuse (Louvain–St-Trond–Hasselt) in order to block the way to Antwerp; and that he wanted to meet Hodges the next day. Clearly Monty was extremely disturbed about all that he had heard, because he told Mather that he must wake him up on his return no matter what time it was: 'On no other occasion', comments Mather, 'can I remember Monty wishing to be disturbed in the middle of the night, even at the height of the Alamein battle.'[23]

Carol Mather delivered Montgomery's 'requests' to General Hodges – fortunately he had been introduced to him the previous day so the general recognised him. Mather says that, because of the wild rumours about German paratroops dressed in Allied uniforms being everywhere, there were a lot of 'trigger-happy checkpoints' in the American zone, so things could be tricky, especially for non-Americans! It is clear that once again he was worried by how out of touch Hodges appeared to be and how he had nothing to say about protecting the Meuse bridges. It was fortunate, therefore, that Montgomery was assembling a corps (XXX Corps) of four divisions (the 43rd, 51st and 53rd

Infantry Divisions, plus the Guards Armoured) and three independent armoured brigades, to which could be added Canadian 4th Armoured Division in 48 hours, with the task of operating along the Meuse from Liège to Namur and Dinant, thus effectively sealing the river line in what was supposedly its most vulnerable area, namely where the *Schwerpunkt* of Dietrich's Sixth Panzer Army was aimed.

The problems between the Allies were not helped when the two senior British generals in Eisenhower's headquarters (Major-General Sir Kenneth Strong, SHAEF's Chief of Intelligence and Major-General Sir John Whiteley, SHAEF's Deputy Chief of Operations), went to see Ike's Chief of Staff, the irascible Lieutenant General Bedell Smith (well-known for his hair-trigger temper!) at midnight on the 19th, to get him out of bed and tell him that control of the northern side of the 'Bulge' should be passed to Montgomery! Accounts as to what happened seem to differ. Some say that Bedell Smith rang Bradley directly and asked him if he would object to this happening: 'Ike thinks it may be a good idea to turn over to Monty your two Armies on the north and let him run that side of the Bulge from 21st Group. It may save us a great deal of trouble, especially if your communications with Hodges and Simpson go out.'[24] Bradley, having thought quickly about it said that it was hard for him to object and that if only Monty were an American general there would be no problem! Others say that Bradley did object and that it was left to Eisenhower to make the decision. What definitely did happen was that Bedell Smith, clearly feeling embarrassed and annoyed at having to question Bradley's ability, then lost his temper with the two Englishmen, calling them 'Limey bastards!' and sacking them both on the spot! Fortunately he would rapidly have a change of heart and the disagreement would be smoothed over. Strong would recall later that, at Eisenhower's meeting at Verdun next day, Bedell Smith had quietly joined them and said that he would recommend the Montgomery 'take-over' to Eisenhower, which is exactly what happened. However, no matter what has been written since, Bradley would not have been human if he had not been deeply hurt. He always prided himself on being the 'Soldier's

General', a down-to-earth 'hands-on' soldier, so to have two-thirds of his Army Group taken away from him and, worse still, put under command of: 'that little Limey fart' (as Patton was wont to call Montgomery) was the ultimate embarrassment. And unfortunately, as we shall subsequently see, Monty's foolishness in being unable to resist, as Bradley politely puts it, 'the chance to tweak our Yankee noses', would rebound upon him, almost ruining what some historians have seen as Montgomery's 'finest hour'.

Notes

1   A document which outlined the use of enemy uniforms, etc., was captured by a unit of US 7th Armored Division near Heckhuscheid early on in the assault.

2   The *Wirbelwind Flakpanzer* IV, mounted either quad 2cm AA cannon or one 3.7cm FlaK 43 in an open-topped turret which replaced the normal turret of a Pz Kpfw IV. They were issued to panzer regiments to provide close AA support.

3   See Reynolds' *Men of Steel*. Peiper's men would also behave in an appalling manner towards innocent civilians in Stavelot, where a total of 138 civilians would be killed on 18 December. One witness (Mde Régine Gregoire) would not only have to put up with their brutality at first hand, but would also hear them boasting about it – such as decapitating one civilian, then sticking the head on a pike and using it for target practice: see, Eisenhower, John. *The Bitter Woods*.

4   Interview with Major Ken Hechler, US Army, in September 1945 and quoted in *Men of Steel*.

5   The dump had originally contained some two million gallons of petrol, but some had been evacuated during the previous night.

6   The engineers had been operating a number of local sawmills, as part of US First Army's 'Winterization & Bridge Timber Cutting Program'.

7   Major Ralph Ingersoll, *US 1st Infantry Division 1939–45*, in Osprey, Vanguard No. 3.

8   US armoured divisions were normally divided into two Combat Commands 'A' and 'B', each based upon an armoured regiment, while there was a third combat command HQ – known as 'CCR', available to control divisional reserves or to be used for special missions.

9   By the afternoon of 17 December, there was little cohesion left within 14th Cavalry Group and they were no longer capable of withstanding the German assault. Devine and his staff had been ambushed near Recht on their way to Jones' CP and, according to the official history, only he and two of his officers had managed to escape on foot. John Eisenhower in *The Bitter Woods* says that Devine's first words as he burst into the CP were: 'General we've got to run, I was practically chased into this building by a Tiger tank!'

10 As quoted in Eisenhower, John. *The Bitter Woods*.

11 As quoted in *Tank Aces – from Blitzkrieg to the Gulf War* by George Forty.

12 General Bruce C. Clarke, 'The battle for St-Vith', in *Armor* magazine, Nov-Dec, 1974.
13 IWM Sound Archive, Tape 3005
14 Cole, Hugh M. *The Ardennes: Battle of the Bulge.*
15 Ibid. General Count Alfred von Schlieffen had been Chief of the German General Staff in December 1905 and had left his detailed plan for a future war against France, Russia and Great Britain. Cannae was of course a major battle between the Romans and Carthaginians in 216 BC. Both, like the Schnee-Eifel battle, were based upon the principle of double envelopment.
16 Arnold, James R. *Ardennes 1944*. Osprey Military Campaign series, No. 55.
17 Cole, Hugh M. op. cit.
18 Merriman, Robert E. *The Battle of the Ardennes.*
19 *The Patton Papers, 1940–45.*
20 Hamilton, Nigel. *Monty – the battles of Field Marshal Bernard Montgomery.*
21 Mather, Carol. *When the Grass Stops Growing.*
22 'Phantom' was a British signals unit which operated in the forward areas, obtaining battlefield intelligence, primarily through interception.
23 Mather, op. cit.
24 Quoted in Bradley, Omar N. *A Soldier's Story.*

8
THE END OF THE BEGINNING

Trouble at the top

General Eisenhower had returned to SHAEF headquarters at Versailles from his trip to Verdun, tired, but happier now that some of the problems of command had been sorted out and positive plans made to deal with the German offensive. However, as his staff car driver and confidante, Captain Kay Summersby, was to record in her book, *Eisenhower was My Boss*, Ike's personal problems were just beginning: 'The morning of December 20 was D-Day in our own SHAEF sector of the breakthrough – Intelligence reported a suicide squad of at least three score Germans headed towards Versailles.' She goes on to explain that she had heard that First Army had caught a German officer in American uniform and given him a: '... good first-degree grilling at Liège'. The officer had finally admitted that he was one of a special band, led by Otto Skorzeny, whose single mission, which was: '... to be accomplished with ruthless, fanatic zeal' was the assassination of her beloved boss Eisenhower. She comments: 'To say that this report upset the SHAEF staff is pure understatement.' Of course the story could not have been farther from the truth, although it is worth remembering that one of Skorzeny's own men while training had been convinced that this was to be their aim, and that Skorzeny had deliberately fostered the idea. The effect which this rumour would have on the freedom of movement of the Supreme Commander was staggering; the headquarters compound was turned into a virtual fortress prison.

Barbed wire appeared. Several tanks moved in. The normal guard was doubled, trebled, quadrupled. The pass system became a strict matter of life and death, instead of the old formality. The sound of a car exhaust was enough to halt work in every office, to start a flurry of telephone calls to our office, to inquire if the boss was all right. The atmosphere was worse than that of a combat headquarters up at the front, where everyone knew how to take such a situation in their stride.[1]

Poor General Eisenhower was forced to vacate the comfortable house he occupied (in which General von Rundstedt had lived when he was OB West), because it was somewhat isolated, and move into the Trianon compound, where he occupied a flat over his office. Kay Summersby and Ruth Briggs (Ike's secretary) were also moved into quarters a short distance away. None of them was permitted to leave the area, even to walk in the garden, for fear that a sniper might have got through the 'toe-to-toe' guard! Kay wrote in her diary:

> Another night tonight of uneasiness. E is just pinned to his office all day; at night he goes upstairs and sleeps in Tex's[2] flat. I stay across the way from the office. Everyone's confined to the compound. What a life. Eisenhower finally got fed up with all the restrictions: 'Hell's fire,' he grumbled, coming out of his 'office cell'. 'I'm going for a walk. If anyone wants to shoot me, he can go right ahead. I've got to get out!'

Movement problems
Another major hindrance to free movement which affected senior and junior ranks alike was caused directly by the jumpiness and increasingly suspicious attitude of MPs on traffic and other duties, and the sentries. It became quite a test of memory to convince an aggressive 'Snowdrop' (an American MP) that you really were who you said you were and not a German in American uniform – even though you didn't know who was the premier batter of the Brooklyn Dodgers, or who Betty Grable's husband was! This caused much frustration and wasted time. For example, on 21 December, while he was in the middle of directing the defence of St-Vith, Brigadier General Bruce Clarke was held by American MPs for five hours, because he wrongly placed the Chicago Cubs in the American League (Baseball). Skorzeny would have been overjoyed!

The emphasis of the attack shifts

Lack of progress by Dietrich's Sixth SS Panzer Army was apparent to the German High Command as early as 20 December and this caused a shift of emphasis to von Manteuffel's Fifth Panzer Army. Major Percy Ernst Schramm, keeper of the war diary at OKW, wrote later:

> Because the counter-pressure exerted by the enemy on the right flank still continued, and threatened to grow sharper, CinC West (von Rundstedt) ordered Army Group B (Model) to clean up the situation as quickly as possible. The intentions of 3rd Pz Gren Div were changed in that it and 12th SS Pz Div were incorporated into the thrust movement of the other units. As the objective to be attained, CinC West was given the capture of St-Vith on the right wing and the extension of the ground gained then to the west, as well as the quickest possible formation of bridgeheads over the Meuse between Huy and Givet, that is on both sides of Namur. For CinC West it was a matter of so building the northern front of the attack arrow that it would run 15 to 20 kilometres north of the roads used by motorised units and thus would make their use unhampered by artillery.[3]

The roads throughout the Ardennes were scornfully described by Jochen Peiper as being '... only broad enough for a bicycle!' – a measure of his frustration at being unable to make the sort of progress he had expected. It must have been galling for the Waffen-SS to realise that because their crack formations could not make the headway that had been expected of them, the ordinary *Panzerwaffe* of the Heer would take over. This was further confirmed when II SS Panzer Corps (2nd and 9th SS Pz Divs) was moved southwards to follow the routes already opened up by Fifth Panzer Army around St-Vith, while the Führer's personal strategic reserve – made up of Führer Begleit and Grenadier Brigades – was earmarked to support von Manteuffel's successful advance. However, even that little pugnacious bundle of energy had not yet overcome Clarke's stubborn horseshoe defence around the key town.

Curtains for Battle Group Peiper

We left Peiper's group on the night of the 20th just three miles from Werbomont, with his Panthers forming a firm base for him at La Gleize. At this juncture the Americans (XVIII Airborne Corps, with under command 30th Inf Div from V Corps, plus a large part of 3rd Armd Div) decided to block, check and then eliminate the dangerous breakthrough. This would be as far west as Peiper would get, and from now on, despite the support which he would receive from the remainder of 1st SS Panzer Division, he would be fighting a losing battle. On the 21st he decided to concentrate his entire force at La Gleize and operate from there, but he soon found that he was trapped in a small pocket, short of fuel and supplies, unable to prevent American action in the area, but determined to keep open the bridge across the Amblève near Cheneux. Fierce fighting took place that day and on the morning of the 22nd there were house-to-house battles in La Gleize itself, which went on well into the afternoon until the panzer grenadiers managed to restore the perimeter. Amazingly the Luftwaffe attempted a supply drop at about 2000 hrs. Most of the supplies dropped into American hands and Peiper reckoned that only some 10 per cent reached his men – the fuel dropped being just sufficient to keep his radio generators operating and not much else. Peiper requested permission to fight his way out, but this was refused at the highest level and the Division was told once again to try to achieve a link-up. By the 23rd the village of La Gleize, a hamlet called La Venne and a group of isolated farmsteads was all the real estate left to the battle group, and the Americans had stepped up their counter-attacks and punishing artillery bombardments. Peiper realised that, with fuel and ammunition supplies running out, the night (23rd/24th) would represent their one and only chance of breaking out. Fortunately for him, higher HQ at long last relented and gave the order he had been waiting so long to hear. At about 0200 hrs on the morning of Christmas Eve, Peiper led what was left of his once proud battle group, on foot, southwards, leaving a small rearguard to hold off the enemy and endeavour to destroy their abandoned vehicles. All the wounded and prisoners were left behind in La Gleize. When they reached the next village (La Venne), they co-opted two Belgian civilians to guide them to safety. However, they were not yet in the clear by any means. They would be forced to hide in woods for most of the 24th to avoid American spotter planes, fight skirmishes with American outposts and ford the bitterly cold River Salm before they at last managed to reach the main body of their division near Wanne just before dawn. Peiper's command was officially disbanded on the following day and what was left – less than a thousand men – rejoined their respective units. At this stage it is worth mentioning the part played in the destruction of this troublesome battle group by the Allied Air Force. Initially, due mainly to the appalling weather, their efforts were fairly ineffectual, but as Peiper pushed farther westwards it became vital that his column be located. This was done by two volunteer pilots who, despite low cloud, went up and eventually found them in the Amblève valley, heading towards Werbomont via La Gleize and Cheneux. The commander of IXth Tactical Air Command, Brigadier General 'Pete' Quesada, imme-diately ordered two fighter groups a total of some thirty-two P-47 Thunderbolts – into the air to attack the German spearhead with 500lb bombs. They attacked and despite suffering casualties from accurate low-level flak, managed to knock out at least three of Peiper's leading tanks and block his advance for an all-important two hours. This so delayed the Germans at the *moment critique* as to have a major effect upon the later destruction of this all-important armoured battle group and thus on the outcome of the entire Ardennes battle.

On the *Hitlerjugend* front, II SS Panzer Corps had, on 23rd December, and in line with the revised plan, now re-assumed command of 2nd and 9th SS Panzer Divisions, and their leading recce elements were well past Marche-en-Femenne and only some ten kilometres from the Meuse. The important Baraque de Fraiture road junction, west of the River Salm, had been captured, but as always, the main advance was being held up by the severe shortage of fuel resulting from increasing Allied air attacks on the long supply routes. Indeed, over the entire battlefield as the weather improved and the daily number of Allied sorties climbed (more than 15,000 were flown during the four days

25–28 December inclusive) the chances of Dietrich's Sixth Panzer Army ever being able to restart their offensive became more and more unlikely, despite Hitler's refusal to give it up. II SS Panzer Corps was ordered to attack once again across the Ourthe around Durbuy and then to continue on to the Meuse, while those forces still to their rear were ordered to join them as quickly as possible. The Führer chose to ignore a joint recommendation from his two most senior generals (von Rundstedt and Model) to curtail the offensive and settle for establishing a firm defensive line along the Meuse – although even now this limited objective was probably impossible to achieve. He did, however, agree that a special effort should be made to eliminate the American garrison at Bastogne, which remained a thorn in the side of any successful armoured thrust by either Fifth or Sixth Panzer Armies.

On to Bastogne

Below Dietrich's stalled Panzer Army, von Manteuffel's panzers were having more success. The 2nd Panzer and Panzer Lehr Divisions of Lüttwitz's XLVII Panzer Corps had made good progress, although they had had to fight through a series of defensive positions and had also been delayed, waiting for replenishment to arrive. The 2nd Panzer's objective was not Bastogne, but rather the River Meuse, still far to the west, so they would bypass the town some distance to its north via Noville. Panzer Lehr was within six miles of Bastogne by the evening of the 18th, so stood a good chance of getting there before American reinforcements (101st Airborne Division) could reach the key town. Totally out of character, however, the divisional commander, Fritz Bayerlein, allowed himself to be misled by wily Belgian civilians both as to the best route to take to avoid possible enemy roadblocks on the way to Bastogne and the size and makeup of any likely opposition he would meet en route. Instead of pushing on, he chose to halt, go on the defensive and wait for first light before continuing, thereby missing his golden opportunity.

Gefreite Guido Gnilsen of 2nd Pz Div remembers that time:

On a hill with a cross roads we stopped. Here was the spearhead, the tanks were all ready to go, all lined up, but could not go any further because they were waiting for petrol. Everything arrived but still no petrol. That was a good opportunity for the enemy artillery, they engaged the cross roads and made our position very uncomfortable. We decided it would be better if we withdrew.

At last the petrol came and we all filled up. It was surprising that we weren't attacked from the air as the sun was shining and the weather was perfect. We would have been a really good prey for them. We hadn't lost too much time because of the stop, then we went off along the main road to Bastogne, passing a burning Sherman and also a good many knocked-out German tanks, lying at the side of the road. At first light we turned off the main road on to a side road, where we passed heaps of cases of ammunition many metres of them all stacked up, there must have been hundreds of thousands of shells. While they were piled there then they couldn't be used against us – that pleased me most of all!

Action at Noville, 20 December 1944

Having stayed the night in a convenient farmhouse, Guido's unit was scheduled to go into the attack early the following morning. He writes:

To assist the assault were several four-barrelled anti-aircraft guns on a gun carriage, also a few turretless tanks. From the road we moved into open fields and saw in front of us a hollow, then rooftops appearing out of the morning mist. We could see the tracer from the AA guns looking like nylon string, fading out in the dark. The firing was getting heavier minute by minute and from all sides came bangs and crashes accompanied by poisonous fumes. There was a dust all around us and then two clouds of earth right in front of our halftrack from near misses. We couldn't see a thing and began to get a bit nervous, so we stationed ourselves close behind tank number four, then took cover behind a haystack. Things then began to happen very fast, as out of the smoke came our grenadiers, retreating as fast as they could with frightened looks on their faces. Tank No 4 was also withdrawing, so we did, convinced that the Amis were counter-attacking. Then we saw that our commander, Major Monschau, had been wounded and had to be evacuated, so we were without a commander. The regimental commander quickly took a hand and ordered his adjutant, Captain Göricke, to take over command of the 11th Battalion, while our Signals Officer, Leutnant Bopp, would take over A Company, as its commander had also been wounded.

We dug ourselves in inside a wood, with all round cover. There was a lot of noise on the road from the movement of heavy trucks. The medics were bringing in the wounded and we got a rest from battle, anyway the immediate danger was over, but we were all like lost sheep, looking for our shepherd – where is the Commander, or the adjutant? ... This day was going to end and it was getting on towards evening, but we did not know whether or not Noville had fallen, so we drove into the middle of the town. What a sight met our eyes in the half light – the last rays of the sun going down mixed with the red glow of burning houses, also the church was on fire and brewed-up tanks were silhouetted against the sky. The sound of fighting in the distance was an accompaniment to this never-to-be forgotten scene, the like of which I have never seen before or since. Now it was night so we made our quarters in a house near the church. It was still light enough to see what damage had been done, so to satisfy my curiosity I made my way, in a trance, through the streets, with a feeling of victory when I saw knocked-out Shermans and other blown-up wagons, and as far as the eye could see cases full of provisions, tins of carrots, etc. I didn't know if some of them were full of chocolate or cigarettes.

All of a sudden a salvo of artillery fire came down and I had to find a place to take cover quickly – I landed up in an old shed, where I found a dead civilian. I can only imagine that he was brought there by mistake with the American casualties and left there hoping someone would find him. Then I wanted to see how we were able to capture Noville and it looked as though heavy tanks had come from the other side of the town and made the enemy pull back towards Bastogne. But you could see by looking at our tanks that they had not had an easy job. Many had been hit time and time again, but they had not been penetrated and that showed that the Panther was much better than the Sherman on which I noticed that many shots had gone through. One thing caught my eye – a Panther had tried to crush an American Jeep and had landed with its tracks pointing skywards and the funny thing was that the Jeep was still standing on its wheels! In a building near the church with the name *Hôtel de Ville* (town hall) I saw all our men who had been killed, lying in rows. One of them was our adjutant whom I had last seen running over the fields – a few days before he had shared his Christmas presents with us that his mother had sent him – cakes and so on.

The fighting around Noville was without doubt the most terrible part of the war for me, in a few hours we had lost twenty tanks and half of the panzer grenadier regiment. ... Our battalion was now only at company strength and we had lost all our senior officers. The tired and weary grenadiers who had not had time to sleep for days, had come to take part in the push on Foy. Now we were standing in the twilight, in a street where the Amis' artillery was pounding us constantly, which was very unpleasant as you can imagine.

But our destination was not Bastogne, but the Meuse. So we moved farther west and after a long drive came to Harsin where we stayed the night to get prepared for the next move to Hargimont. We came in our halftrack behind two tanks by the light of the moon along a road into the town. Up until now it had all been quiet, but as soon as we reached the houses all hell broke loose! We were suddenly hit by the tank in front of us as it reversed while we ran over a motorbike. At that precise moment I could not keep my eyes open any longer and fell into a deep sleep so could hear no more of the war outside. When everything quietened down I had to go on guard so that the others could get a bit of sleep. As Christmas Eve approached we put pickets all around the town so that we could not be surprised in our sleep.

We hoped we would have a bit of peace over Christmas. However, the Amis came down from the high ground and tried to get at us from all sides, but we drove them back. Now we had no time to think about Christmas Eve. Our Sergeant Tönneböhm was very badly hit, they wrapped him in a tent cover and took him with four others to the Command Post ... In the evening it was a bit quieter. We found a little Christmas tree which we trimmed as best we could ...

It was a wonderful Christmas Day, the sun was shining and it was very quiet. We knew things would not stay like this for long. We moved farther west, the convoy making a hell of a lot of noise – no wonder the enemy artillery was landing shells right in the middle. Lieutenant Baier was wounded on Christmas Day and Sergeant-Major Schmelzer took over the company. It was a wonder how we got through the barrage and on the 26th we pushed to the furthest point west. After someone had relieved me on the radio I decided to stretch my legs and get a bit of fresh air. I saw a sign at the end of the road: 'Dinant 9 kms', so that meant it was just 9 kilometres to the Meuse – our objective.

We were very much mistaken if we thought that we would have a quiet night; the tanks were stranded at Celles with the same complaint as always – no petrol and the enemy was preparing to surround us. The fighting went on for three days, then came the fighter-bombers to give us the last push backwards. ... The Ardennes offensive was lost. For two days we were still fighting in Rochefort, with the Americans advancing from all sides. The infantry had been in their foxholes, in the snow and ice, holding their positions as well as they could, pushing back every attack. So ended the year 1944.

Meanwhile, back at St-Vith

'On the morning of 20 December the Americans defending St-Vith held the easternmost position of any organised nature in the centre sector of the Ardennes battleground. The most advanced elements of the German drive by this time were twenty-five airline miles to the south-

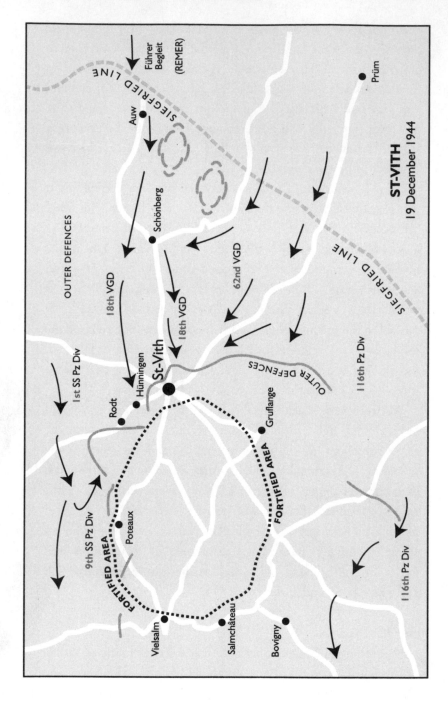

ST-VITH
19 December 1944

west of St-Vith. The St-Vith perimeter, now of substantial size, continued to act as a breakwater holding the LXVI Corps in check while other German units surged westward past its northern and southern extension.' That is how the Army official history succinctly describes the position in which the opposing forces found themselves five days into the offensive in the area of the all-important road centre of St-Vith. While single battle groups, like Peiper's, could, with difficulty, still manage to get forward, any advance by a force of significant size needed a proper road network over which to operate, and on the 20th, this was still not the case, there being just one main supply route to feed the westward advance of von Manteuffel's forces, as has been explained already. The stubborn defence of St-Vith was causing an immense traffic jam to build up, the effects of which were felt at every level (James R. Arnold in his *Ardennes 1944* in Opsrey's Campaign Series, comments that both Model and von Manteuffel were forced to abandon their staff cars on the clogged roads, in order to get to an all-important strategic planning meeting!).

Despite the surrender of the American forces on the Schnee-Eifel, which released considerable German forces for other operations, there was no significant attack on St-Vith on 20 December – 'just a few feeble German jabs' is how the official history puts it, and this undoubtedly gave the defenders time to strengthen their lines. More troops had arrived, including a medium tank battalion, and the divisional artillery of 7th Armored was now much better integrated. Another somewhat unexpected caller had been Brigadier General William Hoge, CG of CCB 9th Armored Division, the next formation to the south of St-Vith. He was far from clear as to what was going on and surprised to find no sign of General Jones with whom he had been completely out of touch. Initially he was all for going back to Bastogne to try to get new orders from the corps commander, but Clarke was able to persuade him to take up a position just to the south of St-Vith and work in co-operation with the garrison. They were able to complete this move without enemy interference because German reports covering the defenders' activities on the 20th had led them to suppose that the garrison was much stronger than it actually was. In addition, the movement of the attacking forces over the muddy, broken-up forest tracks, was extremely difficult. The Führer's own crack *Begleit* Brigade did try a half-hearted assault that was stopped by the fire of 814th Tank Destroyer Battalion which knocked out their leading tanks (the official history says that they knocked out all four leading Panthers with just seven shots!). One of the two divisions of the main attack force, 18th VGD (the other was 62nd VGD) then tried a piecemeal attack on the high ground north of the Schönberg road, with the aim of seizing St-Vith's railway station. The divisional commander, Günter Hoffmann-Schönborn, accompanied this assault, but within a couple of hours it had failed – one of the main problems being the inability of the horse-drawn artillery[4] to get past the armoured vehicles.

Christ cleansing the temple

20 December was also the day on which Field Marshal Montgomery had visited General Hodges at his First Army HQ, at Chaudfontaine. Instead of following the 'incognito' approach which had been adopted by Bradley and others (viz: ditching the staff car in favour of a Jeep, covering star plates, badges of rank, etc.), Monty had gone entirely in the other direction, ordering his aides to find '... the largest Union Jack that will go on the bonnet of the car. Also eight motorcycle outriders.' Consequently when he swept into Hodges' Headquarters, as one observer said: 'It was like Christ Come to Cleanse the Temple!' Both Hodges and Simpson were there, neither of whom had had any contact with Bradley or his staff since the German offensive began. Monty cabled Alan Brooke that evening: 'Ninth Army has three divisions and First Army fifteen, there are no reserves anywhere behind the front. Morale is very low. They seemed delighted to have someone to give them firm orders.'[5] And that is exactly what Montgomery proceeded to do. Simpson's Ninth Army would immediately assume responsibility for the sector to the north of the 'Bulge' above Monschau, taking under command HQ XIX Corps. As far as First Army was concerned, he explained that he wanted to form a tactical reserve corps of at least three divisions under General 'Lightning Joe' Collins who was

undoubtedly Hodges' most aggressive and able corps commander. His HQ VII Corps would be allotted US 84th Inf Div (from First Army), the newly arrived US 75th Infantry Division and US 3rd Armored. The new corps was to assemble in the Durbuy–Marche area and be ready to be used offensively on his orders. Monty, as always, was supremely confident that he could handle any situation. Later, he wrote: 'By 20 December I was sitting pretty. I did not mind much what happened to my right so long as the Germans did not get over the Meuse and I was pretty certain I could stop that.' In addition to forming this mobile reserve, Monty was also anxious to, as he put it: 'tidy up the front' and this would involve giving up St-Vith so as to be able to rescue 7th Armored and 106th Infantry Divisions from their increasingly isolated positions. Here he differed with Hodges, who considered it essential to hold on to St-Vith for as long as possible. However, it was also clear that General Ridgway's XVIII Airborne Corps would have to continue to press on towards St-Vith if they were to be able to provide an escape-route for the beleaguered garrison, while as we have already seen, Clarke's method of defence involving a slow withdrawal would continue to delay the enemy. The situation soon became known to all levels of command, the Supreme Commander sending CG 7th Armd a message which read: 'The magnificent job you are doing is having a great beneficial effect on our whole situation. I am personally grateful to you and wish you would let all of your people know that if they continue to carry out their mission with the splendid spirit they have so far shown, they will deserve well of their country.'[6]

By the morning of 21 December the St-Vith salient was disposed as shown in the sketch-map and was generally in good shape. They were expecting an enemy assault from the east by either or both of the two VGDs, with armoured support from Begleit Brigade. The defence was based on the ridge lines and hills which masked the town from the north-east, east and south-east. There were two obvious lines of approach through these shielding hills, namely along the main road from Büllingen to St-Vith from the north, and the road and rail approach from Prüm in the south-east. When the German attack began at about 1100 hrs it was initially directed at the northern and eastern parts of the defence, held by Clarke and Hoge's combat commands. An hour later and the attack had spread along the entire defence line, with the position on the right flank being just as critical. The Germans threw in attack after attack that afternoon and at about 1700 hrs launched yet another one, this time along the Schönberg road directly from the east, then some 90 minutes later they advanced down the Malmédy road from the north. At 2000 hrs another thrust came from Prüm. The pattern was much the same in all cases, a combined infantry/tank assault following a heavy 15–20 minute artillery barrage. During one of these assaults, Corporal Horace M. Thorne, of Troop D, 89th Cavalry Squadron, was leading a scouting patrol in a heavily wooded area. As he advanced with his light machine-gun, a German Panzer Mark III emerged from the trees and was quickly immobilised by fire from American light tanks. Thorne then killed two of the tank crew as they attempted to bail out. In order to get at the remainder of the crew, Corporal Thorne left his covered position and crept forward alone through intense machine-gun fire, until he was close enough to toss two hand-grenades into the turret, killing the rest of the crew. He then returned for his LMG and, despite heavy mortar fire, set it up on the back deck of the immobilised enemy tank. He then began to engage the enemy from his advantageous, but exposed position, killing eight and knocking out at least two enemy machine-gun posts. Eventually his gun jammed and he was killed by small arms fire while attempting to clear it. He was awarded a Medal of Honor posthumously. As the citation read: 'Corporal Thorne, displaying heroic initiative and intrepid fighting qualities, inflicted costly casualties on the enemy and insured the success of his patrol's mission by the sacrifice of his life.' There were countless other displays of heroism as the defenders faced wave after wave of fresh attacks, both sides taking heavy casualties.

Withdrawal

Inevitably the pressure became too great and at about 2130 hrs Clarke was forced to order the gallant defenders to withdraw, saving what vehicles and weapons they could, and to form a new defence line west of the town. This was very difficult, indeed impossible, for some of the defenders, especially those who were hampered by having a high proportion of wounded. They tried to break up into small parties and to work their way back, but many were eventually taken prisoner. Remer's Begleit Brigade had managed to slip around St-Vith to the north and at about 0200 hrs launched an attack towards the village of Rodt which was held mainly by administrative troops (cooks, drivers, signallers), who defended fiercely but were eventually crushed. This drove a wedge between two elements of the defence (Rosebaum's CCA and Clarke's CCB) and Clarke had to withdraw part of his left flank to protect Hinderhausen – a vital position on the escape route through to Vielsalm.

While the attacks were taking place on the night of 21st/22nd, higher up the chain of command, other plans were being laid. Major General Matthew B. Ridgway, CG of XVIII Airborne Corps, had prepared a plan the main element of which proposed that a perimeter defence taking in both St-Vith and Vielsalm continue to be held. Ridgway was clearly determined not to give up any more ground, despite the fact that his plan would leave both 7th Armored and 106th Infantry Divisions – or what was now left of them – cut off and surrounded. He sent the plan down to Brigadier General Hasbrouck at Vielsalm – who was very worried by it as was Clarke.[7] Clearly such a proposal was quite impossible, not only because of the circumstances now pertaining on the battlefield, but also because it was not in line with the thinking of Field Marshal Montgomery, now commander of the northern flank, who, because he wanted to 'tidy up' the defensive line, would certainly never approve of leaving two divisions in such a vulnerable situation – he did not want any more troops to be sacrificed. Hasbrouck sent a message to Ridgway explaining the desperate position they were in. Ridgway sensibly opted to leave it to the 'man on the ground' to decide, and Monty, having being given precise details of the situation by his LO at Hasbrouck's HQ, immediately sent a message direct to Hasbrouck saying: 'You have accomplished your mission – a mission well done. It is time to withdraw.' Ridgway was told of Montgomery's order soon after midday on the 22nd and immediately came down to Hasbrouck's HQ to plan the withdrawal. By now 82nd Airborne and 3rd Armored Divisions, had made contact with 7th Armored along the River Salm between Vielsalm and Salm-château about two miles to the south. The withdrawal was achieved and by the evening of the 22nd all survivors were safely across without further loss and ready to 'fight another day'. One significant 'casualty' was the unfortunate commander of the decimated 106th Infantry Division, Major General Alan Jones, who, after all the traumas of the past few days, had a heart attack just after midnight on 22/23 December and had to be evacuated to Liège.

American casualties in the defence of St-Vith were considerable, but as the official history has it, they must be: 'measured against their accomplishments. They had met an entire German corps flushed with easy victory and halted it in its tracks. They had firmly choked one of the main enemy lines of communication and forced days of delay on the westward movement of troops, guns, tanks and supplies belonging to two German armies. They had given XVIII Airborne Corps badly needed time to gather for a co-ordinated and effective defense. Finally, these units had carried out a successful withdrawal under the most difficult conditions and would return again to do battle.'[8]

Clarke and von Manteuffel met after the war and discussed the battle on television. It is clear that the German still thought he had been up against far more troops than was the case, as this extract from their conversation shows:

> '*Von Manteuffel*. For success we needed surprise. We needed bad weather to keep your airforce grounded and we needed speed to get the road net at St-Vith and to push on through. My timetable called for occupying St-Vith by 1800 on December 17th.
> *Clarke*. You certainly got the surprise and the bad weather.
> *Von Manteuffel*. But we ran into your corps at St-Vith.
> *Clarke*. Not a corps, General, an armoured combat command.
> *Von Manteuffel*. That's right. I forgot. But you had so many tanks.
> *Clarke*. You were seeing the same tanks over and over again, General, in different places. Our mobile reserve.'[9]

On Elsenborn Ridge

To the north of St-Vith along the Elsenborn Ridge, where the northern shoulder of the American defences lay – made up from a mix of units from 2nd, 99th, 1st and 9th Infantry Divisions – the GIs were holding against all that Dietrich's Sixth SS Panzer Army could throw at them. One of these defenders was J. R. McIlroy, acting squad leader of the 2nd Squad in 34th Platoon, F Company, 393rd Inf Regt, 99th Inf Div, whom we left in Chapter 6, withdrawing after the Roer dams operation had been suspended. He recalls:

Just before midnight [18/19 December] we reached Elsenborn Ridge or near there and were told that they had made a mistake and for us to turn around and go back to our old positions. I was in the lead again, this time carrying a rifle. As a precaution we up front had fixed our bayonets. We were not lucky this time – the Germans were already in our foxholes. We soon took them back, however, after a short bayonet fight. A few years ago I read in an after battle report that we had killed seven at that time. I think our only casualty was Lusk who was bayoneted through his hand. I can't remember who was with me except Lusk and Oxcien. Paul Viscova said he was behind us and witnessed this – in fact he said that he shot two after the balance ran. We held this position all that day [19th]. We had some opposition but our main problem was friendly artillery fire. We had some of this fire from American tanks and anti-tank guns, but a lot of it came from the artillery ... the tree bursts were deadly. Later that night we did pull back. I'm sure we were surrounded, but in the dark you could not tell one side from the other. There was some snow on the ground, the moon came out at times. We could see Krinkelt burning and hear the cows bawling. It was so cold that when we lay down to rest our boots would freeze to the ground. Those of us left were not in good shape. To tell you how close we were to the enemy, I came out wearing German hob-nailed boots, a P-38 revolver strapped to my side and carrying a German burp gun. About 2 a.m. on the 20th we did reach friendly troops on

Elsenborn Ridge. We probably were the last organised troops to pull back. We pulled back to near the town of Elsenborn. After receiving more ammunition, two or three meals and a little sleep we moved back to replace I Company of the 394th. The location was a hot spot – it was the farthest right of all the 99th positions. We started at the north of the road from Wirtzfeld to Elsenborn – the 2nd Division were on the other side. Our F Company CP was in a cistern about 50 yards back from our front line foxholes. We had an outpost about 50 yards in front. This position was held and occupied by us from 22 December 1944 to 30 January 1945, when we went on to the attack. Our biggest problem was German artillery – the landscape was black and white from the artillery craters. We lost several men from direct hits on their holes. The second biggest problem was the weather. It snowed most days and the temperature was near zero for several nights. We didn't have proper winter clothing – we just put on all we had, long underwear, winter issue pants, shirt, sweater, scarf, field jacket, gloves and a wool cap under our helmet liner and helmet. We had a blanket or two and a light sleeping-bag. Our foxhole was covered by our tent or shelter halves, with logs on top. Our GI greatcoat was no good for combat, it would get wet and heavy, then freeze. If we had one we would put it down to absorb the moisture. If you saw a man with an overcoat he was a replacement from the rear. For several days one man stayed awake in each foxhole night and day – two hours up, two hours down. We tried to sleep in the day time. You needed someone with you in your hole just to get body heat.

One of the worst assignments was night patrols, mostly to bring back prisoners. Not all these were successful, but one night about twenty of us went out with Lieutenant Joe Kagen and we did capture one. He was in an outpost and we almost fell into his hole. I don't think that he was going to give the alarm or maybe he was asleep. He was about as scared as I would have been. When we got him back he was giving out more than just his name, rank and serial number. One of the prettiest sights we observed from the Elsenborn Ridge position was late on the 23rd and again on the 24th December. The weather had cleared and it looked like all the Allied air force came out. The sky was filled with planes and there were vapour trails all over. Some P-38s and Mustangs strafed the German lines down below us. This was the first help we had from our air force since the Bulge started, but there had been German planes out strafing us several times.

Christmas 1944 was just another day. We were cold and hungry just like all the days. We had K Rations for breakfast, C Rations for lunch. After dark the cooks sent down canisters of turkey and all the trimmings (cold); we ate it all anyway.

The last attack we had on Elsenborn Ridge came early on the 28th of December. I was in our outpost with Lloyd Peterson. As usual we had fog. When the fog lifted just a little I could see German troops going up the draw to my left front. They had full packs, some horse-drawn equipment, they looked and acted like they were not told we were holding this position – they looked like they were going on a field trip. I fired into them and about the same time our artillery unleashed a heavy barrage on them. We must have had a forward observer call in about the same time as I spotted them. A few of the Germans got close enough to get in a fire fight but they soon withdrew. This fight was mainly an artillery battle. The Germans had a bad day, they were just slaughtered. That night you could hear the wounded calling for water – for their mothers – I'm sure many of the wounded froze to death that night.'

'Nuts!' The defence of Bastogne

Like St-Vith, Bastogne was another important road communications centre which the Germans were determined to capture. Being some distance farther west and thus deeper into the Ardennes than St-Vith, it was an ideal 'hub' from which a number of routes would bring them to the Meuse. Equally, if it were not captured it would provide the Allies with an ideal base from which to mount a counter-offensive. One of the major pluses which had resulted from

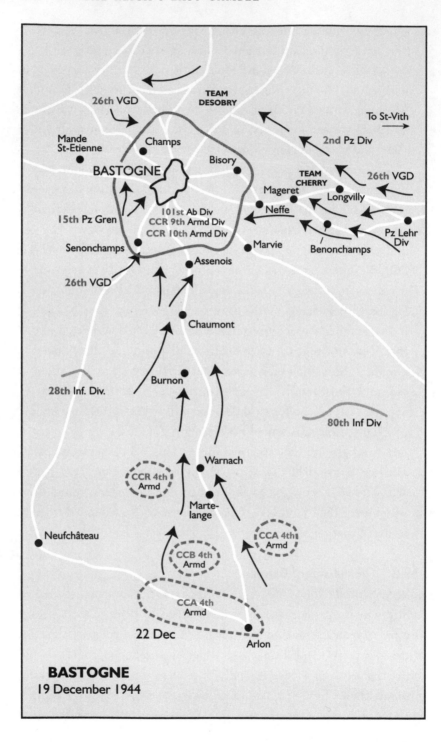

26th VGD

TEAM DESOBRY

To St-Vith

Mande St-Etienne

Champs

BASTOGNE

Bisory

2nd Pz Div

26th VGD

TEAM CHERRY

Mageret

Longvilly

Neffe

15th Pz Gren

101st Ab Div
CCR 9th Armd Div
CCR 10th Armd Div

Pz Lehr Div

Senonchamps

Marvie

Benonchamps

26th VGD

Assenois

Chaumont

28th Inf. Div.

Burnon

80th Inf Div

Warnach

CCR 4th Armd

Martelange

Neufchâteau

CCA 4th Armd

CCB 4th Armd

CCA 4th Armd

22 Dec

Arlon

BASTOGNE
19 December 1944

the spirited defence of St-Vith had been, as we have seen, the buying of time, thus enabling American troop movement and other remedial action to take place. As far as Bastogne was concerned, this consisted of the moving in of 101st Airborne Division ('The Screaming Eagles', so-called after their distinctive insignia of white eagle's head with black eyes, yellow beak and red tongue, facing left in a black shield under a black flash with AIRBORNE inscribed in yellow). Like the 82nd, the 101st had been resting at Reims, after the Arnhem operation. They arrived in Bastogne by road[10] on 19 December and had established defensive lines by the following day. It is worth noting that the organisation of the 101st was ideally suited to all-round defence, there being four infantry regiments: 501st, 502nd, 506th Para Inf Regts, 327th Glider Inf Regt. Smaller than the normal infantry division (11,640 all ranks instead of 14,253), it still had three battalions of field artillery (but armed with the 75mm pack howitzer) plus one battalion of 105mm howitzers in place of medium artillery. In addition there was an AA battalion, engineer battalion, medical company and the usual ancillary services. The division was under the command of Brigadier General Anthony C. McAuliffe, artillery commander of the 101st, because the divisional commander, Major General Maxwell D. Taylor, was in the USA. McAuliffe's orders from General Middleton, given on the morning of 19 December before he left the town for his new HQ at Neufchâteau, were clear and precise: 'Hold Bastogne!'

The other major unit which McAuliffe would have for the defence of Bastogne was CCB of 10th Armored Division under the command of Colonel William Roberts, which had arrived in Bastogne on the 18th, ahead of the Paratroopers. Middleton had immediately ordered CCB to put out three combat teams to cover the most likely routes into Bastogne from the east: Combat Team O'Hara (30 tanks and 500 men under Lieutenant Colonel James O'Hara), which was sent to Wardin (ESE of Bastogne) with orders to hold it at all costs; CT Cherry (Lieutenant Colonel Henry T. Cherry), sent out along the Longvilly road that evening to bolster the remnant of 9th Armd Div's CCR, which were already out to the east and had been becoming more and more vulnerable; CT Desroby (Major William R. Desroby) which was sent NE to Noville. All would quickly find themselves heavily engaged by the rapidly advancing German forces of von Lüttwitz's XLVII Panzer Corps which was now busy surrounding and isolating Bastogne. CCB would lose a fair amount of its tank strength during these early, confused battles, but some of this loss would be made up from remnants of other units, such as what was left of 9th Armd's CCR when they managed to straggle back into the town. Mobile anti-tank support would come from the thirty-six SP tank destroyers of 705th TD Bn (Lieutenant Colonel Clifford Templeton) which arrived in Bastogne on the night of the 19th. They were equipped with the latest American tank destroyer, the M18 GMC Hellcat, which mounted the new and highly effective M1A1C 76mm gun – one of the finest TDs of any nation in WWII. As far as artillery was concerned, the defenders had three additional armoured field artillery battalions all equipped with 155mm medium howitzers: 755th Armd Field Arty Bn (Lieutenant Colonel William F. Hartman), 969th Armd Field Arty Bn (Lieutenant Colonel Hubert D. Barnes), both of which had been originally assigned to other formations; together with 420th Armd Field Arty Bn they would form a group capable of firing (from the west) around the whole of the Bastogne perimeter, which must have gladdened the heart of Brigadier General McAuliffe, who had been 101st's artillery commander. In all there were some 130 artillery pieces of all types ready and able to provide support just as long as the ammunition held out.

McAuliffe went to see General Middleton in the evening of 20 December. He was very upbeat and said that he was confident that he could hold out for at least 48 hours if he were to be completely cut off. No doubt his corps commander briefed him upon what future developments had been passed down, resulting from General Eisenhower's meeting at Verdun on the 19th, namely that US Third Army was already engaged in turning through 90 degrees and that 'Georgie's Boys' would soon be riding to the rescue![11] McAuliffe returned to Bastogne and just managed to get there before the Germans cut the road behind him and isolated the town.

The Germans attack

As we have already seen, not all the German forces approaching the Bastogne area were in fact aiming to attack the town. The 2nd Panzer Division was more interested in reaching the Meuse, so was seeking to bypass Bastogne, but unexpectedly its advance guard made contact with part of 10th Armd CCB at Noville (CT Desroby) and with other elements of the CCB (and CCR), between Noville and Longvilly. On the left, Panzer Lehr Division captured Mageret during the night of 18/19 December, then at first light began attacks towards the centre of Bastogne and against the American outposts. Following behind the panzers were two regiments of 26th VGD, whose panzer grenadiers had somehow managed to keep pace with the tanks but were now exhausted, with their immediate resupply columns well to the rear. Of necessity there would have to be a pause before they were ready for further effective action – and in any case, a considerable amount of planning and co-ordination had to take place. This pause lasted for two days, 21–22 December, while the Germans 'closed the ring' and prepared for an all-out assault. However, it should not be thought that even at the beginning of the siege, the US airborne troops and their armoured support conducted anything other than an aggressive defence, inflicting heavy casualties and convincing such experienced commanders as General Fritz Bayerlein of Panzer Lehr that he was up against far stronger opposition than was actually present. The breathing-space also allowed McAuliffe the time to meld his disparate garrison into a far more cohesive force. In addition, of course, it gave time for the forces concerned in the relief plan to begin their approach.

Fourth Armored is on the way

'For me, memories of Bastogne begin at dusk on 18 December 1944 as I stood beside the road in front of the house which sheltered the Command Post of Combat Command A of 4th Armored Division.' That is how Brigadier General Hal C. Pattison, who was then the executive officer of CCA, recalled the 'Bulge' operation. The division had been preparing for an attack eastwards to penetrate the Siegfried Line and drive north-eastwards with a view to establishing a bridgehead over the Rhine in the vicinity of Worms–Mainz–Darmstadt. They were currently in corps reserve with all their units engaged in a heavy maintenance programme, but all that was to change! He recalls:

As I stood in front of the CP that winter evening the division commander, Major General Hugh Gaffey, with his military police escort, suddenly appeared out of the dusk from the direction of Corps Headquarters. Catching sight of me he signalled for me to come to the road where he stopped long enough to say, 'Pat, we have a change of orders. You will be ready move early tomorrow. Send an LO to Division and we will get him back to you with your instructions before midnight.' For the past 48 hours we had been hearing of a German offensive in the north of us and had disquieting news only that day about the success the Germans were having along with rumours of new, highly effective weapons they were employing. As a consequence, it took no great imagination to guess we were being shifted north to help deal with the situation there. But the magnitude of the whole thing was, at that moment, beyond our expectations. When, around 2300 hrs, our LO returned with orders we were not much enlightened. Essentially, we knew that we were to move north to the vicinity of Longwy in Belgium. We were to move at 0900 on the 19th (CCB which was located to the north of us was to move at midnight), on a route that took us north-west past Metz and across the flooded Moselle. We would receive further instructions en route. We moved on schedule and, shortly before dark, somewhere south-east of Longwy, we were met by a messenger from Division with instructions to bivouac for the night and were given a 'goose egg' (the sign on a map to denote the location and extent of an assembly area/leaguer/harbour/hide) to use. We went into an assembly area around a farm and got busy servicing the vehicles and feeding the troops. Within an hour we were told that we had stopped prematurely and were ordered to move at once to Longwy. En route we were again met with destination orders and a 'goose egg' for our assembly area around a village to the north-east of Arlon. We arrived at the designated area well before daylight on the 20th and established ourselves in the local schoolhouse, but soon had instructions to move again – this time to a village a few miles north of Arlon on the Bastogne highway. By noon we were in place and had established a screen in the north on what turned out to be our line of departure for the advance on the 22nd.

The march itself holds some vivid memories. A sense of apprehension resulting from the dearth of information coupled with the knowledge that such a move could mean a real emergency existed. Pride in the businesslike professional conduct of the troops during what was turning out to be an epic shifting of direction for a field army; columns of troops were moving north, others east and still other logistic units were moving west as we got nearer Luxembourg. The columns were crossing each other at road junctions with never a pause by either crossing column; MP control so perfect that vehicles of crossing columns passed through the intervals of the other with the precision of trained horsemen in a dressage in the riding hall. Exasperation as to the seeming confusion as to destination and assembly area. The murmur and beat of artillery fire and the lightning-like shimmer of the flashes on the northern horizon as we drew nearer to Arlon – the necessity to discipline the imagination as to the meaning of it all. The relief of getting to our destination and getting some 'good information' as to the situation. As I look back with the realisation of the magnitude of the troop movement, the speed with which it was arranged and carried out and the efficiency of it all, I cannot help but be proud to have been a part of one of the great military operations of history. From our standpoint at the time we were chagrined at the number of combat vehicles which we lost on the march for it meant we would be going into action brutally short of firepower. The ordnance people, however, did Herculean work in getting the cripples back to us. Most of them had joined their units before the final relief of Bastogne took place on the 26th.

Twenty-first December was taken up seeking information and getting ready for the attack which was to take place at dawn on the 22nd. Our column was to attack north on the Arlon–Bastogne highway and the other, CCB, to the west of us. The mission was of course to relieve 101st Airborne Division in Bastogne. Our advance got off on schedule in a heavy snowstorm which fortunately stopped by mid-morning. We soon began to pick up stragglers from units which had been overrun in the early momentum of the German attack. All were wet, hungry and cold, some were wounded and many were without weapons. It was heartening to hear most of them ask to join us and fight again, but the several hundred we recovered that day were sent to the rear for a rest, dry clothes and food and eventual return to their own units. By mid-afternoon we had reached Martelange where Corps engineers had destroyed the bridge as part of the barrier plan. This was to hold us up for more than 24 hours. The current in the Sure River and the gorge through which it ran, made a treadway bridge out of the question, so the engineers constructed a Bailey bridge about ninety feet in length. The operation was hampered by freezing rain which had begun and by a company of German Paratroopers, but during the day of the 23rd we got a company of armored infantry across and secured the far bank of the river. Once across, early on the 24th, we expected to make rapid progress towards Bastogne, but the regimental headquarters of the 5th Parachute Division was located in Warnach and it took nearly 24 hours of nip and tuck to drive the Germans out of a warm village into the cold. General Patton had told us to attack all day and all night and not to stop until we got to Bastogne, but the Germans dictated otherwise. We had to call off the attack about midnight for lack of infantry, and regroup. In any case tanks can't keep going on courage alone – they need gas. Early on Christmas Day we did drive the Germans out and continued to advance to the next hard nut – Tintange – which was cleared on Christmas Day. On the 26th we advanced another five or six miles and captured Hollange after another hard fight with a battalion-sized defence force.

Meanwhile our companion CCB had fairly fast going until it hit Chaumont where it suffered heavily from anti-tank fire with the result that its tank battalion was close to non-effective for a 24-hour period. To bolster the attack, Division, on Christmas Eve, moved the Reserve Command (CCR) from the right flank where it had been committed on the 23rd, on a 60-mile march around the left flank to attack north-east towards Bastogne. Late on the 26th elements of the 37th Tank Battalion, commanded by Creighton Abrams, the greatest of several great soldiers in 4th Armored,[12] broke through on the Assenois road to enter Bastogne. By the evening of the 28th, CCA had cleared the length of the Arlon–Bastogne highway and elements of the 35th Division had moved up to hold the shoulder. Access to Bastogne was secure.[13]

First into Bastogne

As Brigadier General Pattison explained in his reminiscences, it was the 37th Tank Battalion that was leading in the final run into Bastogne. Here is how the privately published Divisional history tells of the last dramatic moments.

The final assault was launched from the far edge of Assenois, the last village before Bastogne. In the lead was Company C of the 37th Tank Battalion, followed by Company C of the 53rd Armored Infantry Battalion. Lieutenant Colonel Creighton W. Abrams, then commander of the 37th Tank Battalion, clinched a cold cigar in the corner of his mouth and said, 'We're going in to those people now.' With that, he swept his arm forward and the charge was on. The command tank of Company C, 37th Tank Battalion, moved out first. In the turret was First Lieutenant Charles Boggess, Jr. 'The Germans had these two little towns of Clichmont and Assenois on the secondary road we were using to get to Bastogne,' he recalled later. 'Beyond Assenois the road ran up a ridge through heavy woods. There were lots of Germans there too. We were going through fast, all guns firing, straight up that road to burst through before they had time to get set. I thought of a lot of things as we got set. I thought of whether the road was mined, whether the bridge at Assenois would be blown, whether they would be ready at their anti-tank guns. Then we charged and I didn't have time to wonder!' Meanwhile, four American artillery battalions were slamming barrages into enemy-held Assenois and the woods beyond it. The 22nd, 66th and 94th Armored Artillery Battalions dropped in 105mm shells and a supporting battalion lobbed 155mm howitzer rounds. Under the artillery support, Lieutenant Boggess' medium tanks advanced through shell bursts to the enemy positions. The ground pitched, and houses spilled into the street, but the undaunted American force kept going. 'I used the 75mm like a machine gun,' said Boggess' gunner, Corporal Milton Dickerman. 'Murphy (Private James, the loader) was plenty busy throwing in the shells. We shot 21 rounds in a few minutes and I don't know how much machine gun stuff. As we got to Assenois an anti-tank gun in a halftrack fired at us. The shell hit the road in front of the tank and threw dirt all over. I got the halftrack in my sights and hit it with high explosive. It blew up.' Dirt from the enemy shell burst had smeared the driver's periscope. 'I made out OK, although I couldn't see very good,' explained the driver, Private Hubert Smith. 'I sort of guessed the road. I had a little trouble when my left brake locked and the tank turned up a road we didn't want to go. So I stopped her, backed her up and went on again.'

The armored infantry were also in the thick of the fighting and one of the infantrymen distinguished himself gallantly enough to become the third Congressional Medal of Honor winner in the 4th Armored Division. He was Private James Hendrix, a 19-year-old rifleman with Company C, 53rd Armored Infantry Battalion. His citation read: 'Private Hendrix dismounted and advanced upon two 88mm gun crews, and by the ferocity of his action compelled the German gun crews, first to take cover and then to surrender.' Hendrix, a red-haired,

freckle-faced farm boy from Arkansas, later explained: 'we ran
up to them yelling "come out!" but they wouldn't. One poked
his head out of a foxhole and I shot him through the neck. I got
closer and hit another on the head with the butt of my M-1. He
had American matches on him. The others came out then with
their hands up.' The citation continues: 'Later in the attack this
fearless soldier again left his vehicle voluntarily to aid two
wounded soldiers threatened by an enemy machine gun. Effectively silencing two enemy machine guns, he held off the enemy
by his own fire until the wounded men were evacuated. "I just
shot at the machine guns like all the 50s on the halftracks were
doing," Hendrix said. "A halftrack had been hit pretty bad and
these fellows were wounded and lying in a ditch. Machine gun
fire was mostly towards them, but some bullets were coming my
way." Continuing the attack, Hendrix again endangered himself
when he ran to aid still another soldier who was trapped in a
burning halftrack. Braving enemy sniper fire and exploding
mines and ammunition in the vehicle, he pulled the wounded
man from the conflagration and extinguished his flaming
clothing with his body. Hendrix explained it so: "Grenade
exploded between his legs and everybody got out, but he was
hollering for help. I pulled at him and got him out on the road,
but he was burned bad. I tried to find water to put out the fire,
but the water cans were full of bullet holes, so I beat out the
flames as best I could. He died later."

The four lead tanks in Boggess' column drew ahead as the halftracks were slowed by German shells and debris. The tankers
rolled along, sweeping the wooded ridge with machine gun fire.
Finally they burst through the German defences and into the
101st Airborne perimeter. Lieutenant Boggess ordered the roaring
Sherman tank down to a crawl. In the open fields beyond the
pines he saw red, yellow and blue supply parachutes spilled over
the snow like confetti. Some of the colored chutes, caught in the
tall pines, indicated where ammunition, food and medical
supplies had been dropped to the besieged troops. The column

halted. standing up in his turret, Lieutenant Boggess shouted: 'Come here, come on out!' to khaki-clad figures in foxholes. 'This is the Fourth Armored!'

There was no answer. Helmeted heads peered suspiciously over carbine sights. The lieutenant shouted again. A lone figure strode forward. Lieutenant Boggess watched him carefully. 'I'm Lieutenant Webster of the 326th Engineers, 101st Airborne Division,' the approaching figure called. 'Glad to see you!' The time was 4.45 p.m., 26 December.[14]

Nuts!

While 4th Armored Division were just beginning their epic advance from Arlon, there was an incident in Bastogne which has become the stuff of legends. At about 1130 hrs on the 22nd, a party of four Germans (a major, a captain and two soldiers), bearing a white flag, drove up the road towards the forward positions of 2nd Batt 327th Glider Regt at Marvie. They were carrying a written demand which read:

> To the USA Commander of the encircled town of Bastogne. The fortune of war is changing. This time the US forces in and near Bastogne have been encircled by strong German armoured units ... There is only one possibility to save the encircled US troops from total annihilation: that is the honourable surrender of the encircled town ... If this proposal should be rejected, one German Artillery Corps and six heavy AA Battalions are ready to annihilate the US troops in and near Bastogne ... All serious civilian losses caused by artillery fire would not correspond with the well-known American humanity.
>
> The German Commander.[15]

In a broadcast (now on tape in the IWM Sound Archive[16]) General McAuliffe said that they had thought that the surrender demand, which the German commander had: '... the effrontery to send' was the funniest thing they had ever heard, hence his one word reply 'Nuts'. However, the German major who had brought the demand wanted a formal answer, so he decided that he would still just say nuts, but have it properly written out:

'To the German Commander:
 Nuts!
                    The American Commander.'

Colonel Joseph Harper, CO of the 327th had great pleasure in delivering this note to the waiting German party; they had been kept, suitably blindfolded, at the forward CP of his F Company. Having read it, the Germans appeared puzzled; clearly they had expected the Americans to surrender, so Harper had to explain that the one-word reply definitely meant exactly the opposite! He further told them that if they did attack they would have tremendous losses, then putting them in the back of his Jeep, took them to the outskirts of his positions and, somewhat incongruously, wished them good luck before they departed.

Air Support
In his post-siege radio broadcast McAuliffe also paid tribute both to the offensive air support and to the air supply which the garrison received once the weather had cleared on the third day of the siege. He had special praise for the ground to air liaison officer: Captain 'Maestro' Parker, who talked the Thunderbolt ground-attack fighters onto their targets brilliantly, using 'salty' language – he became such a hit with the troops that they would crowd around him just to listen, until he had to be 'roped off'! The troop-carrying command aircraft which delivered all the ammunition, food and supplies that were needed, also earned his commendation. On the first day alone US Ninth Air Force B-26 Marauder bombers and P-38 Lightnings and P-47 Thunderbolts flew nearly 1,300 attack sorties, one observer likening them to 'shoals of silver minnows in the bright winter sun'. In addition on that first day, 241 transport aircraft dropped their loads to the garrison – 95 per cent of which were recovered. Although the German AA was ready and waiting on

the days that followed, the pilots took no evasive action, but flew straight into the flak so that they could continue to drop accurately, despite taking heavy casualties. The air activity was not all one sided; the Luftwaffe mounted two separate heavy air attacks on Christmas Eve, which resulted in considerable damage to the town and some casualties.

The assault continues

The knowledge that US 4th Armored Division was advancing did not dissuade the Germans from continuing the pressure, For example, before daylight on Christmas Day, 15th Panzer Grenadier Division's 115th Battle Group, which had been attached to 26th VGD for only a couple of days,[17] went in to the attack at Champs (NW of Bastogne). They were banking on the Americans being so occupied with celebrating Christmas morning, that they would be able to break into the town before the dreaded *Jabos* could appear. However, their commander, Oberst Wolfgang Maucke, had not from the outset had his heart in his task, having protested that he had been given no time for reconnaissance or marrying up with the eighteen tanks and two SP artillery battalions which were to support his two panzer grenadier battalions. The attack got to within a mile of the centre of the town, but then petered out, being repulsed by men of 502nd Parachute Infantry and some tank destroyers, the Germans having to withdraw in some confusion. The CO of the 502nd, Lieutenant Colonel Steve Chapuis, was awarded the DSC for his heroism during the action. The Germans would never get any closer and when Lieutenant Boggess and his leading tanks arrived at 1645 hrs on the 26th, the siege was over and the Americans had won a remarkable victory.

The Battered Bastards

For his tenacity Brigadier General McAuliffe was awarded a well-deserved DSC, which was pinned on by Third Army's commander, General George S, Patton, Jr., in Bastogne on the 28th. The modest airborne commander commented on the wonderfully high morale of his troops, explaining how a wounded Paratrooper he was talking to had told him that they all now called themselves 'The Battered Bastards' [he said 'blighters' on the radio so as not offend anyone!] of the Bastion of Bastogne. 'No one should be surprised with what was achieved by the men of the 101st at Bastogne,' said McAuliffe. 'That is just what should be expected anytime of airborne troops. With the kind of troops I had, a commander can do anything.'

The end of the beginning

By Christmas 1944 it is fair to say that 'Wacht am Rhein' had reached the limits of its success. There was still plenty of power and fight left in the three panzer armies, but they had just about shot their bolt. They were running short of fuel, ammunition and supplies, which made the tasks imposed by the Führer even more impossible to achieve, and the clearing weather left them at the mercy of the Allied air power. They had captured the important road centre of St-Vith, but it had taken them far longer than anticipated; they had besieged the other important road hub, Bastogne, but had not managed to take it. Now the siege had been broken. They had almost reached the River Meuse, their first major objective on the way to Brussels and Antwerp – but not quite! Even their most powerful battle group had been thwarted, had acknowledged defeat and turned for home. In nearly every location they had been beaten by the sheer guts and determination of the average American GI, many of whom were 'green' in this their first time in battle; many of whom were scared stiff from having tasted both the actual horrors of war (as well as the imagined ones); some had run in panic westwards, but others had tried to get eastwards to deal with the enemy break-throughs. However, the shambles which the Germans' unexpected assault had created in the Ardennes was rapidly becoming a thing of the past, as the Allies got to grips with the situation and began taking proper remedial action. General Patton's Third Army, in a miracle of co-ordination, control and organisation, had turned 90 degrees and, after a difficult advance, had relieved Bastogne. Now it was the Germans who had to be worried about being outflanked and cut off, as 'Georgie's Boys' prepared to lay into them. In the north, Montgomery's 21st Army Group, now with two US armies under command, had 'tidied up' the front and was ensuring that the enemy would never be able to 'bounce' crossings over the Meuse.

And yet, as we shall see, Hitler had yet another ace up his sleeve and was about to play it.

Notes

1 Summersby, Kay. *Eisenhower Was My Boss.*
2 Captain Earnest 'Tex' Lee was one of Eisenhower's personal aides.
3 Quoted from: *WW II German Military Studies*, OKW War Diary Series, Part IV.
4 Unlike the Allies, the German Army still relied on horses for pulling a considerable proportion of their supply wagons and artillery limbers. While this had some advantages on the steppes of Russia, it made life extremely difficult for them on the Western Front.
5 Hamilton, Nigel. *Monty.*
6 As quoted in *The Bitter Woods*. Eisenhower would award a Presidential citation to all members of the St-Vith garrison.
7 Neither Hasbrouck nor Clarke thought much of the plan; Clarke dubbed it Custer's Last Stand!
8 Cole, Hugh M. *The Ardennes: Battle of the Bulge.*
9 As quoted in *Tank Aces from Blitzkrieg to the Gulf War.*
10 The division had hardly any organic transport because it was normally flown into battle, so sufficient vehicles had to be provided to move them into Belgium.
11 After the battle, the stocky, taciturn McAuliffe said that he had been 'surprised' to hear that they were having to be 'rescued by 4th Armored Division'. In fact he really resented the implication that they needed to be rescued at all! He said that the 101st were in fine shape, that they had given the Germans a licking and were ready to attack straight away!
12 Lieutenant Colonel (later General) 'Abe' Abrams was a capable, brave and inspiring commander, who post-war rose to become Chief of Staff of the US Army. General Patton said of him: 'I am supposed to be the best tank commander in the Army, but I have one peer – Abe Abrams.'
13 As quoted in Forty, George. *Patton's Third Army at War.*
14 Ibid.
15 As quoted in *The Bitter Woods*.
16 IWM Sound Archive, tape 1922/I/c.
17 On 23 December Hitler had agreed to release two fresh divisions (9th Panzer and 15th Panzer Grenadier), but Model decided that they were more needed to bolster up the left flank of Fifth Panzer Army and Seventh Army, than to be used in the assault on Bastogne, so all that was allocated to the siege was the one regimental combat team.

9
FLANK ACTIONS

The battles for Elsenborn Ridge, St-Vith, Bastogne and all the rest which formed the major part of the German Ardennes offensive was not all that was taking place on the Western Front during December 1944 and January 1945, and it is relevant to break off from the main action and to look at what was happening on the flanks and to the rear of the Ardennes. To the north, British Second Army had inevitably become involved, both in its own right and because 21st Army Group now included two US Armies (First and Ninth) under the temporary command of its commander Field Marshal Montgomery. The activities of US First and Ninth Army units have been and will be dealt with later, but here is the place to cover those of British XXX Corps. Their operations against the enemy, although not anywhere near on the same scale as those which were taking place in the Ardennes proper, were just as vital, because when they were moved down behind the Ardennes, along the Meuse, they prevented the panzers from bouncing bridges over the river and ever gaining a foothold on the western bank. This meant that the Germans could not achieve Hitler's aims of splitting the Allied forces and of reaching Brussels and Antwerp.

Also, below the Ardennes in 6th Army Group's sector, there were going to be more unwelcome surprises for the hard-pressed Allies, designed deliberately to take their eyes off the ball at a critical time.

Towards the Meuse
Despite the threat from US Third Army's thrust to relieve Bastogne, which clearly worried Model, von Rundstedt refused to be dissuaded from pressing on towards the Meuse. He was convinced that the Allies could not assemble a sufficiently strong force to defend the river line before 30 December, so the panzers had a week in which to cover the

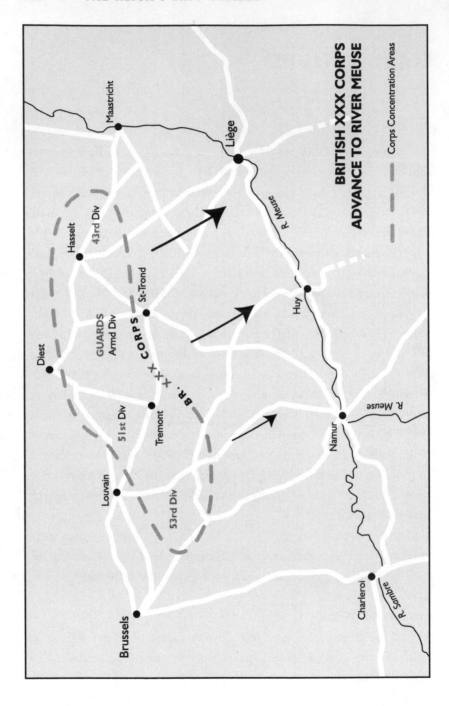

BRITISH XXX CORPS
ADVANCE TO RIVER MEUSE

- - - Corps Concentration Areas

Maastricht

Liège

R. Meuse

43rd Div

Hasselt

St-Trond

Huy

GUARDS
Armd Div

CORPS

Diest

BR. XXX

51st Div

Tremont

R. Meuse

Namur

Louvain

53rd Div

Charleroi

R. Sambre

Brussels

remaining six miles to the river. What he had not realised was that as early as 19 December Montgomery had called a halt to the intended 21st Army Group concentration for the coming Rhineland battle and had put into effect plans to switch British divisions from the Geilenkirchen sector to the west of the Meuse, in order to counter any threat to 21st Army Group's southern flank. The 43rd Infantry and Guards Armoured Divisions were moved westwards from south-east of Maeseyck, while the Welsh 53rd Infantry Division was moved from Roermond to Turnhout. XXX Corps was ordered to assemble in the area Louvain–St-Trond and put in command of the three divisions already mentioned, together with 51st Highland Division and three independent armoured brigades. Monty also took the precaution of getting reconnaissance troops down to the line of the river as quickly as possible, to give immediate cover to the bridges between Liège and Givet. These included SAS troops and even tank replacement personnel, while the armoured regiments of 29th Armoured Brigade, which had been in the process of re-equipping with new British Comet tanks in western Belgium, were ordered to re-draw their old Shermans and get to the Namur area as quickly as possible.

Maxwell Nicholson was a member of Recce Troop, 3 RTR, which had been withdrawn to Poperinghe for the re-equipping of their tank troops with the new British Comet tank, to replace their almost worn out Shermans with which they had fought across France and the Low Countries. His Recce Troop would, however, keep their light American General Stuart 'Honey' tanks. He recalls:

Familiarisation and testing of the new tank in very muddy condi-tions was proceeding apace, when Model's Ardennes offensive broke like a thunder-clap. It was 16 December. The battle seemed to develop slowly at first, and there was a shortage of hard news, in consequence the Americans were slow to realise the seriousness of the situation. Montgomery took command of the northern part of the Ardennes operation on 20 December and 3 RTR was re-activated, moving swiftly back to Brussels to pick up its Sher-mans, while Recce Troop moved with all speed from Poperinghe to the Meuse with its Honeys. Passing through Brussels and the Belgian countryside was like passing through a morgue. The overwhelming atmosphere was of deep gloom and fear, even terror. The streets were foreboding, empty and dark.

Recce Troop arrived at Dinant on the Meuse on the evening of 22 December and took up positions guarding the railway bridge. There were US engineers in position on both the railway and road bridges, and they were presumably ready to blow them. They were very trigger-happy. On the 23rd the Shermans started to arrive and we moved into Dinant itself, put a block on the bridge and established an infantry bridgehead on the other side. On the 24th the Germans announced their presence by shelling the town from the high ground to the east (with showers of impressive shrapnel sparks off the granite road surface) and during the night of the 23rd there was an attempt by Skorzeny's Kommandos to send a flying column of troops dressed as Americans in American Jeeps to seize the Dinant bridges, which was very effectively dealt with by the infantry with necklace mines and Bren fire.

Recce Troop was briefed on Christmas Eve by the Colonel to probe eastwards from Dinant at first light towards the high ground, to establish the whereabouts of the German *Schwerpunkt*. Christmas Day dawned, a dark and misty morning, and as we were pushing out from Dinant up onto the high ground we were soon being passed by panic-stricken Americans fleeing in Jeeps and every other form of transport, carrying many wounded and racing to the rear. They were quite difficult to stop for interrogation and the information gained was not very precise – e.g., 'Dodged through a column of tanks!' We pressed on up the road cautiously and were at one point alarmed to hear very heavy tracks coming towards us. Surely this must be a Tiger! We reversed around a corner and went back to look on foot, but to our relief we saw only a vast caterpillar tractor driven by a very large cigar-smoking black GI!

By this time we were on high ground on the main road overlooking a valley, about 10 kilometres east of Dinant. The fog

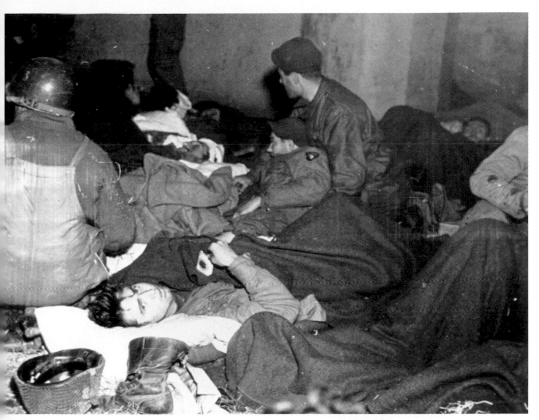

Above: Wounded men of the Bastogne garrison in an improvised emergency ward, 27 December 1944. (US Army)

Below: Armoured vehicles of 4th Armored Division move past the bodies of dead GIs who were killed in the effort to relieve Bastogne, 25 December 1944. (US Army)

Above: Troops of 101st Airborne Division move out of Bastogne to take the battle to the enemy, despite the siege! 29 December 1944. (US Army)

Below: Men of 2nd Battalion, 325th Glider Regiment, 82nd Airborne Division, move up through heavy fog, 30 December 1944. (US Army)

Above: Infantrymen of 10th Armored Infantry Regiment, 4th Armored Division, engage the enemy on their way to relieve Bastogne. They are wearing the special armoured force winter uniform. (US Army)

Bottom left: Dugouts built into a bank near Vaux Chavanne protected men of 82nd Airborne Division from enemy artillery fire – and winter blasts! (US Army)

Below: The battered town of Stavelot in the Amblève valley, as seen from US 30th Infantry Division's positions to the west. The town was occupied by 18th VGD. (US Army)

Above: On the lookout for German snipers, GIs of US Third Army move cautiously through the streets of Moircy, Belgium, 31 December 1944. (US Army)

Below: Tanks and infantry of US 84th Infantry Division en route to Samrée and La Roche, Belgium, 10 January 1944. (US Army)

Right: An excellent photograph of American troops of 83rd Infantry Division in the centre of Bihain, on their way to attack a German position, 11 January 1945. (US Army)

Opposite page, below: Pfc Frank Vukasin of C Coy, 331 Inf Regt, 83rd Inf Div, reloading his rifle at Houffalize, with dead Germans in the snow. (US Army)

Above: A Bazooka team of US First Army's 3rd Armored Division, waiting for the enemy at the edge of a forest clearing, 14 January 1945. (US Army)

Below: Men of a combat patrol from 23rd Infantry Regiment, 2nd Infantry Division, hug the ground to escape enemy fire, near Ondenval, Belgium, 16 January 1945. (US Army)

Above: Major General Maxwell D. Taylor, CG 101st Airborne Division, hands over control of Bastogne to Major General Troy Middleton, CG VIII Corps, on 18 January 1945. (US Army)

Below: Houffalize, 18 January 1945, two days after the linking there between First and Third Armies. (US Army)

7th Armored Division tanks at St-Vith. (US Army)

Above: Tank crews having a coffee break in the snow. Note the right hand man wears a composition crash helmet and goggles – he is probably the tank driver. (US Army)

Below: Men of 317th Infantry Regiment, 80th Infantry Division, stop for chow in Bockholz, Luxembourg, 27 January 1945. (US Army)

Right: Tanks of 740th Tank Battalion, with troops of 82nd Airborne Division on their back decks, push on through thick snow towards Herresbach, Belgium. (US Army)

Below: Lieutenant Colonel 'Abe' Abrams (centre) and Lieutenant Colonel Harold Cohen (Patton Museum)

Left: Lieutenant General Alexander M. Patch, Jr., CG US Seventh Army, congratulates 36th Infantry Division's 2nd Lieutenant Stephen R. Gregg of Bayonne, New Jersey, having just presented him with the Medal of Honor. (US Army)

Below: Infantrymen of US Seventh Army on patrol in the forest of Dominale, south of Bitche, 15 January 1945. (US Army)

Above: Combat engineers of US 36th Infantry Division sit around a small blowtorch, heating up their coffee! 27 January 1945. (US Army)

Below: Men of a signals team from 3rd Algerian Infantry Division, complete with wire-laden mule, in the foothills of the Vosges Mountains. (IWM–EA 432953)

Above: Gun cleaning in progress on a British-manned Sherman. 3 RTR had hurriedly to redraw their old Shermans which they had just handed in for exchange when the 'Bulge' flap blew up suddenly. (Author's collection)

Below: Shermans of 29 Armoured Brigade on the edge of a forest near the Meuse. (Tank Museum)

Above: The end of the 'Bulge'. A column of German prisoners passing a US Third Army tank. (US Army)

Below right: 'German spearhead halted' was the original caption given to this evocative photograph of a frost-bound German 88mm gun, probably the most feared anti-tank gun of the war, now abandoned to the elements in a forest in the Ardennes. (Author's Collection)

Left: Captured Germans (probably Grief commandos) in Allied uniforms could well be shot as spies (IWM–PL 68548)

Below: Sign at the Celles cross-roads in the Ardennes. (L. Brooksby)

BATTLE OF THE BULGE

A CELLES, en décembre 1944, lors de la Bataille des Ardennes, l' avance allemande fut définitivement stoppée grâce à l' assaut victorieux de la 2nd Armored Division US et du 3th Royal Tank Regiment UK

was worse now, but we could hear suspicious sounds from below. The CO therefore brought up the tank squadrons and our more lightly armoured Honeys were pulled back. It was now late morning and the fog and mist started to clear. Gradually the picture unfolded in the valley below where German troops were having their breakfast, with infantry carriers and other vehicles. There was mutual recognition and the Shermans took cover and opened fire. There was complete panic among the enemy, who were racing to their vehicles and endeavouring to return fire at the same time. They extricated themselves but sustained casualties. The Regiment was unable to pursue because there was no way down into the steep valley, but later on, at about 2 p.m., an American task force appeared below and pursued the enemy, firing constantly with all weapons – the noise gradually fading into the distance until an uneasy quiet descended on the scene. This was not the very best Christmas Day I have ever experienced!

However, had we NOT been at Dinant, I am sure the Germans could have captured the Dinant bridges and made an effort to penetrate towards Brussels – it would have caused a panic not seen since the days of the Benghazi Harriers!

The Third then spent some considerable time occupying a blocking position at the west end of the Ardennes salient. Arctic weather descended and the Shermans were unable to move on the icy roads and unable to move off them because of the soft ground under the snow. The Honeys, with rubber track pads, were able to run on ice, so that the whole task of patrolling and reconnoitring naturally fell on our shoulders. Each day we conducted long patrols in the extensive areas of No Man's Land. The Germans often patrolled the same areas at night and there were occasional contacts. The superior speed and manoeuvrability of the Honeys saved our skins on more than one occasion. Later, when American infantry came into the area, we moved in support. There were many frozen German dead lying about and we investigated one farm where we found an abandoned Panther tank in the farmyard. I climbed in. The radio was still running. I knew then that the German offensive was finished!

Another member of 3 RTR was Lawrence Brooksby, a tank driver, who recalls that he was just getting settled down: 'in comfortable, warm billets in Poperinghe, waiting for Christmas, when we heard some disheartening stories about FM von Rundstedt pushing the Americans back in the Ardennes, but did not think that it would have anything to do with us.' He was of course mistaken and very soon afterwards, they got orders to go back to Brussels and to pick up their old tanks. 'To my dismay', he goes on, 'I found my tank wouldn't start as the battery was flat. So we got the battery charger going, but in the meantime the other tanks were ready to go. They pulled out leaving us behind, with orders to follow on as quickly as possible.' Lawrence and his crew did so, and after an eventful, but reasonably trouble-free journey through Belgium ('we could see that the people were digging in and expecting the worst') they eventually reached Namur, then received orders to press on towards Dinant:

The road we took runs parallel with the Meuse – a nice bit of country with some nice scenery, but on the way we didn't see many people, I think they had all fled from the coming Germans. I did speak to one man who said he was very pleased to see us. We had a quiet drive, but kept our eyes open as we had no idea where the enemy was. We were now in touch with the rest of the squadron, but I don't think they knew much more as there was a general shortage of maps. There were three bridges to defend in our sector – at Namur, Dinant and Givet. The 8th Battalion of the Rifle Brigade had come up from Holland to secure these bridges, with orders that if they couldn't hold them they were to blow them up – leaving 3 RTR on the wrong side! We pushed on to the high ground and, as it started to get lighter we could see the Germans coming up the road towards us, but they were too far away for us to be certain of hitting them. However, when they got nearer we were able to knock out several trucks and halftracks and we had some casualties as well. We also had great difficulty with the severe frost and cold – some nights the tracks were frozen solid to the ground and we had to throw petrol on them, then set fire to it to free them. When we had to sleep outside the tank, we would dig a hole just deep enough and large enough to accommodate the five-man crew side by side. Then we laid down a tank cover at the bottom of the hole and covered ourselves up with all the others, put on all our clothes, balaclava helmets, etc., and cuddled together to keep warm, dreaming about our nice warm billets in Poperinghe and the girls we had left behind there. When we woke our noses were blue and we were all white and frozen!

Peter Parnwell of Dorchester was then serving in the 7th Argyll and Sutherland Highlanders in the 51st Highland Division and his memories of the Meuse battles were much the same as Maxwell and Lawrence's, but he did also write this most evocative description of life amid the snow and bleakness of the Ardennes where:

No man can live in the open more than a day or two. The temperature during the last week has not risen above 20 degrees Fahrenheit and the foot of snow has increased to about 18 inches. Regardless of being made a target by enemy artillery, our forward troops invariably set fire to any ruined building they come across, for the sake of a few minutes' warmth. The contents of our water-bottles has been frozen for ages, the tins of food in our packs are solid, socks stick to paralysed feet, and tears from our eyes freeze to our lashes. Such is the state of existence in the Ardennes battle; we fight eternally exhausted with a desperate desire to reach the next ex-habitation where a fire and perhaps some shelter may be found.

He also told me that one morning near Beaulieu, 'while ... exercising frozen limbs after a night in the open', they were disturbed to hear the noise of two tank engines coming from a minor cross-roads less then half a mile away towards the enemy. 'Two Tigers coming this way,' was the report. 'A diminutive Scotsman, who had driven the Battalion ammunition truck much of the way from Alamein, was with us, having passed beyond 'A' Echelon in error. He took a PIAT from his vehicle with just one bomb and trudged ahead through the snow. After perhaps half an hour we were wondering who could turn the ammunition truck on the narrow road with its snow-filled ditches, when the driver came back, pushed his PIAT under the canvas, turned to us with the very expressive gesture of vertically rinsing his hands, accompanied by the memorable words: "Och, tha's anither ain awa." (The 7th Argylls' war diary for 13 January 1945 records that two Panthers were located in the battalion area and that one was knocked out. It seems a pity that a fearless and independent action by a private soldier was not noted).

Allied solidarity

Monty later wrote that the Ardennes battle displayed many good examples of Allied solidarity and cites, in particular, the passage of XXX Corps across the south flank of US First Army, and its subsequent deployment into blocking positions east of the Meuse, saying that it had been 'an operation of tremendous complications achieved without serious difficulty'.

Monty re-organises

At the same time as he was organising XXX Corps to protect the Meuse bridges, Montgomery had carried out some regrouping within the US First and Ninth Armies which General Eisenhower had placed under his command on 19 December. His first priority was to halt the enemy advance and oppose it with a firm front, linking up with 12th Army Group to the south below him. This required certain regrouping and the creation of a suitable reserve within US First Army that would then be available for offensive operations. Monty chose Major General 'Lightning Joe' Collins' VII Corps for the task. There was a mutual respect on both sides, although they argued as to how the situation should be tackled. Collins quite agreed with Eisenhower's decision to put 21st Army Group in charge of the northern 'Bulge' area, saying later that: 'a dangerous front had been opened, which would have made it difficult if not impossible for Bradley to have controlled operations north of the Bulge from his Headquarters in Luxembourg.'[1] He went on to say that Monty deserved much credit for the success in driving back the enemy from the Ardennes, but that the same result could have been achieved quicker and with more casualties to the enemy, had he (Monty) acted more boldly and with more confidence in the abilities of the American troops. This was always a bone of contention between the two generals, Montgomery preferring to 'tidy up' the front by giving up real estate and establishing a proper defensive line, while Collins thought that he should have counter-attacked boldly towards St-Vith, in order to inflict maximum casualties upon the enemy – neglecting to consider of course the resulting heavy losses of American life which would have inevitably ensued in such an operation – and one can imagine how that would have been reported in the American Press.

By Christmas, the enemy offensive had been sealed off roughly along the line Elsenborn–Malmédy–Hotton–Marche–St-Hubert–Bastogne, with all routes to the Meuse securely blocked. The danger was far from over, but clearly the German offensive would now never cross the Meuse, let alone reach Brussels or Antwerp. However, more problems were about to blossom to the south.

Operation 'Nordwind' (North Wind)

And I wish to tell you something here and now gentlemen: our forces are certainly not inexhaustible. It meant taking an incredible risk to mobilise these forces for this offensive and the coming blows, a risk that on the other hand also contains the greatest dangers. ... The overall plan of the operation is clear – to liquidate the American divisions. The destruction of these American divisions must be the objective ... exterminate division by division ... Our only concern is to destroy and eradicate the enemy forces wherever we find them ... We will then fight the third battle there, and there we will knock the Americans to pieces. That must be the fanatical goal.[2]

Adolf Hitler

These extracts are taken from a briefing given by Hitler to some 20 to 30 of his generals who had been called to his HQ at Ziegenberg Castle, not far from Giessen, on 28 December 1944, in connection with the new offensive 'Nordwind', which he was planning to launch at midnight on 1 January 1945 in Lower Alsace, with the aim of regaining the Saverene Gap and of killing as many American troops as possible in the process. Those who attended – and who had to go through the indignity of being stripped of their weapons and briefcases by SS guards! – said that Hitler, despite being in poor physical condition, had lost none of his personal magnetism and spoke brilliantly, emphasising that the destruction of enemy forces was the main aim of 'Nordwind'.

A Rousing New Year
General George S. Patton, Jr., celebrated the arrival of New Year 1945 with a massive artillery barrage, when every available gun in the US Third Army fired on the stroke of midnight. It must have sounded a death knell to the exhausted German soldiers still fighting in the snow-clad Ardennes as they endeavoured to reach the River Meuse on their impossible road to Antwerp. On the 'other side of the hill', the Führer too was full of surprises, as he gave a New Year broadcast to the German people, promising them that the Fatherland would rise to ulti-mate victory like a phoenix from the rubble of its ruined cities. After-wards he entertained his closest associates with glasses of champagne at a private party in his bunker – Hitler did not touch alcohol of course, but was still very upbeat and cheerful after his broadcast. At about 0430, he left the gathering so that he could listen at first hand to the reports filtering in about his latest offensive.

While the eyes of the world had been firmly fixed on the Ardennes the Führer had launched yet another surprise offensive, this time against the Allied southern flank in the Alsace, held by 6th Army Group (Devers), which was basically composed of US Seventh Army

(Patch) and French First Army (de Lattre de Tassigny). 'Nordwind' did not come as such a complete surprise to Allies as had 'Wacht am Rhein', because this time they were partly forewarned by Ultra; nevertheless, it was a nasty New Year's present for the unfortunate GIs and *poilus* on the ground who would have to do the fighting.

The Allied Forces

Commanding 6th Army Group was Lieutenant General Jacob L. 'Jake' Devers, who had been a classmate of Patton's at West Point in 1909, and had been commissioned into the field artillery prior to WWI. Early in WWII General Eisenhower had commented that Devers had a reputation as a 'fine administrator', but that he lacked 'battle experience'. Indeed, it would appear that Ike did not think very highly of him at all; for example, when asked by the US War Department to rate 38 of his most senior officers, he had put Devers down as 24th, lower even than some of his corps commanders. He also commented that Devers: '... was often inaccurate in statements and evaluations ... he has not, so far, produced among the seniors of the American organisation here a feeling of trust and confidence'.[3] Devers did, however, have a 'guardian angel' in the person of General George C. Marshall, Chief of Staff of the US Army, so Ike could not (and anyway would not for purely patriotic reasons) consider sacking him. US Seventh Army commander, Major General Alexander McCarrell 'Sandy' Patch, on the other hand, had seen a great deal of action since he graduated in 1913, having been on the Punitive Expedition to Mexico, then going to France in WWI, rising in little more than a year from captain to lieutenant colonel commanding a machine-gun battalion. He commanded a corps on Guadalcanal in late 1942, doing so well that he was then given command of US Seventh Army in March 1944 and remained their Commander all the way through the fighting in southern Europe from the 'Dragoon' landings on the French Riviera, through the Vosges, Alsace and on into Germany. Ike rated Patch ahead of his other Army Commanders such as Hodges and Simpson. The third senior Allied commander on this part of the front was the extremely able, but extremely autocratic, French commander, General Jean-Marie Gabriel de Lattre de Tassigny, known behind his back as 'King Jean'! He had commanded the French 14th Division in the Armistice Army, went to Tunisia in September 1941, was later imprisoned for 'attempted treason' by the Vichy authorities, but managed to escape to England and was selected to command all French forces for the invasion of southern France. Early in the Alsace campaign de Gaulle would order him to ignore any Allied orders and to take matters into his own hands to ensure the security of Strasbourg – this would not make things any the easier for

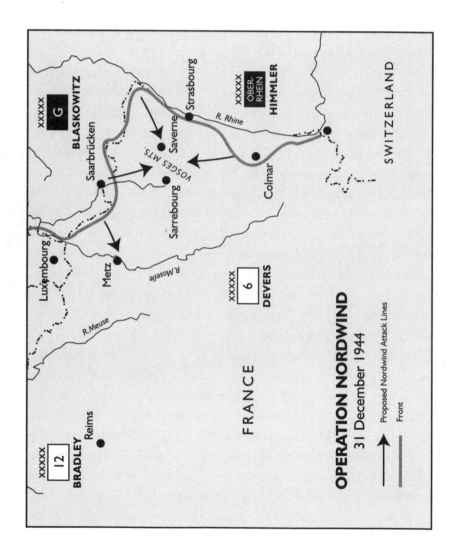

OPERATION NORDWIND
31 December 1944

Eisenhower, who already found 'Joan of Arc' (as American President Roosevelt called the other French 'prima donna' General Charles de Gaulle!) very difficult to manage.

In total, in mid-December 1944, Devers' Army Group was comprised of some eighteen divisions – two armoured and six infantry in US Seventh Army and three armoured and seven infantry in French First Army. For further details see Appendix 4, but in outline they were: US Seventh Army: 12th and 14th Armored Divisions, 36th, 44th, 45th, 79th, 100th and 103rd Infantry Divisions. French First Army: 1st, 2nd, 5th Armoured Divisions, 1st, 16th Infantry, 3rd Algerian, 2nd Moroccan, 4th Moroccan Mountain, 9th Colonial Divisions, plus US 3rd Infantry Division.

All these divisions were 'combat effective' on paper, but some were relatively green and untested, while others had suffered from a difficult winter campaign, especially the French colonial troops who detested the cold weather. All were short of supplies, equipment and manpower because priority had been given to the troops of the northern armies who were dealing with the 'Bulge'. Furthermore, 6th Army Group had been prevented by General Eisenhower from putting in another attack to try to clear the Colmar pocket (on the western side of the Rhine below Strasbourg) and instead had been required to take over a large slice of US Third Army's responsibilities, leaving Patton free to conduct his famous '90-degree wheel' northwards. As the map shows, this had left 6th Army Group with a long, convoluted front line that featured not one but two vulnerable 'bulges' which had to be covered.

German Forces

Opposing them, the Germans were, initially anyway, in just as bad a state if not worse. Most of the more 'up to scratch' units in manpower and equipment had been absorbed into Army Group B for the Ardennes operation. 'Wacht am Rhein' had also been given priority for vehicles, weapons, equipment, ammunition and fuel, so the major proportion of supplies of all types had long been diverted northwards. To make everything more complicated, a new Army Group HQ was formed in early December – Army Group Oberrhein (Upper Rhine) which controlled Generalleutnant Siegfried Rasp's Nineteenth Army – which was still dug in *west of the Rhine*, tenaciously holding the Colmar Pocket, together with XIV SS Corps and various military and paramilitary units east of the Rhine. The formation of this independent HQ did not help the command and control because it divided the forces facing Allied 6th Army Group. The new HQ was also given an unqualified commander, namely Hitler's ardent crony, SS Reichsführer Heinrich Himmler. At least his considerable influence did cause the manpower and supply shortages to be addressed to some extent, but inevitably 'Nordwind' continued to take second place to 'Wacht am Rhein'. On paper, some twenty German divisions were involved in 'Nordwind', thereby outnumbering the Allied forces, but many units and formations were at half strength or under. As in 'Wacht am Rhein', there was also a severe lack of older, well-trained NCOs and of company and battalion commanders. They would not begin to receive a realistically larger share of military resources until the Ardennes offensive had stalled.

In overall charge was Army Group G under General-Oberst Johannes Blaskowitz – an extremely able soldier of the 'old guard', who had been an opponent of some of Hitler's early policies, but, like so many others, had acquiesced in the Nazi 'take-over', though without much enthusiasm. He had done extremely well as a corps commander in Poland in 1939, but, having been appalled by the catalogue of SS atrocities there, he had naïvely sent a detailed memo to Hitler, thinking that the SS had acted without proper authority – this did little to endear him to the Führer! However, his military ability was such that he remained in high command posts throughout the war. He would be the real military intelligence behind 'Nordwind' – and a convenient scapegoat when things went wrong.

Between 27 and 30 December, the selected assault divisions belonging to Generalleutnant Hans von Obstfelder's First Army were carefully withdrawn from their front-line positions, while those remaining endeavoured to cover the gaps – the signal units of those departing remained in position and worked overtime to give the impression of normalcy. In the north, opposite US XV Corps, who were defending the Sarre valley, elements of XIII SS Corps (under SS Gruppenführer und Generalleutnant der Waffen-SS Max Simon) were prepared as the primary assault force. This comprised: 17th Panzer Grenadier Division, 36th *Volks* Grenadier Division, 404, 410 *Volks* Artillery Corps, 20 *Volkswerfer* Brigade, plus miscellaneous units (see Appendix 2 for details). In the Bitche area the assault force was to be, on the right (the western wing): XC Corps (under Luftwaffe Generalleutnant der Flieger Erich Petersen) comprising 559th and 257th VGD; on the left (the eastern wing): LXXXIX Corps (under Generalleutnant Gustav Hoehne) comprising 361st, 256th VGDs. The Vosges forces were also strengthened with additional SP and assault guns, plus army artillery and engineer battalions. Later they would be reinforced by the experienced 6th SS Mountain Division from Finland.[4] In reserve under direct control of Army Group G was XXXIX Panzer Corps (under Generalleutnant Karl Decker) comprising 21st Pz and 25th Panzer Grenadier Divisions. Other formations also being assembled as a reserve and for possible future operations (such as Operation 'Zahnarzt' (Dentist) which proposed a series of attacks on Luneville and Metz, to the rear of Patton's Third Army), were 10th SS Panzer Division and 7th Parachute Division. 'Zahnarzt' did not get off the ground and the forces were used elsewhere.

All the German forces were short of AFVs, weapons and equipment, despite their running of 'Arrow Flash' convoys – the German equivalent of the American 'Red Ball Express',[5] but these were unable to negotiate the bombed bridges and shot-up roads just behind the front line. However, just before the attack 17th Pz Gren Div did receive ten Panthers from 21st Pz Div, and other heavy armour to arrive included a small number of Jagdtiger (the SP version of the Tiger II which mounted a 128mm gun in its massive fixed turret). In total Blaskowitz had about 80 tanks, mainly heavies, which were held to exploit any breakthrough.

Meanwhile, as the Germans prepared for their offensive, the Americans were busy adopting their new defensive positions, taking over large portions of Third Army's front, so that US Seventh Army soon found itself holding a 126-mile stretch; 84 miles from the Saarbrücken area east to Lauterbourg, then a further 42 miles southwards along the Rhine. To hold this territory they had just six divisions, so their allotted frontage was some 20 miles per division, six per regiment or two per battalion, with the two armoured divisions being held in reserve (12th Armd behind XV Corps and 14th Armd behind VI Corps). Patch placed his HQ at Saverne, just behind the centre of his line. Before this layout was finalised, however, SHAEF ordered two divisions to go into theatre reserve, so, although they were desperately short, Patch had to nominate 36th Inf Div from the Rhine frontage and 12th Armd Div from XV Corps reserve, which, as the official history comments, left his defensive lines 'paper thin'. In order to help with these problems, Devers brought in Leclerc's French 2nd Armd Div and the leading regiments of the newly arriving, completely 'green' young GIs of 42nd, 63rd and 70th Divs. They were literally rushed up to the front direct from the jetties at Marseilles, where they had just arrived, without waiting for their attached artillery, armour and other supporting elements. They were then organised into three task forces, each comprising three infantry regiments and a small command group – TF Linden (42nd), TF Harris (63rd) and TF Herren (70th). All these changes meant that General Patch had to re-organise his defences considerably, and he initially put the three inexperienced TFs along the Rhine front, but later transferred two of the regiments from TF Harris, plus the entire French 2nd Armd Div north to the Sarre valley to beef up XV Corps. He next inserted a mechanised screening force (TF Hudelson, comprising two cavalry sqns, a detached inf bn, with some supporting elements including a TD company) from the Bitche area on the west to Neunhoffen on the east, then put a similar screening force on his extreme left, to cover between the left of his XV Corps and the right of Third Army. His only reserves now were 14th Armd still behind VI Corps and French 2nd Armd now reserve for XV Corps. The SHAEF reserves (12th Armd and 36th Inf) were located around Sarrebourg in Seventh Army's rear area.

Problems with Strasbourg

Although Devers and his commanders appeared confident that Seventh Army could halt any German attack, the Supreme Commander was clearly not so convinced. 'Devers was instructed to give up any forward salient in his area,' Eisenhower later wrote in his autobiography *Crusade in Europe*. 'That would permit saving troops on his northern flank, even if he had to move completely back to the Vosges. This, however, implied that in the event of such a step, the city of Strasbourg might have to be given up, albeit temporarily, and this caused great concern among French military and governmental circles. The 'Strasbourg Question' would (in Eisenhower's own words) '... plague me throughout the duration of the Ardennes battle'. There was also a command and control problem within the French forces, General Leclerc being most reluctant to place his French 2nd Armoured Division under control of 'King Jean', giving publicly his reason as being purely that the Americans could provide much better logistic support. The real reason, which was much more deeply rooted, concerned the fact that the '... ghost of Marshal Pétain's Vichy regime had already begun to cast its long shadow over France', Leclerc considering that some of the senior French officers were little better than turncoats. However, the question of the defence of Strasbourg was far more important than these internal squabbles and seriously threatened to split the Americans and French at the highest level, until Eisenhower acceded to de Gaulle's urging and issued new orders to General Devers on 3 January, giving 6th Army Group the responsibility for defending the city. Devers was at Seventh Army CP when the new SHAEF orders were received and agreed that VI Corps should hold the Maginot–Rhine line, with a series of defensive lines to the rear in case a sudden withdrawal became necessary. XV Corps would hold its present positions and be ready to counter any possible enemy penetration.

Help from Ultra?

Bletchley Park operators had, thanks to Ultra, heard Generalfeldmarschall Gerd von Rundstedt's stirring call to arms for the 'Wacht am

Rhein' offensive on 16 December, breaking as it did some two months
of silence on the Enigma machines. Since then some traffic had been
resumed, including order of battle information for the coming offensives farther south, but there was nothing specific that could pinpoint
where 'Nordwind' would strike exactly and for the most part the
German assault formations maintained strict radio silence. In his book,
The Ultra Secret, F. W. Winterbotham does say that he learnt later that
the warning about an attack in Alsace by Blaskowitz's Army Group G
against US Seventh Army had '... enabled Eisenhower to make some
quick moves to straighten out and reduce the Seventh Army front
where a salient might have enabled the Germans to cut it off '. In addition, Patch did meet his two corps commanders at Fénétrange (CP HQ
XV Corps) just prior to the New Year and warned them to expect a
major enemy attack during the early hours of New Year's Day, so
clearly some intelligence data was available.   ·

The Germans attack

In the opening hours of the New Year, the Germans launched a two-
pronged attack, with XIII SS Corps pushing south across the Sarre
valley, while XC and LXXXIX Corps struck roughly in the same direction through the wooded Lower Vosges. The more northerly attack was
met by determined resistance from the troops of US 44th and 100th
Infantry Divisions who were deployed in depth and well dug in. The
German SS troops attacked: 'in suicidal open waves, cursing and
screaming at the American infantrymen who refused to be intimidated
... Allied artillery and, when the weather broke, Allied air attacks,
together with the bitter cold, soon sapped the strength of the attackers.'
They were unable even to dent the American positions and three days
later, on 4 January, they called off that particular attack, the attacking
corps commander (Simon) observing that all the attack had shown was
that the German soldier '... still knew how to die, but little else'.[6]

The second attack was launched from the Bitche area through the
lower Vosges and this was more successful because it had appeared to
be a less likely line of assault because of the rough terrain. The assault
force had hidden in the Maginot Line bunkers which were still in their

hands, while the absence of a preliminary bombardment, the thick forests and overcast skies had all contributed to the element of surprise. The leading elements of 559th, 257th, 361st and 256th VGDs easily penetrated the mass of small American positions established by TF Hudelson who were defending in this area. The wheeled and tracked armoured vehicles of this light mechanised unit found it impossible to move on the snowy, icy tracks and many had to be abandoned. During the next four days, the VGD infantry pushed through the Vosges for some ten miles, but on the western edge of their advance the US 100th Inf Div positions held firm and were reinforced. Elsewhere, with fewer uncommitted reinforcements available, the defence was more patchy and a variety of units found themselves trying to work together, while piecemeal 'backstopping' and complex switching of units completely entangled the forces of 45th, 79th and 70th Infantry Divisions. The official history quotes, for example, the position of Major General Robert T. Frederick (CG 45th Inf Div) who found himself having to try to control eight different infantry regiments, half of which had never been in combat before! These included elements of TF Harris and TF Herren, both of which had been withdrawn from across the Vosges. The history goes on to explain that: 'as American reinforcements met German attackers, the battle quickly turned into a bitter winter infantry fight focusing on the towns that lay along the snow-covered mountain roads'.

It would be wrong to think that there was no panic among the defenders. Just as in the Ardennes, in addition to the many acts of heroism, there were also examples of service and supply units 'bugging out' as the history of at least one US division recalls: 'Rear echelons, remembering the fate of the 1st Army echelons, 7th Army HQ, 12 TAC HQ, huge trucking and ordnance outfits, all packed up and fled! Leaving food uneaten on the table, they "partied" [GI slang French for 'left'] and never stopped until they had reached Luneville.'[7] The four VGD divisions were now also bolstered by the arrival of 6th SS Mountain Division Nord which, as already mentioned, was an experienced formation that had been trained and equipped for cold-weather warfare, on top of which they were fresh, and at full strength. Nevertheless, the GIs stubbornly held on to all the vital Vosges exits, constantly counter-attacking the German forces who were by now becoming dangerously over-extended.

To make up for his withdrawal of the inexperienced, *ad hoc* Task Forces, General Patch decided to move 103rd Inf Div from the far north-western corner of XV Corps' area over to the eastern shoulder of the German advance through the Vosges, thus relieving pressure on the hard-pressed defenders. The attackers carried out a very similar manoeuvre, moving 36th VGD from XIII SS Corps in the Sarre area to LXXXIX Corps. However, despite this, the untried American troops proved themselves both brave and competent, continuing to deny the Vosges exits, which meant that OKW could not and would not commit their mobile reserves. In essence, this brought 'Nordwind' to a full stop, but as both sides still had their mobile reserves uncommitted, the action was far from over; indeed Patch was planning to use the 103rd in an offensive in the Vosges.

Additional attacks

'Nordwind' was only the first of the German attacks. During the next three weeks (5–25 January) it was followed by four more offensives, each mounted by more than one division against US Seventh and French First Armies. Hastily planned and poorly executed, they were still sufficient to threaten the inexperienced and exhausted Allied troops who opposed them. The first two were:

a. Starting on 5 January 1945, 553rd VGD (XIV SS Corps), reinforced with armour and Commandos, attacked across the Rhine at Gambsheim, some ten miles north of Strasbourg.

b. Starting on 7 January 1945, 198th VGD and 106 Pz Bde (LXIV Corps) with some 40–50 heavy tanks and assault guns, attacked just south of Strasbourg at Rhinau on the northern edge of the Colmar pocket. This attack, also known as 'Sonnenwende' (Winter Solstice), not only threatened the southern flank and rear of VI Corps, but also the city of Strasbourg. The initial objective was a triangular area between the rivers Rhine and Ill, from Sélestat to Erstein, which would then be extended north to take in a small bridgehead at Rhinau and thence to invest Strasbourg. However, the commander of LXIV Corps (Thumm) was unhappy about the operation, as was his Army Commander, Rasp, and despite some early success 'Sonnenwende' petered out a week later. These two attacks also rapidly persuaded General Patch to give up any ideas of deploying 103rd Division for an offensive in the Vosges.

The next assault against US Seventh Army began on 7 January along the northern sector of the Lauterbourg salient, with 21st Pz, 25th Pz and 245th VGD under XXXIX Panzer Corps' control. This clearly endangered the entire American line, but the GIs put up a spirited defence, especially in the centre of the salient. Worried by the slow progress of his panzers, Blaskowitz paid a personal visit to the front and threatened to court-martial all the senior panzer commanders. His threats had the desired result and, on 9 January, XXXIX Panzer Corps finally penetrated US VI Corps' centre. This forced General Brooks to commit his corps reserve (14th Armored Division) near Hatten and Rittershoffen, German and American armour battling it out. The official history describes the next ten days (10–20 January) as resembling a 'general mêlée' and there was bitter, hand-to-hand fighting in the small towns with:

> dismounted panzer grenadiers and armored infantrymen fighting side by side with the more lowly foot infantry. Almost every structure was hotly contested and at the end of every day each side totaled up the number of houses and buildings it controlled in an attempt to measure the progress of the battle. Often in the smoke, haze and darkness, friendly troops found themselves firing at one another and few ventured into the narrow but open streets, preferring to advance or withdraw through the blown-out interior walls of the gutted homes and businesses.[8]

Typical of the heroism in this period is the citation for the Congressional Medal of Honor awarded to Master Sergeant Vito R. Bertoldo of Company A, 242nd Infantry in 42nd Infantry Division while defending two command posts against enemy infantry and armour, which reads:

> On the close approach of enemy soldiers, he left the protection of the building he defended and set up his machine gun in the street, there to remain for almost twelve hours driving back attacks while in full view and completely exposed to 88mm, machine gun and small-arms fire ... He then moved back inside the command post, strapped his machine gun to a table and covered the main approach to the building by firing through a window. One shell (from an 88mm tank gun) blasted him across the room, but he returned to his weapon. When two enemy personnel carriers led by a tank moved toward his position, he calmly waited for the troops to dismount and then, with the tank firing directly at him, leaned out of the window and mowed down the entire group of more than twenty Germans.

When the CP was moved to another building Bertoldo volunteered to remain behind, covering the withdrawal of his comrades, and remained there all night. In the morning he moved to a building being used as a CP by another battalion and began a day-long defence of that position also:

> He broke up a heavy attack, launched by an SP 88mm gun covered by a tank and about fifteen infantrymen. Soon afterwards another 88mm weapon moved to within a few feet of his position, and, placing the muzzle of its gun almost inside the building, fired into the room, knocking him down and seriously wounding others. An American Bazooka team set the German weapon afire and MSgt Bertoldo went back to his machine gun and, dazed as he was, killed several of the hostile troops as they attempted to withdraw.

The enemy then began an intensive assault supported by a devastating barrage, but he remained at his post, throwing white phosphorous grenades at the advancing enemy until they broke and ran. Next a tank fired at him from under 50 yards away, destroying the machine-gun and once again blowing him across the room. Nevertheless, the intrepid GI returned to the fight, now with just his rifle, and single-handed covered the withdrawal of his comrades.

> With inspiring bravery and intrepidity MSgt Bertoldo with-stood the attack of vastly superior forces for more than 48 hours without rest or relief, time after time escaping death only by the slightest margin while killing at least 40 hostile soldiers and wounding many more during his grim battle against the enemy hordes.[9]

The last enemy attack began on 16 January, when XXXIX Panzer Corps spearheaded a final drive from Lauterbourg down the west bank of the Rhine with 10th SS Panzer Division and 7th Parachute Division, with two assault gun brigades in support, together with Himmler's escort battalion. The American division which caught the brunt of their attack was Major General Roderick Allen's 12th Armored Division, which was operating on the western side of the Gambsheim bridgehead. That day, 12th Armd had begun an attack to try to capture Herrlisheim, which would have seriously affected north-south communications within the enemy bridgehead. However, their attack would run unex-pectedly into the leading elements of 10th SS Panzer Division with disastrous results, the 43rd Tank Bn of 12th Armored being virtually wiped out. The rest of 12th Armored would fare little better.

One American tanker, then a young platoon commander, who remembers these battles very well indeed is Colonel (USA Ret) Owsley Costlow, who was commanding 3rd Platoon (four M4 Sherman medium tanks) in the 23rd Tank Battalion. He told me:

> On the night of 16/17 January 1945 we were just outside of Strasbourg, at the little town of Weyersheim, firing indirect fire

missions into Stainwald Woods [*sic*]. An artillery survey team had come up that afternoon to get the four tanks of my Third Platoon into firing positions. A tank with a bulldozer blade had dug a hole behind each tank so by backing each tank into the hole we would have additional elevation for our tank cannons (75mm). Our mission was to fire one 75mm round sometime during each half an hour throughout the night into Stainwald Woods to harass the German troops in the woods. This we understood was to keep them awake all night, the only problem was it kept us awake too.

Close to midnight I was called to an officers' meeting to learn of our, the Battalion's, plan to attack the bridgehead the Germans had established around the little town of Offendorf on the Rhine River. The overall plan was that the 17th Armored Infantry Battalion would take Herrlisheim and the 66th Armored Infantry Battalion would clear the Stainwald Woods. The 23rd Tank Battalion would drive between them with my platoon leading. We were not to move out until both infantry objectives had been achieved. Then we were to stop at the railroad tracks, pick up some of the infantry from the 66th and attack Offendorf. Our 'intelligence' said there was nothing out there but old men and young boys wanting to give up. Ha! Needless to say it but the units turned out to be the 10th SS Armored Division and the 553rd *Volks* Grenadier Division and they certainly were not about to give up. In fact they had all but destroyed the 43rd Tank Battalion the day before, however, we had not been told this before we began our attack.

We started out from Weyersheim a little after midnight and made a blackout night march up to the Zorn River. The Division's 119th Armored Engineer Battalion had built a Bailey bridge over the river where we crossed. From there we moved to a large open field and waited for the code word 'Zippo' over the radio before we moved into the attack. The move was supposed to be at first light and after Herrlisheim and Stainwald were in US hands. We waited and waited, dawn came and no 'Zippo'.

Certainly the element of surprise was gone so I went back to my Company Commander, Captain Albert Lange, to ask him about the delay and to find out if our orders had been changed. He said that he had not received the order to go and really didn't know why there was a delay.

Well, there we were out in the middle of a large open field, just like sitting ducks! I really don't remember the exact time but it seems to me it was sometime between 10 a.m. and 11 a.m. when over the radio came the waited word 'Zippo'.

As you may know a tank platoon in WWII consisted of five tanks, but when we moved out that morning we only had four, because we had lost one at Rimling, France about two weeks before. So now believing that both our flanks were secure we moved out toward Offendorf using the technique called 'by leaps and bounds'. Two tanks move forward while the other two form a base of fire and 'overwatch' the moving tanks. Then the moving tanks stop and become the base of fire for the others to pass through them. Then the technique is repeated again and again until changed. After about ten or fifteen minutes of this manoeuvre the Company Commander called me on the radio and said we were moving too slow, to pick up the pace, so we abandoned the leaps and bounds and moved in a wedge formation. This placed two tanks abreast leading with the other two also abreast to each other but several yards back and spread out to the sides.

As we got nearer to the area between Herrlisheim and Stainwald I began to see through my binoculars many American tanks in various stages of destruction, some burned while others were in pieces. I immediately called Captain Lange and told him what I was seeing. He said that they had been knocked out on a previous day and were not mined and said for me to ignore them. Then I began to see individuals in long overcoats jump up out of a foxhole, then run over to another one and drop into it. I again called Captain Lange and told him about this and asked if these could be Germans. Is everything in front of me enemy?

The answer was yes! Then I asked permission to fire – 'Granted' was the reply.

I then gave the command to my gunner: 'Gunner, doughs [dismounted infantry] 800 yards, direct front, 30 caliber fire!' 'On the way' was given by the gunner and he pressed the trigger, but the solenoid that fires the coaxial machine gun had slipped and did not engage the trigger. This was the only time the solenoid had failed to engage the trigger during the entire war. Nevertheless, the loader immediately began to adjust the solenoid as the tank continued to move forward. The long-coated infantrymen were still getting up out of one foxhole and moving very quickly to another hole and dropping out of sight. Since they were always moving facing us it looked very suspicious to me, but it was still too far away to see clearly who they were and Captain Lange had said that everything in front was enemy, we continued to move forward. As we moved I kept watching them through my binoculars and to my horror I now began to see that the doughs were our own infantry, the 17th AIB. 'Cease fire! Cease fire!' I commanded. The Good Lord was with us and them too and I truly believe it was Divine Intervention that caused the solenoid to fail, otherwise we would have shot our own infantry.

Then as we passed them they just waved and made no sign to warn us of the anti-tank guns to our front. This I shall never forgive them because we could have been better prepared and perhaps it would not have been such a surprise.

In approaching the road and railroad tracks, both of which were on a hill above the large flat field we were in, I noticed movement on the other side of the railroad – it was a gun firing. I could not see the recoil and could not tell which way it was firing and at first thought it was 17th AIB firing their 57mm anti-tank guns away from us towards Offendorf. Then I saw my Number Two tank [Sergeant Frank Chruma was tank commander] stop, shudder and their left track broke and started to peel off the driving sprocket. Next within a second I saw the hatch cover open and someone – probably Sergeant Chruma, try to get out but just fall on to the top of the turret. Smoke then began to rise out of the hatch opening and then I knew for certain they had been hit by the gun I saw firing.

I immediately ordered my driver to stop and to begin to back up. Then I told my gunner to fire at the small railroad station across the raised road. I believe that we did get off two or three rounds, but then from nowhere I saw a streak of yellow fire coming straight at my tank, then crash, sparks flew and the tank rocked violently. We too had been hit! The 88mm projectile entered our left side just above the track and below where the loader sits. I said 'We've been hit, let's get out of here!' or something like that and we did! The loader, Pfc Ralph Ritter, was wounded in the legs by flying metal and the gunner, Sergeant Willard J. Smith had flash burns on his face. Everyone else was all right but shaken.

Well, I could go on and on about what happened to us after that, but suffice it to say that it was a very bad day for my platoon and me. We lost all four tanks and out of the twenty men involved, eight were killed and three were wounded. The 17th AIB never did capture Herrlisheim and the 66th AIB did not take or even get into Stainwald Woods and of course we were not to attack until those units had accomplished their missions. We were really set up, something I believe that should never have happened.

In a later interview with the Inspector-General of 12th Armored Division, Owsley had this to say:

If proper liaison had been maintained with the 66th AIB and the 17th AIB we could have obtained information concerning the woods to our right flank and would have taken precautions against enemy fire from the woods. Also, we could have obtained information from the friendly infantry in front of us as to the situation in front and to their right front. Also, we could have kept friendly infantry out of our line of attack so that we could bring fire upon all suspicious-looking objects to our front. After talking with my platoon sergeant, it was learned that we had AT fire directed at us from both Herrlisheim and the Stainwald Forest along with direct fire from the railroad station previously mentioned.

The End in Alsace

On 26 January 1945, as suddenly as it had begun, the German offensive came to an end. By the end of the month Hitler had replaced Blaskowitz with SS General Paul Hauser, having labelled Blskowitz's reports 'too pessimistic' and then saying that he did not display sufficient initiiative.[10] He then sent most of the German formations opposite 6th Army Group to the Eastern Front, leaving General Devers facing far weaker forces than he had ever done – even before the offensive began. Hitler also issued a directive which made all senior commanders responsible for reporting in advance to him all decisions affecting operational movement – even down to tactical level. After the failure of 'Nordwind' and the other follow-up offensives, the front lapsed into a state of static defence. The Germans had, however, suffered grievously for the failure of this 'Other Bulge' campaign – the casualty estimate for the month of January 1945 being some 23,000 Germans as compared with about 14,000 Allied losses. What was perhaps even more important about this butcher's bill was that, while the Allied casualties could be and would be replaced, the German casualties could not. On 9 February, the Germans abandoned their remaining foothold west of the Rhine. Hitler's last gamble had failed.

Notes

1 Quoted in Hamilton, Nigel. *Monty.*
2 Heiber, Helmut. 'Hitler's Briefings. Fragments of the Minutes of his Military Conferences 1942–45' as quoted in Joachimsthaler, Anton. *The Last Days of Hitler.*
3 As quoted in Irving, David. *The War Between the Generals.*
4 The SS 6th Mountain Division was based on the SS Brigade *Nord* which originally was formed from the Totenkopf concentration camp guards. It had disgraced the Waffen-SS with its panicked rout by the Red Army at Salla, Finland, in July 1941. It remained on the Finnish front until autumn 1944, then retreated into northern

Norway and returned to Germany via Oslo and Denmark in November and December. Despite their background, they fought well enough in 'Nordwind'.

5　This was a one-way loop highway system between St-Lô and Chartres on which every available truck was used running non-stop throughout the day and night during the battle for France. From 25 to 29 August 1944, for example, just under 6,000 trucks delivered 12,500 tons of supplies.

6　Clarke and Smith. *Riviera to the Rhine.*

7　Quoted by Whiting, Charles, in 'The Other Battle of the Bulge' from the *History of 45th Infantry Division.*

8　Clarke and Smith, op. cit.

9　As quoted in Jordan, Kenneth N. Sr. *Yesterday's Heroes.*

10　This did not stop von Rundstedt asking for Blaskowitz to command Army Group H in place of Generaloberst Student.

THE ALLIED COUNTER-OFFENSIVE

Another Allied Crisis

While, to quote Bradley, 'the Bulge spilled harmlessly westward through the empty Ardennes', the Allied High Command was busily engaged in manufacturing what was probably the most serious rift that occurred between the top American and British commanders during the entire war. It was as though they were willing Hitler's prophetic statement about the parlous state of the Allied Command's 'Common Front', which I mentioned at the start of this book, to come true, and that it would, as he had predicted 'suddenly collapse with a giant clap of thunder'.

Ever since the early days of the advance across France, there had been two opposing schools of thought as to how best to proceed with the overall strategic battle. Should the advance be on a broad front, with all armies sharing the supplies (and the glory!), or should it be by means of a bolder, swifter advance on a much narrower front, by only a select element of the Allied strength to which would be given the lion's share of everything? Ever the diplomat, Eisenhower favoured the broad approach, reasoning that the more cautious advance with all armies keeping roughly in line, and with 'fair shares for all', would be safer, easier to handle and be a much better way of keeping the peace between his Army Group and Army commanders, in particular between Montgomery on the one hand and Bradley and Patton on the other. Until the 'Bulge' Eisenhower had strenuously supported the broad front approach and the general Allied success seemed to have vindicated his handling of the problem, although Montgomery was continually vocal in his support for the narrow front, as was Patton when he felt that Third Army wasn't getting its fair share of ammunition, fuel and supplies. To make matters even more controversial and difficult, Montgomery also advocated the establishment of a single ground force commander directly below Eisenhower, who would control all the Army Groups and be subordinate only to the Supreme Commander. Although he did not say so in as many words, it was obvious that he saw himself as that single ground force commander, back in charge once more as he had been for the 'Overlord' landings. This difference of opinion had already come to a head at least once and Ike had been forced to reprimand the Field Marshal: 'Steady Monty! You can't speak to me like that, I'm your boss', he had said to his diffi-cult subordinate.[1] Matters had really come to a head in October, again over the single ground force commander issue, prompting Eisenhower to tell Monty that he was well aware of the powers and limitations of the Allied Command and that if he (Monty): '... as the senior Commander in this theater of one of the great Allies, feel that my conceptions and directives are such as to endanger the success of oper-ations, it is your duty to refer the matter to higher authority for any action they may chose to take, however drastic.'[2] Fortunately, Monty saw in the nick of time that Eisenhower was not bluffing and backed off – in fact he wrote to the Supreme Commander apologising and promising that he would not raise the subject of command again! However, he had a conveniently short memory as far as that particular topic was concerned, as he showed just two months later, when Eisen-hower appointed him to command the northern sector of the 'Bulge'. This was, in Monty's opinion, proof positive that what he had been advocating for so long, was the right and proper solution. Once again he allowed his judgement to be completely clouded by this single issue, just as he had done before and could not – or would not – see what offence he was giving to the senior American commanders from Eisen-hower downwards.

Monty had begun Boxing Day by lecturing Bradley, whom he had invited to visit him to 'co-ordinate tactics' for the coming offensive against the Germans, and had finished up by scolding him 'like a schoolboy' about what had gone wrong in the Ardennes so far. Although he did not blame Eisenhower personally, he made it clear that he considered incompetent generalship to be at the root of the débâcle: 'Monty was more arrogant and egotistical than I have ever seen him,' wrote Bradley later. 'Never in my life had I been so enraged and so utterly exasperated. It required every fiber of my strength to restrain myself from an insulting outburst ... However, to avoid a potentially crippling breakdown in the Allied command, I kept my counsel.' Monty for his part, appears to have been blissfully unaware of Bradley's true feelings: 'Poor chap,' he wrote that evening to the British CIGS, Field Marshal Alan Brooke. 'He is such a decent fellow and the whole thing is a bitter pill for him. But he is man enough to admit it and he did.'[3]

If that were not bad enough, Monty then wrote a highly critical letter to the Supreme Commander in which, having listed the errors he considered had been made over the previous three months, reiterated that, in his opinion, if the command structure of one single ground commander was not instituted immediately the Allies would be bound to fail yet again: 'One commander must have powers to direct and control operations; you cannot possibly do it yourself, and so you have to nominate someone else.' The imperious British Field Marshal then rubbed salt into the wound by telling Ike that it would be necessary for him (Eisenhower) to be 'very firm' in assigning him (Montgomery) operational control in the north, because any loosely worded state-ment would be 'quite useless'! Coupled with the BBC news broadcasts and British Press reports which were both making Monty the hero of the hour, it was all too much for the Supreme Commander to stomach any longer – something had to give and it was not going to be he!

Fortunately, an opportunity to prevent an irreversible situation occurring presented itself fairly rapidly. Major-General Freddie de Guingand, Monty's brilliant and devoted Chief of Staff, in whom the Field Marshal had complete confidence, had been sent by Monty to SHAEF HQ to explain why he had decided to delay US First Army's launching a counter-attack against the now weakened German offen-sive. It had been expected that this counter-attack by General 'Light-ning Joe' Collins' corps would take place in the north at the same time as Patton's Third Army launched its assault in the south, but now Monty wished to delay it until 4 January at the earliest. General de Guingand sensed immediately that something was badly wrong because of the extremely frosty reception he received at SHAEF and it soon became abundantly clear to him that General Eisenhower had lost all patience with Monty and was preparing to send a cable to the Combined Chiefs of Staff stating bluntly that they must choose between him and the Field Marshal once and for all. De Guingand was shocked at the depths to which the relationship between the two commanders had sunk – at least as far as Eisenhower was concerned – and realised that unless Monty retracted immediately, he was likely to be replaced, the name of Field Marshal Alexander being quoted as his likely successor; there was absolutely no chance that the Americans (or any of the other Allies for that matter) would countenance the loss of General Eisenhower. Fortunately de Guingand managed to persuade Eisenhower to hold off from sending the cable until he had a chance to speak to Monty personally.

On his return to HQ 21st Army Group, de Guingand carefully spelt out the situation to his boss and it would appear that for the very first time Monty realised just how close he was to self-destruction! 'It was one of the few times that I saw Montgomery really worried and disturbed, for I believe he was genuinely and completely taken by surprise,' said de Guingand later. 'I don't think I had ever seen him so deflated.' He explained to his master what he considered had to be done, indeed, some say that he had already drafted a letter of apology for Monty's approval. Montgomery hastily sent off the following enciphered cable:

Dear Ike. Have seen Freddie and understand you are greatly worried by many considerations in these difficult days. I have given you my frank views because I have felt you like this. I am sure there are many factors which may have a bearing quite beyond anything I realise. Whatever your decision may be you can rely on me one hundred per cent to make it work and I know Brad will do the same. Very distressed that my letter may have upset you and I would ask you to tear it up.

Your very devoted subordinate,

MONTY'[4]

On one of the very few occasions in his life, Montgomery was having to eat humble pie, but at least he did it with good grace and then immediately dismissed it from his mind and got back to the job in hand. Unfortunately, his change of heart did not last for long and Anglo-American relations hit another all time low a week later when, at a Press conference on 7 January, he put his foot into it yet again! Initially he had said all the right things, emphasising how devoted he was to Eisenhower and that he was disappointed whenever he read uncomplimentary remarks about Ike in the British Press: 'He bears a great burden. He needs our fullest support. He has the right to expect it and it is up to us to see that he gets it. Let us rally round the captain of the team.'

Next Monty paid a fulsome tribute to the fighting qualities of the American soldier: 'He is a very brave fighting man and he has that tenacity in battle which stamps a first-class soldier. He is basically responsible for Rundstedt not doing what he wanted to. During this battle I tried to identify myself very closely with the American soldier, so that I shall take the correct action with these great Allied armies which are now under my command. I now have an American identity card, which identifies me in the Army of the US. My fingerprints are registered in the War Department at Washington – I would sooner have them there than at Scotland Yard.'

Had he left it at that, all would have been well, but Monty could not resist having a dig at Bradley's poor handling of the initial days of the Bulge campaign, and to make matters worse the British Press once more over-egged the part he had played, with such headlines as the one that appeared in the *Daily Mail* on 8 January, which implied that Monty had taken over command of the armies along the whole of the northern flank on his own initiative and had done so days before it had been confirmed by SHAEF. 'MONTGOMERY FORESAW ATTACK' trumpeted the banner headline. 'His troops were all ready to march. ACTED ON HIS OWN TO SAVE THE DAY.'

It was left to Churchill to endeavour to heal the wounds, with a ringing tribute to the Americans and to the part they had played in defeating 'Wacht am Rhein'. Speaking in the House of Commons on

17 January, he spelt out the true facts: that, while the British had just one corps in action, the Americans had some 30 divisions engaged, with 30 to 40 men *continuously* in action for every one British soldier. 'Care must be taken,' warned the Prime Minister, 'in telling our proud tale, not to claim for the British Army an undue share of what is undoubtedly the greatest American battle of the war and will, I believe, be regarded as an ever famous American victory.' General Eisenhower would later write that the incident had caused him more distress and worry than any similar problem in the entire war.

Operation 'Bodenplatte' (Baseplate)

The Allies were so used to having things their own way as far as the air war was concerned, that 'Bodenplatte', the last Luftwaffe offensive of the war, which took place on New Year's Day, 1945, came as a complete shock to everyone. All available Luftwaffe aircraft – some 850–900 – attacked and caused considerable damage to some 27 Allied airfields in Belgium and Holland. One German report estimated 467 Allied planes destroyed, but other reports put accurate losses considerably lower at 144, plus 62 damaged. Even if one accepts the lower figures, the losses were considerable, though insufficient to make any difference to overall Allied control of the air. In fact, during the operation the Germans lost nearly 300 aircraft every one of which would be quite impossible to replace. Even more serious for them was the fact that 237 of their best pilots were killed or reported missing from operations on that one day. These included three Wing Commanders, seventeen Group Commanders and 39 Squadron Commanders.[5] Perhaps even more distressing for the Luftwaffe was the fact that many of these casualties were victims of 'friendly' AA fire by the German Flak units protecting the V-2 launch sites, over which many of the aircraft had flown on the way to their targets. This was a direct consequence of tight security, the AA gunners having been kept completely in the dark about the operation. Also, being unused to seeing so many of their own aircraft in the sky at any one time, they had naturally assumed that the planes were hostile. Added to these considerable losses were the equally heavy casualties which had been the result of

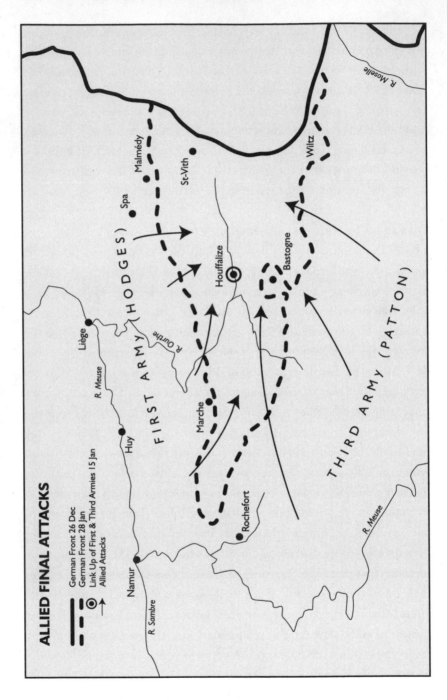

ALLIED FINAL ATTACKS

German Front 26 Dec
German Front 28 Jan
Link Up of First & Third Armies 15 Jan
Allied Attacks

R. Sambre

Namur

R. Meuse

Huy

Liège

R. Meuse

FIRST ARMY (HODGES)

Spa

Malmédy

St-Vith

R. Ourthe

Houffalize

Marche

Rochefort

Bastogne

Wiltz

R. Moselle

THIRD ARMY (PATTON)

the mainly indecisive strikes against scattered ground targets during the Bulge offensive. 'The Luftwaffe received its death blow in the Ardennes,' the great fighter ace Adolf Galland is said to have lamented – and he was right!

High-water mark – Blunting the German Spearhead

'Traditionally the Battle of the Bulge is told in terms of the gallant American defenders at St-Vith; "Nuts", the one-word rejection of the surrender offer at Bastogne; and the Third Army's turn from their attack eastward to attack northward against the south flank of the German salient. All that is true; those units deserve the credit and glory earned. However, little is said about the actions on the northern flank, perhaps because it was under the supervision of British Field Marshal Bernard Montgomery. It was on that northern flank where the attack of the 2nd Armored Division, temporarily in the American First Army and VII Corps, stopped the German advance three miles short of the Meuse River and blunted the German spearhead. Had the 2nd Armored Division failed, the Germans would most probably have realized their goal of splitting the Allies and may have been able to achieve a stalemate on the western front.'

That is how Donald E. Houston, in his very detailed and accurate history of 2nd Armored, one of the US Army's crack formations, and nicknamed 'Hell on Wheels', begins the chapter on the Bulge battles.

From the end of November until 19 December, 2nd Armored had been manning defensive lines along the River Roer, while planning an attack across the river and on towards the Rhine. However, 'Wacht am Rhein' had changed all that and on the afternoon of the 19th, they were told that 29th Infantry Division would relieve them and they were put on a 6-hour alert to be ready to move. Next day they were first attached to Ninth Army, then to First Army, and then ordered to prepare to move to new assembly areas some 100 miles to the west. They would form part of General 'Lightning Joe' Collins' VII Corps together with 3rd Armored, 75th and 84th Infantry Divisions, which were assembling in the Marche–Hotton–Modave area, ready to counter-attack the panzers once they had lost their momentum. On the 21st 'Hell on Wheels' under its hard-driving Commander Major General Ernest 'Old Gravel Voice' Harmon began to prepare for what their history describes as being: 'one of the most spectacular moves of the war'. At 1500 hrs it was put on alert, and an hour later ordered to move, but there was some delay while suitable maps were obtained and issued, so they did not begin their momentous drive to the new assembly area until 2300 hrs. The move created enormous traffic problems which can only be appreciated when one realises that at a regulation 50-yard interval, the 3,000 vehicles of the division would form a convoy one hundred miles in length! Using two routes halved this length, but the march still had to be completed over roads encrusted with ice, snow and mud, and without lights. However, just 22 hours later, the leading elements began to arrive at Huy in Belgium. Immediately patrols were sent to locate the enemy and to guard the Meuse bridges, first contact with the enemy being made at 1130 hrs on the 23rd, when an armoured car patrol of 82nd Reconnaissance Battalion, was shot up by enemy tanks some four miles from Ciney. As soon as he received the patrol's report General Harmon's reaction was immediate and he sent his CCA to take Ciney. Task Force A of CCA reached the town at about 1515 hrs and was ordered to remain there while recce elements were sent towards Namur and Dinant. Later they were told to head towards Buissonville, where the armour would pose a double threat to the Germans. If the enemy continued to move north-westwards they would meet the rest of 2nd Armored head on and if they continued west, they would have CCA on their left flank which would still pose a serious threat.

Ambush!

We left 2nd Panzer Division with its leading elements at the 'high-water mark' just nine kilometres short of the Meuse, but with most of its tanks stranded a few miles further back at Celles through lack of petrol. Gefreite Guido Gnilsen of 2nd Pz had said that he had realised at that moment that the Ardennes offensive was lost – and he was right, even though he was unaware that US 2nd Armored Division now not only lay across their path, but was also moving ever closer. Task Force B of 2nd Armored's CCA arrived at Ciney at about 1900 hrs and took over from TF A which then moved on towards Buissonville, via Lengonne. As Major Herbert Long, who was leading in his Jeep, rounded a sharp curve he drew anti-tank fire which 'almost parted his hair'! The lead tank engaged the gun crew and then crushed the gun. The TF commander was told by local civilians that there were some 600 enemy and a few tanks in Buissonville, so he decided to divide his task force into two columns, sending one half along the main road and the other via another road about 1,000 yards to the east. After about three miles, both columns were fired upon by elements of 2nd Pz Div's reconnaissance battalion. They dealt with the enemy and pressed on, the leading tank platoon commander on the secondary route having a hair-raising ride through one small village where his lead tank had fired at an anti-tank gun which had been illuminated by light from the open doors of two nearby houses whence the gun crew were hastening, but they were too late and both the gun and its crew were 'flattened'. The leading tank continued on through the village, calling to the rest to follow him. The second Sherman moved off, down a steep hill and around an S-bend, when it was apparently hit by a shell which exploded on the turret but did not knock it out, although all could feel the tremendous heat generated. Then a German halftrack came 'barrelling down' a side-street and crashed into a nearby house. It was subsequently crushed by the tank backing over it and the tanks then temporarily withdrew, while a platoon of 41st Armd Inf Regt appeared and secured the village house by house.

On the main route the remainder of the Task Force was moving smoothly along, the night was bright, there was a thin blanket of snow everywhere and the temperature was below freezing point. F Company, 41st Armored Infantry was leading on foot, followed by its halftracks, then two other infantry companies and a tank company. The leading elements suddenly heard the unmistakable sounds of approaching armour, so the company commander quickly deployed his men off the roadsides and waited. The result was total surprise, the burning enemy vehicles lighting up the area for the infantry, tanks and TDs to engage many new targets. Some twelve armoured vehicles were destroyed, 30–40 German troops were killed and a similar number captured. After the successful ambush the TF 'coiled' for the rest of the night, ready to resume the advance next morning. They were now only about eight miles from Rochefort.

The advance was resumed at 0630 hrs on Christmas Eve, with TF A on the main road and TF B attacking cross-country. They were engaged by anti-tank guns and Panther tanks, flushed several out of their positions and saw several German columns in the area, but reached and captured Buissonville without too much trouble, TF A entering the town while TF B overwatched from a nearby hill. From this position they had an unrestricted view for about ten miles 'right down the Germans' throats', as one observer put it, so they were able to bring artillery fire to bear on large numbers of enemy forces at ranges of between 4,000 and 10,000 yards, knocking out 38 wheeled vehicles, four anti-tank guns and six artillery pieces. An unknown number of enemy were killed and more than 100 surrendered. Similar actions took place later that day and again on Christmas Day, when Celles was taken. The thrust to the Meuse had been stopped and it was a fine Christmas present for 2nd Armored, in General Harmon's words, 'The bastards are in the bag!' In all the 'bag' contained some 2,500 Germans killed, more than 1,200 taken prisoner, masses of tanks, other AFVs, trucks and artillery pieces knocked out or captured – with only some 1,500 panzer grenadiers and a handful of tanks escaping to fight another day. To all intents and purposes as far as the 'Bulge' operation was concerned, 2nd Panzer Division was no more. The enemy offensive had effectively been sealed off and it would now be the Allied turn to advance. And they would be supported both by massive air and artillery strikes which would inflict crippling losses on the Germans, as one by one, the panzer divisions disengaged and fell back towards Bastogne, which Hitler still saw as the essential prize to be taken at all costs, even though the siege had already been partly broken and a tenuous supply line established via the Assenois road. Larger and larger numbers of German formations were still trying to beat down the defences, though with little chance of success.

While the Germans were still trying to get into Bastogne, one senior American officer, Major General Maxwell D. Taylor, the commanding general of 101st Airborne Division, was also trying desperately to get through the defences and rejoin his 'Screaming Eagles'. Taylor had been in the USA, pleading the case for more airborne troops in the US Army, when he first heard of the unexpected German offensive and that his division was under siege in Bastogne. He hitched a lift back to Europe on a cargo plane and travelled by Jeep to Luxembourg, where the CG of 4th Armored Division had tried hard to dissuade him from going any further. He could have saved his breath because General Taylor was determined to get there; he turned down the offer of a tank, and his Jeep driver got him to Bastogne where he was able to tell his incredulous Paratroopers that they were now world-renowned heroes!

A DUAL ASSAULT

Third Army's attack

As we recorded in the last chapter, Montgomery had brought up British XXX Corps on the right flank of the US First Army to take over the Givet–Hotton sector, so that he could release his reserve corps (Collins' US VII Corps) to thrust towards Houffalize on 3rd January. This was also the objective of US Third Army which was now widening its salient in the Bastogne area, so that between the two offensives the enemy salient could be destroyed. Patton had received orders from 12th Army Group to continue his attack to the north-east and effect a junction with First Army in the Houffalize area. Additionally, he was to destroy the Germans trapped in the Third Army zone of operations, continue the attack towards St-Vith, protect the right flank of First Army and, lastly, continue to defend the line of the rivers Saar, Moselle and Sauer. Despite the intensity of the battle, there were occasional examples of what could be termed 'civilised warfare', such as when the Germans asked VIII Corps' artillery to stop firing on an important cross-roads which was located near a hospital. After a thorough investigation General Patton decided to hold fire in that sector, but to ensure fair play he sent officers through the enemy lines to see that the roads were being used exclusively for hospital traffic – which fortunately was the case.

On 8 January Patton issued another operational directive to his Army which confirmed his previously issued verbal orders. In part they stated that:

a. 94th Infantry Division was assigned to XX Corps.

b. III Corps would relinquish control of 4th Armored Division, assume control of 90th Infantry Division and attack next day south-east of Bastogne.

c. III Corps would seize Noville and Houffalize (if VII Corps of First Army had not done so already), or continue to the north-east towards St-Vith, maintaining contact with First Army.

d. VIII Corps would maintain the defence of the Meuse line, assume control of 4th Armored and on the 9th attack and capture Noville and the high ground around Houffalize.

e. XII Corps was ordered to continue its mission of clearing enemy west of the Moselle and Sauer, and to attack north on orders.

f. XX Corps to continue with its present mission.

H-Hour for these attacks would be 1000 hrs on 9 January. The 9th Armored and 28th Infantry Divisions were to be assigned to US Fifteenth Army[6] and placed in SHAEF reserve.

Patton launched his attack from the Bastogne salient with emphasis initially on the eastern shoulder of the enemy area, west of Bras. This was a combined pincer movement by 6th Armored and 35th Infantry Divisions from within the Bastogne perimeter, and by 90th Infantry Division from the Café Schumann cross-roads. Fighting was hard and 90th Infantry in particular took heavy casualties, but by 11 January the two claws of the pincer had linked up at Bras, trapping some 15,000 enemy, mostly from 5th Parachute Division. Simultaneously, 4th Armored and 101st Airborne also moved out of the Bastogne perimeter northwards, attacking towards Noville and Houffalize. Typical of the hard-fought actions in these attacks was that in which SSgt Archer T. Gammon of Company A, 9th Armored Infantry Battalion, 6th Armored Division, was awarded the Medal of Honor posthumously on 11 January 1945. Gammon was a squad leader with A Company and had been advancing steadily through woods south-west of Wardin, clearing them of enemy. When his platoon was held up by machine-gun fire, he charged 30 yards through hip-deep snow, firing his 'grease' gun' and throwing grenades which knocked out the 3-man MG crew. No sooner had his platoon resumed their advance when another machine-gun, supported by riflemen opened up, and a massive Tiger II tank, also supported by infantry, began firing its 88mm gun at the GIs from the flank. Gammon rushed forward, then ran out to the left, crossing the width of the platoon's skirmish line in an attempt to reach the Tiger II and its protecting infantry, who began concentrating their fire on him. He charged and wiped out the machine-gun crew with his grease gun and grenades. Then he went for the tank! Amazingly the Tiger began to withdraw, stopping every few yards to fire its gun at the lone soldier. He was killed instantly by a tank shell, but his self-less and heroic act had cleared the way for his platoon to advance without further delay.

The Battle of Bastogne was now just about over, but there were several more days of fighting for the Longvilly area. On 16 January, 6th Armored Division took Michamps and Longvilly and next day cut the Bourcy–Longvilly road. Having secured its objectives, the division reorganised, consolidated and prepared to refit as quickly as possible. On the 21st it resumed its advance to the north-east, and on that day recorded the longest advance (9,000 yards) they had made since the summer. During the next few days the north-eastward advance continued, the division keeping up constant pressure upon the retreating enemy. Soon they reached the area of Weiswampach and made an attempt to secure the high ground on the west bank of the Our but failed. On the 26th they tried again and this time not only secured their objective but also cut Skyline Drive east of the town. The last Germans had now been driven back behind the Siegfried Line and the Ardennes salient had completely collapsed.

First Army's attack

VII Corps also 'jumped off' on 3 January as planned, against a well-organised defence, with dug-in tanks and anti-tank guns, and in the most atrocious weather possible, with sub-zero temperatures, deep snowdrifts and appalling visibility. Some gains were made that first day until heavy snow brought everything to a standstill until the 5th. VII Corps was supported on its left flank by Ridgway's XVIII Airborne Corps, which also made satisfactory gains, reaching Vielsalm and Salmchâteau by the 7th. On 4 January British XXX Corps on the other flank also attacked, on a two-divisional front (53rd Welsh Division on the left and 6th Airborne Division on the right). The Paratroopers had a fierce battle at Bure, but succeeded in taking it and the surrounding area on the 5th, while the Welsh secured Grimbiermont two days later, thus keeping pace with the Americans to their north.

VII Corps had advanced with 2nd and 3rd Armored Divisions abreast, followed by 84th and 83rd Infantry Divisions. The aim of their attack was to drive rapidly to the south-east with the armour leading, take Houffalize and its vital road net and link up with Third Army. In 3rd Armored Division's zone, the advance was made with CCA and CCB abreast, CCB being to the west. Each combat command was divided into two task forces, while the division was bolstered by the attachment of 330th Inf Regt, 83rd Inf Div, and three additional artillery battalions. The first phase of the attack (3–9 January) consisted of a slow advance against a strong enemy rear-guard, reaching the line Provedroux–Ottré–Regne. From 9–13 January 83rd Inf Div took over the attack to the south-east, through a heavily wooded area some three to four miles deep. They were to establish a bridgehead on the southern edge of the woods on the line Bovigny–Baclain–Montleban. However, this line had not been fully reached before 3rd Armd resumed the lead on 13 January and there followed numerous bitter battles over strongpoints in villages, culminating in the taking of Brisy and the high ground in its vicinity, north of the Ourthe, on the 19th. The area of the German salient west of Houffalize had now been cleared, but it had taken fifteen days of stubborn rearguard actions, as graphically explained in this short extract from the unofficial history of Task Force Lovelady entitled 'Five Stars to Victory':

The 1st Battalion task force was in Regne and, working together, it was quickly secured. We lost one tank to anti-tank fire, one to a mine and one to a German tank destroyer. After defending Regne for two days under harassing artillery fire and rocket fire, we moved administratively to Hebronval, from whence the remainder of the attack on Cherain would be launched. Here we thawed out, re-equipped partially and on the 12th of January, hastily moved out towards Langlir, there to engage a stubborn foe in the final phases of an attack which was gradually reducing the unsightly bulge into Belgium. Arriving at the outskirts of Bihain, our jump-off to Langlir was delayed overnight while infantry attacks routed the enemy from acres of bazooka defended woods.

Before dawn, the tanks charged into action, skirting Langlir and plunging down the road to Lomre. Here D Company lost a tank to mines, but evened the score by knocking out a self-propelled gun. Casualties were heavy, especially among infantrymen, because of the artillery and mortar fire, which, during the past two weeks had been showered upon us in greater profusion than we had heretofore believed was in the realms of enemy capability. Twenty-seven prisoners were captured, another SP gun was destroyed and an 88mm ground mount, in addition to a signal truck and a half-track. A smoothly operated bazooka team from our infantry disabled two Mark IVs and two Mark Vs. Before dawn on the 14th of January, our tanks and infantry were creeping along the fringe of the woods south-east of Lomre. Across the fields of snow lay Cherain, our objective. The lead tank hit a mine but the attack moved on and the task force knocked out a Mark IV, a 20mm AA battery mounted on a half-track and a Volkswagen. Another Sherman died of wounds inflicted by an anti-tank gun, when it poked its nose out of the woods. Direct fire was coming from every angle, rapidly thinning our ranks. E Company tried to dash into Cherain and lost two more tanks. Angrily, Task Force Lovelady coiled again at the edge of the woods, organised a co-ordinated attack and struck with all their might. Three more tanks from E Company were lost along with most of their crews and many more infantrymen shed their lives in what was swiftly becoming only a monument to the memory of Task Force Lovelady.

To be sure, these were days to try the very souls of men! The grimness of the day before was multiplied on the 15th of January. Bitterly, the ten tanks left in our two companies, with the remnants of the infantry battalion again marched in the face of death. One tank returned, while the larger part of a hundred doughboys guarded the other nine with their lifeless bodies. Cold, wet, miserable with trench foot, frozen fingers and battle weary minds, men whose tanks had been knocked out would walk back into the aid station at Lomre. Here they stripped, sat by a hot stove whilst their clothes dried, ate and drank hot coffee. In a few hours they were fighting mad again, apparently offended by the effrontery of any German force who dared to defy the tanks of Task Force Lovelady. What Shermans could be repaired and others which could be mustered from maintenance company, were manned by these crews, who plunged back into the fray more than once never to return. To them we can but offer humble thanks.

When all else failed B Company's light tanks, charged into that deadly German target range, dashing wildly about, purposely drawing fire so that others could localize it, permitting artillery to be brought upon the offending pieces. This was no more successful than previous attempts. Finally, with two TDs from the 703rd TD Battalion, three light tanks and about 60 infantrymen left in the Task Force, we were withdrawn to Lomre, while other units attacked the defiantly held town of Cherain from every side until it eventually crumbled.

Task Force Lovelady was down but not out. This once great and powerful war machine was shattered but not irreparably. It was defeated but unashamed. Victory, like success, sometimes thrives in the face of adversity and oftimes is gained only by a series of defeats. TF Lovelady would rise again, as it had before, to avenge the lives of its comrades with the same forceful blows that had been dealt to Hitler's finest troops in three countries. No sooner had we withdrawn to Lomre and been attached to Combat Command A, than our maintenance teams set about recovering salvageable tanks and putting them into fighting order. By the 18th of January we had seventeen Shermans and ten light tanks ready for combat. The infantry battalion was relieved and a similar unit from the 335th Infantry Regiment of the 84th Division was attached. We were alerted to move through our nemesis, Cherain, and proceed to Sterpigny, where another mission awaited us.

On 20–21 January, 3rd Armored was relieved by elements of 84th Infantry Division and 4th Cavalry Group and withdrawn into reserve.

The 2nd Armored Division had just as difficult an action as 3rd Armored. In their History they make a striking comparison between the December and January phases of the 'Bulge'. It took six days to stop the German advance in the relatively open terrain over which they had fought in December 1944, while fourteen days were needed to oust the Germans from the more rugged, heavily wooded eastern Ardennes. Also the weather was surprisingly different – in the December days it had been good flying weather so air support was plentiful, but not once during January had conditions allowed the aircraft to fly. Also, in December the snow had just begun to fall, but by January it was deep enough to make the going almost impossible for men on foot, let alone for vehicles. Finally, and probably most telling, had been their orders. Initially they had been told to attack and destroy the enemy, in January this became to advance and clear the enemy from the zone, and they had to do this against an enemy who continually put up a very good rearguard defence.

Heavy armour losses

The heavy tank losses that were sustained in the Battle of the Bulge resulted in a critical shortage of tank crewmen. The normal crew for the M4 Sherman was five men: in the hull were the driver and assistant driver who sat next to him and manned the ball-mounted .30 machine-gun; in the turret were, in addition to the commander, the gunner, who sat on the right side of the gun, and the assistant gunner, who sat on the left side and loaded the main gun and coaxially-mounted machine-gun. As casualties became more acute the assistant driver had first to be eliminated which denied the tank the use of the ball-mounted machine-gun, which had been particularly effective against enemy infantry. Later on, the assistant gunner also had to be eliminated which meant that as well as all his other jobs, which included navigating, giving orders to the rest of the crew and operating the radio, the tank commander had also to load the main armament. The 3-man crew was the bare minimum to operate the tank and could not be sustained for very long.

Link-up

By the 15th the offensives of First and Third Armies had all but joined up, with patrolling taking place in the same area, but a proper junction did not take place in Houffalize until the following morning when a task force belonging to CCA of 2nd Armored Division, under the command of Lieutenant Colonel Hugh O'Farrell, met up with a patrol from 41st Armored Reconnaissance Squadron, 11th Armored Division, whose CO, Lieutenant Colonel Miles Foy, was close on their heels. Their meeting was filmed for posterity by both a motion picture cameraman (SSgt Douglas Wood) and a still photographer (Pfc Ernest Brown). To the considerable surprise of both officers they discovered that they had previously been classmates at the School of Armor at Fort Knox. Their link-up could be said to have sealed the end of the Battle of the Bulge, but the true end came a week later, when, on the afternoon of 23 January, 7th Armored Division attacked and retook St-Vith. The privilege of being the first unit to enter the town was rightly given by CG 7th Armored, Major General

Hasbrouck, to Brigadier General Bruce C. Clarke's Combat Command B, which had defended it so gallantly just a month previously. CCB received a Unit Presidential Citation for its outstanding performance at St-Vith, First Army Operations Report for the period reading: 'Without control of the communications center of St-Vith, focal point of five main highways and three rail lines, the enemy's armored, infantry and supply columns were all practically immobilized ... The salient of St-Vith not only threatened the whole of Fifth Panzer Army's northern flank, but continued to prevent the movement of Sixth SS Panzer Army. This afforded US First Army sufficient time to bring up reinforcements to a new defense line.' Undoubtedly it had been a major factor – perhaps *the* major factor in ensuring the failure of 'Wacht am Rhein'. And remember, that after this failure, despite the fact that the war would still drag on for a number of months, the Germans had no more operational reserves left, so they were no longer capable of successfully offering proper resistance on either the Western or the Eastern Fronts.

Now that the battle was won, SHAEF ordered US First Army to revert to 12th Army Group command, but left US Ninth Army under Montgomery's operational control. He wasted no time in withdrawing all British troops in order to regroup for the Rhineland: 'Now was the opportunity', he wrote later, 'to proceed with the utmost despatch to carry out our plans, in order to take full advantage of the enemy's failure.'

Notes

1 Gelb, Norman. *Ike and Monty, Generals at war.*
2 Ibid.
3 Ibid.
4 As quoted in *Monty* by Nigel Hamilton
5 The basic German air combat unit was the Squadron of between 9–16 aircraft led by a Lieutenant. Three Squadrons formed a Group of some 30–60 aircraft commanded by a Major. Three Groups, plus a staff element, the CO being a Lieutenant Colonel, formed a Wing of 90–150 aircraft.
6 US Fifteenth Army, which became operational in January 1945, with two corps and six divisions, was destined to serve primarily as an occupation force as the Allies swept through Germany.

11
CONCLUSIONS

A good example from the German side
As I mentioned in the opening chapter, Major (later Generalmajor,
German Cross in Gold, Knight's Cross with Oakleaves) Otto Ernst
Fritz Adolf Remer, was given command of the Führer Begleit (Escort)
Brigade and promoted first to Oberst, then to Generalmajor, for his
prompt and loyal action after the assassination attempt on his Führer
had failed. His brigade, which contained elements of most arms and
services, was initially in OKW reserve, but from 18 December onwards
fought on the left flank of von Manteuffel's Fifth Panzer Army
throughout the remainder of 'Wacht am Rhein', so it forms a useful
microcosm of the German forces involved in the Bulge operations.
Remer later wrote a study of his part in the operation, making some
valuable and penetrating comments on why the operation failed. I
believe that by studying this 'microcosm' one will be able to extract a
list of useful 'Conclusions' that apply to the operation as a whole from
the German point of view.

Preparation. At the end of November 1944, the Begleit Brigade,
which had been guarding Hitler's HQ at Rastenburg, was transferred to the west for operational duty. Hitler divulged neither the
purpose of the new task nor the exact destination, Remer being
merely ordered to assemble the brigade in the Eifel for 'training and
re-organisation'. He was, however, given some explicit instructions
by Hitler. First, that his brigade would only be employed as a
complete brigade; secondly, that he should take care that it was not
thrown prematurely into local operations; thirdly, and most intrigu-
ingly, that he was to send back daily reports (via an assigned radio
station, and presumably for his Führer's personal consumption)
giving details of the condition and potential commitment of the

brigade (this link to OKW did not prevent his receiving conflicting orders from Heeresgruppe, HQ Fifth Panzer Army and LXVI Corps *all* at the same time during operations!). However, from his original instructions he surmised that a major offensive was being planned, but at this stage he was not told anything precise, although later (some few days prior to 16 December) he was told that his brigade would initially be part of Army Group Reserve. They arrived at Daun in the Eifel at the beginning of December and he was immediately struck by the high state of security – only single vehicles were allowed to move by day; major movement was strictly controlled during the night. If columns had not reached their destinations during one night they must halt, clear the road and camouflage themselves from the air. And there were many other restrictions: units had to suspend training activities when enemy aircraft were near; postal communications were totally suspended; command posts were forbidden to be signed; complete radio silence was imposed, etc. The conspicuous concentration of troops in the Eifel was explained away by deceptive information that they were there to counter possible enemy attacks, yet it must have seemed strange to any of the soldiers who thought about what they were doing, that the tactical training concentrated on river crossings, fighting for defiles and roadblocks, night attacks on a company scale, assault patrolling, quick penetration of forests and villages, etc., in fact all primarily offensive rather than defensive operations. On the maps, a line some kilometres behind the front line, was indicated as 'only to be crossed on foot'. Potentially unreliable soldiers[1], who might desert were weeded out during this training period.

All these precautions accorded with what was happening in the rest of the Army Group and clearly they were highly successful in preventing the Allies from learning about the coming offensive. However, restrictions, such as no mail from home, must have had an adverse effect upon the morale of officers and soldiers alike.

Battlefield Replacements. Before the offensive Remer put about 20 per cent of his Brigade's allocated personnel and *matériel* into a field replacement battalion. He also had the foresight to detach some of his ablest officers and NCOs to train them, which paid dividends. During the offensive, replacements reached the front three times from the field replacement battalion, so the brigade, which had considerable losses during the continuous hard days of combat, was kept up to strength and was able to expand into a small panzer division in February 1945, prior to their transfer to the Eastern Front. Based on operational experience in Russia, it had been ordered that rifle companies should not exceed 40 men, because stronger companies could not be properly led in battle by young company commanders, and would only cause unnecessary concentrations which resulted in casualties. 'The combat strength of large companies, especially inexperienced, youthful units, dropped to about a third of their original strength after the first battle and then usually remained at this level for some time.'[2] Remer also makes the point that infantry should only remain in their armoured personnel carriers until contact was made, because a direct hit on an APC usually resulted in the loss of the entire crew. Additionally, weapons such as mortars and machine-guns which were temporarily out of use because of casualties, should be recovered and not just left on the battlefield.

Organisation. On arrival at the assembly area Remer's brigade was 're-organised', its weapons, tanks and guns being brought up to full authorised strength, although some of their equipment did not arrive until the offensive had already begun. Furthermore, while that part of the brigade which he had brought from the Führer's HQ was in excellent shape as far as composition, education, training and personal weapons handling, were concerned, the newly added units lacked battle experience and were not so well equipped. He does, however, make the distinction that the Panzer Battalion Grossdeutschland was the exception as it had always been part of an élite force since the formation of Panzer Division Grossdeutschland in May 1942. The assault gun battalion had been issued with new guns, but some of these had been left damaged on the road between the railway station and the assembly area, because the drivers were inadequately trained. Workshop facilities and recovery services were completely inadequate. For security reasons the tanks and assault guns could not be 'broken-in', so guns were first adjusted by trial firings only two days before the offensive began. Remer makes no mention of ammunition shortages, but it is a fact that in December 1944 the German *total* 105mm gun/howitzer ammunition stock was less than half of what it had been on 1 September 1939, so clearly they were experiencing shortages from the outset of the campaign. The Flak Regiment Hermann Göring was probably the best-equipped and best-trained flak unit in the entire Wehrmacht, but it was hard to use within the framework of a relatively small brigade; moreover it was extremely difficult to move in the difficult country-side of the Ardennes and Eifel, because of its large 12ton tractors and 10.5ton guns. Needing relatively firm soil and good roads, they frequently blocked the advance routes. Their anti-tank capability was excellent, being able to knock out enemy tanks at 3,000 metres. The light flak battalion, on the other hand, was much more manoeuvrable and provided good air defence, though Remer admits that there were: '... repeatedly over the brigade area, attacks by low-flying planes and fighter planes', one of the major problems once the weather cleared.

The brigade had only one light artillery battalion (containing two light batteries and one heavy) whose tractors could get across country 'only to a limited extent', and he says that he would have preferred to have a second artillery battalion – preferably SP – than the cumbersome heavy AA battalion. Clearly the brigade was short of integrated artillery, which they found to be a major drawback during offensive operations. A similar drawback was the lack of sufficient means of communication – he had only one signals company (half wire, half radio) with which to control the operations of three independent battalions and the remainder of his brigade. Other major drawbacks included: no integrated combat engineers, so they always had to rely upon corps/army engineers; a shortage of military police for traffic control; transportation space allocated was only one fifth of what was needed.

Losses. A scrutiny of the casualties sustained is illuminating: in total there were almost 2,000 casualties of whom 450 were killed and about 100 were missing in action. Some 60–70 per cent of these losses were the result of hand-grenade splinters (indicating the severity of the close-quarter fighting). What was feared most of all was the American ability to put down concentrated, flexible artillery fire. About 15–20 per cent of their casualties were from aerial attack – bombs or low-level strafing – though these losses were mainly sustained by the supply troops and reserves, the forward troops having, as has already been mentioned, excellent AA resources. Among the fighting troops, approximately 10 per cent of the casualties were caused by tank fire and the rest by infantry fire. Of the brigade's nine commanding officers, three were killed and four injured, so clearly Remer's commanders led from the front in typical German fashion.

Of his 100 tanks, the brigade had 25–30 in operational condition after their part in the offensive was over. Of the casualties, 10–12 were knocked out by tank/anti-tank gunfire; 5–10 ran over mines; the remainder had to be destroyed during operations because they lacked fuel or could not be towed away because of lack of recovery vehicles. (This was an Army Group-wide shortage. It was estimated that, for the total 1,700–1,800 tanks and assault guns in Army Group B, there were *only six* tank repair companies!) So far as Remer's artillery was concerned, they lost only two of their ten light guns – one from a direct hit, the other run over by a tank. One of the heavy guns had to drop out after being hit by a bomb, while of the 24 heavy AA guns three were lost by enemy action. Of their 135 APCs, 45 were lost, mostly to artillery fire; in the rear areas a relatively high number of supply trucks were lost to fighter ground-attack sorties.

Enemy Casualties. On the credit side, Remer claims that the brigade put 140–150 enemy tanks out of action and that before they were obliged to destroy their own tanks when abandoning territory they had gained, the ratio of losses between the two sides was one to eight – Remember 'You always haff eleven!' – so it was based on fact not supposition. Some 20–30 enemy artillery pieces were captured or destroyed. Something they did find remarkable was the large number of serviceable enemy soft-skinned vehicles that they captured – some 60–70 Jeeps and about the same number of trucks: 'But the joy was short-lived because these vehicles consumed too much fuel.' A total of sixteen enemy aircraft were shot down, thirteen by the flak battalion and three by the infantry. The brigade took 400–500 prisoners. The major item which they did not capture was fuel, although 'fuel finding details' always accompanied fighting troops. On the other hand they did live almost exclusively on the considerable quantities of food, clothing and equipment that were taken.

Fuel. 'The brigade had continuous fuel difficulties after 20 December and most of the tactical decisions were dependent on the fuel situation.' The planning allowed for 4.2 daily issues of fuel for the brigade, one 'daily issue' being the amount of fuel needed for every vehicle per 100 kilometres of travel, and when they began to advance out of the Daun area on Day 3 of the offensive they had only two daily issues. The entire transport section had been sent four days previously to collect the rest of their agreed fuel allocation from a location far in rear of the River Rhine – they never received it, although there were individual vehicles arriving sporadically , but never whole convoys. The fault lay in a variety of problems, such as road congestion, vehicle breakdowns, enemy action (on some days as much as 50 per cent was 'set aflame') and there were a certain number of cases of a unit stealing another's fuel supplies. Enemy stocks were captured, but never enough as had been optimistically expected. It was standard practice to siphon all fuel from captured vehicles. However, Remer comments critically that 'tactical decisions were dependent on the fuel situation'.

Reasons for the failure of the offensive

Remer gives the following as being, in his opinion, the reasons for failure of the offensive:

a. **Weather.** The start date for 'Wacht am Rhein' was deliberately chosen (a period of overcast skies was expected) so as to eliminate as far as possible enemy air action, because of their own inferiority. This became even more important once the Eifel region was chosen as the assembly/initial combat area, because it involved channelling heavy traffic through relatively few roads. Then, contrary to all the weather forecasters' predictions, the skies cleared after the first week – *just when the fighting troops and their immediate back-up were trying to negotiate the worst of the road network.*

b. **Adverse terrain and bad road conditions.** Everywhere, but especially in those areas where snow had already fallen, road conditions deteriorated rapidly and to add to the misery most units did not have winter equipment for their vehicles, in particular, for their AFVs. Remer quotes an example of the chaotic road conditions which his Brigade encountered in the St-Vith area, where it was impossible to commit a mobile panzer unit, like his brigade, in time, even when one made allowance for the technical inexperience of his young tank drivers. 'It was impossible to launch a panzer unit on a road which at places could be used only in a single file. Moreover, the entire road was required by the *horse-drawn* 18th VGD, which was just moving up toward the front. Columns of the Sixth SS Army were also using it. *Yet I was ordered to advance along this road from Roth via Auw and Schönberg to St-Vith.*'

c. **Lack of Fuel.** Coupled with the adverse weather and terrain difficulties, Begleit Brigade suffered from lack of fuel from the third day onwards. Because of the state of the roads, fuel vehicles had to be towed forward by tracked vehicles, thus increasing fuel usage, indeed *twice* as much POL was used as had been allowed for and of course, nowhere near as much fuel was being delivered as anticipated because of bad roads, enemy air activity, etc. After Christmas, except for a few days, enemy air activity prevented almost every movement of whole units on the roads. Assemblies and major operations were also attacked with increasing severity. Units had been directed to do their marching, transferring and part of their fighting by night.

d. **Underestimating the enemy.** Remer makes the point that as far as the 'St-Vith episode' was concerned, he believed that the enemy resistance was considerably underestimated. This is perhaps a major criticism that can be laid at the door of all the German commanders. They were so positive that the young, 'un-blooded' GIs would give in quickly, that their unfounded optimism coloured all their plans, in particular, their timings.

e. **Lack of combat troops.** Despite the fact that on paper three Armies were employed in the offensive, Remer considers that a smaller number of combat units were actually available than had been planned for. Some units were prevented from taking part because they were urgently needed in other endangered sectors; others were probably never despatched at all, after High Command realised that the Meuse would not be reached and crossed in the four to five days as was originally planned.

f. **Quality of Units.** Personnel and *matériel* did not reach the anticipated standards in many units. All the panzer divisions were short of tanks and some VGD and *Volks* artillery corps were short of horses. Consequently there was no substantial support by corps or army artillery at vital times, such as at St-Vith and Bastogne. The Brigade never received additional artillery support, so was always dependent upon its single artillery battalion. The US artillery, on the other hand, with its large expenditure of ammunition, was always superior. 'This cost us much blood in difficult attacks,' Remer comments bitterly. A number of divisions and units had no combat experience or experience in teamwork, and there was a general lack of experienced NCOs and junior officers in many units, though not in his Brigade.

g. **Air Support.** Remer comments that there was no notable support from the Luftwaffe. Indeed he goes so far as to say: 'The complete lack of air support on the one hand and the continuous enemy air activity on the other had a considerable effect on the morale of our troops.'[3] Without the 'airborne artillery' of the *Bltzkrieg* era, the boot was very much on the other foot. It must be remembered, however, that from the Luftwaffe perspective the view was somewhat different. Galland, as has already been mentioned, lamented that the Ardennes offensive had given the air force its 'death blow' and he puts this down to the unfamiliar conditions, lack of training and combat experience as much as to numerical strength.

Conclusion

Generalmajor Remer closes his short treatise on the failed offensive with the following 'Conclusion', which I believe is well worth quoting in full as it encapsulates what were undoubtedly the hopes and fears of the German soldiers who fought in the Ardennes:

Every officer and every soldier who took part in this operation knew its significance. Through a lightning-like advance across the Meuse River in four to five days, to Antwerp in about fourteen days, it was to lead to the destruction of about half of the invasion armies and the elimination of the important supply post of Antwerp. Hitler's warning, that we would either take Antwerp or in 1945 be faced with a war of *matériel*, which we would not be equal to, clearly defined the stakes. The supreme command's goal, to induce the West through a clear offensive victory to step out of the war or agree to negotiations which would allow a free hand in the East, had failed.

Another reason for a speedy success, and also a reason for the early beginning on 16 December even though preparations had not yet been completed, was that the date of the beginning of the Russian offensive out of the Baranov bridgehead was known. By this date the Eastern Front, which according to Hitler had been weakened to the limit in favour of the Ardennes offensive, was to be furnished the bulk of the panzer divisions no longer needed in the west. Instead, the departure of the divisions earmarked for the east was delayed by weeks after the failure of the offensive for lack of fuel.

It was further hoped that this offensive would diminish attacks on Germany and her paralysed key industries. The industries could again attain the full capacity output of armaments in the construction of new types of aeroplanes, production of synthetic gasoline, etc. But these hopes were also frustrated.

The optimism wakened by the first success of the Ardennes offensive both at home and with the men at the Eastern Front turned to dejection. Among the units participating in the offensive the initially excellent psychological attitude of the soldiers was profoundly shocked. When I reported to Hitler on 30 January 1945, I frankly stated that the frustration of hope had had a paralysing effect on the troops, that with the decimated units I had seen everywhere after the offensive, the race could no longer be won. With the great hopes of the offensive abandoned, we all now hoped that the Government would find a political solution for ending the war.

If the German officer, like any soldier, continued to do his duty, true to his oath and resigned himself to fight on in compliance with orders, he did so in the belief that any hour a political solution would come. On the Eastern Front, however, he fought with the knowledge that every yard of German soil trodden and defiled by Bolshevism signified the annihilation and destruction of German and Occidental culture.

And on the other side of the hill

In the Epilogue to his book: *The Ardennes: Battle of The Bulge*, in the official United States Army in WWII series, Hugh M. Cole draws many similar conclusions to Otto Remer, but of course from the other side of the hill, so most of the minuses are now pluses. Nevertheless, some major factors such as weather and terrain made life equally unbearable for both sides. For an army that was so magnificently equipped as the American, it was surprising, for example, that one of their major casualty producers was not the hand-grenade splinter, but rather the inadequacy of their footwear. Trench foot, caused by the fact that the GIs' footwear was not anywhere near as good as the German jackboot, accounted for a significant number of casualties.

Tactical reasons why the offensive failed.

Hugh Cole lists the following reasons why the German armoured advance failed to come forward as planned:

a. The initial US defence had been much more stubborn and tenacious than had been anticipated, so the rapid penetration of their positions had not been achieved (cf., Remer's point about underestimating the enemy).

b. Tactical support and resupply had not kept pace with the advance of the fighting troops. (As Remer has pointed out there were many reasons for this but mainly inadequate road network, terrain, weather and air attack.)

c. Denial of a free road net to use for control and ease of movement, this was especially because of the Americans retaining control over the two key road hubs of St-Vith and Bastogne.

d. The shoulders of the offensive had not been brought forward in time with the central thrust, the lack of forces and proper control causing the 'shoulders' to jam.

e. The slow build-up had prevented any real depth being achieved in time for the offensive to succeed before the Allies reacted sufficiently to halt it.

f. The tactical reaction of the Allied forces as a whole, especially the commitment of reserves had been much faster than anticipated.

Peripheral effects

In the North. There has probably been more argument about the British involvement on the northern flank of the 'Bulge' than in any of the major battles elsewhere in the Ardennes offensive. Such arguments range at one end of the spectrum from those that claim that the British 'saved the day' after the American lines had been breached and they were in headlong retreat, to those who deny any knowledge of British participation whatsoever. Both are of course miles from the truth. British units of XXX Corps were sent hurriedly to the Meuse and undoubtedly helped to prevent the Germans from capturing their hoped-for bridgeheads – an important deployment certainly, but not the turning-point of the Bulge offensive. Undoubtedly, however, Field Marshal Montgomery did play a key role in sorting out the defence of the northern shoulder and it was clearly the correct decision to put him in albeit temporary command of US First and Ninth Armies because

Bradley was out of communication with them and clear, precise orders were needed from someone who could appreciate the 'Big Picture'. However, his actions afterwards in what he unwittingly (or deliberately?) said to the Press did considerable harm to Anglo-American relations in SHAEF just at a critical moment in the war. He was indeed fortunate to be able to recant before an irreparable split took place.

In the South. Hitler's 'Nordwind' offensive was designed to take the pressure off the Ardennes front and prevent US Third Army from being able to disengage, swing to the north and relieve Bastogne. It failed because it was too weak and not properly co-ordinated and, more importantly, just as they had done in the Ardennes, the German High Command totally underestimated the American ability to fight a defensive battle. Although the numbers of German troops involved in this operation were considerably less than those employed in the Ardennes – they were also undoubtedly less well equipped – they did outnumber the Allied defenders. However, the fighting ability of the American and French soldiers and the effective defensive deployments in which they were positioned, plus their commanders' good use of interior lines of communication, certainly paid off. As the official history says: '... the German offensive was a close call. Had the attackers been able to articulate their units with the speed and, most important, with the unity of purpose that characterised the movements of their opponents, the results might have been far different.'

Summary

As I said in the Introduction, I believe that Hitler never really wanted just a limited military success, which was realistically the best he could have hoped to achieve with the forces he had available. Instead, he was far more interested in bringing about a major political change that would act in Germany's favour and would lead to a cessation of hostilities in the West. Then he could concentrate the Fatherland's dwindling assets upon the *real* enemy in the East. The 'Battle of the Bulge', however, was doomed to failure from the very beginning because the German ground troops were too weak to achieve their task and they lacked any credible air support, the Allies having virtually absolute air superiority once the weather had cleared. Other reasons which had also led to failure were the hampering effect of weather and terrain, which limited the attackers' freedom of action, in particular that of his better-equipped armoured troops; Hitler's system of High Command which gave only minimal freedom of action to his army commanders two of whom, Model and von Manteuffel, showed skilful leadership; while the choosing of the Ardennes as the correct place to carry out his counter-offensive was brilliant strategically, the actual selection of the *Schwerpunkt* in Sixth SS Panzer Army's area was completely wrong, because of the unforeseen difficulties with the terrain; their opponents had reacted far faster and with greater determination than had ever been imagined, being able to bring in uncommitted forces quickly, while the determined resistance of the American units – many without any battle experience – had been completely unexpected and had led, for example, to the failure of the attacking force to keep to their timetable; finally, the shortage of supplies, in particular fuel, had led to early failure being inevitable.

Even the Russians wanted to get into the act!
The proximity of timings between the Ardennes offensive and the beginning of the Red Army offensive on the Oder Front, caused Stalin to boast the following month that the victories they had achieved had materially affected the results of 'Wacht am Rhein': 'The success of this [Soviet] drive resulted in breaking the German attack in the West,' he said. Later the Soviets would refuse to pay back American wartime shipping loans on the grounds that they had saved the American forces in the Ardennes. The final straw came in a series of articles published after the war in which it was alleged that the Soviet attack in January 1945 '... averted the danger of the rout of the Anglo-American armies'.[4]

A last word from the Supreme Commander
In early November 1944, General Eisenhower had told a reporter of the *New York Times* that this phase of the war was like: 'climbing

the last and hardest ascent of a high mountain in a thick fog. You can't see where the top is and you won't until you suddenly reach the turn and begin to go down the other side.' Undoubtedly the German Ardennes offensive could well be likened to an unforeseen deep chasm suddenly encountered in the last part of the Allied ascent 'Up the Mountain', but once it was safely crossed the Allies could reach the top safely and start down the other side. It is interesting that Eisenhower claimed responsibility, both for the policy which led to the offensive taking place and for its successful conclusion, remarking to the US Secretary of War, Henry L. Stimson, a year later: 'From my viewpoint the German winter offensive of December 1944, was the outcome of a policy for which I was solely responsible... which, starting from the most meagre prospects in the minds of many doubters, ended in complete and unqualified victory. I consider myself solely responsible for this portion of the campaign (the Bulge) just as I do for all other parts of the campaign that were waged under my direction.'[5]

And as one who helped 'Scale The Mountain' recalled:

We advanced up the valley from Hotton under continual shell-fire, bombing and strafing – the road, and there is really only one, runs in places with a drop of hundreds of feet on one side and high, ice-covered cliffs on the other. Not a few tanks and vehicles, hit by shells or sliding in the snow and ice, crashed down into the frozen river in the valley. On the pine-covered slopes around the town masses of German tanks, self-propelled guns and vehicles lie shattered and snow-covered where the Allied bombers caught them as they concentrated for a further thrust. Along the road above the town, in the ditches or run over by tanks, lie the mutilated bodies of many of Hitler's followers. Squashed flat in the roadway are the remains of a fanatical youth who tried to stop a tank with a hand grenade. In a ditch lies a corpse of an oldish man, hit by a shell as he sheltered – twenty yards away is his helmet and his head. Young or old, fanatical or frightened, their fate is the same. Horrible it is perhaps, though its witnesses, callous and hard, are unaffected by such sights; and what does it matter to the victim whether he dies sleeping in his bed or finishes his chapter scattered in a hundred pieces on an Ardennes mountainside.'[6]

Notes

1 The report lists Alsatians, Lorrainians and *Volkliste III* (persons of German descent but of foreign nationality and considered to be politically unreliable).
2 WW II German Military Studies vol 12, Part V. The Western Theatre.
3 The post-war estimate of the number of Luftwaffe first-line aircraft on 16 December was about 1,500, so arguably there were enough to support the attack. Göring promised adequate support, but it never materialised.
4 As quoted from the USSR Information Bulletin of 12 May 1948 in *The Ardennes: Battle of the Bulge.*
5 As quoted in Miller, Merle. *Ike the Soldier As I knew Him.*
6 Peter Parnwell, late 7th Argylls.

Appendix 1
OPERATION 'WACHT AM RHEIN' GERMAN FORCES

Organisation (as at December 1944)
OB WEST
OB West had been formed in Paris in 1942 to control Army Groups B, C and H on the Western Front. By mid-December 1944 much of the territory that had been under their control had been lost, the Allies having pushed the Western Front back towards the border areas of Germany along the West Wall. Feldmarschall Gerd von Rundstedt was now back once more in overall command of OB WEST.

Army Group B
Under OB WEST was Army Group B (Feldmarschall Walther Model) which had been formed in the spring of 1942 to control the armies advancing on Stalingrad, then reformed in southern Germany in August 1943 and finally sent to France in January 1944, where it then controlled Seventh and Fifteenth Armies plus the Armed Forces in The Netherlands. By December 1944 it too had lost much of its strength on the Western Front. It was thus the obvious choice to command the Ardennes counter-offensive. The senior staff of Army Group B were:
Chef der Generalstab: General der Infanterie Hans Krebs
Ia: Oberstleutnant iG Reichhelm (iG shows him to be a member of the 'General Staff')
O Qu: Oberst iG Bloch von Blettnitz
Artilleriekommandeur: Generalleutnant Karl Thoholte
Below Army Group B was the 'Wacht Am Rhein' attack force made up of three Armies composed as follows:

Fifth Panzer Army
This was formed in Tunisia in December 1942, destroyed May 1943, reformed in Normandy 6 August 1944 from HQ Panzer Group West
Kommandeur: General der Panzertruppen Hasso von Manteuffel
Chef der Generalstab: Generalmajor Carl Wagener
Ia: Oberstleutnant iG Neckelmann
Ic: Oberstleutnant iG von Zastrow
O Qu: Oberstleutnant iG Birk
Artilleriekommandeur: Generalleutant Eduard Metz

Army Troops
Artillery
  19 Anti-Aircraft Brigade
  653 Heavy Anti-Tank Battalion
  669 Ost Battalion
  638, 1094, 1095 Heavy Artillery Batteries
  25/975 Fortress Artillery Battery
  1099, 1119, 1121 Heavy Mortar Batteries
Engineer
  207, 600 Engineer Battalions
  3 Organisation Todt Brigade (paramilitary engineers)

XLVII Panzer Corps
Formed in Danzig as an infantry corps, then dissolved and reformed in summer 1940 as a panzer corps, served on Eastern Front 1941–44, then transferred to France in June 1944 and fought in Normandy, Falaise and Ardennes. It would be finally destroyed in Ruhr pocket April 1945.

Kommandeur: General der Panzertruppen Heinrich von Lüttwitz
Chef der Generalstab: Oberstleutnant iG Count Bernstorff
Artilleriekommandeur: Oberst Langenbeck

XLVII Panzer Corps Troops
 15 *Volks* Mortar Brigade
 182 Anti-Aircraft Regiment
 766 *Volks* Artillery Corps

2nd Panzer Division
Kommandeur: Oberst Meinrad von
 Lauchert
Ia: Oberstleutnant iG Welz

 3rd Panzer Regiment
 2, 304 Panzer Grenadier Regiments
 74 Artillery Regiment
 273 Anti-Aircraft Battalion
 2 Reconnaissance Unit
 38 Anti-Tank Battalion
 38 Engineer Battalion
 38 Signals Battalion

Home Station: Würzburg (Wehrkreis XIII), later Vienna (Wkr XVIII). Formed in 1935, it was transferred to Vienna in 1938 and by the start of WWII most of the men in the division were Austrians. It suffered heavy losses in Poland in 1939, took part in the French campaign of 1940, then served on the Eastern Front until withdrawn to France to rest and refit in 1944. Re-organised in the Eifel area at Wittlich after suffering heavy losses in Normandy (by August it had only 25 tanks left), it absorbed men from the broken 352nd ID. At the time of the Ardennes offensive it still had a fair number of veterans in its ranks manning some 100 tanks and other AFVs. It would again suffer heavy casualties and by early 1945 was reputed to be down to just four tanks, three assault guns and 200 men. Ended the war defending Fulda in April 1945.

9th Panzer Division
Kommandeur: Generalmajor Harald
 von Elverfeldt
Ia: Maj iG von Grolmann

 33 Panzer Regiment
 10, 11 Panzer Grenadier Regiments
 102 Artillery Regiment
 9 Reconnaissance Battalion

 50 Anti-Tank Battalion
 287 Anti-Aircraft Battalion
 86 Engineer Battalion
 81 Signals Battalion
 Attached to 9th Pz Div: 301 Heavy
  Panzer Battalion

Formed as 4th Light Division in Vienna (Wkr XVII) in 1938 and took part in the invasion of Poland in 1939; that winter it was converted and redesignated 9th Panzer Division. Fought in 1940, playing a major role in taking The Netherlands. Fought in the Balkans, then on the Eastern Front in heavy combat, so that by January 1944 it was down to thirteen tanks. Sent to Nîmes, in South of France to be rebuilt and absorbed 155 Reserve Panzer Division. Fought in Normandy and managed to break out of the Falaise pocket but suffered heavy casualties there and then again around Aachen, where it lost two-thirds of its remaining combat strength. It was then sent to Army Group B's reserve at about the end of September 1944 to be rehabilitated. Its strength was made up by more than 11,000 reinforcements, and 178 AFVs which included some 22 of the late model Pz Kpfw VI Tiger tanks. It would play a major role in the Ardennes offensive. Later it was forced into the Ruhr pocket and surrendered there in April 1945.

Panzer Lehr Division (130th)
Kommandeur: Generalleutnant Fritz
 Bayerlein
Ia: Oberstleutnant iG Kaufmann

 130 Panzer Regiment
 901, 902 Panzer Grenadier Regiments
 130 Artillery Regiment
 130 Reconnaissance Battalion
 311 Anti-Aircraft Battalion
 130 Engineer Battalion
 Signals Battalion
 Attached to Pz Lehr Div: 559 Anti-
  Tank Battalion
 243 Assault Gun Brigade

Home Station was Wkr III; it was formed from the demonstration *(Lehr)* units of the tank training schools at Potsdam and the Bergen manoeuvre area in Wkr XI. After being sent to eastern France in early 1944, it went to Hungary where it absorbed 901 Lehr Inf Regt, then returned to France first in the Orléans then Le Mans areas in early June 1944. On D-Day it was one of the strongest divisions in the German Army and was rushed into the area around Caen where it was soon reduced to 20 per cent of its original strength. Sent to the St-Lô area, it was heavily attacked by USAAF bombers and virtually annihilated. Withdrawn and rebuilt once again in the Paderborn area, it first helped Army Group G against US Third Army, then was committed to the 'Bulge' operation, besieging Bastogne. By the end of the offensive it had just 300 men and fifteen tanks left.

26th *Volks* Grenadier Division
Kommandeur: Oberst (later General-major) Heinz Kokott
Ia: Major iG von Tisenhausen

39 Fusilier Grenadier Regiment
77, 78 *Volks* Grenadier Regiments
26 Artillery Regiment
26 Reconnaissance Battalion
26 Anti-Tank Battalion
26 Engineer Battalion
26 Signals Battalion

Home Station: Cologne, Wkr VI. Originally 26th Inf Div, it was to be rebuilt numerous times after heavy fighting on the Eastern Front. It was known as the 'Dom' Division after its divisional emblem which was patterned on Cologne Cathedral. Finally rebuilt in October 1944 in the Warthelager manoeuvre area in Poland, with recruits from Westphalia and the Rhineland, also from the Kriegsmarine and Luftwaffe, it had a strength of more than 17,000 men at the start of the Ardennes offensive. By the end the division had been whittled down to

fewer than 1,800, but it remained in action right up to the end of the war.

Führer Begleit Brigade
Kommandeur: Oberst (later General-major) Otto Remer
Ia: Oberstleutnant iG Raithel

102 Panzer Battalion
100 Panzer Grenadier Regiment
828 Grenadier Battalion
120 Artillery Regiment
120 Reconnaissance Unit
Anti-Tank Battalion
673 Anti-Aircraft Regiment
120 Engineer Battalion

Home Station: Berlin (Wkr III). Created for the Ardennes offensive (later, in 1945, it became the Führer Begleit Division), this formation had Hitler's personal escort brigade as its nucleus to which was added a tank battalion and some infantry from Panzer Division Gross Deutschland. It was also strongly reinforced with artillery (88mm and 105mm pieces) and assault guns (Sturmgeschütz).

LXVI Corps
Formed in autumn 1942 and saw service on the Eastern Front in 1943, then sent to SE France in early 1944 and took part in the withdrawal from the Mediterranean coast in front of the 'Dragoon' landings. Upgraded in 1944, it would fight in the Ardennes offensive, then later be destroyed in the Ruhr pocket.

Kommandeur: General der Artillerie Walther Lucht
Chef der Generalstab: Oberst iG Siewert
Corps Troops
  16 Mortar Brigade (comprising 86, 87 Mortar Regiments)
  244 Assault Gun Brigade
  460 Heavy Artillery Battalion

18th *Volks* Grenadier Division[1]
Kommandeur: Oberst Günter Hoffmann-Schönborn

293, 294, 295 *Volks* Grenadier Regiments
1818 Artillery Regiment
1818 Anti-Tank Battalion
1818 Engineer Battalion
1818 Signals Battalion

Home Station Wkr V. Formed in Denmark in September 1944, chiefly from Kriegsmarine personnel who had been transferred to the Army, together with men of 571st Grenadier Division and 18th Luftwaffe Division which had been decimated. It first saw action in the Trier area of France, then in the Roer dams battle before being committed to the Ardennes offensive, still roughly at full strength and with two months 'blooding'. It would take heavy casualties. It was still fighting two months later against the Allied drive on Prüm, before surrendering at the end of the war.

62nd *Volks* Grenadier Division
Kommandeur: Oberst Friedrich Kittel

164, 183, 190 *Volks* Grenadier Regiments
162 Artillery Regiment
162 Anti-Tank Battalion
162 Engineer Battalion
162 Signals Battalion

Home Station: Glatz, Wkr VIII. Mobilised from Silesian reservists in 1939, it fought in Poland and France, then on the Eastern Front where it suffered heavy losses at Stalingrad and Kursk. Withdrawn in September 1944 to refit and be re-organised in the Neuhammer manoeuvre area, with many Czech and Polish conscripts who spoke no German, it was transferred to the Western Front, and would fight in the Eifel and Monschau battles of the Ardennes offensive and be virtually annihilated at Monschau by US 9th Inf Div. It was finally destroyed in the Ruhr pocket.

LVIII Panzer Corps
Formed in 1943 in France; in August 1944 was in southern France. Fought in the Ardennes from December 1944.

Kommandeur: General der Panzertruppen Walter Krüger
Chef der Generalstab: Oberst iG Dingler

Corps Troops
7 *Volks* Mortar Brigade (84, 85 Mortar Regiments)
401 *Volks* Artillery Corps
1 Anti-Aircraft Regiment

116th Panzer Division
Kommandeur: Generalmajor Siegfried von Waldenburg
Ia: Oberstleutnant iG Guderian

16 Panzer Regiment
60, 156 Panzer Grenadier Regiments
146 Artillery Regiment
146 Reconnaissance Battalion
226 Anti-Tank Battalion
281 Anti-Aircraft Battalion
675 Engineer Battalion

Home Station: Rhine, Wkr VI. Formerly 16th Motorised (Pz Gr) Division, created in 1940 and fought in the Balkans, then on the Eastern Front. After receiving heavy casualties it was finally withdrawn in late 1943 to France, where it was amalgamated with 179th Reserve Panzer Division to form 116th Pz Div. The division was then in action in France in July 1944 at Mortain, then encircled at Falaise, but managed to break out with heavy casualties. The 'Greyhound' Division (named after its symbol) was down to just twelve tanks and some 600 men by the end of August. Withdrawn to the Düsseldorf area, it was reformed in September–October to 11,500 strong, but still had a shortage of tanks. By the time it was committed to the Ardennes offensive its tank strength was over 100, but would suffer heavy casualties spearheading the southern prong of the attack. Later it was withdrawn to

Kleve, then used in The Netherlands. Finally it was destroyed in the Ruhr pocket.

560th *Volks* Grenadier Division
Kommandeur: Oberst Rudolf Langhauser

1128, 1129, 1130 *Volks* Grenadier
  Regiments
1560 Artillery Regiment
1560 Anti-Tank Battalion
1560 Engineer Battalion
1560 Signals Battalion

Home Station: Wkr X. Formed initially from a mix of unit personnel and Luftwaffe personnel stationed in Norway and Denmark, it was located in southern Norway, but then upgraded and earmarked for the Eastern Front. Hitler cancelled this order and transferred the division to Denmark. It was committed into the Ardennes offensive as part of LVIII Panzer Corps. Later it would be switched to under command II SS Panzer Corps and fight in the Eifel near St-Vith, then go into Army Group B reserve, to be used in the battle for Echternach after 212th VGD collapsed. It would be finally destroyed in the Ruhr pocket.

XXXIX Panzer Corps
Kommandeur: Generalleutnant Karl
  Decker

This headquarters would be brought up from OKW Reserve towards the end of December 1944, to control some of the troops trying to take Bastogne, which included 1st SS Pz Div, Pz Lehr Div and 167th VGD. Despite his protests, it would, for a few days, be placed under command of Gen der Pztr von Lüttwitz, the German Orbat showing both corps under: 'Army Group Lüttwitz'.

167th *Volks* Grenadier Division
Kommandeur: Generalleutnant Hans-
  Kurt Hoecker

331, 339, 387 *Volks* Grenadier Regiments
167 Artillery Regiment
167 Anti-Tank Battalion
167 Engineer Battalion
167 Signals Battalion

Home Station: Wkr VII. Formed from Bavarian replacement/training units in 1939, the first 167th Infantry Division was practically wiped out on the Eastern Front, officially disbanded and its remnants absorbed by 376th Inf Div. The second 167th VGD was formed in Hungary in September 1944, consisting mainly of recruits from the partly formed 585th VGD and what remained of the shattered 17th Luftwaffe Field Division. Transferred to Belgium in December 1944, it was used in the later stages of the Ardennes offensive and then remained on the Western Front until February 1945, when US Third Army crushed it in the Siegfried Line battles. Remnants remained until it was totally destroyed in the Ruhr pocket.

Sixth SS Panzer Army
This was formed in the autumn of 1944 in the vicinity of Paderborn. After the Ardennes offensive it served in Hungary, then Austria where it was defeated by the Red Army in the Battle of Vienna.

Kommandeur: Obergruppenführer der
  Waffen SS Josef 'Sepp' Dietrich
Chef der Generalstab: Brigadeführer
  der Waffen-SS Fritz Krämer
O Qu: Standartenführer der Waffen-
  SS Ewert
Artilleriekommandeur: Gruppenführer
  der Waffen-SS Kruse

Army Troops
Artillery
  683 Heavy Anti-Tank Battalion
  741 Anti-Tank Battalion
  394, 667, 902 Assault Gun
    Battalions
  1098, 1110, 1120 Heavy Howitzer
    Batteries

428 Heavy Mortar Battery
1123 K-3 Battery
2nd Anti-Aircraft Division (41, 43
   Regiments)
Panzer
   506 Heavy Panzer Battalion
   217 Assault Panzer Battalion

Parachute Battalion Von der Heydte
4 Engineer Organisation Todt
   Brigade

I SS Panzer Corps
Formed in Germany in 1942, then
served on Eastern Front until 1944
when sent to Western Front (Normandy,
Falaise and then the Ardennes). In
January 1945 it was transferred to the
Eastern Front and fought in Hungary
and Austria.

Kommandeur: Gruppenführer der
   Waffen-SS Hermann Priess
Chef der Generalstab: Sturmbann-
   führer der Waffen-SS Lehmann
Artilleriekommandeur: Oberstleutnant
   Knabe

Corps Troops
   4 *Volks* Mortar Brigade (51, 53
      Mortar Regiments)
   9 *Volkswerfer* Brigade (14, 54
      Mortar Regiments)
   388, 402 *Volks* Artillery Corps
   501 SS Heavy Artillery Battalion
   501 SS Artillery Observation
      Battalion

1st SS Panzer Division
Kommandeur: Oberführer der Waffen-
   SS Wilhelm Mohnke

   1 SS Panzer Regiment
   1, 2 SS Panzer Grenadier Regiments
   1 SS Artillery Regiment
   1 SS Reconnaissance Battalion
   1 SS Anti-Tank Battalion
   1 SS Anti-Aircraft Battalion
   1 SS Engineer Battalion
   1 SS Signals Battalion
   Attached 501 Heavy Panzer
      Battalion

Home Station: Berlin. The 'Liebstandarte (Personal Flag/Standard) Adolf
Hitler' was formed in 1934 from
volunteers, as a bodyguard unit for the
Führer. It served as an independent
motorised unit in Poland and France
before being expanded into a fully
motorised infantry division early in
1941. After service in the Balkans and
then Russia, it was decimated at the
Battle of Rostov in 1941–42, pulled
out and sent to rest and refit in
northern France. It returned to the
Eastern Front and took part in much
heavy fighting until again being withdrawn to Belgium where it was reinforced to nearly 22,000 men. It fought
in Normandy, at Caen and Falaise,
until it was down to fewer than thirty
tanks when it was again withdrawn to
Germany to be rebuilt once more to
almost its old strength. Placed in
reserve behind Aachen, it would take
part in the Ardennes offensive then be
sent to Hungary, where, Hitler, who
was displeased by the division's performance, ordered them to remove their
'Adolf Hitler' cuff-titles. They are
reputed to have replied by sending him
a latrine bucket full of their decorations and medals! Retreating into
Austria, they fought in the Battle of
Vienna and ended the war on the
Eastern Front.

12th SS Panzer Division
Kommandeur: Standartenführer der
   Waffen-SS Hugo Kraas

   12 SS Panzer Regiment
   25, 26 SS Panzer Grenadier Regi-
      ments
   12 SS Artillery Regiment
   12 SS Reconnaissance Battalion
   12 SS Anti-Tank Battalion
   12 SS Anti-Aircraft Battalion
   12 SS Signals Battalion

The 'Hitler Jugend' (Hitler Youth)
Division was formed mainly from
Hitler Youth organisations[2] and its
training cadres came from the 1st SS

Panzer Division. First activated in June 1943, when the average age of its soldiers was 17, it was used primarily to train recruits for other SS divisions. In April 1944 it went to France and was rushed to Normandy on D-Day. It fought well, displaying both skill and courage, but sustained nearly 90 per cent casualties against British and Canadian troops in 21st Army Group sector. It prevented an Allied breakthrough at Falaise, was surrounded and down to some 300 men and ten tanks, but managed to escape complete destruction. Withdrawn and rebuilt to a strength of some 22,000, it was short of experienced junior officers. After the Ardennes offensive it moved to Hungary, then took part in the Battle of Vienna, and finished the war on the Eastern Front.

12th *Volks* Grenadier Division
Kommandeur: Generalmajor Gerhard Engel

48, 89 *Volks* Grenadier Regiments
27 Fusilier Regiment
12 Artillery Regiment
12 Anti-Tank Battalion
12 Engineer Battalion
12 Signals Battalion

Home Station: Schwerin Wkr II. The 12th VGD took part in nearly every major campaign of the war, fighting in Poland, France and on the Eastern Front. Rebuilt in East Prussia during the summer and early autumn of 1944 to nearly 15,000 men, it was redesignated a VGD and sent to Aachen in mid-September, then would fight in the Ardennes offensive as part of I SS Panzer Corps. During the retreat afterwards, it came under II SS Panzer Corps, but remained on the Western Front after Sixth SS Panzer Army went east. In February 1945 it opposed US Ninth Army's advance across the Roer. Finally destroyed in the Ruhr pocket in April 1945.

277th *Volks* Grenadier Division
Kommandeur: Oberst Wilhelm Viebig

289, 990, 991 *Volks* Grenadier Regiments
277 Artillery Regiment
277 Anti-Tank Battalion
277 Engineer Battalion
277 Signals Battalion

Home Station: Stuttgart, Wkr V. The first 277th VGD was formed in June 1940 and disbanded two months later. It was not until December 1943 that the second received any manpower and in January 1944 it went to Croatia, then to Narbonne in southern France. Sent to Normandy in mid-June, it fought well around Caen, but was badly mauled until it was down to fewer than 1,000 combat troops (plus a further 1,500 administrative personnel). Sent to Hungary, it was rebuilt as a VGD, although it contained many ethnic Germans from conquered border regions. After the Ardennes the remnants were trapped in the Ruhr pocket and surrendered.

3rd Fallschirmjäger (Parachute) Division
Kommandeur: Generalmajor Wadehn

5, 8, 9 Parachute Regiments
3 Artillery Regiment
3 Reconnaissance Unit
3 Anti-Tank Battalion
3 Engineer Battalion
3 Signals Battalion

Formed in the Reims area of France during late 1943 with a cadre from 1st Fallschirmjäger Division, and brought up to a strength of some 17,000 men. It did not take part in airborne operations but fought as an infantry division. Almost completely destroyed in Normandy and then surrounded at Falaise, where its commander (Generalmajor Schimpf) was seriously wounded but carried to safety by the handful of men who escaped. It went on fighting under the direct command of Generalleutnant Meindl, commander II Fallschirmjäger Corps and was again surrounded (in the Mons pocket) but again managed to break out. Withdrawn, it was sent to Oldenzaal, Holland, to be rebuilt, mainly with inexperienced Luftwaffe ground troops, so it was short of experience at all levels. However, it would fight well in the Ardennes, suffer more casualties, then get caught near Eifel by one of Hitler's 'no withdrawal' orders and most of its personnel would be killed, wounded or captured. A few escaped but were finally encircled in the Ruhr pocket.

150 Panzer Brigade
Kommandeur: Obersturmbannführer der Waffen-SS Otto Skorzeny

According to Skorzeny's own narrative in his memoirs, the brigade was to consist of:
  two tank companies each of ten tanks
  three reconnaissance companies each of ten scout cars
  three motorised infantry battalions, each with two rifle and one heavy machine-gun company
  one light anti-aircraft company
  one Commando company
Headquarters staffs at brigade and battalion would be kept as small as possible, while they dispensed with the usual administrative services so as to save on manpower. Total strength was to be 3,000 all ranks.[3] However, according to Jean-Paul Pallud[4] the final strength was only about 2,500 of which 500 were from the Waffen-SS, 800 from the Luftwaffe and the remaining 1,200 from the Army. (See elsewhere for more details of the brigade personnel, weapons, equipment and vehicles, including the use of US and British vehicles/equipment/ uniforms).

II SS Panzer Corps
Kommandeur: Obergruppenführer der

Waffen-SS Willi Bittrich
Chef der Generalstab: Obersturmbannführer der Waffen-SS Keller
Artilleriekommandeur: Oberführer der Waffen-SS Bock

The Corps was formed in Germany in May 1942 and sent to northern France in July. In January 1943 it went to the Eastern Front, six months later to Italy, then back to France, back to the Eastern Front and finally to Normandy in June 1944. After being surrounded at Falaise and Mons it was sent to the Arnhem area to refit and was instrumental in foiling the Allied airborne offensive which should have culminated in the capture of the bridge. Next it took part in the Ardennes Offensive, then fought in Hungary and Austria.

Corps Troops
  502 SS Panzer Battalion
  502 SS Heavy Artillery Battalion
  502 Artillery Observation Battalion

2nd SS Panzer Division 'Das Reich'
Kommandeur: Brigadeführer der Waffen-SS Heinz Lammerding

  2 SS Panzer Regiment
  3 SS Panzer Grenadier Regiment 'Deutschland'
  4 SS Panzer Grenadier Regiment 'Der Führer'
  2 SS Artillery Regiment
  2 SS Reconnaissance Battalion
  2 SS Anti-Aircraft Battalion
  2 SS Engineer Bataillon
  2 SS Signals Battalion

The division had two home stations: 3 Regt at Munich and 4 Regt at Vienna. Formed during the winter of 1940/41 it was initially designated as a pz gren div and fought on the Eastern Front, where by the end of 1941 it was down to less than 40 per cent of its combat strength. Withdrawn to rest and refit in Vichy France in the summer of 1942, when it was converted to tanks. Returned to the Eastern Front and again suffered heavily, was again transferred to SW France (around Toulouse), then ordered to Normandy[5] where it was used as a 'fire brigade' to plug gaps. By mid-August it was down to about 450 men, fifteen tanks and six guns. Rebuilt, it would take part in the Ardennes offensive, then be sent to Hungary. It was still in action on the Eastern Front when the war ended.

9th SS Panzer Division 'Hohenstaufen'
Kommandeur: Oberführer der Waffen-SS Sylvester Stadler

9 SS Panzer Regiment
19, 20 SS Panzer Grenadier Regiments
9 SS Artillery Regiment
9 SS Reconnaissance Battalion
9 SS Anti-Tank Battalion
9 SS Engineer Battalion
9 SS Anti-Aircraft Bataillon
9 SS Signals Battalion
Attached: 519 Heavy Anti-Tank Battalion

Formed in late 1942/early 1943 in NE France, then moved first to the Mediterranean area, then to the Eastern Front in March 1944 and on to Poland. Soon after D-Day it returned to France and was heavily engaged in Normandy. Like 2nd SS Pz Div, it fought hard and was soon down to some 450 men plus a handful of tanks and guns. Posted to the Arnhem area with 10th SS Pz Div in late August, it was in the perfect position to thwart British 1st Airborne Division's attempt to capture and hold 'a bridge too far'. They would then take part in the Ardennes offensive, followed by Hungary then Austria. At the time of the Ardennes the division was very short of motor transport.

LXVII Corps
Kommandeur: Generalleutnant Otto Hitzfeld
Chef der Generalstab: Oberst iG Warning

Formed in 1940 and converted to a reserve corps in France in late 1942, it moved to the Somme area in the summer of 1944 and took part in the withdrawal from France. Upgraded that autumn, it was in the Aachen area in late 1944, then took part in the Ardennes offensive and was destroyed at Eifel and Remagen.

Corps Troops
17 *Volks* Mortar Brigade (88, 89 Mortar Regiments)
405 *Volks* Artillery Corps
1001 Heavy Assault Gun Company

3rd Panzer Grenadier Division
Kommandeur: Generalmajor Walter Denkert

8, 29 Panzer Grenadier Regiments (motorised)
103 Panzer Battalion
3 Artillery Regiment (motorised)
103 Reconnaissance Battalion
3 Anti-Tank Battalion
3 Engineer Battalion (motorised)
3 Anti-Aircraft Battalion
3 Signals Battalion (motorised)

Home Station: Frankfurt, Wkr III. Originally 3rd Inf Div in the peacetime army, it fought in Poland and France, then re-organised and fully motorised. Took part in Operation 'Barbarossa' and stayed on the Eastern Front until surrounded and surrendered to the Red Army at Stalingrad. A new division – now known as 3rd Pz Gren Div – was formed in SW France in the spring of 1943 and was sent to Italy in June, where it opposed the Allied landings at Salerno. Fought well in Italy and was transferred to France in August 1944. Suffered heavy casualties during the withdrawal, then at Nancy and Metz. Withdrawn and rebuilt in Germany, it still lacked a high percentage of troops and equipment. It would fight in the Ardennes, and in the Eifel battles and finally be destroyed in the Ruhr pocket.

246th *Volks* Grenadier Division
Kommandeur: Oberst (later Generalmajor) Peter Koerte

352, 404, 689 *Volks* Grenadier Regiments
246 Artillery Regiment
246 Anti-Tank Battalion
246 Engineer Battalion
246 Signals Battalion

Home Station Trier, Wkr XII. A
Hessian unit, mobilised in 1939 as
246th Inf Div, it took part in the invasion of France in 1940. It returned
there in late 1941, then in January
1942 went to the Eastern Front where
it remained until surrounded and
destroyed in July 1944. A second
246th Inf Div, this time a VGD, was
formed in Prague; it contained a few
survivors, ex-Kriegsmarine personnel,
etc. It first saw action in western
France in late September 1944,
relieving 116th Pz Div at Aachen in
early October. Much of the division
surrendered when the city fell and the
remnant was reformed under Oberst
Peter Koerte. It was earmarked to take
part in the Ardennes offensive, but was
heavily engaged in the Hürtgen Forest,
where by November its fighting troops
had been decimated. It was taken out
of action, boosted with a large number
of ex-Luftwaffe reinforcements and
went back into action in the Monschau
area in January 1945. It was sent to
Seventh Army in the February
following US Third Army's breakthrough at Prüm and ended the war on
the southern sector of the Western
Front.

272nd *Volks* Grenadier Division
Kommandeur: Oberst Eugen
  Kosmalla, then Generalmajor Eugen
  König from 13 December 1944

980, 981, 982 *Volks* Grenadier Regiments
272 Artillery Regiment
272 Anti-Tank Battalion

272 Engineer Battalion
272 Signals Battalion

Home Station: Wkr III. The original
272nd Inf Div was formed in June
1940, but disbanded after two months
and its soldiers (all older men) released
to civilian employment. Another
272nd Inf Div was organised three
years later in December 1943. Badly
under strength, it was sent to fight in
Normandy where it had been virtually
destroyed by August 1944. Withdrawn
to Wkr III, it was rebuilt later that
summer and designated a VGD, then
returned to the Western Front where it
would fight in the Hürtgen Forest, the
Ardennes and the Roer river battles. It
was scheduled as part of the assault
force for 'Wacht am Rhein', but was
actually engaged defensively against US
78th Inf Div. By January 1945, it was
all but completely destroyed and
finished its existence in the Ruhr
pocket in April 1945.

326th *Volks* Grenadier Division
Kommandeur: Oberst (later Generalmajor) Dr. Erwin Kaschner

751, 752, 753 *Volks* Grenadier Regiments
326 Artillery Regiment
326 Anti-Tank Battalion
326 Engineer Battalion
326 Signals Battalion

Home Station: Wkr VI. Organised in
late 1942, 326th Inf Div was part of
the occupation troops in Vichy France,
it was eventually sent to northern
France in July 1944, where it relieved
2nd Pz Div. Overrun at Caumont, it
was then trapped in the Falaise pocket
and only a few stragglers escaped. Sent
to Hungary, it was rebuilt as a VGD
and arrived back on the Western Front
in mid-December during the Roer river
battles. Generally poorly trained and
inexperienced, it would not do well in
the Ardennes offensive and would
eventually end up in the Ruhr pocket.

Seventh Army

Formed in 1940 for the campaign in the west, spent 1940–44 on occupation duties in western France. Fought in Normandy, then in the Ardennes offensive. Surrendered to the Americans in Czechoslovakia.

Kommandeur: General der Panzertruppen Erich Brandenberger
Chef der Generalstab: Oberst Freiherr Rudolf-Christoph von Gersdorff
O Qu: Oberstleutnant iG Fussenegger
Artilleriekommandeur: Generalmajor Riedel

Army Troops
  44 Machine-Gun Battalion
  999 Penal Battalion
  657, 668 Heavy Anti-Tank Battalions
  501 Fortress Anti-Tank Battalion
  1092, 1093, 1124, 1125 Mortar Batteries
  660 Heavy Artillery Battery
  1029, 1039, 1122 Heavy Mortar Batteries
  15 Anti-Aircraft Regiment
  47 Engineer Battalion
  1 Organisation Todt Brigade

LIII Corps
Kommandeur: General der Kavallerie Edwin Graf von Rothkirch und Trach
Chef der Generalstab: Oberst iG Bodenstein

Formed in late 1940, fought on the Eastern Front 1941–44 until destroyed. Reformed in 1944 and thereafter fought on the Western Front. On 22 December it would be brought forward to take command of 15th Pz Gren Div, Führer Grenadier Brigade and 5th Fallschirmjäger Div (from LXXXV Corps)

9th *Volks* Grenadier Division
Kommandeur: Oberst (later Generalmajor) Werner Kolb
  36, 57, 116 *Volks* Grenadier Regiments

  9 Artillery Regiment
  9 Anti-Tank Battalion
  9 Engineer Battalion
  9 Signals Battalion

Home Station: Giessen Wkr IX. Formed in 1935 as 9th Inf Div from men of Hessen–Nassau. Guarded Germany's western flank during the invasion of Poland and fought well in France, then spent three years on the Eastern Front until almost completely destroyed. Taken out of the line and rebuilt, it absorbed 584th VGD and became a VGD for the Ardennes offensive, being committed on 28 December. By April 1945 it had been almost completely destroyed – down to just the divisional commander and his staff. It surrendered after defending Nuremberg.

15th Panzer Grenadier Division
Kommandeur: Oberst (later Generalmajor) Hans-Joachim Deckert

  104, 115 Panzer Grenadier Regiments
  115 Panzer Battalion
  33 Artillery Regiment (motorised)
  115 Reconnaissance Battalion
  33 Anti-Tank Battalion
  33 Anti-Aircraft Battalion
  33 Engineer Battalion (motorised)
  33 Signals Battalion (motorised)

Home Station: Kaiserslautern Wkr XII. Originally formed in Sicily from remnant of 15th Pz Div (ex-Tunisia) so it contained a mix of units. It then served in Italy and took part in the withdrawal to the Gothic Line. It was transferred to southern France in the late summer of 1944 to assist in holding up the Allied advance. Pulled out of the line after months of continuous action, it was rebuilt so that by early November its manpower strength was some 13,000 men, but with little armour and few vehicles. It then fought around Aachen and Geilenkirchen, followed by the Ardennes offensive when it would take part in the siege of Bastogne. Afterwards it would retreat to the Kleve area and then end the war in northern Germany.

Führer Grenadier Brigade
Kommandeur: Oberst (later Generalmajor) Hans-Joachim Kahler

99 Panzer Grenadier Regiment
101 Panzer Battalion
911 Assault Gun Brigade
124 Anti-Tank Battalion
124 Reconnaissance Unit
124 Anti-Aircraft Battalion
124 Engineer Battalion

Composed with a nucleus of troops from those who guarded the outer defence of the Führer's headquarters, it had served for a short while on the Eastern Front before coming to the Ardennes.

LXXX Corps
Kommandeur: General der Infanterie
Franz Beyer
Chef der Generalstab: Oberst iG
Koestlin

First formed in Poland in September 1939 as 'Grenzkommando', then sent to Denmark, followed by the campaign in France in 1940. Stayed in France as XXXI Corps until converting to LXXX Corps in early 1942. Fought on the Western front 1944–45.

Corps Troops
408 *Volks* Artillery Corps
8 *Volks* Mortar Brigade
2 Mortar Regiment

212th *Volks* Grenadier Division
Kommandeur: Generalmajor Franz
Sensfuss

Home Station: Munich, Wkr VII. The 212th Inf Div was originally formed in southern Bavaria and took part in both the Polish and French campaigns, then the attack on the Soviet Union.

By the summer of 1944 it had been decimated, was withdrawn to Poland to be rebuilt as a VGD with a fair number of experienced men, so it was better than average; in fact one of the best VGD divisions to fight in the Ardennes. Nevertheless it would take heavy casualties, rifle companies soon being down to fewer than 30 men. The remnants would continue to resist in southern Germany until the end of the war.

316, 320, 423 *Volks* Grenadier Regiments
212 Artillery Regiment
212 Anti-Tank Battalion
212 Engineer Battalion
212 Signals Battalion

276th *Volks* Grenadier Division
Kommandeur: Generalleutnant Kurt
Moehring (from 18 December 1944
Oberst (later Generalmajor) Hugo
Dempwolff)

986, 987, 988 *Volks* Grenadier Regiments
276 Artillery Regiment
276 Anti-Tank Battalion
276 Engineer Battalion
276 Signals Battalion

Home Station: Wkr XI. The original 276th Inf Div was formed and disbanded early in the war. A second was formed in December 1943, then sent to SW France to finish training. Committed to Normandy, it was virtually destroyed in the Falaise pocket after which it was re-organised in Poland as a VGD. It would fight in the Ardennes offensive, again suffer heavy casualties including its commander, Moehring. Later it would oppose the American attempts to cross the Rhine, now down to 410 men only. It would be finished off in the Ruhr pocket.

340th *Volks* Grenadier Division
Kommandeur: Oberst (later Generalleutnant) Theodor Tolsdorf

694, 695, 696 *Volks* Grenadier
Regiments
340 Artillery Regiment
340 Anti-Tank Battalion
340 Engineer Battalion
340 Signals Battalion

Home Station: Königsberg, Wkr I. The original 340th Inf Div was mustered in East Prussia, then stationed in the Hamburg area until mid-1941 when it was moved to France. It then went to the Eastern Front where it was eventually practically destroyed. Rebuilt as a VGD in September 1944 by absorbing 572nd VGD, it fought around Aachen, then was attached to I SS Panzer Corps, taking heavy casualties in the Battle of the Bulge. Its remnants were probably absorbed into various shattered SS formations.

LXXXV Corps
Kommandeur: General der Infanterie
Baptist Kniess
Chef der Generalstab: Oberstleutnant
iG Lassen
Arko: Oberst Beisswaenger

Formed in 1940, it was on occupation duties for most of the war, then from 1944–45 on the Western Front. It surrendered in May 1945 near Pilsen in Czechoslovakia.

Corps Troops
406 *Volks* Artillery Corps
18 *Volks* Mortar Brigade (21, 22
Mortar Regiments)

5 Fallschirmjäger (Parachute) Division
Kommandeur: Oberst (later Generalmajor) Ludwig Heilmann

13, 14, 15 Para Regiments
5 Para Artillery Regiment
5 Reconnaissance Battalion
5 Para Anti-Aircraft Battalion
5 Para Engineer Battalion

Formed at Reims in March 1943 from XI Air Corps' Para Demonstration

Battalion, it was posted to Normandy where it was heavily engaged and trapped in the Falaise pocket and virtually destroyed. Later the Luftwaffe decided to rebuild the division from ground personnel, so it was no longer really a parachute division. It would be assigned to LXXXV Corps for the Ardennes offensive, take part in the siege of Bastogne and suffer heavy casualties while performing well considering the inexperience of its troops and commanders. By February 1945 it was down to less than a battle group in strength. Trapped against the Rhine it was almost totally destroyed and its divisional commander was captured.

352nd *Volks* Grenadier Division
Kommandeur: Oberst (later Generalmajor) Erich Schmidt

914, 915, 916 *Volks* Grenadier Regiments
352 Artillery Regiment
352 Anti-Tank Battalion
352 Engineer Battalion
352 Signals Battalion

Home Station: Wkr XI. Formed from elements of two other divisions in November 1943, it was deployed against the Allied landings in Normandy and after a few days was down to battle group strength. It held Caen against Allied assaults and was just about completely destroyed and its survivors absorbed into 2nd Pz Div. Rebuilt as a VGD in northern Germany, absorbing large numbers of Luftwaffe and Kriegsmarine personnel, it returned to the Western Front and played a full part in the Ardennes and Rhineland battles despite its lack of experienced troops. Surrendered to the Allies at the end of the war.

79th *Volks* Grenadier Division
Kommandeur: Oberst (later Generalmajor) Alois Weber

208, 212, 226 *Volks* Grenadier Regiments

179 Artillery Regiment
179 Anti-Tank Battalion
179 Engineer Battalion
179 Signals Battalion

Home Station: Koblenz Wkr XII. The 79th Inf Div was raised in 1939 and first saw action on the Saar front, then in France 1940. On the Eastern Front from 1941, it was encircled and destroyed at Stalingrad. A second was created in early 1943, sent to the Eastern Front where, again, it was destroyed (only one man lived to tell the tale). In the autumn of 1944 a third division was formed in Poland, this time as a VGD. Transferred to the Western Front, it would fight in the Ardennes offensive, earning considerable praise from its opponents, despite its lack of artillery.

Notes

1 Not to be confused with the original 18th Infantry Division which was converted first to motorised infantry, then to a pz gren div which served on the Eastern Front.

2 The 'Hitler Jugend' was the Nazi Party organisation for all German boys aged 15 to 18. It was made compulsory by the 'Hitler Jugend' Law of 1936, which banned all other youth organisations. The girls' equivalent was the 'Bund Deutscher Maedel'.

3 See *Skorzeny's Special Missions*

4 See Pallud, *et al*. Ardennes 1944: Pieper and Skorzeny.

5 En route to the front it committed a series of atrocities (e.g., hanging 95 men at Tulle and killing more than 400 men, women and children at Oradour in reprisal for the murder of their reconnaissance battalion commander).

Appendix 2
OPERATION 'NORDWIND'
GERMAN FORCES

Army Group G
Occupying the area below Army Group B was Army Group G, initially formed in southern France in May 1944 and commanded by Generalleutnant Hermann Balck, but during 'Nordwind' it was commanded by General Johannes Blaskowitz who took over on 22 December 1944 and so was responsible for the planning phase as well as its execution.

Army Group Oberrhein
Kommandeur: SS Reichsmarschall Heinrich Himmler
Formed on 10 December 1944 and completely independent of von Rundstedt's OB West and Army Group G, reporting instead direct to OKW and in practice direct to Hitler. It was to control Nineteenth Army in the Colmar pocket, as well as XIV SS Corps and various military and paramilitary units east of the Rhine.

First Army
Kommandeur: Generalleutnant Hans von Obstfelder

Initially formed for the French campaign in 1940, it spent 1940–44 on occupation duties in SW France then withdrew across southern France and along the Loire and upper Seine. In early 1945 fought in the Saar then retreated across SW Germany and surrendered in May 1945 south of Munich.

Nineteenth Army (in the Colmar pocket)
Kommandeur: General Friedrich Wiese, replaced on 15 December 1944 by Generalleutnant Siegfried Rasp.

Initially formed at Avignon in February 1943; controlled all German troops in French Mediterranean 1942–44; withdrew north in August 1944, retreated across SW Germany in 1945 and surrendered at Innsbruck on 5 May.

There were ten divisions in Nineteenth Army, although some of them were unable to muster more than a few thousand men – the equivalent of just one or two battalions. The divisions were (reading clockwise from the south): 30th SS Division; 338th, 189th, 159th Infantry Divisions; 269th, 16th, 708th *Volks* Grenadier Divisions; 716th, 198th Infantry Divisions; Division Buercky. There were also two Corps HQ involved: LXIV Corps and LXIII Corps

ASSAULT FORCES FOR 'NORDWIND'

XIII SS CORPS
Kommandeur: SS Gruppenführer und Generalleutnant der Waffen-SS Max Simon
17th SS Panzer Grenadier Division (Goetz von Berlichingen)
Kommandeur: SS-Standartenführer und Oberst der Waffen-SS Hans Lingner (captured 8 Jan 1945). His place was taken by SS-Standartenführer und Oberst der Waffen-SS Fritz Klingenberg.

17th SS Panzer Battalion
37, 38 SS Panzer Grenadier Regiments
17 SS Panzer Artillery Regiment
17 SS Reconnaissance Battalion
17 SS Anti-Tank Battalion
17 SS Engineer Battalion

17 SS Signals Battalion
17 SS Anti-Aircraft Battalion

Named after a German robber baron of the Middle Ages, this élite division was formed in France in October 1943. As well as Germans it included Volksdeutsche, Belgians and Roumanians. Practically destroyed in Normandy (St-Lô), it was withdrawn and rebuilt at Chartres, absorbing both 49th and 51st SS Panzer Grenadier Brigades. Fought in the battle of Metz and later in the Saar battles. Surviving fragments unsuccessfully defended Nuremberg.

36th *Volks* Grenadier Division
Kommandeur: Generalmajor August
  Wellm

Formed in 1935–36 as the 36th Infantry Division of the peacetime German army, in 1940 it became a panzer grenadier division, but after suffering heavy casualties in Russia it was first reformed as a two-regiment infantry division, then returned to Germany and was reformed as a three-regiment *Volks* grenadier division. Fought in 'Nordwind', then the Saar and finally in southern Germany.

Other troops in this element of the 'Nordwind' forces included:

404, 410 *Volks* Artillery Corps
20 *Volks* rocket-launcher Brigade
2 Armoured flame-thrower
  Company
2 Army artillery battalions
1 Artillery Observation Battalion

LXXXIX CORPS
Kommandeur: Generalleutnant Gustav Hoehne.

Formed as the 'Scheldt' Corps in Belgium in the summer of 1942, then upgraded to LXXXIX Corps in early 1943. Fought on the Western Front 1944–45 until destroyed.

256th *Volks* Grenadier Division
Kommandeur: Generalmajor Gerhard Franz.

The original 256th Infantry Division had been formed in 1939 and destroyed in the Soviet summer offensive in July 1944. A second 256th Div was formed as a VGD in September 1944 in Saxony. It took part in the Saar battles, northern Alsace, Bitche and in the Saar–Moselle, until it ended the war in southern Germany.

456, 476, 481 Grenadier Regiments
256 Artillery Regiment
256 Anti-Tank Battalion
256 Reconnaissance Battalion
256 Engineer Battalion
256 Signals Battalion

361st *Volks* Grenadier Division
Kommandeur: Oberst (later Generalmajor) Alfred Philippi

Formed in Denmark in late 1943, badly mauled in Russia in 1944, rebuilt in Germany incorporating 569th Grenadier Division. Fought in the Arnhem battles, then transferred to the Saar, where it absorbed remnant of 553rd Inf Div, before itself being absorbed by 559th Inf Div in January 1945.

951, 952, 953 Grenadier Regiments
361 Artillery Regiment
361 Anti-Tank Battalion
361 Engineer Battalion
361 Signals Battalion

XC CORPS
Kommandeur: Generalleutnant Erich Petersen

Formed in the winter of 1942/43 as IV Luftwaffe Feldkorps. Served in Russia, then in early 1944 transferred to French Mediterranean coast and took part in retreat to Alsace. Late 1944 redesignated XC Corps, fought on southern sector of Western Front until destroyed west of the Rhine in March 1945.

257th *Volks* Grenadier Division
Kommandeur: Generalmajor Erich
  Seidel

257th Infantry Division was formed in 1939, fought and suffered heavy losses on the Eastern Front and in the autumn of 1944 was rebuilt in Poland as a VGD, having absorbed 587th VGD, then fought in the Saar and on the Western Front until the war ended.
  457, 466, 477 Grenadier Regiments
  257 Artillery Regiment
  257 Anti-Tank Battalion
  257 Reconnaissance Battalion
  257 Engineer Battalion
  257 Signals Battalion

559th *Volks* Grenadier Division
Kommandeur: Generalmajor Freiherr
  Kurt von Muehlen

Formed in mid 1944 as a grenadier division, it was upgraded to VGD status and fought in eastern France, then in the Saar and Alsace, followed by the West Wall battles and was finally cut off and destroyed west of the Rhine.

  1125, 1126, 1127 Grenadier Regiments
  1559 Artillery Regiment
  1159 Anti-Tank Battalion
  1159 Reconnaissance Unit
  1559 Engineer Battalion
  1559 Signals Battalion

A later arrival was:
6th SS Gebirgs (Mountain) Division
(Nord)
Kommandeur: SS Gruppenführer und
  Generalleutnant der Polizei Kurt
  Brenner

Originally raised in Austria as an SS regiment in late 1940, then upgraded to a brigade and finally to a division in April 1941. It included many *Volks-*

deutsche mountaineers. Served in Finland and Russia from 1941, but initially did not do well. Remained in northern Russia until autumn 1944 and took part in the retreat from Lapland to Norway. Fought in the Saar and was then cut off west of the Rhine in March 1945. Put up a spirited resistance until captured in early April 1945.

  11 SS Gebirgs Regiment 'Reinhard
    Heydrich'
  12 SS Gebirgs Regiment 'Michael
    Gesimar'
  6 SS Gebirgs Artillery Regiment
  6 SS Gebirgs Anti-Tank Battalion
  6 SS Gebirgs Reconnaissance
    Battalion
  6 SS Gebirgs Engineer Battalion
  6 SS Gebirgs Anti-Aircraft Battalion
  6 SS Gebirgs Signals Battalion
  Attached: 506 SS Panzer Grenadier
    Battalion

**In reserve, under direct control of
Army Group G was:**
XXXIX Panzer Corps
Komandeur: Generalleutnant Karl
  Decker

21st Panzer Division
Kommandeur: Generalleutnant Edgar
  Feuchtinger

The original 21st Panzer Division was formed in late 1940 as 5th Light Division, sent to North Africa and destroyed in Tunisia in May 1943. A second 21st Panzer was formed in Normandy in mid-1943, equipped with obsolete foreign tanks and considered 'unfit to serve on the Eastern Front'. Nevertheless it fought well in Normandy and later was assigned to Army Group G; it was involved in the drive on Strasbourg and was eventually sent to the Eastern Front where it remained until the end of the war.

  22nd Panzer Regiment
  125, 192 Panzer Grenadier Regiments

21 Panzer Reconnaissance Battalion
220 Anti-Aircraft Battalion
220 Panzer Engineer Battalion
200 Panzer Signals Battalion

25th Panzer Grenadier Division
Kommandeur: Generalmajor Arnold
   Burmeister

Originally formed pre-war as an
infantry division and in late 1940 was
re-organised as a motorised unit.
Fought on the Russian Front until the
summer of 1944, then withdrawn to
Germany after heavy losses and rebuilt.
Opposed American advance at Metz,
then held the Bitche area and finally
defended a sector north of Berlin.

35, 119 Panzer Grenadier Regiments
125 Panzer Battalion
25 Artillery Regiment (motorised)
25 Anti-Tank Battalion
25 Panzer Reconnaissance Unit
25 Engineer Battalion (motorised)
25 Signals Battalion (motorised)

Later assembled for Operation
'Zahnarzt' (Dentist), but used elsewhere when the operation was
cancelled.

10th SS Panzer Division 'Frundsberg'
Kommandeur: SS Oberführer und
   Generalmajor der Waffen-SS Heinz
   Harmel

Formed in SW France in the winter of
1942/43, it transferred to SE France
and then to Normandy in late 1943,
and to Russia in March 1944. It

returned to France, via Poland, and was
badly mauled in Normandy (Falaise).
Sent to Arnhem to regroup, it was
responsible for the destruction of
British 1st Airborne Div there. Fought
at Aachen and then the Saar; the
survivors returned to the Eastern Front,
defended Berlin and then fought in
eastern Germany and Czechoslovakia.

10th SS Panzer Regiment
21, 22 SS Panzer Grenadier Regiments
10 SS Panzer Artillery Regiment
10 SS Anti-Tank Battalion
10 SS Panzer Reconnaissance
   Battalion
10 SS Panzer Engineer Battalion
10 SS Panzer Signals Battalion
10 SS Anti-Aircraft Battalion
10 SS Rocket-Projector Battalion

7th Fallschirmjäger (Parachute) Division
Kommandeur: Generalleutnant Wolfgang Erdmann

Formed in September 1944, it was in
action almost immediately to prevent
British XXX Corps from relieving
Arnhem. Upgraded to full parachute
division status, it took part in operations on the Western Front, first in the
north, then later opposing the Rhine
crossings.

19, 20, 21 Parachute Jäger Regiments
7 Para Artillery Regiment
7 Para Anti-Tank Battalion
7 Para Engineer Battalion
7 Para Signals Battalion

Appendix 3
OPERATION 'WACHT AM RHEIN'
ALLIED FORCES

This gives details of those Allied Forces that were primarily dealing with the 'Battle of the Bulge', namely. the German Operation 'Wacht am Rhein'. See Appendix 4 for details of those Allied Forces that opposed the German operation 'Nordwind'.

NB. Divisions were switched between Corps as the battle dictated and were added to the 'Bulge' forces from elsewhere; for example, when XVIII Airborne Corps was created US 7th Armored and 30th Infantry Divisions came from US Ninth Army, then 17th, 82nd and 101st Airborne Divisions from SHAEF reserve. They are shown below under the corps in which they were serving at the beginning of 1945.

SHAEF
Supreme Headquarters Allied Expeditionary Force (SHAEF) had been formed in the UK in February 1944, and the next month was set up near London in the Bushey Park area. Early in May, a forward HQ was established near Portsmouth, then after the invasion, the Supreme Commander, General Dwight D. Eisenhower, established a small advanced HQ near Tournières, south-west of Bayeux. On 20 September, SHAEF Main opened at the Trianon Palace Hotel, Versailles, with some 5,000 all ranks. It was still in this location throughout the 'Battle of the Bulge'. By early February 1945, the size of the staff had more than tripled, the lion's share being provided by the US military. Some of the main staff appointments were:

Supreme Commander: General
   Dwight D. Eisenhower

Deputy Supreme Commander: Air
   Chief Marshal Arthur W. Tedder
Naval CinC: Admiral Bertram H.
   Ramsay
Air CinC: Air Chief Marshal Trafford
   Leigh-Mallory

Chief of Staff: Lieutenant General
   Walter Bedell Smith
Deputy Chiefs of Staff: Lieutenant
   General F. E. Morgan;
   Lieutenant General Humfrey M.
   Gale;
   Air Vice Marshal J. M. Robb

G1 Division (Personnel): Maj Gen
   Ray W. Barker
G2 Division (Intelligence): Maj Gen
   K. W. D. Strong
G3 Division (Operations): Maj Gen
   Harold R. Bull
G4 Division (Supply): Maj Gen
   Robert W. Crawford
G5 Division (Civil Affairs): Lt Gen A.
   E. Grasett

Below SHAEF there were, by the time of the Ardennes Offensive, the following Army Groups (reading from north to south): British/Canadian 21st Army Group (Montgomery); US 12th Army Group (Bradley); US 6th Army Group (Devers). Within these Army Groups, the following formations and units were those directly concerned with halting the German assault (again reading from north to south).

BRITISH FORCES

HQ 21st Army Group
Formed in the UK on 9 July 1943 to command Canadian First Army and

British Second Army for the coming invasion of NW Europe. General (later Field Marshal) Sir Bernard Law Montgomery had been in command of 21st Army Group ever since its formation and would continue to be so when it became the main ground forces HQ for all Allied troops concerned with the invasion. However, as we shall see, his HQ would command British, Canadian and American troops during the Ardennes battle. His Chief of Staff was Major-General Francis Wilfred de Guingand.

NB. At the start of the Battle of the Bulge, HQ 21st Army Group was in command of both Canadian First Army and British Second Army. Later, on orders from SHAEF, it also took over command of US First and Ninth Armies. However, the only British troops to be involved in the battle were those in XXX Corps.

British Second Army
Army Commander: Lieutenant-
  General Sir Miles Dempsey
XXX Corps
GOC: Lieutenant-General Sir Brian
  Gwyne Horrocks

Chief of Staff: Initially Brigadier (later Major-General Sir Harold) 'Pete' Pyman. When he was promoted his place as BGS was taken by Brigadier (later General Sir Charles) C. B. 'Splosh' Jones.

HQ Location: Boxtel, Holland from 13 December 1944.

Corps Troops
  2nd Household Cavalry Regiment
  11th Hussars
  4th and 5th Royal Horse Artillery
  7, 64, 84 Regiments, Royal Artillery
  73 Anti-tank Regiment, RA
  27 LAA Regiment, RA

6th Airborne Division
GOC: Major-General Eric L. Bols

3rd, 4th Parachute Brigades
6th Airlanding Brigade

Divisional Troops
  6th Ab Div Reconnaissance Regi-
    ment, RAC
  3rd, 4th Airlanding Anti-tank
    Batteries, RA
  53rd Light Regiment, RA
  249 Ab Field Company, RE
  3, 591 Para Sqns, RE
  3, 9 Ab Sqns, RE
  286 (Ab) Fd Pk Coy, RE
  6 Ab Div Sigs, R Sigs
  22 Indep Para Coy, AAC

Formed in May 1943, its first commander was Major-General R. N. Gale. The division jumped and fought on D-Day and thereafter, until returning to the UK in early September 1944. On 20 December, it was given orders to move to Belgium and two days later the main body left its Wiltshire bases. By 26 December, it was concentrated between Dinant and Namur. It was withdrawn to Holland at the end of January 1945 and remained there until 24 February when it again returned to the UK. It would later be used in Operation 'Varsity' – the Rhine crossings, 23 March–1 April 1945.

51st Highland Infantry Division
GOC: Major-General T. G. Rennie

  152, 153,154 Infantry Brigades

Divisional Troops
  2 Derbyshire Yeomanry, RAC
  126, 127, 128 Field Regiments, RA
  61 Anti-tank Regiment, RA
  40 LAA Regiment, RA
  274, 275, 276 Field Companies, RE
  239 Field Park Company, RE
  16 Bridging Platoon, RE
  51 Divisional Signals, R Sigs
  1/7 Battalion, Middlesex (MG Bn)

51st Highland Div was first formed in September 1939, then captured in

France in June 1940, less 154th Infantry Brigade Group. On 7 August 1940, it was reconstituted by redesignating 9th (Highland) Inf Div a duplicate TA division. Before the NW European campaign, the division had fought in North Africa and Sicily. Prior to the Ardennes it had landed in Normandy and fought hard battles at Bourguébus Ridge and Falaise. A battle-proven division.

53rd Welsh Infantry Division
GOC: Major-General R. K. Ross

71, 158, 160 Infantry Brigades

Divisional Troops
53 Reconnaissance Regiment, RAC
81, 83,133 Field Regiments, RA
71 Anti-tank Regiment, RA
25 LAA Regiment, RA
244, 282, 555 Field Companies, RE
285 Field Park Coy, RE
22 Bridging Platoon, RE
53rd Inf Div Sigs, R Sigs

Formed in September 1939 as a first line TA infantry division. It was re-organised in May 1942 as a mixed division, then in October 1943 it was again re-organised and became an infantry division. It had been in the UK for the first four years of the war, moving to NW Europe 21 June 1944. Prior to the Ardennes it had fought hard battles in Normandy (The Odon, Caen, Mount Picon and Falaise) and then in Holland, so it was a battle-proven formation.

29 Armoured Brigade
Brigade Commander: Brigadier C. B. C. Harvey

23 Hussars
2 Fife & Forfar Yeomanry
3 Royal Tank Regiment
8 Rifle Brigade

Formed on 29 December 1940 in the

UK, 29 Armd Bde was part of 11th Armoured Division until 14 December 1944, when it was put under direct command of 21st Army Group for five days (15–20 Dec 1944), then 53rd Inf Div (20–22 Dec), XXX Corps (22–27 Dec), 6th Ab Div (28 Dec –13 Jan 1945), then back to 11th Armd Div via 21st Army Group. The Brigade had just handed in all its tanks prior to receiving new ones, so had to redraw the old ones post-haste!

33 Armoured Brigade
Brigade Commander: Brigadier H. B. Scott

1 Northamptonshire Yeomanry
144 Regiment, RAC
1 East Riding Yeomanry

Formed in the UK on 17 March 1944 by the redesignation of 33 Tank Brigade, it was a battle-proven brigade which had been in NW Europe since 13 June 1944. On 22 December 1944 it came under command of XXX Corps until 18 January 1945.

34 Army Tank Brigade
Brigade Commander: Brigadier W. S. Clarke

9 Royal Tank Regiment
107 Regiment, RAC
147 Regiment, RAC

HQ formed in December 1941, then in June 1942 it was redesignated 34 Army Tank Brigade in the UK. Entered NW Europe on 3 July 1944 and fought in Normandy and in the Scheldt Estuary prior to the Ardennes. Under command of XXX Corps from 27 Dec 1944 until 1 Feb 1945.

NB. In reserve within XXX Corps were: the Guards Armoured Division, 43rd (Wessex) Infantry Division and 50th (Northumbrian) Infantry Division.

AMERICAN FORCES

US 12th Army Group

Commander: Lieutenant General
  Omar N. Bradley
Chief of Staff: Major General Leven
  C. 'Lev' Allen
G-2: Brigadier General Edwin L.
  Sibert
Aides to General Bradley: Captain
  (later Lieutenant Colonel) Lewis
  Bridge; Captain (later Lieutenant
  Colonel Chester B. Hansen

One of three US Army Groups formed
overseas during the war, 12th Army
Group commanded US First, Third,
Ninth, and later, Fifteenth Armies.
During the Ardennes offensive it was
located in Luxembourg City. It would
lose US First and Ninth Armies to 21st
Army Group for part of the offensive
(see text).

US First Army

Commander: Lieutenant General
  Courtney H. Hodges
Chief of Staff: Brigadier General (later
  Major General) William Benjamin
  Kean, Jr.
G2: Colonel Benjamin A. Dickson

General Hodges' First Army comprised
V and VII Corps, then later also XVIII
Airborne Corps. Its location during the
Ardennes Offensive was initially in
Spa, Belgium, but it moved, hastily,
from there on 20 December 1944 to
Chaudefontaine.

Army Troops (attached from SHAEF
Reserve)
  143, 413 Mobile AAA Gun
    Battalions
  526 Armored Infantry Battalion
  Belgian 5 Fusilier Battalion
  Norwegian 99 Infantry
    Battalion

US V Corps

Commander: Major General Leonard
  T. Gerow

Activated at Camp Beauregard, La, on
20 October 1940, it went overseas on
23 January 1942. It fought in
Normandy, northern France and the
Rhineland, before taking part in the
Ardennes operations. It returned to
USA in July 1945.

Corps Troops
  102 Cavalry Group (mechanised) –
    with 38 and 102 Cav Rcn Sqdns
    attached
  613 Tank Destroyer (TD) Battalion
  186, 196, 200, 295 Field Artillery
    (FA) Battalions
  187 FA Group (motorised) (751,
    997 FA Battalions)
  190 FA Group (motorised) (62, 190,
    272, 268 FA Battalions)
  406 FA Group (motorised) (76, 941,
    953, 987 FA Battalions)
  254 Engineer Combat Battalion
  1111 Engineer Combat Group (51,
    202, 291, 296 Engineer Combat
    Battalions)

1st Infantry Division
CG: Brigadier General Clift Andrus –
  in command from December 1944

  16, 18, 26 Infantry Regiments
  5, 7, 32, 33 FA Battalions
  1 Engineer Combat Battalion
  Attached: 745 Tank Battalion, 634,
    703 Tank Destroyer Battalions,
    103 AAA Automatic Weapons
    Battalion.
(NB. In this and all subsequent US divisions I have for simplicity not included
such standard divisional units as
medical battalions, military police
platoons, ordnance maintenance units,
QM companies, signal companies,
etc.).

'The Big Red One' had fought in North
Africa, Sicily and then Normandy,
landing on Omaha Beach on D-Day,
led by 16th Inf. They fought through to
take Caumont, and were relieved by
5th Inf Div. Next attacked as part of
the 'Cobra' breakout on 26 July, then

on across France and into Belgium, crossing the Meuse on 9 September and besieging Aachen. After various periods of heavy fighting around Aachen and in the Hürtgen Forest battle, it was in reserve when the Ardennes offensive started and was sent to the Malmédy sector.

2nd Infantry Division
CG: Major General Walter M. Robertson

9, 23, 38 Infantry Regiments
12, 15, 37, 38 FA Battalions
2 Engineer Combat Battalion
Attached: 741 Tank Battalion, 612, 644 Tank Destroyer Battalions, 462 AAA Automatic Weapons Battalion.

'Indianhead' landed in France on 7 June across Omaha Beach, fought through Normandy (St-Lô) and across the Vire, then was moved into Brittany and assaulted Brest which surrendered after a 39-day battle. On 26 September moved by rail and road to St-Vith and took up defensive positions in this 'quiet' part of the front. In early December it was selected together with 9th and 78th Inf Divs, plus 3rd Armd Div, to assault the Roer and Urft dams. It was withdrawn from the Ardennes front on 11 December and began its attack on the 13th. By the night of 15/16 December it had captured Wahlerscheid, so was 'out on a limb' when the German counter-offensive began.

9th Infantry Division
CG: Major General Louis A. Craig

39, 47, 60 Infantry Regiments
26, 34, 60, 84 FA Battalions
15 Engineer Combat Battalion
Attached: 746 Tank Battalion, 376, 413 AAA Battalions (one Gun, one Automatic Weapons)

'Octfoil' fought in North Africa and Sicily, then landed across Utah Beach

on 10 June, fought through Normandy reaching the west coast of the Cotentin Peninsula on 17 June and blocking German withdrawals. It fought on through Normandy, helping to block the Falaise Gap. Prior to the Ardennes offensive it was engaged in the Hürtgen Forest. On 7 December it relieved 1st Inf Div, then returned to the offensive with 3rd Armd Div, going forward towards the Roer as the central 'prong' of the assault on the Roer and Urft dams.

78th Infantry Division
CG: Major General Edwin P. Parker, Jr.

309, 310, 311 Infantry Regiments
307, 308, 309, 903 FA Battalions
303 Engineer Combat Battalion
Attached: 709 Tank Battalion, 628, 893 TD Battalions
552 AAA AW Battalion
(CCR of 5th Armd Div and 2nd Ranger Bn were also attached)

The 'Lightning' Division had landed in France on 22 November, moved to Tongres in Belgium then to Roetgen, Germany. After relieving 1st Inf Div in the line, it fought its first battle, for the Roer and Urft dams, on 12 December. It blocked the strategic road junction near Monschau in response to the German offensive.

99th Infantry Division
CG: Major General Walter E. Lauer

393, 394, 397 Infantry Regiments
370, 371, 372, FA Battalions
324 Engineer Combat Battalion
Attached: 801 TD Battalion, 535 AAA AW Battalion

The 'Checkerboard' Division had landed at Le Havre on 3 November, moved to Aubel in Belgium and then to the Ardennes, where it took over positions from 9th Inf Div between Höfen and Lanzerath. The 2nd Inf Div would move through their lines for the assault on the Roer dams. 99 Div would be hit hard by the German counter-offensive.

VII Corps
CG: Major General Joseph Lawton 'Lightning Joe' Collins

Activated at Fort McClellan, Alabama on 25 November 1940, it moved overseas on 9 October 1943 and fought in the Normandy, northern France, Rhineland, Ardennes–Alsace and Central Europe campaigns, returning to the USA to be inactivated at the Presidio of San Francisco on 1 March 1946.

Corps Troops
  4 Cavalry Group (mechanised)
  29 Infantry Regiment
  509 Parachute Infantry Battalion
  298 Engineer Combat Battalion
  740 Tank Battalion
  18, 83, 87, 183, 193, 957, 991 Field Artillery Battalions
  18 FA Group (containing 188, 666, 981 FA Bns)
  142 FA Group (195, 266 FA Bns)
  188 FA Group (172, 951, 980 FA Bns)
  342, 366, 392, 1038, 1313 Engineer General Service Regiments

2nd Armored Division
CG: Major General Ernest Nason 'Old Gravel Voice' Harmon

  66, 67 Armored Regiments
  82 Armored Reconnaissance (Recon) Battalion
  41 Armored Infantry Regiment
  14, 78, 92 Armored FA Battalions
  17 Armored Engineer Battalion
  Attached: 702 TD Battalion, 195 AAA AW Battalion. Elements of 738 Tank Battalion (Mine Clearing) were also attached 12–17 Jan 1945.

'Hell on Wheels' had fought in North Africa and Sicily before landing in Normandy on 9 June 1944. It fought in

Normandy and northern France, then on into the Rhineland, attacking Aachen and finally taking up defensive positions along the Roer until released to help counter the Ardennes offensive.

3rd Armored Division
CG: Major General Maurice B. Rose
  32, 33 Armored Regiments
  83 Armd Recon Squadron
  36 Armored Infantry Regiment
  54, 67, 391 Armored FA Battalions
  23 Armored Engineer Battalion
  Attached: 643 (then 703) TD Battalion, 486 AAA AW Battalion.

The 'Spearhead' Division arrived in Normandy on 23 June 1944, fought first near St-Lô then through Normandy and in the pursuit across France, on into the Rhineland. Heavily committed in the battles for Aachen, it was, with 9th Inf Div, part of the central 'prong' of the assault on the Roer dams.

83rd Infantry Division
CG: Major General Robert Chauncey Macon

  329, 330, 331 Infantry Regiment
  322, 323, 324, 908 FA Battalions
  308 Engineer Combat Battalion
  Attached: 774 Tank Battalion (until 24 Dec), 772 TD Battalion, 453 AAA AW Battalion.

The 'Thunderbolt' Division landed on Omaha Beach on 19 June, then fought through Normandy, taking part in Operation 'Cobra' and assaulting St-Malo and Dinard (including an amphibious assault on the Ile de Cézembre. After France it took part in the Rhineland campaign, helping to clear the west bank of the Roer on 10 December. From 3 January it was part of VII Corps.

84th Infantry Division
CG: Major General Alexander R. Bolling

333, 334, 335 Infantry Regiment
325, 326, 327, 909 FA Battalions
309 Engineer Combat Battalion
Attached: 701 (then 771 from 20
Dec) Tank Battalion, 638 TD
Battalion, 557 AAA AW Battalion.

The 'Railsplitters' landed in France between 1 and 4 November 1944, moved to Holland and from there to attack the Geilenkirchen salient north of Aachen (supported by British 79th Armd Div flail tanks and searchlights) on 18 November. On 29 November they began a drive on the River Roer. From there they were moved to Marche in Belgium to counter the German Ardennes offensive.

XVIII Airborne Corps
CG: Major General Matthew Bunker
  Ridgway

On 9 October 1943 II Armored Corps had been redesignated XVIII Corps, then on 25 August 1944 it was redesignated XVIII Airborne Corps. It took part in the Rhineland, Ardennes and Central Europe campaigns, not returning to USA until 1951 and being inactivated at Fort Bragg on 21 May of that year.

Corps Troops
  14 Cavalry Group (mechanised)
  254, 275, 400, 460 FA Battalions
  79 FA Group (153, 551, 552 FA
    Battalions)
  179 FA Group (259, 965 FA Battal-
    ions)
  211 FA Group (240, 264 FA Battal-
    ions)
  401 FA Group (187, 809 FA Battal-
    ions)

7th Armored Division
CG: Major General Robert W.
  Hasbrouck

  17, 31, 40 Tank Battalions
  23, 38, 48 Armored Infantry Battal-
    ions
  434, 440, 489 Armored FA Battalions

33 Armored Engineer Battalion
87 Cavalry Recon Squadron (mecha-
  nised)
Attached: 814 TD Battalion, 820 TD
  Bn (from 25 to 30 Dec 1944), 203
  AAA AW Battalion

The 'Lucky Seventh' landed in Normandy on 11 August 1944 and took part in the pursuit across France, then in fierce fighting in the Metz area in September and again in Holland the following month. On 16 December they were committed to the vital defence of St-Vith.

30th Infantry Division
CG: Major General Leland S.
  Hobbs

  117, 119, 120 Infantry Regiments
  113, 118, 197, 230 FA Battalions
  105 Engineer Combat Battalion
  Attached: 743 Tank Battalion, 803
    TD Battalion, 448 AAA AW
    Battalion.

'Old Hickory' landed at Omaha Beach on 10 June 1944, fought in Normandy and in Operation 'Cobra', then featured in forcing back German gains around Mortain. In October it had attacked between Aachen and Geilenkirchen and completed the encirclement of Aachen on 16 October with 1st Inf Div. The division was rushed to the Malmédy–Stavelot area on 17 December.

75th Infantry Division
CG: Major General Fay B. Prickett

  289, 290, 291 Infantry Regiments
  730, 897, 898, 899 FA Battalions
  275 Engineer Combat Battalion
  Attached: 750 Tank Battalion, 629,
    772 TD Battalions, 440 AAA AW
    Battalion

Landed at Le Havre and Rouen on 13 December 1944, moved to Yvetot. Initially part of VII Corps. On 23

December they were rushed to the front and took up a defensive position along the River Ourthe.

82nd Airborne Division
CG: Major General James M. Gavin

504, 505 Parachute Infantry Regiments
325 Glider Infantry Regiment
376, 456 Parachute FA Battalions
319, 320 Glider FA Battalions
80 Airborne AA Battalion
307 Airborne Engineer Battalion
Attached: 507, 508 Parachute Infantry Regiments, 551 Parachute Infantry Battalion, 740 Tank Battalion (30 Dec–11 Jan 1945), 628 TD Battalion (2–11 Jan 1945), 643 TD Battalion (4–5 Jan 1945).

Activated on 25 March 1942, the 'All Americans' had landed at Casablanca in May 1943, trained and then taken part in the invasion of Sicily. Part of the division had also dropped at Salerno and again in Normandy behind Utah Beach on 6 June. They took part in the airborne assault in the Nijmegen–Grave area on 17 September, taking the Grave bridge. On 17 December the division was brought up to the front in response to the German offensive.

106th Infantry Division
CG: Major General Alan W. Jones

422, 423, 424 Infantry Regiments
589, 590, 591, 592 FA Battalions
81 Engineer Combat Battalion
Attached: 820 TD Battalion, 440 AAA AW Bn (8 Dec–4 Jan 1945), 563 AAA AW Bn (9–18 Dec) and 634 AAA AW Bn (8–18 Dec)

The 'Golden Lions' landed on 6 December 1944 and replaced 2nd Inf Div in the Schnee–Eifel sector on 11 December. The division would suffer heavily in the Ardennes offensive.

US Third Army

CG: Lieutenant General George Smith Patton, Jr.
Chief of Staff: Brigadier General Hobart R. Gay
DCOS (Opns) Colonel P. D. Harkins
G-2 (Intelligence) Colonel Oscar W. Koch

Like US First and Second Armies, the Third had been in existence pre-war. Patton had taken command in January 1944 in the UK during the pre-invasion period. Although a total of six corps and 42 divisions would serve under Third Army from 1 August 1944 to 8 May 1945, the organisation for the period of the Ardennes Offensive is as shown here, namely III, VIII and XII Corps. Its location from 20 December was Luxembourg City.

Army Troops
109, 115, 217, 777 AA Gun Battalions
456, 465, 565 AAA AW Battalions

III Corps
CG: Major General John Millikin

Activated at the Presidio, San Francisco, Ca, on 18 December 1940, it went overseas on 5 September 1944, took part in the northern France, Rhineland, Ardennes-Alsace and Central Europe campaigns, returning to USA to be inactivated on 10 October 1946. Located at Arlon during the Ardennes battles.

Corps Troops
6 Cavalry Group (mechanised)
179, 274, 276, 777 FA Battalions
193 FA Group (177, 253, 696, 776, 949 FA Bns)
203 FA Group (278, 742, 762 FA Bns)
1137 Engineer Combat Group (145, 188, 249 Engr C Bns)
467, 468 AAA AW Battalions

4th Armored Division[1]
CG: Major General Hugh J. Gaffey

8, 35, 37 Tank Battalions
10, 51, 53 Armored Infantry Battalions
22, 66, 94 Armored FA Battalions
24 Armored Engineer Battalion
25 Cavalry Recon Squadron (mechanised)
Attached: 704 TD Battalion, 489 AAA AW Battalion

Landed on Utah Beach on 13 July 1944 and entered combat on 17 July, taking Coutances then Avranches. Heavily engaged in Lorraine then in the drive towards the River Saar. When the Ardennes offensive began it moved 150 miles to the Arlon–Luxembourg area and would later relieve Bastogne. Normally operated the usual armd div 'CCA, CCB and CCR' combat command structure.

6th Armored Division
CG: Major General Robert W. Grow

15, 68, 69 Tank Battalions
9, 44, 50 Armored Infantry Battalions
128, 212, 231 Armored FA Battalions
25 Armored Engineer Battalion
86 Cavalry Recon Squadron (mechanised)
Attached: 691 TD Battalion (15–23 Dec 1944), 777 AAA AW Battalion.

The 'Super Sixth' landed at Utah Beach on 19 July, fought through Normandy, then swung into Brittany on 1 August, CCA investing Brest, while CCB and CCR relieved 4th Armd Div at Vannes and Lorient. Fought through Lorraine and by 5 December were at the River Saar. At the start of the offensive they were given responsibility for the sector Ettelbruck–Mostroff.

26th Infantry Division
CG: Major General Willard S. Paul

101, 104, 328 Infantry Regiments
101, 102, 180, 263 FA Battalions
101 Engineer Combat Battalion
Attached: 735 Tank Battalion, 818 TD Battalion, 390 AAA AW Battalion

The 'Yankee' Division arrived in France on 7 September 1944 and relieved 4th Armd Div in the Salonnes–Moncourt area. It fought on through France and by early December had reached the Maginot Line fortifications. When the German Ardennes offensive began it was training reinforcements near Metz and was sent north to Luxembourg on 20 December.

35th Infantry Division
CG: Major General Paul W. Baade

134, 137, 320 Infantry Regiments
127, 161, 216, 219 FA Battalions
60 Engineer Combat Battalion
Attached: 654 TD Battalion, 448 AAA AW Battalion

Crossed Omaha Beach 5–8 July 1944. The 'Santa Fe' Division fought in Normandy, holding a series of German counter-attacks near St-Lô, then fought throughout the autumn in the Lorraine area. On 26 December, the division moved from Metz to Arlon, Belgium, to help in the relief of Bastogne.

90th Infantry Division
CG: Major General James A. Van Fleet

357, 358, 359 Infantry Regiments
343, 344, 345, 915 FA Battalions
315 Engineer Combat Battalion
Attached: 773 TD Battalion, 774 TD Battalion (21 Dec–6 Jan 1945), 537 AAA AW Battalion

Landing on D-Day on Utah Beach, the 'Tough Hombres' fought in Normandy and suffered heavy casualties through France and onwards. By October they were in the Metz area, taking part in the thrust to the River Saar.

VIII Corps
CG: Major General Troy H.
 Middleton

Activated at Fort Sam Houston, Texas, on 14 October 1940, it went overseas on 13 December 1943 and returned to the USA to be inactivated exactly two years and two days later, having fought in the Normandy, northern France, Rhineland, Ardennes–Alsace and Central Europe campaigns.

Corps Troops
 174 FA Group (965, 969, 700 FA
  Battalions)
 333 FA Group (333, 771 FA Battalions)
 402 FA Group (559, 561, 740 FA
  Battalions)
 422 FA Group (81, 174 FA Battalions)
 687 FA Battalion
 1102 Engineer Combat Group (341
  Engineer Service Battalion)
 1107 Engineer Combat Group (159,
  168, 202 Engineer Combat Battalions)
 1128 Engineer Combat Group (35,
  44, 158 Engineer Combat Battalions)
 178, 249 Engineer Combat Battalions
 467, 635, 778 AAA AW Battalions
 Attached: Six French light infantry
  battalions

9th Armored Division
CG: Major General John W. Leonard

 2, 14, 19 Tank Battalions
 27, 52, 60 Armored Infantry Battalions
 3, 16, 73 Armored FA Battalions
 9 Armored Engineer Battalion
 89 Cavalry Recon Squadron (mechanised)
 Attached: 811 TD Battalion, 482
  AAA AW Battalion

'Phantom' landed in France on 3 October 1944 and initially patrolled a quiet sector of the Germany–Luxembourg frontier. When it was hit by the Ardennes offensive, CCA defended near Emsdorf, CCB at St-Vith and CCR along the Bastogne–Trois Vierges road.

11th Armored Division
CG: Brigadier General Charles S.
 'Rattlesnake Pete' Kilburn

 21, 41, 42 Tank Battalions
 22, 55, 63 Armored Infantry Battalions
 490, 491, 492 Armored FA Battalions
 56 Armored Engineer Battalion
 41 Cavalry Recon Squadron (mechanised)
 Attached: 602 TD Battalion (from
  29 Dec 1944), 575 AAA AW
  Battalion

'Thunderbolt' landed in France on 17 December 1944 and was immediately deployed to defend the Givet–Sedan sector against the German offensive.

28th Infantry Division
CG: Major General Norman D. Cota
 109, 110, 112 Infantry Regiments
 107, 108, 109, 229 FA Battalions
 103 Engineer Combat Battalion
 Attached: 707 Tank Battalion,
  602 TD Battalion (24–31 Dec
  1944), 630 TD Battalion and
  447 AAA AW Battalion (from 19
  Jan 1945)

The 'Keystone' Division landed in Normandy on 22 July 1944 and fought through Normandy, then was involved in heavy fighting against the West Wall (Siegfried Line) near St-Vith and in the Hürtgen Forest. They were resting and holding a 25-mile stretch along the River Our in Luxembourg when the German offensive struck them.

87th Infantry Division
CG: Brigadier General Frank L. Culin,
 Jr.

345, 346, 347 Infantry Regiments
334, 335, 336, 912 FA Battalions
312 Engineer Combat Battalion
Attached: 761 Tank Battalion, 610
TD Battalion (14–22 Dec 1944),
691 TD Battalion (22–24 Dec
1944, 8–26 Jan 1945), 704 TD
Battalion (17–19 Dec 1944), 549
AAA AW Battalion

'Golden Acorn' landed in France from
1 to 5 December 1944 and took over a
sector in the Metz area from 5th Inf
Div. They were later transferred to help
counter the German offensive, their
first major action being in the area to
the west of Bastogne.

17th Airborne Division
CG: Major General William M. Miley

507[2], 513 Parachute Infantry Regi-
    ments
193, 194 Glider Infantry Regiments
466 Parachute FA Battalion
680, 681 Glider FA Battalions
139 Airborne Engineer Battalion
155 Airborne AAA AW Battalion

The 'Golden Talon' Division was flown
to the Reims area 23–25 December
1944 by night and assembled at
Mourmelon. Their first action was
west of Bastogne later that month.

101st Airborne Division
CG: Major General Maxwell D.
    Taylor (he was away when the divi-
    sion was rushed to Bastogne and
    Brigadier General Anthony C.
    McAuliffe was in command)

502, 506 Parachute Infantry Regi-
    ments
327 Glider Infantry Regiment
377, 463 Parachute FA Battalion
321, 907 Glider FA Battalion
326 Airborne Engineer Battalion
81 Airborne AA Battalion
Attachments: 501 Parachute
    Infantry Regiment, 705 TD
    Battalion

The 'Screaming Eagles' dropped both
on D-Day in Normandy and again in
Holland on 17 September 1944, to
capture bridges north of Eindhoven. It
was withdrawn to France for rest and
rehabilitation in late November.
Released from theatre reserve on 17
December, it arrived at Bastogne two
days later.

XII Corps
CG: Major General Manton S. Eddy
Activated in Columbia, South Carolina
on 29 August 1942, they went overseas
on 10 April 1944 and participated in
the campaigns of northern France,
Rhineland, Ardennes–Alsace and
Central Europe. The Corps was inacti-
vated on 15 December 1945 in
Germany. Its HQ was at Luxembourg
City during the Ardennes operations.

Corps Troops
2 Cavalry Group (mechanised)
177 FA Group (215, 255, 775 FA
    Battalions)
182 FA Group (802, 945, 974 FA
    Battalions)
183 FA Group (695, 776 FA Battal-
    ions)
404 FA Group (273, 512, 752 FA
    Battalions)
161, 244, 277, 334, 336, 736 FA
    Battalions
1303 Engineer Service Regiment
452, 457 AAA AW Battalions

4th Infantry Division
CG: Major General Raymond O.
    Barton

8, 12, 22 Infantry Regiments
20, 29, 42, 44 FA Battalions
4 Engineer Battalion
Attached: 70 Tank Battalion, 802,
    803 TD Battalions, 377 AAA AW
    Battalion

The 'Ivy' Division landed on Utah
Beach on D-Day, fought in Normandy,
taking Cherbourg, then helped to
liberate Paris and penetrated the

Siegfried Line in the Schnee–Eifel. After severe fighting, it was relieved and sent to Luxembourg to rest. It was thus subjected to the full force of the Ardennes offensive.

5th Infantry Division
CG: Major General Leroy S. Irwin

  2, 10, 11 Infantry Regiments
  19, 21, 46, 50 FA Battalions
  7 Engineer Battalion
  Attached: 737 Tank Battalion, 654
    TD Battalion (22–25 Dec 1944),
    803 TD Battalion (25 Dec 1944
    onwards), 807 TD Battalion
    (17–21 Dec 1944), 818 TD
    Battalion (13 July–20 Dec 1944),
    449 AAA AW Battalion

The 'Red Diamond' Division crossed Utah Beach on 11 June 1944, fought in Normandy, opening the offensive towards Nantes and taking Angers on 10 August. Later it was heavily involved in the fighting around Metz. When the Ardennes offensive began it relieved 95th Inf Div and attacked out of the Saarlautern bridgehead on 18 December.

80th Infantry Division
CG: Major General Horace L. McBride

  317, 318, 319 Infantry Regiments
  313, 314, 315, 905 FA Battalions
  305 Engineer Combat Battalion
  Attached: 702 Tank Battalion, 610
    TD Battalion (23 Nov–6 Dec, 21
    Dec–28 Jan 1945), 808 TD
    Battalion (25 Sept–21 Dec 1944),
    633 AAA AW Battalion

The 'Blue Ridge' Division landed in France across Utah Beach on 3 August 1944. Fought in Normandy, assisting in the battle of the Falaise Gap, crossed the Moselle in September and had more hard fighting in November 1944 in the drive to the River Saar. It was withdrawn for rest and rehabilitation on 7 December, but was thrust into action again a fortnight later after assembling in the Arlon area on 20 December.

10th Armored Division
CG: Major General William H. H. Morris, Jr.

  3, 11, 21 Tank Battalions
  20, 54, 61 Armored Infantry Battalions
  419, 420, 423 Armored FA Battalions
  55 Armored Engineer Battalion
  90 Cavalry Recon Squadron (mechanised)
  Attached: 609 TD Battalion, 796
    AAA AW Battalion

The 'Tiger' Armored Division landed at Cherbourg on 23 September 1944 and entered the line on 2 November, taking part in the siege of Metz and the advance towards the River Saar. It moved to Luxembourg City on 17 December 1944.

Notes
1 4th Armored Division did not have a nickname, indeed they always said that '4th Armored' was 'name enough'.
2 The 507th were attached to 17th Airborne from 27 August 1944, but not officially assigned until 1 March 1945.

Appendix 4
OPERATION 'NORDWIND'
ALLIED FORCES

HQ SIXTH ARMY GROUP
Consisting of US Seventh Army and French First Army, it was formed for the landings in the South of France.
Commander: General Jacob L. Devers

US SEVENTH ARMY
Commander: Lieutenant General Alexander M. Patch

Activated overseas initially as Force 343 during the planning for Operation 'Husky' (the invasion of Sicily), it became HQ US Seventh Army on 18 July 1943 and then went on to command Operation 'Anvil' (later changed to Operation 'Dragoon'), the landings on the French Riviera coast on 15 August 1944. It continued to command the US forces in Sixth Army Group for the rest of the war. During Operation 'Nordwind', US Seventh Army initially comprised of two armoured and six infantry divisions: 12th and 14th Armored Divisions, plus 36th, 44th, 45th 79th, 100th and 103rd Infantry Divisions, as shown below. However, it would lose 12th Armored and 36th Infantry Divisions to SHAEF reserve and gain French 2nd Armoured, plus US 42nd, 63rd and 70th Infantry Divisions.

HQ XV Corps
CG: Major General Wade H. Haislip
When the Corps passed from US Third Army to under command of US Seventh Army on 29 September 1944, its main elements were at that time: US 79th Infantry Division, French 2nd Armoured Division and US 106th Cavalry Group. When 'Nordwind' began, XV Corps was occupying a narrow strip across the Saar valley, between Saarbrücken and Bitche and was commanding one armoured and three infantry divisions: 12th Armd and 44th, 100th, 103rd Inf Divs.

HQ VI Corps
CG: Major General Edward H. Brooks

When 'Nordwind' began, VI Corps was holding the Lauterbourg salient. It was commanding one armoured and three infantry divisions: 14th Armd and 36th, 45th, 79th Inf Divs.

HQ XXI Corps
During 'Nordwind' this new HQ, which had only recently arrived in Sixth Army Group's area, supervised a miscellaneous collection of units.

12th Armored Division
CG: Major General Roderick C. Allen

23, 43, 714 Tank Battalions
17, 56, 66 Armored Infantry Battalions
493, 494, 495 Armored Field Artillery Battalions
119 Armored Engineer Battalion
92 Cavalry Recon Squadron (mechanised)
82 Medical Battalion, Armored
Attached: 827 TD Battalion, 572 AAA AW Battalion

Activated on 15 September 1942, the 'Hellcat' Division landed at Le Havre on 9 November 1944, moved to the front on 5 December and attacked towards the Maginot Line. CCA took Singling on 9 December and the division had reached Utweiler by 21 December. It attacked the Rhine strongpoint of Herrlisheim on 8 January 1945, but sustained heavy casualties soon afterwards.

14th Armored Division
CG: Major General Albert C. Smith

    25, 47, 48 Tank Battalions
    19, 62, 68 Armored Infantry Battalions
    499, 500, 501 Armored Field
      Artillery Battalions
    125 Armored Engineer Battalion
    94 Cavalry Recon Squadron (mechanised)
    64 Armored Medical Battalion
    Attached: 398 AAA AW Battalion

Activated on 15 November 1942, it landed at Marseilles on 30 October 1944 and sent elements to guard the Franco-Italian border on 14 November. Fought up from southern France through Obernai, to block the exits from the Vosges mountains, capturing Barr on 29 November. Attacked across the River Lauter on 12 December and was later assigned defensive positions south of Bitche near Neunhoffen. The 'Liberator' Division was hit by a strong German attack on 1 January 1945 and involved in heavy fighting for the next two weeks.

36th Infantry Division
CG: Brigadier General Robert I.
    Stack

    141, 142, 143 Infantry Regiments
    131, 132, 133, 155 Field Artillery
      Battalions
    111 Engineer Combat Battalion
    111 Medical Battalion
    Attached: 753 Tank Battalion, 636
      TD Battalion, 443 AAA AW
      Battalion

The 'Texas' Infantry Division was inducted into Federal service on 25 November 1940, landed in North Africa on 13 April 1943 and fought in North Africa. Landed at Salerno, Italy on 9 September 1943 and in May 1944 landed at Anzio. It landed in southern France on 15 August 1944 and fought with Sixth Army up the Rhône valley. By September it was in the Vosges foothills. In early December it began a drive on the Colmar pocket. Assembling at Montbronn on 1 January 1945, it took up defensive positions in the Rohrweiler–Weyersheim region on 19 January 1945.

42nd Infantry Division
CG: Major General Harry J. Collins

    222, 232, 242 Infantry Regiments
    232, 392, 402, 542 Field Artillery
      Battalions
    142 Engineer Combat Battalion
    122 Medical Battalion

The 'Rainbow' Division was activated on 14 July 1943, arrived at Marseilles on 8–9 December 1944 and elements of the division entered combat near Strasbourg on 24 December 1944, but did not fight as a complete division until 14 February 1945.

44th Infantry Division
CG: Major General Robert L.
    Spragins

    71, 114, 324 Infantry Regiments
    156, 157, 217, 220 Field Artillery
      Battalions
    63 Engineer Combat Battalion
    119 Medical Battalion
    Attached: 749 Tank Battalion, 776
      TD Battalion, 895 AAA AW
      Battalion

Inducted into Federal service on 16 September 1940, it landed at Cherbourg on 15 September 1944, fought in northern France in Ninth Army, then joined XV Corps on 14 October and by December 1944 was in defensive positions east of Sarreguemines when 'Nordwind' struck and drove them back to the Rimling area.

45th Infantry Division
CG: Major General Robert T. Frederick

157, 179, 180 Infantry Regiments
158, 160, 171 Field Artillery Battalions
120 Engineer Combat Battalion
120 Medical Battalion
Attached: 101, 191 Tank Battalions, 645 TD Battalion, 106 AAA AW Battalion

The 'Thunderbird' Infantry Division was inducted on 16 February 1940, fought in North Africa, Sicily and Italy, including Salerno and Anzio. It assaulted Ste–Maxime in southern France on 15 August 1944, then fought with Seventh Army for the remainder of the war.

63rd Infantry Division
CG: Brigadier General Frederick M. Harris

253, 254, 255 Infantry Regiments
718, 861, 862, 863 Field Artillery Battalions
263 Engineer Combat Battalion
363 Medical Battalion

The 'Blood & Fire' Division was activated on 15 June 1943, advanced elements reached Marseilles on 8 December 1944 and was organised initially as Task Force Harris, defending the Vosges and the Maginot Line area 22–30 December.

79th Infantry Division
CG: Major General Horace L. McBride

313, 314, 315 Infantry Regiments
310, 311, 312, 904 Field Artillery Battalions
304 Engineer Combat Battalion
304 Medical Battalion
Attached: 781 Tank Battalion, 813 TD Battalion, 463 AAA AW Battalion

The 'Cross of Lorraine' Division was activated on 15 June 1942 and landed across Utah Beach on 14 June 1944, attacking towards Cherbourg and fought with Third Army in Normandy and northern France. It passed, with the rest of XV Corps, to Seventh Army from Third Army on 29 September 1944.

100th Infantry Division
CG: Major General Withers A. Burress

397, 398, 399 Infantry Regiments
373, 374, 375, 925 Field Artillery Battalions
325 Engineer Combat Battalion
325 Medical Battalion

The 'Century' Infantry Division was activated on 15 November 1942 and arrived at Marseilles on 20 October 1944, going into combat at St-Rémy in the Vosges Mountains on 1 November. They were holding positions south of Bitche when 'Nordwind' began.

103rd Infantry Division
CG: Major General Charles C. Haffner, Jr.

409, 410, 411 Infantry Regiments
382, 383, 384, 928 Field Artillery Battalions
328 Engineer Combat Battalion
328 Medical Battalion

The 'Cactus' Infantry Division was activated on 15 November 1942 and arrived at Marseilles on 20 October 1944, relieving 3rd Inf Div at Chevry on 9th November and continued to fight with Seventh Army. They were relocated to the Sarreguemines area in mid-December to defend against the Ardennes offensive, but it never reached them; they were later involved in 'Nordwind'.

FRENCH FIRST ARMY

CG: General Jean de Lattre de Tassigny

At the time of 'Nordwind', this comprised of three armoured and seven infantry divisions, as shown below. Two Corps HQs were deployed: French II Corps in the north from the Rhine to the High Vosges, and French I Corps in the south above the Belfort Gap.

1st Armoured Division

2nd Armoured Division
CG: General Jacques Leclerc

This division was transferred to US Seventh Army in late December 1944, to make up for the loss of an armoured division to SHAEF reserve.

5th French Armored Division

1st Infantry Division

16th Infantry Division

Algerian 3rd Division

Moroccan 2nd Division

Moroccan 4th Mountain Division

Colonial 9th Division

US 3rd Infantry Division (attached to French II Corps)

CG: Major General John E. 'Iron Mike' O'Daniel

7, 15, 30 Infantry Regiments
9, 10, 39, 41 Field Artillery Battalions
10 Engineer Combat Battalion
3 Medical Battalion
Attached: 756 Tank Battalion, 601 TD Battalion, 441 AAA AW Battalion

The 'Marne' Division fought in Algeria, French Morocco, Tunisia, Sicily and Italy, before assaulting southern France on 15 August 1944, with VI Corps until 15 December 1944, when it was attached to First French Army.

Appendix 5
THE PRINCIPAL PLAYERS

NB. These short pen-pictures endeavour briefly to trace careers up to and in some cases after the Ardennes offensive, so that readers can place anyone who is unfamiliar to them.

GERMAN

Bayerlein, Generalleutnant Fritz (1899–1970), holder of the Knight's Cross with Oakleaves and Swords, plus the German Cross in Gold. Commander of Panzer Lehr Division, in XLVII Panzer Corps, described by Desmond Young as being: '... a stocky little terrier of a man, full of energy and enthusiasm'. He rose to prominence with Rommel in North Africa. He took command of the élite Panzer Lehr Division (made up of instructors from the panzer training schools) in January 1944 a few days after his 45th birthday. His division spearheaded von Manteuffel's 5th Panzer Army, bypassed Bastogne to the south and got to within ten miles of the Meuse, before being virtually annihilated. After the Ardennes he commanded LIII Corps until captured in the Ruhr on 15 April 1945.

Beyer, General der Infanterie Dr. Franz (1892–?), holder of the Knight's Cross. He commanded LXXX Corps (212, 276, 340 VGD) in Seventh Army and had a wealth of battle experience from the Eastern Front.

Bittrich, General der Waffen-SS Wilhelm 'Willi' (1894–1979), holder of the Knight's Cross with Oakleaves (awarded Swords in May 1945) and the German Cross in Gold. A fighter pilot in WWI, then a stockbroker, he joined the SS in 1934 and rose steadily in the Waffen-SS to command III SS Panzer Corps in Normandy, then was responsible for 'squeezing out' the British airborne forces at Arnhem. His Corps would follow up the main assault, with the aim of striking for Antwerp once across the Meuse.

Blaskowitz, General Johannes (1883–1948), began his military service at the age of 16, serving in an infantry company and being awarded the Iron Cross First Class during WWI. Having escaped Hitler's 1938 army purges, his professional ability became evident while commanding Eighth Army in southern Poland. Later became CinC of occupied Poland. His political naïvety, however, caused him to condemn SS activities in Poland, which put him on Himmler's blacklist! Nevertheless, his undoubted military ability – he was the holder of the Knight's Cross with both Oakleaves and Swords (one of the last recipients) and the German Cross in Silver – ensured that he was made commander of Army Group G by von Rundstedt in May 1944. He would also be a convenient scapegoat for the failure of 'Norwind'. Died in suspicious circumstances just before his trial for war crimes in 1948.

Brandenberger, General der Panzertruppen, Erich (1892–1955), holder of the Knight's Cross with Oakleaves. Commissioned into the artillery in 1913, he was COS XXIII Corps in 1939, then took over 8th Panzer Division. Promoted Generalleutnant then General der Panzertruppen in August 1943, he replaced Eberbach (when he was captured in France) as commander

Seventh Army in August 1944. Bespectacled and heavily jowled, his schoolteacher appearance belied his ability. He would hold the southern shoulder until forced back by Patton (Operation 'Lumberjack'), retiring on a broad front through the Eifel and across the Moselle. Hitler relieved him of command for 'defeatism' in March 1945. He then took over Nineteenth Army in the Black Forest.

Decker, Generalleutnant (later General der Panzertruppen) Karl (1897–?), holder of the Knight's Cross with Oakleaves and the German Cross in Gold. He was a very experienced officer with a reputation for prudence and determination. He commanded HQ XXXIX Corps which was sent up from OKW reserve to handle the siege of Bastogne.

Deckert, Oberst Hans-Joachim (1904 –?), holder of the German Cross in Gold. He was Commander of 15th Panzer Grenadier Division, LIII Corps, and later commanded 19th Panzer Division.

Dempwolff, Oberst (later Generalmajor) Hugo (1898–?), commanded 276 VGD after Generalleutnant Moehring was killed.

Denkert, Generalmajor Walter (1897– 1957), holder of the Knight's Cross and the German Cross in Gold, was commander of 3rd Panzer Grenadier Division which had had to be rebuilt after France, to a total of some 12,000 men, then took part in the fighting in the Eifel battles of January 1945.

Dietrich, Oberstgruppenführer Joseph 'Sepp' (1892–1966), holder of the Knight's Cross with Oakleaves, Swords and Diamonds. A roughneck ex-butcher who rose to become a General in the Waffen-SS, he had participated in the Beer Hall *Putsch* in 1923 and from then on was a loyal member of the Nazi Party. Strong and fearless, he was not a brilliant soldier, so he was despised by the regular army generals. His top level of command should have been divisional, but he was chosen by Hitler to command Sixth SS Panzer Army which would then supposedly play the leading role in the Ardennes operation, but be outclassed by Manteuffel's Fifth Panzer Army. Hitler appreciated his loyalty, but was aware of his lack of soldierly expertise, so he was given the very capable General Fritz Kraemer as his deputy.

Elverfeldt, Generalmajor Harald Gustav Freiherr von (1900–45), holder of the Knight's Cross with Oakleaves and the German Cross in Gold. He commanded 9th Panzer Division and played a prominent part in the Ardennes battle, but his division was decimated when Hitler refused to allow them to withdraw. He was killed in action in March 1945 in battles over the Rhine bridgeheads.

Engel, Generalmajor Gerhard (1906–?), holder of the Knight's Cross with Oakleaves. In the Ardennes he was commanding 12 *Volks* Grenadier Division in First SS Panzer Corps. Together with 3rd Fallschirmjäger Division their task was to break into the American positions near the Losheim Gap. Engel had been Hitler's adjutant since 1937, but was promoted to major general in late 1944. He was seriously wounded in the Ardennes offensive, but returned to duty in February 1945.

Galland, Generalleutnant Adolf (1912– 96), holder of the Knight's Cross with Oakleaves, Swords and Diamonds. This dashing fighter pilot, whose black cigar and black moustache were his trademarks, was the youngest major general in the German Armed Forces when he was promoted in November 1942, aged 30. An ace who had shot down more than 100 Allied aircraft, he was relieved of his command as General der Jagdflieger after a particularly stormy meeting when the Reichsmarschall accused the fighter pilots of cowardice. He then appointed himself commander of the élite Messerschmitt Me 262 jet fighter unit.

Gersdorff, Generalmajor Rudolf Christoph Freiherr von (1905–?), holder of the Knight's Cross and the German Cross in Silver. He was Chief of Staff of Seventh Army during the Ardennes operations. It is said that he was one of a group of officers who tried unsuccessfully to persuade Field Marshal Fedor von Bock to arrest Hitler when he visited his Army Group headquarters in 1943.

Heilmann, Oberst (later Generalmajor) 'King' Ludwig, Commander 5th Fallschirmjäger Division, LIIIV Corps and holder of the Knight's Cross with Oakleaves and Swords. He was taken prisoner when his division was trapped with its back to the Rhine.

Heydte, Oberst Friedrich August Freiherr von der (1907–?), holder of the Knight's Cross with Oakleaves. Commanded 1st Battalion of 3 Fallschirmjäger Regiment in Crete then in 1944 was commanding the Parachute School when Hitler selected him to command a special Parachute force in the Ardennes, known as 'Battle Group von der Heydte'. Inexperienced pilots and Paratroopers made a shambles of the operation and von Heydte was captured on 23 December 1944. A lawyer by profession, post-war he became a Fellow of the Carnegie Endowment for International Peace.

Himmler, Heinrich (1900–45). Reich Leader of the SS from 1929. Hitler made 'Faithful Heinrich' the commander of Army Group Oberrhein on 26 November 1944, despite his lack of military knowledge, and would do the same again on 25 January 1945 with Army Group Vistula. Committed suicide soon after his capture in May 1945.

Hitzfeld, General der Infanterie Otto (1898– ?), holder of the Knight's Cross with Oakleaves. He commanded 102nd Infantry Division in 1943, then from 1 December 1944 LXVII Corps (246, 326 VGD) on the north flank of Sixth SS Panzer Army and would attack the Allied line north and south of Monschau. Despite being a highly experienced commander, especially in tank–infantry co-operation, his corps would fail to take its objectives.

Hoecker Generalleutnant Hans-Kurt (1894–?), holder of the Knight's Cross and German Cross in Gold. A Generalmajor in 1942, he commanded 258th Infantry Division, then 17th Luftwaffe Field Division from November 1943. As part of Fifth Panzer Army (Europe), his division helped to defend Paris. On 28 August it was virtually destroyed by US First Army and officially dissolved. Its remnants were sent to Hungary and absorbed into the newly forming 167 VGD in September 1944. He then took the reformed division to the Ardennes.

Hoehne, Generalleutnant Gustav (1893–?). He joined the army in 1911 and later served in WWI and in the Reichswehr, rising to Oberst in 1938. Holder of the Knight's Cross with Oakleaves, he would command LXXXIX Corps from 1 December 1944.

Hoffmann-Schönborn, Oberst (later Generalmajor) Günter (1905–?), holder of the Knight's Cross with Oakleaves. An artilleryman, he was the only commander of 18 VGD from its inception, which contained naval personnel, the remnant of 18th Luftwaffe Field Division and was formed in Denmark in September 1944. Assigned to Fifth Panzer Army, the division would suffer heavy losses in the Ardennes. He had also served as an inspector of Sturmgeschütz (assault gun artillery).

Hummel, Oberst Kurt, Commander of 79th *Volks* Grenadier Division, whose infantrymen proved to be formidable opponents, he was a veteran infantry regimental commander. He briefly commanded 353rd Infantry Division in early 1945.

Jodl, Generaloberst Alfred (1890–1946), holder of the Knight's Cross with Oakleaves. Chief of the OKW and Hitler's chief military adviser throughout the war. He embraced National Socialism and had a high regard for Hitler's 'military genius'. A desk-bound soldier, it was estimated that he dealt with some 60,000 papers a year! It was he to whom Hitler gave the task of studying the feasibility of the Ardennes offensive. Although he always maintained that he had 'merely followed orders', he was found guilty of war crimes at Nuremberg and hanged.

John, Generalleutnant Dipl. Ing. Friedrich-Wilhelm (1895–?), holder of the German Cross in Gold. Chief of Supply and Administration at OB West, he was 'let in' on the plan by von Rundstedt early on.

Kahler, Oberst (later Generalmajor) Hans-Joachim (1898–?), holder of the Knight's Cross with Oakleaves. He was Commander of the Führer Panzer Grenadier Brigade from 1 July 1944 until the end of hostilities.

Kaschner, Generalmajor Dr. Erwin (1897–?), holder of the German Cross in Gold. Having previously commanded 486th Grenadier Regiment in 262nd Infantry Division in Russia, he next commanded 326th *Volks* Grenadier Division which would be part of the costly German assault in the Monschau–Höfen sector, then after failing in the bloody battles at Höfen, turn south to take a secondary role in the battle for Elsenborn ridge. It would be 'smashed' in the second battle of the Schnee–Eifel.

Keitel, Generalfeldmarschall Wilhelm 'Lakeitel' (a pun on *'Lakai'* = footman/ lackey/flunkey) (1885–1946), holder of the Knight's Cross. Obnoxious, servile 'mouthpiece' to Hitler as his minister of war and chief of staff of the Wehrmacht from 1938. He presided over the court that condemned to death the officers involved in the attempted assassination of Hitler. Found guilty of war crimes at Nuremberg, he was hanged.

Kittel, Oberst (later Generalmajor) Dipl. Ing. Frederich (1896–?), holder of the Knight's Cross and the German Cross in Gold. He was the younger brother of the defender of Metz. He commanded 62 VGD which had, as 62nd Infantry Division, sustained heavy casualties in Russia, then been made up with inexperienced recruits and redesignated as a 'VGD'. They would fight well and achieve a breakthrough in the Schnee–Eifel, only to be virtually wiped out in the battle for Monschau.

Kniess, General der Infanterie Baptist (1895–?). Commander of LXXXV Corps in Brandenberger's Seventh Army, which initially comprised 5th Fallschirmjäger Division and 352nd VGD, both of which had been 'rebuilt'. Experienced, his division had played a part in the invasion of France in 1940 and he had then been stationed there until being posted to the Eastern Front in 1941, where he was promoted to Command of LXVI Corps in November 1942.

Koerte, Oberst (later Generalmajor) Peter (1896–?), holder of the Knight's Cross. He commanded 246th VGD from August 1944 onwards. Some records say that he was killed in action in early 1945, but others that he was alive and well long after the war had ended.

Kokott, Oberst (later Generalmajor) Heinz (1890–?), holder of the Knight's Cross. He commanded 26th VGD in

Fifth Panzer Army's XLVII Panzer Corps which would cross the Our, take part in the siege of Bastogne and suffer heavy casualties once again. Kokott had considerable armoured experience, having served with the crack Panzer Lehr Division.

Kolb, Oberst (later Generalmajor) Werner (1895–?), holder of the Knight's Cross with Oakleaves and the German Cross in Gold. A reserve officer, he was Commander of 9th *Volks* Grenadier Division.

Kraemer, Standartenführer (later Brigadeführer) der Waffen-SS Fritz (1900–59), holder of the Knight's Cross and the German Cross in Gold. He was seconded to the Waffen-SS to be Sepp Dietrich's Chief of Staff of I Panzer Corps in 1943. Later he commanded 12th SS Panzer Division and in October 1944 became Chief of Staff, Sixth Panzer Army. Sepp Dietrich relied heavily on his expertise because, although he had transferred to the SS, Kraemer had a solid Army background. He forged a close working relationship and friendship with Dietrich, so was able to prevent his army commander from making too many mistakes! Guderian thought highly of him. After the war he was tried for his part in the Malmédy massacre and sentenced to ten years' imprisonment.

Kraas, SS Brigadegeneral Hugo (1911–80), holder of the Knight's Cross with Oakleaves. He was commanding 2nd SS Panzer Grenadier Regiment in the Liebstandarte when he was promoted to command 12th SS Panzer Division (Hitler Jugend) in I SS Panzer Corps. His division would follow 277th VGD and would assault north of the Losheim Gap. Extremely brave, he was among the best infantry commanders of the Waffen-SS.

Krebs, General der Infanterie Hans (1898–1945), holder of the Knight's

Cross with Oakleaves and the German Cross in Gold. He was Army Group B's Chief of Staff. He had been attached to the Soviet Embassy during the period of German–Soviet 'friendship', so was lacking in field experience, yet he must have been extremely able because he remained Model's COS for two years.

Kreipe, General der Flieger Werner (1904–?). From 1941 to 1943 he was COS Fliegerkorps I, then General in charge of training, after which he became Chief of Staff of the OKL in August 1944 on the death of Generaloberst Korten. After the failure of the Luftwaffe to influence events in the Ardennes, he was banished by Hitler and spent the rest of the war in command of the Air Warfare College in Berlin.

Krüger, General der Panzertruppen Walter (1892– ?), holder of the Knight's Cross with Oakleaves and the German Cross in Gold, he commanded LVIII Panzer Corps in Fifth Panzer Army. His Corps had the task of crossing the Our near Lützkampen, capturing Houffalize, then continuing past the River Ourthe to capture crossings over the Meuse. He was an able, proven corps commander, with plenty of armoured experience.

Lammerding, Generalleutnant der Waffen-SS Heinz (1905–71), holder of the Knight's Cross. He commanded 2nd SS Panzer Division (Das Reich) from the start of the Normandy campaign until he was wounded on 26 July 1944. Command devolved briefly to Christian Tychsen, Commander of 2nd SS Panzer Regiment, then to Oberführer Otto Baum. On 24 October Lammerding returned to lead the division throughout the Ardennes offensive until 20 January 1945 when he was assigned as Chief of Staff to Himmler's Army Group Weichsel. He was an experienced and capable engineering officer, personally courageous, but out of his depth as a divisional commander.

Langhauser, Oberst Rudolf. Commander of 560 *Volks* Grenadier Division for its entire combat existence – he had previously commanded 1130th Grenadier Regiment in 560th Grenadier Division in Scandinavia, before it became 560th VGD.

Lauchert, Oberst (later Generalmajor) Meinrad von (1905–58), holder of the Knight's Cross with Oakleaves and the German Cross in Gold. He was Commander of 2nd Panzer Division in the Ardennes.

Lucht, General der Artillerie Walther (1882–1949), holder of the Knight's Cross with Oakleaves and the German Cross in Gold. A solid and reliable leader with vast experience from the Eastern Front, he commanded LXVI Corps in Fifth Panzer Army.

Lüttwitz, General der Panzertruppen, Heinrich Freiherr von (1896–1970), holder of the Knight's Cross with Oakleaves and the German Cross in Gold. He commanded XLVII Corps in Manteuffel's Fifth Panzer Army, operating on the left flank (south). It was his corps which surrounded Bastogne. On Hitler's orders he pressed on towards the Meuse and his corps was virtually destroyed.

Manteuffel, General der Panzertruppen, Hasso von (1897–1978), holder of the Knight's Cross with Oakleaves, Swords and Diamonds. Short of stature (only 5ft 3in tall) and weighing only 120 pounds, he was a bundle of energy and a 'passionate soldier' with a deep understanding of the capabilities of the average German soldier. A brilliant, dashing and brave cavalry officer with a capacity to inspire troops, he was one of the few Prussian generals to whom Hitler

listened (on occasions!) and who would speak his mind if he considered the Führer to be wrong. Before the offensive he made numerous foot recces of the front in disguise. He commanded Fifth Panzer Army in the offensive and was awarded the Diamonds to his Knight's Cross for his success (the 24th member of the Wehrmacht to receive this, the highest, German military honour). Leading from the front as always, his Kübelwagen (Jeep) was shot from under him on three occasions! After rapid initial success, his attack would bog down in front of Bastogne. After the Ardennes, he went on to command Third Panzer Army on the Oder Front.

Model, Generalfeldmarschall Walther (1891–1945), holder of the Knight's Cross with Oakleaves, Swords and Diamonds and the German Cross in Gold. Nicknamed: 'Hitler's Fireman', this brilliant Prussian, who had joined the German Army in 1909, was a major general at the start of WWII and by early 1944 was a field marshal. He got on well with Hitler, who appreciated his abilities. For his part Model was perfectly prepared to argue with the Führer if he disagreed with his orders. An energetic commander and a brilliant tactician, he was admired by all ranks, but had few friends and little social life, being a totally dedicated soldier, a committed Christian and a family man. In August 1944, he took over both as CinC Army Group B and CinC Army Group West, from von Kluge but found the job very difficult until von Rundstedt was reinstated. He was responsible for much of the detailed planning for the Ardennes assault, but fundamentally disagreed with it as an empty gesture, favouring, like von Rundstedt, a lesser solution. After the Ardennes, he was trapped in the Ruhr pocket and chose to commit suicide rather than surrender.

Moehring, Generalleutnant Kurt (1900–44), holder of the Knight's Cross and

German Cross in Gold. Commander of 276 VGD. Re-organised in Poland from 276th Infantry Division which had been virtually destroyed in the Falaise pocket in Normandy, it would lose more than 2,000 men and its commander in the Ardennes. It would be first employed between Wallendorf and Bollendorf on the German left wing. He was killed trying to capture Medernach during the night of 17/18 December 1944.

Mohnke, SS Oberführer (later Brigadeführer und Generalmajor) der Waffen-SS, Wilhelm (1911 – alive in 1998). He was commanding 26th SS Panzer Grenadier Regiment in 12th SS Panzer Division when he was selected to command (when the previous commander, Priess, took over I SS Panzer Corps) the crack 1st SS Panzer Division (Leibstandarte Adolf Hitler) which would lead the assault through the Losheim Gap area once 3rd Para and 12th VGD had broken through the Allied line. He had to relinquish command in February 1945 after receiving ear damage during an air raid. Energetic and hard-driving, he was not well liked by his subordinates or army field commanders, although Dietrich praised him for his combat leadership.

Obstfelder, Generalleutnant (later General der Infanterie) Hans von (1886–?), holder of the German Cross in Gold and Knight's Cross with Oakleaves and Swords. A pre-war soldier in the Reichswehr, he was promoted to Generalleutnant in 1938 and initially commanded 28th Inf Division. In command of First Army (1 December 1944), he would eventually command Nineteenth Army.

Peiper, Obersturmbannführer Jochen (1915–76). This Lieutenant-Colonel of Waffen-SS had a reputation for professional competence and efficiency. Well educated, fluent in English and French, he joined Sepp Dietrich's Liebstandarte-SS (LSSAH) in 1934. He was one of

Himmler's personal adjutants in 1938–39 and at the start of the war commanded an SS company in Poland, then was promoted to command a battalion at the age of 25. He next became a regimental commander and won his Knight's Cross, then the Oakleaves (March 1943, then January 1944), both on the Eastern Front. In the Ardennes Offensive, he commanded a 5,000-strong task force built around his 1st SS Panzer Regiment, which spearheaded Dietrich's Sixth SS Panzer Army. A fanatical Nazi, his 'fame' sprang from his association with the infamous massacre of nearly 100 American troops at Malmédy. His task force would be encircled later and only 800 all ranks would escape.

Pelz, Generalmajor Dietrich, Commander II Flieger Corps.

Petersen, Generalleutnant Erich, Commander XC Corps which had been formed in late 1942 as IV Luftwaffe Feldkorps.

Pickert, Generalleutnant Wolfgang, Commander III FlaK Korps.

Priess, SS Gruppenführer und Generalleutnant der Waffen-SS Hermann (1901–85). A highly experienced and respected commander, who had commanded both 1st and 3rd SS Panzer Divisions. From October 1944 he commanded I SS Panzer Corps in Sixth SS Panzer Army, which contained 1st and 12th SS Panzer Divisions, 12th and 3rd Parachute Divisions and 277th VGD, plus also under command, Skorzeny's 150 Panzer Brigade. His Corps' main effort would be made in the south of the army sector, where the relatively open, rolling country of the Losheim Gap was best for armoured exploitation. Quiet, reserved and private, he gained a deserved reputation as a tenacious combat commander. Tried for the Malmédy massacre, he was imprisoned until 1954.

Rasp, Generalleutnant Siegfried (1898–?), holder of the Knight's Cross and the German Cross in Gold. Commissioned in 1915, he was an Oberstleutnant when WWII began and eventually rose to the rank of General der Infanterie. Took over as Commander of Nineteenth Army from General Weise on 15 December 1944.

Remer, Oberst (later Generalmajor) Otto-Ernst (1912–?), holder of the Knight's Cross with Oakleaves and the German Cross in Gold. He was commander of Führer Begleit Brigade (later Führer Begleit Division), and had been commanding the escort (*Begleit*) battalion protecting Hitler at his HQ when the bomb attempt was made on his life. His prompt reaction in rounding-up suspects brought him into favour with Hitler, hence his rapid promotion.

Rothkirch und Trach, General der Kavallerie Edwin Graf von (1888–?). He was probably the least well qualified of the nine corps commanders taking part in the offensive, most of his previous experience having been in command of static units in Russia, looking after fortifications, etc. He commanded LIII Corps until captured by the Americans in March 1945.

Rundstedt, Generalfeldmarschall Karl Rudolf Gerd von (1875–1953), holder of the Knight's Cross with Oakleaves and Swords. Orthodox, competent but uninspiring, he was a general officer from the 1920s onward and commanded Army Group A in Poland and France. In June 1941, as part of Operation 'Barbarossa', his Army Group South thrust slowly and steadily towards the Caucasus. Later he was relieved of his command, having unexpectedly withdrawn from Rostov, but when Hitler was informed that he had had a heart attack he was retired with a large 'golden handshake'. Recalled in May 1942 and put in charge of the occupation of Vichy France, he became CinC West until he was sacked again in July 1944 when he clashed with Hitler over the 'no withdrawal' order. Reinstated in September 1944, again as CinC West, he was responsible for stabilising the front and was nominally in command of the Ardennes operation. He favoured a much more modest attack, but was overruled by Hitler. He would be 'sacked' once again in March 1945 (for losing the Remagen Bridge). He was always contemptuous of Hitler and the Nazi Party, never seeking to curry favour with them, and remaining non-political to the end.

Schmidt, Generalleutnant Josef 'Beppo'. He was Luftwaffenkommando West, in charge of the ten fighter groups operating in support of troops on the Western Front, a post he had taken over from Adolf Galland.

Schmidt, Generalmajor Erich-Otto (1899–?), Knight's Cross holder and commander of 352nd *Volks* Grenadier Division, yet another reformed division that fought in the Eifel battles.

Sensfuss, Generalmajor (later Generalleutnant) Franz (1891–?), holder of the Knight's Cross with Oakleaves. He was Commander of 212th *Volks* Grenadier Division, rebuilt with recruits from Upper Bavaria, mainly 17-year-olds. They would sustain more than 4,000 casualties during the offensive.

Simon, SS Gruppenführer und Generalleutnant der Waffen-SS Max (1899–1961). Served during WWI, being awarded the Iron Cross 2nd Class. Joined the SS from the Reichsheer in 1933 and by the time the 'Totenkopf' Division was formed, he was the commander of its 1st Infantry Regiment. A strict disciplinarian and able tactical commander, he was ruthless in the field. Tried as a war criminal, he was sentenced to death, but this was commuted to life imprisonment. Released in 1954, he died of a heart attack in 1961, while awaiting another trial for killings on the Russian front.

Skorzeny, Obersturmbannführer Otto (1908–67). A burly giant of a man, he was Hitler's favourite commando, having been responsible for rescuing Mussolini. This rescue and his other escapades earned him the nickname: 'the most dangerous man in Europe'. In the Ardennes, for an operation thought up by Hitler, Operation 'Greif' (Griffon), he commanded a hodge-podge of troops (known as 150 Panzer Brigade) charged with the task of capturing certain bridges over the Meuse and holding them until relieved, while other, English-speaking troops dressed in GI uniforms with US vehicles and equipment spread chaos and confusion among genuine US troops encountered.

Stadler, SS Oberführer Sylvester (1910–95), holder of the Knight's Cross with both Oakleaves and Swords (the latter personally presented by Sepp Dietrich on 6 May 1945, just after he was promoted to SS Brigadeführer and Generalmajor der Waffen-SS). In 'Wacht am Rhein' he was Commander of 9th SS Panzer Division Hohenstauffen in II SS Panzer Corps. It is said that he developed a fine tactical brain, thanks to combat experience in the field under the watchful eyes of senior commanders like Paul Hauser, to add to exceptional bravery and tenacity.

Tolsdorf, Oberst (later Generalmajor) Theodor (1909–78), holder of the Knight's Cross with Oakleaves, Swords and Diamonds. As a colonel he commanded 340th *Volks* Grenadier Division, he became a general at the age of 35 on 18 March 1945, at the same time receiving his Diamonds for outstanding personal bravery and his division's accomplishments. His men called him 'the great Tolsdorf' or the 'Lion of Vilna'.

Toppe, Generalmajor Alfred (1940–?), holder of the German Cross in Silver. He entered the Army in 1923, and from June 1940 held senior O. Qu posts. From 22 July 1944 he was General Qu.d.H at OKH and thus responsible for the 'supply miracle' for 'Wacht am Rhein'.

Viebig, Oberst (later Generalmajor) Wilhelm (1899–?), holder of the German Cross in Gold. Commander of 277th *Volks* Grenadier Division, he was promoted to major general in late 1944. After the Ardennes, he was captured on the western bank of the Rhine when his command post was overrun on 9 March 1945.

Wagener, Generalmajor Carl Gustav (1901–?), holder of the Knight's Cross and the German Cross in Gold. He was Hasso von Manteuffel's Chief of Staff in Fifth Panzer Army.

Wadehn, Generalleutnant. He took over 3rd Fallschirmjäger (Parachute) Division when the previous commander was wounded near Falaise, and commanded the division during the Ardennes offensive.

Waldenburg, Generalmajor Siegfried von (1898–?), holder of the Knight's Cross. He commanded 116th Panzer Division throughout 1944–45. He had previously served as Military Attaché in Rome in 1943, then as Ia at LXXX Corps HQ.

Warlimont, Generalmajor (later General der Artillerie) Walter (1894–?). Having joined the army in 1913, he also served during the inter-war period in the

Reichsheer. A Knight's Cross holder, he was Chief of the operations staff at OKW from 1 January 1942 onwards.

Westphal, Generalleutnant (later General der Kavallerie) Siegfried (1902– ?), holder of the Knight's Cross and the German Cross in Gold. He was Rommel's Chief of Staff in the desert at various levels from DAK upwards, and in 1944 was von Rundstedt's COS at OB West. Described as being the perfect staff officer, his code of honour was that General Staff Officers must be entirely anonymous, acting always in the name of the commander and naturally in his best interests. He was as sceptical about the proposed offensive as was his master von Rundstedt.

Zimmermann, Generalleutnant Bodo (1886–?), holder of the German Cross in both Silver and Gold. He was Operations Officer OB West and so was 'let in' on the plan for the Ardennes offensive early on.

AMERICAN

Anderson, Major General Samuel E., CG IX Bombardment Division, USAAF.

Andrus, Brigadier General (later Major General) Clift (1890–1968). He was commissioned in 1912, rose to become CG US 1st Infantry Division, V Corps. Decorations included DSC, DSM, Silver Star with Oakleaf cluster, Soldiers Medal and Bronze Star with Oakleaf cluster. He retired in 1952.

Baade, Major General Paul William (1889–1959). He was commissioned into the infantry in 1911 and served in France with the AEF during WWI from September 1918 onwards. At the start of WWII he was commanding 16th Infantry Regiment, then commanded Fort Buchanan in Puerto Rico until being made Assistant Divisional Commander of 35th Infantry Division guarding the coast of Southern California. He was appointed CG US 35th Infantry Division in January 1943, landed on Omaha beach on D-Day and led his division through France and Germany until April 1945, when his division was the closest British or American unit to Berlin. Post-war he was appointed Director of Military Training. He was awarded the DSM in 1944.

Barton, Major General Raymond O. (1889–1963). Commanding General US 4th Infantry Division, XII Corps. He was commissioned into the infantry in 1912, served in France during WWI and at the start of WWII was COS IV Army Corps. He assumed command of 4th Motorised Division in June 1942. This division subsequently became 4th Infantry Division and he remained as CG until March 1945, when he was made CG of Infantry Training at Fort McClellan. He retired in 1946. He was awarded the DSM in 1944. At the start of the Ardennes offensive his division was in a holding position 35 miles from the right flank of XII Corps front, abutting US Third Army. Having distinguished themselves in the bloody battles of the Hürtgen Forest operation, they were battle weary and had sustained many casualties. When his G-2 reported that there were large enemy forces to their south in Bitburg, he assumed that the Germans might be planning a big raid but had no inkling of a major enemy offensive.

Bolling, Major General (later Lieutenant General) Alexander R. (1895–1964). He attended the US Naval Academy 1915–16, but then switched to the Army and graduated in 1917. He rose to become the Commanding General of 84th Infantry Division which was part of Collins' VII Corps. During the battle Collins was very impressed by his 'calm approach to the situation'. His decorations included the DSC, DSM, Silver Star,

Bronze Star, Legion of Merit and numerous foreign decorations from France, Belgium, Holland, Russia and Czechoslovakia. He retired in 1955.

Bradley, Lieutenant General (later General of the Army) Omar Nelson 'Brad' (1891–1981). Commissioned from West Point in 1915, he rose swiftly to prominence during WWII, first as Patton's deputy in II Corps during Operation 'Torch' in North Africa, then took over in Tunisia. Appointed senior US ground force commander for the Normandy invasion, he initially commanded First Army then US 12th Army Group. Known as 'the soldiers' general', he has been castigated by some for his apparent inaction at the start of the 'Bulge' assault, a charge he strongly denied. His relations with Montgomery were at the best of times 'difficult'!

Brooks, Major General Edward H. He assumed command of US VI Corps on 25 October 1944, having served briefly as the commander of V Corps. An artilleryman and developer of the M7 105mm SP howitzer, he had commanded the 2nd Armored Division 'Hell on Wheels' since March 1944.

Clarke, Brigadier General (later General) Bruce Cooper Clarke (1901–88). Joined the Army in 1918 and was commissioned into the Engineers in 1925. In 1940 he was appointed CO of 24th Engineer Battalion and became acting engineer officer for the Armored Force on its formation. Later he was chief of staff 4th Armored Division, then CO CCA 4th Armd. He was awarded both the DSC and Silver Star in heavy fighting in August 1944. In November 1944, he was CO CCB 7th Armored Division and was sent to St-Vith to command a hodge-podge of units which he welded into a cohesive force and carried out a masterly defence that seriously delayed Manteuffel's Fifth Panzer Army.

Collins, Major General (later General) Joseph 'Lightning Joe' Lawton (1896–1987). Commissioned in 1917 (youngest in his class), he was appointed chief of staff VII Corps in January 1941, then was detached to help organise the defences of Pearl Harbor and later commanded 25th Infantry Division at Guadalcanal. He later commanded VII Corps in NW Europe, landing at Utah Beach, capturing Cherbourg and going on to take part in Operation 'Cobra', the breakout from the beachhead. Bold, unorthodox generalship made him, with Troy Middleton, one of the two best US Corps commanders according to the Germans. His counter-attack on the northern shoulder of the German Ardennes offensive would cut their major escape route.

Cota, Major General Norman Daniel 'Dutch' (1893–?). Commissioned in April 1917, he became Chief of Staff of 1st Infantry Division in June 1942 when they went overseas, then served at the British Combined Ops HQ in London before being assigned as assistant divisional commander 29th Infantry Division. His outstanding performance on the Normandy beaches earned him promotion to command 28th Infantry Division in August 1944. He commanded the division in the Hürtgen Forest and was still in command when they were sent to 'rest' in the Ardennes, holding the centre of VIII Corps front on the River Our. In August 1945 he returned to USA with his division and retired in June 1946 due to a physical disability, then later returned for a period of active duty. His decorations included the Legion of Merit, the DSC (for his outstanding courage and leadership on the Normandy beaches on D-Day), the British DSO, Silver Star and Bronze Star with Oak Leaf Cluster, DSM – the last of these for Hürtgen Forest and the Ardennes actions.

Craig, Major General Louis A., CG 9th Infantry Division, US V Corps.

Culin, Brigadier General Frank Lewis, Jr. (1892–1967). He was commissioned in 1915 and rose to become CG 87th Infantry Division, VIII Corps. His decorations included the Silver Star with two Oakleaf Clusters, Bronze Star, Air Medal, DSM and various decorations from France and Belgium. He retired in 1946.

Dager, Brigadier General Holmes Ely (1893–1973). He was commissioned into the New Jersey National Guard in 1912 and served in France during WWI, taking part in the Meuse–Argonne Offensive with 51st Infantry Division. In January 1942 he was assigned to 8th Armored Division, then became a combat commander in 4th Armored Division in August 1942. He commanded CCB of 4th Armored Division, US Third Army and was detached to command VIII Corps when they arrived first in Arlon on 19 December – the divisional commander (Gaffey) was not best pleased! He next commanded 11th Armored Div, then 5th Armored Division until leaving the army in February 1946. His decorations included the Silver Star with Oak Leaf Cluster, the Bronze Star with two Clusters, the DSC, DSM, French *Légion d'honneur* and *Croix de Guerre*, the Belgian *Croix de Guerre*, the Luxembourg *Croix de Guerre* and the USSR 'Defence of the Fatherland' (1st Degree).

Devers, General Jacob Loucks (1887–1979). Led US 6th Army Group from southern France all the way into Germany. Not one of Eisenhower's favourites, because he lacked combat experience. However, he was a 'Marshall man' so eventually was promoted to four star rank. Last appointment was as Commander Army Ground Forces. He retired in 1949.

Dickson, Colonel Benjamin Abbot 'Monk'. G-2 of US First Army, handsome sixfooter, who had maintained his weight at the same level as when he had played football at West Point in 1917. Graduating during WWI, he had resigned post-war because he could see no future in the Army, but retained a reserve commission. He took an engineering degree and then went into business in Philadelphia. He returned to active duty in 1940 as a Captain and soon rose to become Bradley's G-2 in North Africa and stayed with him when Bradley took command of First Army. He was very upset when, instead of moving up with Bradley to HQ 12th Army Group, he remained in his current post. To his associates at the higher levels of intelligence, he was a 'volatile man, a pessimist, an alarmist' yet he was clearly extremely able and some said he had a photographic memory. He had a continuous bad relationship with the G-2 of HQ 12th Army Group, Colonel Edwin L. Sibert, whose job he thought should have been his! Nevertheless, he had the last laugh over his detractors, when his now famous 'G-2 Estimate No 37' which contained clear warnings about the forthcoming German attack in the Ardennes was ignored, but proved to be correct.

Doolittle, General James Harold 'Jimmye' (1896–1993), USAAF. A flying cadet, he was commissioned in 1917. Became a public hero for bombing Tokyo 18 April 1942. He commanded Eighth Air Force at the time of the Ardennes, with 2,000 heavy bombers and nearly 1,000 fighters at his disposal.

Earnest, Brigadier General Herbert L., commanded CCA of US 4th Armored Division. His force had many cases of frostbite as a result of exposure in the worst winter weather in the area for 30 years.

Eddy, Major General (later Lieutenant General) Manton Sprague 'Matt' (1892–1962). A veteran of WWI, he was promoted to Major General in 1942 to command 9th Infantry Division in Operation 'Torch'. Plump and 'high-tensioned', he showed considerable boldness and skill in North Africa, then fought in Sicily and later in Normandy, crossing Utah Beach on D+4. In August 1944 he took over command of XII Corps in General Patton's US Third Army, when Major General Cook became ill. He continued to lead XII Corps for the remainder of the war until 20 April 1945. To quote from the Corps history: 'Day in day out, his energy, aggressiveness and personal courage were inspirations to those who came in contact with him.'

Eisenhower, General of the Army Dwight David 'Ike' (1890–1969). Graduating from West Point in 1915, he served as a trainer in the US Tank Corps during WWI, so saw no active service. In the early 1930s he served on General MacArthur's staff and in June 1942 was selected to command the US Army in the European Theatre. Overall command in North Africa followed (Operation 'Torch') and in 1943 at the Teheran Conference, he was selected to command the Allied Expeditionary Force for the invasion of Europe. His strong, amiable personality made him the ideal choice for this difficult job. He was promoted to Five Star General of the Army on 16 December 1944. From 1953 to 1961 he was America's 34th President.

Gaffey, Major General Hugh Joseph (1895–?). He took over command of US 4th Armored Division from 'Tiger Jack' Wood when he was hospitalised in December 1944, Gaffey having been Patton's Chief of Staff from April 1944. An artilleryman, who had been commissioned in 1917, he was COS II Corps in North Africa for which he was awarded the DSM. His

division would break the siege of Bastogne.

Gavin, Major General James Maurice 'Jumping Jim' (1907–90). Youngest general in the US Army when he was promoted to command 82nd Airborne Division on 20 October 1944. His division counter-attacked the northern shoulder of the 'Bulge' (by truck) on 19 December 1944. A hero with two DSCs and two Silver Stars, he was also an innovative thinker and advocate of sky cavalry and satellite communications.

Gerow, Major General (later General) Leonard Townsend 'Gee' (1888–1972). Commissioned in 1911, he was US Chief of War Plans from 1935 to 1939, commanded 29th Infantry Division in 1942 and then V Corps from July 1943. Omaha Beach, the liberation of Paris, then the northern shoulder of the Ardennes, were all operations which his corps took in its stride, while spearheading Hodges' US First Army. His 2nd and 99th Divisions produced some of the stiffest opposition to the German assault in the Elsenborn Ridge area. Described as being: 'testy, outspoken and somewhat impetuous', he nevertheless showed himself to be an extremely able commander.

Grow, Major General Robert W., CG 6th Armored Division, III Corps, US Third Army, began his army career as a private in the Minnesota National Guard, in 1914. He was S3 of the first Mechanised Force of 1930 and after being appointed commander of CCB 8th Armored Division in April 1942, took over 6th Armored Division in May 1942 and commanded them for the rest of the war. Patton described him as being: 'one of the best armored force commanders the war produced'.

Haislip, Major General Wade Hampton 'Ham' (1889–1971). Graduated from West Point into the infantry in 1912, rose to the rank of Lieutenant Colonel with the AEF. Attended the French War College between the wars. His first divisional command was 85th Infantry Division – one of the first divisions to be made up primarily of draftees. By the time of 'Nordwind' he was commanding XV Corps. He was promoted to Lieutenant General in 1945, and retired in 1949 after receiving his fourth star.

Harmon, Major General Ernest Nason 'Old Gravel Voice' (1894–1945). Commanded 2nd Armored Division and spearheaded US VII Corps' drive into the flank of 2nd SS Panzer Division on its north flank around Celles, halting Fifth Panzer Army's drive to the Meuse. *Newsweek* called him 'probably the most profane, wisest and sprightliest tank commander in the army'.

Hasbrouck, Major General Robert Wilson (1896–1985). Graduating from West Point in 1917 into Coast Artillery, he transferred to Field and in April 1941, when the Armored Force was formed, became CO 22nd Armored Field Artillery Battalion in 4th Armored Division. After serving with both 1st and 8th Armored Divisions briefly, he became chief of staff of First Army Group (later Twelfth Army Group) in August 1943. A year later he took command of 7th Armored Division. His division would earn special praise from both Eisenhower and Montgomery for holding out against six German divisions until being ordered to withdraw on 23 December, having been credited with splitting the German offensive. His decorations included the DSM, Legion of Merit, Bronze Star and Silver Star plus the French *Légion d'honneur* and *Croix de Guerre* with Palm, and the Polish War Cross. He would go on to become Deputy COS Army Ground Forces in December 1945 and retired from the Army in 1947.

Hobbs, Major General Leland Stanford (1892–1966). He was commissioned in 1915, rose to command US 30th Infantry Division which was resting in the Aachen area on 16 December, when he heard about the German attack along V and VIII Corps' boundary and was ordered to relieve part of 1st Infantry Division around Eupen, but ran into Kampfgruppe Peiper on the way. Hobbs was a determined and resourceful commander who demanded the very best from his men and led by example.

Hodges, Lieutenant General (later General) Courtney Hicks (1887–1966). Enlisted as a private soldier and served three years in the ranks. He rose to command X Corps in 1942, then Third Army (both in the USA). His most important wartime command followed, when he took over US First Army from Bradley. Quiet, almost too self-effacing, he was a careful, meticulous soldier, well-liked by his men (he was known as 'the soldiers' soldier'). His Army would bear the brunt of the German assault in the Ardennes and, like Bradley, he has been criticised for apparent inaction.

Hoge, Brigadier General William M., who was commanding CCB US 9th Armored Division, which was reserve for the Roer dams attack. A competent armoured commander, he would be involved in the fighting for St-Vith. His division would later win renown when elements of his command captured the Remagen bridge over the River Rhine. Later he would go on to command 4th Armored Division.

Huebner, Major General (later General) Clarence R. (1888–1972). Commander of US V Corps. He was described by Patton as being the 'tops'. CG of 1st Infantry Division ('The Big Red One'), he had brought them to UK, then landed at 'Bloody Omaha' in the first wave. His decorations included the DSC with Oak Leaf Cluster, the DSM with two Oak Leaf Clusters, the Silver Star, Legion of Merit and the Bronze Star. Post-war he was CG US Army Europe.

Irwin, Major General S. LeRoy 'Red' (1893--?). An artilleryman, who was commissioned in 1915, he was commanding 5th Infantry Division in US Third Army throughout XII Corps' operations in the ETO. He went on to command XII Corps in April–May 1945. Known as 'the fighting general', his division would be heavily involved in counter-attacks on the southern shoulder of the enemy assault. His decorations included the British CBE, French *Légion d'honneur* and *Croix de Guerre*, plus the Belgian *Croix de Guerre*.

Jones, Major General Alan W. He commanded the 'green', newly arrived US 106th Infantry Division, which took over the positions from the veteran 2nd Infantry Division, on the left of VIII Corps. His division would be practically destroyed and he would be evacuated having suffered a heart attack.

Kean, Major General William G. Strong-willed, imperious US First Army Chief of Staff (known by his staff as 'Captain Bligh'!).

Kilburn, Brigadier General Charles S. 'Rattlesnake Pete' (1895–1978). He was Commander of 11th Armored Division from early in 1943. His division would trap large numbers of German troops near Bastogne.

Koch, Colonel (later Brigadier General) Oscar W. (1897–1970). General Patton's brilliant, quiet-spoken, scholarly and hardworking G-2 (Intelligence) at HQ Third Army, who was the 'sparkplug' of the HQ and, to quote Patton: 'the best damned intelligence officer in any United States Army Command!'

GSP had brought him to 2nd Armored Division, then took him to North Africa as COS of one of the Task Forces. Later he made him his Army G-2. Together with Colonel 'Monk' Dickson at HQ First Army, he predicted the German assault in the Ardennes which enabled a forewarned Patton to put his plans into speedy execution.

Lauer, Major General Walter E., was the CG of 99th Infantry Division, a 'green' division in General Gerow's V Corps, which had been holding a sector on the southern end of the corps' front in the Ardennes only since mid-November.

Leonard, Major General John William (1890–?) was commissioned into the infantry in 1915, served extensively during WWI in France and was awarded the DSC, the Purple Heart and two French decorations for bravery. He was CO 18th Tank Battalion in 1921 and by July 1941 was CO 6th Armored Infantry Regiment. On activation of 9th Armored Division in July 1942 he became commander CCB as a Brigadier General, then in September 1942 he became CG and continued to command them for the remainder of the war. His division would become famous by assisting 101st Airborne Division to hold Bastogne during the Ardennes offensive. Later it seized the Ludendorff railway bridge at Remagen. Post-war he commanded the Armored School and Post of Fort Knox. His decorations included the DSC, DSM, Legion of Merit, Silver Star, Bronze Star and Purple Heart, together with the French *Légion d'honneur* and the *Croix de Guerre* with Palm (won in both world wars).

Macon, Major General Robert Chauncey (1890–?) was commissioned into the infantry in 1916. By August 1940, he was serving with 6th Infantry (Armored), then was CO 80th

Armored Regiment. He went on to command 7th Infantry Regiment and took them to North Africa in 1942. In April 1943 he became Assistant Divisional Commander US 83rd Infantry Division, then in January 1944 he became CG and continued to command the 83rd until its deactivation in April 1946. His first post-war appointment was as Military Attaché in Moscow.

Marshall, General George C. (1880–1959). He was Army Chief of Staff from 1939 to 1945. A man of genius and a master of organisation, his influence over the US Army was immense. Post-war he would become Secretary of State and be responsible for the European recovery plan (known as the 'Marshall Plan').

McAuliffe, Brigadier General (later General) Anthony Clement (1898–1975). He graduated from West Point in 1918 and by August 1942 was commanding the divisional artillery of the 101st Airborne Division, parachuting into France on the night of 5 June and commanding the force that captured Carentan. After taking part in Operation 'Market-Garden' where he commanded the Glider echelon of the 101st, he was acting divisional commander when the Ardennes operation began. His taciturn reply of 'Nuts' to a German demand to surrender Bastogne was typical of the man and made him an instant celebrity.

McBride, Major General Horace L. (1894–?), CG 80th US Infantry Division. He was commissioned in 1916 into the field artillery and served in France, then Holland during WWI, then in Poland as a Military Attaché. He was commanding 2nd Field Artillery Battalion in 1940, became artillery commander 80th Infantry Division and finally took command

of the division in March 1943. Post-war he commanded XX Corps in southern Bavaria. His decorations included the DSM, Legion of Merit, Silver Star with Oak Leaf Cluster and Bronze Star, plus Cross of the Brave (Poland), *Croix de Guerre* with Palm and Star (France), *Croix de Guerre* (Luxembourg), Order of Alexander Novsky and the Order of War of the Fatherland (USSR).

McLain, Major General Raymond S. Commander of US XIX Corps.

Middleton, Major General (later Lieutenant General) Troy H. (1889–1976). A full colonel of infantry in WWI, he retired in 1937, but was recalled to active duty and rose to command first 45th Infantry Division in Sicily, then VIII Corps until the end of the war in Europe. Eisenhower once said: 'I would rather have Troy Middleton commanding VIII Corps from a stretcher than anyone else I know in perfect health!' Calm and efficient, he was probably Patton's most methodical corps commander and an able tactician.

Miley, Major General William Maynadier (1897–?) was commissioned into the infantry in June 1918. By October 1940 he had assumed command of 501st Parachute Battalion and in July 1942 activated and commanded 503rd Parachute Regiment. In August 1942 he was assistant divisional commander of 82nd Infantry Division, then in April 1943 became CG 17th Airborne Division and took them to the UK. When the Ardennes offensive began the division was flown to France and was soon heavily engaged. His decorations included the DSM, Silver Star with Oak Leaf Cluster, Bronze Star Medal with Cluster; foreign decorations included the British DSO and the Belgian *Croix de Guerre* with Palm. Post-war one of his appointments was a CG US Army in Alaska.

Millikin, Major General John (1888–?). A cavalryman, he was commissioned in 1912 and served in the AEF during WWI. In 1941 he was in command of 2nd Cavalry Division, in 1942 83rd Infantry Division and in 1943 33rd Infantry Division, being appointed CG III Corps in that year. Patton was opposed to his appointment because he had never commanded a division in battle, but after initial misgivings rated him highly.

Morris, Major General William Henry Hamish (1890–1971), CG US 10th Armored Division, holder of the DSC, DSM, Silver Star, Legion of Merit, Bronze Star and numerous foreign decorations from France, Belgium, Brazil, Panama and Ecuador. He would be given command of a provisional corps on 16 December, comprising his own division and 9th Armored Division plus 4th and 109th Infantry Divisions, and charged with unifying defensive measures behind which US Third Army's counter-attack forces could gather.

Nugent, Major General Richard E., CG of XXIX Tactical Air Command, whose fighter-bombers, with those of IX TAC, supported the US ground troops in the Ardennes.

Parker, Major General Edwin P., Jr., CG US 78th Infantry Division.

Patch, Lieutenant General Alexander McCarrell 'Sandy' (1889–1945). Commissioned in 1913 into the infantry, he took part in the Punitive Expedition to Mexico and rose to the rank of Lieutenant Colonel during WWI, commanding a machine-gun battalion – post-war this became his speciality. Rose to prominence in WWII, first forming the Americal Division, then commanding XIV Corps on Guadalcanal. Promoted to command US Seventh Army for the invasion of southern France, he remained in

command for the rest of the war. Rated very highly by Eisenhower, he commanded Fourth Army on his return to the USA, until his untimely death at 55. He was promoted to full general posthumously.

Patton, Lieutenant General (later General) George Smith, Jr. 'Ole Blood 'n Guts' (1885–1945). Charismatic, volatile and brilliant, he was the only high-level armoured commander of WWII who had commanded tanks at brigade level in WWI. In 1942 he commanded the Western Task Force in Operation 'Torch' and then II Corps in Tunisia. Spectacular success followed in Sicily where he commanded US Seventh Army, then he nearly ruined his career by slapping a soldier in a field hospital. He was 'rescued' by his old friend 'Ike' and appointed to command US Third Army which led the race across France after the breakout from the Normandy beachhead. His greatest moment came during the Ardennes battle when he turned his entire Army 90 degrees in order to go to the relief of Bastogne ('If Georgie's coming we've got it made!') was the reaction among the beleaguered garrison. Considered to be the best Allied armoured commander by the Germans, he was to die in a car accident in Germany in 1945.

Paul, Major General (later Lieutenant General) Willard Stewart (1894–1966), CG, US 26th Infantry Division.

Piburn, Brigadier General Edwin W., Commander CCA US 10th Armored Division.

Prickett, Major General Fay B., CG US 75th Infantry Division.

Quesada, Major General Elwood R. 'Pete'. Commander of US IX Tactical Air Command. At forty years of age (in 1944), he was the youngest US general officer in the ETO and can be considered to have been the 'father of the Tactical Air Command'.

Ridgway, Major General (later General) Matthew Bunker 'Matt' (1895–1993). Older than most airborne generals, he had graduated in 1917 and became assistant divisional commander of US 82nd Infantry Division in March 1942, just before its conversion to airborne. In April 1943, now divisional commander, he launched the first major US airborne assault on Sicily. On D-Day he parachuted into Normandy and then commanded XVIII Airborne Corps from September 1944 onwards. During the Korean War he took over command of US Eighth Army when General Walton Walker was killed and then succeeded MacArthur when he was dismissed in April 1951, as head of all US and UN forces. He was Supreme Allied Commander in Europe from 1952 to 1953 and then US Army Chief of Staff in 1953.

Robertson, Major General Walter M. (1888–?). He had graduated from West Point in 1912, but saw no action during WWI. Between the wars he served as an instructor at both the Staff and War Colleges. Older (56) than most other divisional commanders, he was usually mild-mannered and relaxed, but had a formidable temper when roused; he was a teetotaller and something of a loner. He was CG of 2nd Infantry Division from May 1942 and had brought them ashore on Omaha Beach on D+1.

Rose, Major General Maurice B. (1899–1945). CG US 3rd Armored Division, he was more than 6ft tall, with finely chiselled features, always immaculate, one war correspondent described him as looking like Hollywood's idea of a soldier. Invariably he led from the front and was killed near Paderborn in late March 1945, when his command group 'bumped' a Panther tank.

Simpson, Lieutenant General William Hood 'Big Simp' (1899–1961), Commander of US Ninth Army. Tall and completely bald, he was very well thought of by Eisenhower – 'If Simpson ever made a mistake as an army commander, it never came to my attention,' he wrote in his memoirs. His army would come under Montgomery's command when the British field marshal took over the northern flank.

Smith, Lieutenant General Walter Bedell (1895–1961), SHAEF Chief of Staff, well-known for his hair-trigger temper!

Spaatz, General Carl A. 'Tooey' (1891–1974). A fighter pilot in WWI, in 1929 (with Captain Eaker) he established an aircraft endurance record. His rise during WWII was meteoric, commanding in turn Air Combat Command, US Eighth Air Force and NW Africa Strategic Air Force. In 1944 he became chief of US Strategic Air Forces in Europe.

Taylor, Major General Maxwell Davenport (1901–87). He was commissioned into the engineers in 1912 and later transferred to the field artillery. Pre-war service included stints as military attaché in both Japan and China. His first airborne appointment was as Ridgway's COS in 82nd Infantry Division which then became 82nd Airborne. He became CG 101st Airborne Division and dropped with his division behind Utah Beach and captured Carentan. He took part in Operation 'Market-Garden', but was on leave in the UK when his division took part in its epic defence of Bastogne (see McAuliffe). He was one of the most brilliant airborne commanders of the war, and went on to become a five star general and to hold a series of high appointments post-war, including Chief of Staff of the Army (1955–1959), then Chairman of the

Joint Chiefs of Staff (1962-1964) and Ambassador to South Vietnam.

Vandenberg, Lieutenant General Hoyt S. He had joined the US Army Air Corps in 1923 and became Commander of Ninth Air Force. Postwar he was head of military intelligence, then head of the CIA, before returning to take over from Spaatz as COS of the USAF.

Van Fleet, Major General James A. (1892–?). He was commissioned into the infantry in 1915 and commanded 17th Machine Gun Battalion in the AEF and was wounded in the Meuse–Argonne offensive. On D-Day he landed on Utah Beach as CO 8th Infantry Regiment in US 4th Infantry Division, distinguished himself during the capture of Cherbourg, then was promoted to Assistant Commander 2nd Infantry Division. After the siege of Brest (Aug–Sept 1944) he was appointed CG 90th Infantry Division in US Third Army. Patton thought highly of him and he went on to command III Corps in April 1945. Post-war he was CG US Eighth Army in Korea after Ridgway, and retired from the Army in February 1953. He was the recipient of three DSCs and the DSM among numerous other awards.

Weyland, Brigadier General Otto P. 'Opie'. He was CG XIX Tactical Air Command which supported Patton's Third Army. He was highly regarded by GSP who wrote: 'The co-operation between the Third Army and XIX TAC ... has been the finest example of the ground and air working together that I have ever seen.' He became a full general in 1952, as CG Tactical Air Command.

Williams, Major General Paul L. Was Commander of US IX Troop Carrier Command and thus in charge of all C-47s flying out of the UK. His Command would play a major role in supplying Bastogne during the siege.

BRITISH

Bols, Major-General Eric Louis, CB, DSO (1904–?). Commissioned into the Devons in 1924, he then transferred to The King's Regiment as a Captain in 1935 and by 1941 was a local Lieutenant-Colonel. He was GOC British 6th Airborne Division at the time of the Ardennes offensive.

Clarke, Brigadier William Stanhope, CBE, DSO (1899–?). He was commissioned into the Royal Artillery in 1919, then transferred to the Tank Corps in 1921, later RTC and RTR. Commanded British 34 Army Tank Brigade from 3 July 1943 until the end of the war. Post-war he commanded D & M School, RAC Centre, then RAC Centre.

Coningham, Air Marshal Sir Arthur (1895–1948), Commander 2nd Tactical Air Force, RAF.

De Guingand, Major-General Sir Francis Wilfred 'Freddie' (1900–79), KCB, CB, CBE, DSO. Commissioned into the West Yorks in 1919. As Montgomery's brilliant COS he was largely responsible for 'pulling his master's chestnuts out of the fire', after the row between Monty and Eisenhower over certain aspects of command during the Battle of the Bulge.

Harvey, Brigadier Charles Barnet Cameron, DSO and Bar (1900–?). He was commissioned into the 10th Hussars in 1920. He commanded British 29th Armoured Brigade from 22 February 1943 until the end of the war.

Horrocks, Lieutenant-General Sir Brian Gwynne (1895–1985). British commander of XXX Corps, who had previously commanded first XII, then IX and X Corps in the Western Desert where he was badly wounded in 1943. Criticised for apparent inaction during the Arnhem battle after a spectacularly fast advance through Belgium and Holland, it would be his corps that would be employed to defend the northern crossings of the Meuse. Montgomery would – surprisingly – send him home in December 1944 just when the battle was reaching a critical phase. However, Monty had appreciated that the worst was over and the battle won, so wanted his key corps commander to rest before the next vitally important phases, namely the battle of the Reichswald, followed by the Rhine crossing.

Montgomery, Field Marshal Bernard Law, 1st Viscount Alamein (1887–1976). One of the longest-serving and most successful Allied field commanders of WWII, he came to prominence when he took command of British Eighth Army in North Africa and subsequently won the Battle of Alamein. Success in North Africa, Sicily and Italy made him the obvious choice to command 21st Army Group in NW Europe. His somewhat abrasive, 'cocky' attitude made him an extremely difficult person to deal with – especially for the Americans! Normally a careful and methodical planner, the Arnhem débâcle was totally out of character. His insistence that there should be a single field commander (himself!) for Allied forces in Europe, directly below Eisenhower, was a bone of contention which would almost cause the break up of the Alliance and he would be forced to back down. He was promoted to Field Marshal on 1 September 1944.

Rennie, Major-General Thomas G., late Black Watch, was GOC 51st Highland Infantry Division during the period of the Ardennes offensive. Previously he

had commanded 154 Highland Brigade in the division during the fighting in Sicily. He would be killed on 24 March 1945, during the crossing of the Rhine.

Ross, Major-General Robert Knox, DSO, MC (1893–?). He was commissioned into The Queen's Regiment in 1913 and served throughout WW1, winning both a DSO and MC. Between the wars he served with the Sudan Defence Force which he commanded from 1940–1942. He then became GOC 53rd (Welsh) Infantry Division from 12 September 1942 until the end of the war, except for two short periods in February and May 1944.

Scott, Brigadier Harry Balfour, DSO and Bar (1907–?). He was commissioned in The Royals in 1927, and was commander of British 33 Armoured Brigade from March 1944 until the end of the war. He had also been the last commander of 33 Army Tank Brigade before it was converted to an armoured brigade.

Strong, Major-General Sir Kenneth William Dobson, KBE, CB (1900–?) He was commissioned into the Royal Scots Fusiliers in 1920. He was SHAEF's (British) Chief of Intelligence, and was to propose the division of responsibility for the front between Bradley (southern shoulder) and Montgomery (northern), the latter 'taking under his wing' various US Army formations from Bradley's 12th Army Group.

Whiteley, Major General Sir John Francis Martin, KCB, CBE, MC (1896–?). He was commissioned into the Royal Engineers in 1915 and served during WWI. He was General Eisenhower's (British) deputy Chief of Operations at SHAEF from 25 April 1944 until the end of the war in Europe. In 1943 he received the American Legion of Merit.

FRENCH

Lattre de Tassigny, General Jean-Marie Gabriel de (1889-1952). Gazetted from St-Cyr in 1908 into the 12th Dragoons, he transferred to the infantry in 1915 and by the end of the war had been wounded four times and won eight citations. A General de Brigade by the start of WWII, he was commanding 14th Infantry Division in the Armistice Army. Ordered to Tunisia in September 1941, he had serious disagreements with Juin and was recalled. Later, while at 16th Infantry Division's HQ in SE France, he was arrested 'for attempted treason', but escaped on the night of 2 September 1943 and was flown to England. He became largely responsible for the re-organisation and retraining of the Free French Forces. Appointed Commander of all French forces for the invasion of southern France, he commanded French First Army until the end of the war. Created a Marshal of France, at his death, he had been CinC French forces in Indo-China, but had developed cancer of the hip in March 1951 and was obliged to relinquish his command.

BIBLIOGRAPHY

Allen, Colonel Robert S. *'Lucky For-ward'*. The Vanguard Press Inc., 1947

Arnold, James R. *Ardennes 1944 – Hitler's Last Gamble in the West*. Osprey Campaign Series No. 5, 1990

Baker, David. *Adolf Galland: The Authorised Biography*. Windrow & Greene, 1996

Bradley, Omar N. *A Soldier's Story*. Henry Holt & Co., 1951

Clarke, Jeffrey J., and Smith, Robert Ross. *United States Army in WWII – Riviera to the Rhine*. Center of Military History, US Army, 1993

Cole, Hugh M. *United States Army in WWII – The Ardennes: Battle of the Bulge*. Center of Military History, US Army, 1965

Eisenhower, Dwight D. *Crusade in Europe*. William Heinemann, 1948

Eisenhower, John S. D. *The Bitter Woods*. Putnam, 1969

Elstob, Peter. *Hitler's Last Offensive*. Secker & Warburg, 1971

Forty, George. *The Armies of George S. Patton*, Arms and Armour Press, 1996

— *Patton's Third Army at War*. Arms and Armour Press, 1990

— *Tank Aces from Blitzkrieg to the Gulf War*. Sutton Publishing, 1997

Gelb, Norman. *Ike and Monty: Generals at War*. Constable, 1994

Hamilton, Nigel. *Monty*. Hodder & Stoughton, 1981

Irving, David. *Hitler's War*. Focal Point Publications, 1991

Keilig, Wolf. *Die Generale des Heeres*. Podzun-Pallas-Verlag GmbH, 1983

Liddell-Hart, B. H. *The Other Side of the Hill*. Cassell & Co. Ltd., 1948

Lucas, James. *The Last Year of the German Army*. Arms and Armour Press, 1994

MacDonald, Charles B. *United States Army in WWII – The Last Offensive*. Office of Chief of Military History, US Army, 1973

— *The Battle of the Bulge*. Weidenfeld & Nicholson, 1984

Mather, Carol. *When the Grass Stops Growing*. Leo Cooper, 1997

Merriman, Robert E. *The Battle of the Ardennes*. Souvenir Press, 1958

Miller, Merle. *Ike The Soldier As I Knew Him*. G. P. Putnam, 1987

Pallud, Jean Paul, *Battle of the Bulge Then and Now*, After the Battle, 1984

Reynolds Michael. *Men of Steel*. Spellmount, 1999

Skorzeny, Otto. *Skorzeny's Special Missions*. Greenhill Books, 1997

Speer, Albert. *Inside the Third Reich*. Weidenfeld & Nicholson, 1970

Summersby, Kay. *Eisenhower was my Boss*. Werner Laurie, 1949

Toland, John. *Adolf Hitler*. Doubleday, 1976

Whiting, Charles. *The Battle of the Bulge – Britain's untold story*. Sutton Publishing, 1999

— *The March on London*. Leo Cooper, 1992

Winterbotham, F. W. *The Ultra Secret*. Weidenfeld & Nicholson, 1974

World War II German Military Studies The OKW War Diary Series continued: vol. 10, Part IV; vol. 11, Part IV; vol. 12, Part V (The Western Theater). Garland Publishing Inc., 1979

Minutes of Hearing HR 407 held before the Military Personnel Subcommittee of Armed Services, House of Representatives, 96th Congress, First Session, 11 July 1979

INDEX